What Job's Friends Could Have Done

What Job's Friends Could Have Done

Facilitating Post-Traumatic Remaking in the Theodrama of Salvation

BY

Stephen C. Torr

◆PICKWICK *Publications* · Eugene, Oregon

WHAT JOB'S FRIENDS COULD HAVE DONE
Facilitating Post-Traumatic Remaking in the Theodrama of Salvation

Copyright © 2025 Stephen C. Torr. All rights reserved. Except for brief quotations in critical publications or reviews, no part of this book may be reproduced in any manner without prior written permission from the publisher. Write: Permissions, Wipf and Stock Publishers, 199 W. 8th Ave., Suite 3, Eugene, OR 97401.

Pickwick Publications
An Imprint of Wipf and Stock Publishers
199 W. 8th Ave., Suite 3
Eugene, OR 97401

www.wipfandstock.com

PAPERBACK ISBN: 979-8-3852-2756-3
HARDCOVER ISBN: 979-8-3852-2757-0
EBOOK ISBN: 979-8-3852-2758-7

Cataloguing-in-Publication data:

Names: Torr, Stephen C., author.

Title: What Job's friends could have done : facilitating post-traumatic remaking in the theodrama of salvation / by Stephen C. Torr.

Description: Eugene, OR : Pickwick Publications, 2025 | Includes bibliographical references.

Identifiers: ISBN 979-8-3852-2756-3 (paperback) | ISBN 979-8-3852-2757-0 (hardcover) | ISBN 979-8-3852-2758-7 (ebook)

Subjects: LCSH: Bible.—Job—Criticism, interpretation, etc. | Psychic trauma. | Psychic trauma—Biblical teaching. | Suffering in the Bible. | Suffering.

Classification: BS1199.P88 .T67 2025 (paperback) | BS1199.P88 (ebook)

VERSION NUMBER 08/18/25

Unless otherwise indicated, Scripture quotations are taken from the New Revised Standard Version Updated Edition. Copyright © 2021 National Council of Churches of Christ in the United States of America. Used by permission. All rights reserved worldwide.

To Holly, Isla, and Seth.
Thank you for your love.

Contents

Acknowledgments | ix
Abbreviations | xi

1 Introduction | 1
2 Trauma and Theology | 31
3 A Christocentric Theodramatic Anthropology | 66
4 A Theodramatic Ecclesiology | 105
5 Donald Winnicott's Object Relations Theory | 151
6 Developing a True Christlike Self | 190
7 The Facilitating Eucharistic Church | 223
8 What Job's Friends Could Have Done | 253
9 Conclusion | 293

Bibliography | 295

Acknowledgments

INEVITABLY, MORE PEOPLE HAVE influenced the writing of this work than I can name (or perhaps remember, sorry!) here. However, I'm particularly grateful for the church family at St. Bert's in Runcorn who often showed me and others what it means to offer Christlike love to those in need, and in so doing inspired me to explore the topic of this book in greater detail.

During the COVID-19 pandemic a dear friend living in Texas suggested we start a virtual Bible study just for Lent 2020. It was open to anyone and was called "Hitchhiker's Guide to the Bible" as we saw ourselves as trying to make our way with Jesus and with one another along roads we had not traveled, with people we had not met before, and to a destination unknown. That Lent group lasted just over three years until we decided to take a break! Words cannot express how grateful I am to all those I had the privilege of journeying with during that time, and who perhaps unknowingly carried and held me through some of my darkest days to date. Thank you to you my fellow hitchhikers!

The friend who suggested the aforementioned group is Matt Russell, who is more like a brother to me. We don't get to meet in person much but via all manner of communication methods we have laughed and cried together through the joys and woes we have experienced, and I am deeply grateful for his wisdom, his openness, his love, and his friendship. We have talked almost endlessly about trauma and how we might care better for each other and those we encounter and so those conversations have informed the material produced in this work.

I also want to mention Peter Mackriell and Brendan Callaghan. The former has been my counselor and pastoral supervisor, and the latter has been my faithful spiritual director. Both of them continue to open up safe space for me to explore my own inner world and help me search for an authentic life as a follower of Christ. I am grateful for their care and their companionship on the journey.

This manuscript has been a long time coming and, as with any creative piece of work, it is never really finished. Instead—perhaps following the theme of Winnicott—I decided I had done enough! I am grateful to those who gave their time to look over it and offer constructive feedback to help me get it to this point. In no particular order, thanks to Kevin Vanhoozer, Stephen Parker, Chris Cook, and Joanna Collicutt, not to mention the team at Wipf & Stock who have been generous with deadlines!

Last but not least, my thanks go to my family, particularly to my children, Isla and Seth, and my wife, Holly. I am not the easiest to live with! I am therefore grateful for the longsuffering love and care that they continue to offer.

Abbreviations

ANF   *The Ante-Nicene Fathers: Translations of the Writings of the Fathers Down to A.D. 325*. Edited by Alexander Roberts and James Donaldson. 10 vols. Repr., Grand Rapids: Christian Classics Ethereal Library, 1885–87.

NPNF   *A Select Library of Nicene and Post-Nicene Fathers of the Christian Church*. Edited by Philip Schaff and Henry Wace. 28 vols. in 2 series. Repr., Grand Rapids: Christian Classics Ethereal Library, 1886–89.

1

Introduction

Setting the Scene

"To seek life and to flourish as a human is futile if unrelated to living in a right relationship with the God who alone gives life."[1] Tim Harris's statement in an essay reflecting upon the nature of *shalom* in the Bible and the possible interaction between positive psychology and theology points to something crucial that lies at the heart of what follows. The impetus for this project came from two intermingling streams of experience that found agreement with Harris's statement. The first comes from an earlier book I wrote, published in 2013, *A Dramatic Pentecostal/ Charismatic Anti-Theodicy*. In that volume, I aimed to recover the practice of lament as a fitting response to experiences of seemingly innocent suffering and do so in a way conducive to Pentecostal/Charismatic theology and practice. Since that work was completed, a significant reoccurring question I have wrestled with as I have reflected on personal experience and the experience of others is, "Why does the practice of lament feel like such an alien and counter-intuitive practice to engage in for individuals and churches?" There are, I suspect, many contributing factors to the answer to that question, and a significant number of them will be specific to the context of a particular person and community. However, key factors that I suspect are likely to be transcontextual, at least in the UK where I am based, are whether churches have a clear understanding of what healthy processing of suffering means, what the role

---

1. Harris, "*Shalom*," 79.

of the church community is in supporting that process and, therefore, what specific place lament has within that process. If lament is a practice that enables an honest relationship with God in the midst of suffering, it is no wonder that it feels so alien if church communities are uncomfortable with, and ill-equipped for, sharing in one another's suffering, and providing good care for one another when such experiences come. A former colleague once noted in conversation that the practice of lament is present in the Psalms of Ascent.[2] This suggested to him that as these psalms were intended to be used regularly on the climb to worship at the temple, psalms of lament were therefore regularly rehearsed and embedded within Israel's worship. The people of God in the Old Testament seem to inhabit a worldview that recognizes suffering, questions, and doubts as part of life. The result is that ways of remaining in honest relationships with the self, others, and God when life is tough must also be embedded, rehearsed even, in day-to-day life.

As the title of this work suggests, a particularly well-known biblical example of what I am attempting to highlight as a problem in contemporary culture is that of Job's friends. Having sat in silence with Job for seven days and nights (Job 2:13), bearing witness to the suffering he is experiencing from the recent tragic events he has encountered, they can contain their desire to speak no longer. What ensues from the mouth of the friends in much of the rest of the book are unhelpful attempts to explain and resolve the suffering by placing the blame at Job's door, while at no point seeking to talk to God about the situation. This, of course, only heightens Job's suffering as Job eventually turns to God in an act of lament. Without entering into the complex poetry and prose of the book, what is apparent as the book draws to its rather inconclusive conclusion is that Job's response to God is considered by God as right speech and action, while Job's friends are instructed to ask Job to make sacrifices on their behalf and pray for them as they have not spoken rightly of God (42:7–8). Isabelle Hamley describes the book of Job as about a "crisis of the language of faith, a crisis of theology, as well as a story of trauma and how the community of faith may facilitate or hinder constructive responses to psychological pain."[3] Previously I have explored what it might

---

2. The Psalms of Ascent consist of Pss 120–34 and were likely used as processional psalms when on the way to the temple. Of these fifteen psalms, Leslie Allen notes that Pss 123, 125, 126, and 130 are psalms of lament. See Allen, *Psalms 101–150*, 193–97.

3. Hamley, "Patient Job," 85.

mean to speak rightly of God in such circumstances.[4] In the present work I want to offer an answer to the question, "What could Job's friends have done to help Job?" in order to provide guidance for church communities dealing with suffering that can shape a culture in which lament finds a natural home among other healing practices.

In addition to this first stream of exploring roadblocks to embedding the practice of lament, a second stream that has contributed to the shape and content of this project springs from my contexts of parish ministry, theological education, and a priest ordained in the Church of England more generally. When this project began, I was part-time Priest-in-Charge of a Church of England parish in the northwest of England, while also holding a part-time post at a Church of England theological training institute. The parish where I served was both large and diverse in terms of its socio-economic makeup. I lived in the poorest part of the parish and in the poorest civic ward in the borough, where statistics at the time suggested that 45 percent of children in that ward lived in poverty. In addition, the data also suggested that there were significant challenges in all the usual categories of deprivation such as health and education. Having lived there for several years my experience suggested that social cohesion was often lacking in a community that displayed somewhat of a fragmented existence including various ruptures in complex family units. Although I also experienced honesty, generosity, and the embodied presence of love that more often than not made it a rewarding church and community to be part of, there were many who lived, on my metaphorical doorstep, with a lack of hope of finding life in its fullness.

Where local non-faith-based agencies or charities were involved in delivering projects or providing facilities and opportunities, the results varied, but, as Harris notes, what they offered ultimately fell short of the life God wants for the people who lived there because none of the projects, facilities, or opportunities aimed at enabling living in right relationship with God and all that that entails. Let the reader understand that I am not suggesting that provisions by non-Christian agencies or charities are therefore useless, far from it. The Spirit blows where God wills, both inside and outside the church, and all that enables the flourishing of creation is of God whether it is acknowledged by those caught up in it or not. The challenge for me was that the church should be paving the way regarding enabling and encouraging the flourishing of creation and, at the heart of

---

4. Torr, *Dramatic*.

that, enabling and encouraging lives lived in relationship with God, and yet, the church is often behind the curve. I am not here casting blame on anyone but merely highlighting the seeming fact, derived from my experience, that when it comes to those who are suffering, the church should be on the cutting edge of life-changing care, yet is often ill-equipped or trained to offer that, myself included as the leader.

Using more specific examples, some of those who came to be part of the church community that I was leading during that period had experienced what I have now come to recognize as trauma and were searching for hope and healing. Although statutory agencies have a duty of care and are better equipped to deal with aspects of the healing process than churches, I could not shake the niggling feeling that the church should be and could be better at contributing to the care package that such individuals and families need. I do need to say here that what was remarkable was how many in the church family, instinctively and without training, were often able to offer loving, Christlike care. But, this project emerged partly because I needed clarity about what should be offered, why, and how. What I had glimpsed in action needed a clearer definition for me, and most likely for others.

In the context of theological education, I was also aware that although I was given permission and resources to teach a whole module on Christian responses to evil and suffering, primarily to soon-to-be-ordained-deacons in the Church of England, such concentrated teaching on that subject area was, and likely still is, a rarity in the training process. When such input is vying for a place alongside other subject areas that are more likely to equip future leaders to put a sticking plaster over the declining numbers of attendance in churches that those in positions of power in the Church of England are so obsessed with, it is unlikely that such training will get the attention it so desperately needs. Unfortunately, when we do not take the problem of evil and suffering seriously and the linked question of how to offer Christlike care to those who are hurting, and we do not make this a priority in the training of leaders, we may well fill our churches by way of the latest fad and sales pitch, but what people will eventually discover is that the community they have joined does not know how to help individuals walk with God in a sustainable and life-giving way when life gets messy. As if further evidence were required, the recent highlighting of institutional racism and the vast cover-up of non-recent and current abuse cases in the Church of England, not to mention the failings in pastoral care for clergy and their families who are encountering possible disciplinary measures, displays a church that is poorly equipped to both perceive and respond well to situations of evil and suffering. This point was further driven home when the Church of England produced a booklet of prayer for COVID that contained no sign of anything that resembled lament. When prayers for reopening churches were produced by the Liturgical Commission, the few prayers of lament that were included were so wordy and neat that they were neither accessible nor able to suitably convey the deep well of emotions that many who needed such resources were most likely feeling. The bottom line that sums up this second stream of inspiration for this project is that the evidence suggests that at local and national levels the church is often found wanting when it comes to genuinely offering what can rightly be called a Christlike response of care and healing to those who so desperately need it. That is not to say that others have not had experiences like mine of seeing others naturally and instinctively offer such care. It is more to make the point that such care is likely sporadic and largely absent from church culture on a large scale with the associated underpinning theology that should inform and reflect it being equally limited in impact if not volume.

I realize that I will likely come under fire here from those who feel I have overlooked all the good things about the church. I may well also come under fire from those who think I have unfairly placed too much responsibility on fallen humans when it is Jesus and he alone who is the savior of the world. To the first, you have unfortunately proved my point. Although I am of course not against pointing to where the body of Christ lives our vocation out well, the instinct to swiftly shift our attention to the good things so that we do not linger too long on the painful things betrays our inability to bear witness to those who are hurting and take their hurt, the causes of their hurt, and good Christlike care seriously. I am not against celebrating what is good unless it is done as an excuse to ignore what needs improving, and there seems to be too much of such an approach.[5] To the second, Jesus is indeed the savior of the world and God alone can make all things new. However, there is a clear biblical mandate that will be explored further in this work for humans to partner with God in God's work of redeeming and salvaging

---

5. For a helpful introduction to the benefits of gratitude from a Christian perspective see Ford and Ford, "Gratitude." However, my point here is that although the practice of gratitude is valuable and healthy, it must sit alongside healthy acknowledgment and processing of pain and suffering.

creation for communion with Godself. Humans are given responsibility and will be held accountable for what they do with what God has given them, so although Jesus is the savior of the world, that is not an excuse for damaging theology, attitudes, and practices.

Having said all that, in attempting to respond to these two streams of influence, taking Harris's point seriously as attention is turned to Job's friends, this book emerges from a place of hope and possibility that I trust the Spirit of God to have created. In recent years, thanks to the influence of Walter Brueggemann in particular, I have been introduced to the work of the British pediatrician and psychoanalyst Donald Winnicott. Following in the footsteps of Brueggemann and others, I have had my eyes opened to how Winnicott's particular brand of Object Relations Theory may provide a helpful tool to aid in enriching various aspects of Christian theology and practice. The hope and possibility I have is regarding what engagement with Winnicott's work might mean for aiding the church in fulfilling her calling and particularly her calling to be involved in the flourishing of the image of God in individuals and, therefore, in the church and the world. More will be said about the interdisciplinary work of theology and psychology in this project in the "Method" section below.

An added layer of definition to this project comes from the particular tradition and theology from which I emerge. This will not simply be a case of engaging with Winnicott from within a Christian theological discourse but, more precisely, from within a theodramatic discourse that I continue to suggest, following my previous book, is compatible with, and reflective of, Pentecostal theology. Diane Chandler asks, "Given the realities of sin, temptation, and personal brokenness in an imperfect world, how might the body of Christ cooperate with the Spirit in order to bring each facet of life into conformity to Christ through the freedom offered by the Spirit?"[6] In seeking to explore and produce guidance for what Job's friends could have done to help Job, I am aiming to provide something of an answer to Chandler's question that could easily be accommodated in Pentecostal theology and practice. To do this I am continuing my conversation with the model of theodrama engaged with in my previous work, and more specifically, with the work of Kevin Vanhoozer. In what follows, a conversation will form between the work of Vanhoozer and Winnicott, with other voices contributing where appropriate, as I seek to navigate a path toward direction for good pastoral care in the church.

6. Chandler, Introduction to *The Holy Spirit*, 6.

Before sharpening the focus of this project further, a lingering question remains that requires addressing, namely, who is this book directed at? I confess to an element of selfishness and narcissism here in that the main person I set out to write this for was myself! As a church leader desiring to care well for those I encounter, and guide the congregations I lead to do the same, I began exploring how and why I might do that. As will become apparent below in the brief exploration of the existing field, having encountered the situations and people that I had, as well as seeing and participating in much good (and some not so good) practices, I struggled to find a text that provided the theological foundations for the practices we were already exploring, and so I began to write my own in conversation with Vanhoozer and Winnicott. My intent was therefore to construct those foundations and possibly correct some of our beliefs and practices along the way. The present work is an attempt to answer my own questions about what it means, from a particular Christian theological perspective, to speak of the impact of trauma on humans, what healing might look like, and how and why the church might participate in that healing. Although the end goal is therefore better pastoral practice, the focus of the present work is more on the theological foundations that have helped me to gain a clearer sense of what I/we are aiming at and why, which then leads to outworking that in practice. My hope is that those who choose to take this journey with me might also find it useful for their reflections and care of others.

Sharpening the Focus: Trauma and Post-Traumatic Remaking[7]

As the subtitle of this work alludes to, to hone the term "suffering" down and give it some tighter definition I will be focusing on how church

---

7. Contrary to many resources that explore trauma and the care of those who have been traumatized, I am consciously steering away from the terms "post-traumatic recovery" or "post-traumatic growth" opting instead for what Karen O'Donnell following Hilary Scarsella refers to as "post-traumatic remaking" (see O'Donnell, "Eucharist," 184). In a more developed way than O'Donnell, my reason is that "recovery" potentially suggests getting back something that was lost or taken, and "growth" could be construed as an overly optimistic linear upward trajectory following the experience of trauma. The first of these is unhelpful because although what was, before the experience of trauma, is not entirely lost, neither is it possible to simply return to who that person or community once was, including their context and relationships. The second of these is unhelpful because the path of healing beyond trauma is likely not a constant linear upward one, and the idea that it should be, implicit in the language used, may well add unnecessary expectations, leading to unhelpful disillusionment and disappointment,

communities can be better equipped to respond specifically to those who are experiencing trauma. The area of trauma research and response has seen a recent surge in both secular theory and practice as well as in theological works. The present work seeks to add to the growing corpus as a further useful exploration of constructive trauma response for church communities. What I am *not* suggesting is that church communities should replace or work in opposition to professional therapeutic provision. Bessel van der Kolk, a pioneering psychiatrist in the area of trauma response, states, "Study after study shows that having a good support network, constitutes the single most powerful protection against becoming traumatized."[8] He continues, "Our attachment bonds are our greatest protection against threat."[9] Unless the source of the trauma is the caregiver, families and communities of friends potentially provide the most important resource for responding well to experiences of suffering that can work as complementary to specific therapeutic work. Van der Kolk notes,

> Traumatized human beings recover in the context of relationships: with families, loved ones, AA meetings, veterans' organizations, religious communities, or professional therapists. The role of those relationships is to provide physical and emotional safety, including safety from feeling shamed, admonished, or judged, and to bolster the courage to tolerate, face, and process the reality of what has happened.[10]

Research would suggest, therefore, that church communities offering a particular type of care and environment can contribute in important ways to protecting against trauma and enabling healthy recovery from trauma. Peter Levine suggests that "how we handle trauma (as individuals, communities, and societies) greatly influences the quality of our lives. It ultimately affects how or even whether we will survive as a

---

to the survivor. Instead, the language of "remaking" suggests a unique process undertaken by the individual or community whereby something positive and of worth is constructed from the shattered pieces of life in the aftermath of trauma. As will become apparent toward the end of this project, the model and method used here will mean that this remaking can be done in the presence, and with the help, of God and that the hope of the Christian faith is the final and complete eschatological remaking of all who are "in Christ."

8. Van der Kolk, *Body*, 210.
9. Van der Kolk, *Body*, 210.
10. Van der Kolk, *Body*, 210.

species."[11] This work aims not simply to provide another reflection on the importance of community for resilience and trauma recovery but, instead, to offer a distinctly Christocentric interpretation and response to trauma that is shaped by the theodrama in which we find ourselves and particularly the performance at the heart of that drama found in the incarnate Christ.[12]

There is a danger that "trauma" is falsely perceived to be understood as a term that refers to a universally accepted definition. This is far from the case as the discipline and worldview from within which one addresses the phenomena to which this term refers will shape how the term is defined and used. Lucy Bond and Stef Craps highlight points in history where the cause of symptoms of what would later be identified as "trauma" were relabeled depending on the cost or benefit to wider organizations of the acknowledgment of such experiences. In particular, they note the possible impact foreseen by various affected parties in nineteenth- and early twentieth-century Germany, Italy, France, the UK, and the USA if governments or organizations were to have to pay out insurance or early pensions due to the evolving awareness of alternative causes to certain presenting symptoms. In such contexts, "hysteria" could be cured, "cowardice" addressed accordingly, but what would go on to be defined as trauma was potentially far more costly to a powerful system that would be affected by it.[13] Similarly, Judith Herman connects the development of trauma diagnosis with particular wider cultural trends that affected the research.[14] The point here is that there is considerable slippage in defining trauma as well as a vested interest in the details of the definition and methods of diagnosis and treatment. As Bond and Craps note, "Trauma . . . is slippery: blurring the boundaries between mind and body, memory and forgetting, speech and silence. It traverses the internal and the external, the private and the public, the individual and the collective."[15]

---

11. Levine and Frederick, *Waking the Tiger*, 2.

12. Although I am drawing heavily on Vanhoozer's work and related theodramatic sources in this project, I perhaps need to mention my indebtedness to Brian McLaren for phrases such as "the theodrama in which we find ourselves" and similar. Although I am not aware that McLaren uses the language of theodrama, it is the main title of his second book in the *A New Kind of Christian* trilogy—*The Story We Find Ourselves In*—that influenced my own phrasing. See McLaren, *New Kind*, *Story*, and *Last Word*.

13. Bond and Craps, *Trauma*, 14–33.

14. Herman, *Trauma and Recovery*, 9–47.

15. Bond and Craps, *Trauma*, 5.

However, one has to choose to enter the discourse somewhere. The primary concern of this project is the provision of a distinctly Christian understanding of trauma and direction for the positive and life-giving pastoral care of individuals by church communities. With that in mind, it is important to lay out early in this project where I stand, and through which lenses I am engaging with the subject and people in hand. It is also important to provide a sense of method—how I will proceed to reach the aim of offering guidance on how church communities can better care for and support those who have experienced trauma. So, in what remains in this chapter I will lay out in greater detail the model and method to be used throughout the rest of this work followed by an outline of what will unfold in the ensuing chapters and how each will contribute to the overall aim.

Method and Model: First Theology, Theodrama, and Psychology

For clarity's sake, it is important to note at this point the field in which this work is to be primarily located with further contextualization to follow in the next chapter. Although, as will be discussed below, this is interdisciplinary work, dialoguing theology and psychology, I am primarily writing from within the discipline of theology and so locate this work within that field. Given that my approach to this project seeks to highlight, reflect on, and respond to a particular experience or group of experiences that humans have, this project is intended to be a work of pastoral theology within the broader area of practical theology. Definitions of pastoral and practical theology vary greatly and, for many working in these fields, there is significant overlap if not interchangeable use of the terms. As this is somewhat of a rabbit hole, I do not wish for the exploration of these terms to become a distraction from the focus of this project. Therefore, I will simply note that by "pastoral theology" I mean something akin to Deborah van Deusen Hunsinger's definition of it as "first and foremost a theology of *God's care* for the world in Jesus Christ, in which we are invited to participate."[16] Practical theology, by contrast, describes exploration of and reflection on Christian practices more generally—hence

---

16. Van Deusen Hunsinger, *Bearing*, 2. All italics in quotes are original unless otherwise noted.

pastoral theology as a sub-discipline of practical theology.[17] The present project falls under the category of pastoral theology because it is intended to contribute to the resources available that aim at guiding the people of God into good theology and practice regarding the care of those who have experienced trauma. With that in view, we can proceed to explore in greater detail the method and model to be used.

First Theology and Theodrama

There is no obvious place to start in terms of prioritizing method or model, as the two are intertwined, informing each other. Vanhoozer has suggested that in pre-modern philosophy, "first philosophy" focused on metaphysics and the question of what constitutes ultimate reality. In modernity, this shifted to the subject of epistemology and the question of how it is possible to know what is claimed to be true. In postmodernity, a further shift occurred that involved the deconstruction of systems of language, ethics, or aesthetics as a way of unveiling the subjective way reality is engaged with or even, constructed.[18] To some degree, as will be seen, the latter is evidenced in constructive theological approaches to trauma. The aim there appears to be that theology is to be done from the viewpoint of the traumatized, forming or discarding theological beliefs based on the survivor's perceived needs. The upside of such an approach is that it pushes back against unhelpful and problematic theological positions and beliefs that cause more harm than good. However, from within a model (and the postmodern turn, ironically, seems to reveal the undeconstructable truth that everyone, at the very least, interprets or perhaps constructs reality and thus engages with the world through some sort of lens or model) that believes God to be the only one who absolutely knows what is best for each individual, and in which individuals are thought to be hampered, to a greater or lesser extent, by sin and a limited perspective, the suggestion that the survivor ultimately knows best is fraught with problems. But we are getting ahead of ourselves in terms of the use of models. The reason for noting the trends in first philosophy is to follow Vanhoozer and his engagement with David Kelsey highlighting a method that he

17. See Miller-McLemore, "Introduction"; Pattison and Woodward, "Introduction" for helpful introductory discussions regarding definitions of practical and pastoral theology.

18. Vanhoozer, *First Theology*, 16–24.

labels "First Theology." In light of the trends in philosophy, how does one begin doing theology? And in terms of this project, how does one approach providing direction for good Christian post/trauma care? As noted, there is no abstract position of absolute objectivity from which to view and assess the self and the world, and so one begins in the middle.[19] However, this does not mean that all that exists is our experiences from which we construct a sense of coherence and meaning. Instead, it is possible to suggest that our experiences gain meaning when seen in the light of the prior activity of God. But this raises the challenge of deciding whether to start with the doctrine of God, or with the doctrine of Scripture, or somewhere else.

From a Christian perspective, Vanhoozer highlights the possible quandary of having to choose between these two starting points. "God" has little substantial definition without further revelation (making God in our own image falls preys to the criticisms of Marx, Freud, and Feuerbach to name but a few!), and Scripture is just a book, without saying more about the author (and is therefore problematic in terms of accessing an interpretation that carries more weight than simply what it means to an individual or community). However, for Vanhoozer, Kelsey's work draws attention to the possibility that first theology need not choose between the two but instead comprise both. "What Kelsey discovers is that theologians in fact formulate their views of God and Scripture *together*."[20] The result is that "*first theology concerns the nature of the relation between God and Scripture.*"[21] What this means is that a hermeneutical circle emerges—Scripture is considered authoritative because of who the author is, and God is known by way of the revelation of Scripture. One informs and shapes the other in an ongoing circle of interpretation where knowledge of God is deepened and fitting interpretation and use of Scripture is honed. This is a circle that follows Augustine and Anselm along the road of faith seeking understanding leading to wiser living.[22]

However, although a community or individual may enter this circle of God and Scripture interpreting each as first theology through a lens that sees both as foundational to a theological enterprise that follows, the outworking in Christian interpretation, beliefs, and practices is not

---

19. Pete Ward highlights and engages with this observation in the work of Rowan Williams. See Ward, *Introducing*, 9–25.
20. Vanhoozer, *First Theology*, 29.
21. Vanhoozer, *First Theology*, 30.
22. Migliore, *Faith Seeking Understanding*, 2.

universal agreement. The reason for this is that "pre-text judgements" take place regarding how to engage with Scripture. The result is that if certain texts or genres are privileged over others—didactic, historical, poetic; Luke-Acts, Pauline letters, the Gospels—then differences in outcomes—interpretation and use of Scripture leading to particular doctrines and actions—results. How does one proceed through this maze to a more satisfying conclusion? Here the model or lens of Scripture and God together as first theology needs refining further to better enable an equally refined method of engagement to develop. If taking God and Scripture together as a way of proceeding appears to produce various results, perhaps the way to reach a more definite conclusion regarding the best way to proceed is to consider what Scripture consists of in total, in order to determine how God uses it and engages with the world. To put it another way, what lens or model appears to do justice to the content of Scripture and the revelation of God in Scripture? Or how might the content of Scripture guide engagement with it? What becomes apparent following this method in the pursuit of answers to these questions is that there are multiple genres in Scripture through which God does things with words—speech acts—to communicate God's self to creation with the intent of communion with creation.[23] Rather than a pre-text construal that results in reading Scripture in a way that fits imposed models but likely does not do full justice to the content, this method aims at allowing the content of Scripture to guide the construal model to be employed. Using such a method, Vanhoozer concludes, "God is present in Scripture precisely as a communicative agent, its ultimate author"[24] and further, "What God ultimately wants to communicate to us is salvation, a share in the divine life; he wants to communicate the Spirit of Christ."[25] Standing on the shoulders of various scholars who have reached a similar conclusion regarding Scripture, a method that allows the content of Scripture to determine how it should be read results, for this author, with a theodramatic model.

Vanhoozer presented his most extensive engagement with a theodramatic model in *The Drama of Doctrine*.[26] As a follow-up that turned

---

23. For helpful explorations of "speech act theory," see Austin, *How*; Searle, *Speech Acts*. For Vanhoozer's development of speech act theory in theological hermeneutics, see Vanhoozer, *Meaning*, particularly 201–80.
24. Vanhoozer, *First Theology*, 34.
25. Vanhoozer, *First Theology*, 35.
26. Vanhoozer, *Drama of Doctrine*.

attention specifically to discipleship and "doing church" and the role of doctrine within that (and also as a response to the reception of *The Drama of Doctrine*), he further fleshed out his dramatic approach to theology with *Faith Speaking Understanding*.[27] In this later work, he offers the following definitions: "a 'drama' delivers a unified sequence of action that a 'script' preserves or prescribes in writing, which human enactors bodily represent and enact by a 'performance' in a 'theatre' (*theatron* = a place for seeing)."[28] In this approach, the drama—from the Greek word *draō*, meaning to do, act, or take action—is that which is captured in the script as text and brought to life in the embodied vocal and visual performance of the actors. Having said that, he also recognizes a fluidity to definitions, noting that actors can "dramatize" a script in a theatrical performance.[29] He further states of theatre that it "happens whenever one or more persons present themselves to others in space and time."[30] It is, then, "*communicative action in word and deed.*"[31]

The move to using this as a helpful model with which to understand God's relationship to the world and how humans are to respond is relatively straightforward for Vanhoozer. In terms of theology, he understands the subject matter to be "intrinsically dramatic, a series of actions united by a plot." He further suggests, "The drama of God's self-communication structures theological understanding" and that "the drama of redemption orients and prompts human action."[32] Similarly, Wesley Vander Lugt and Trevor Hart have described theology as theatrical in how it reflects on a "God who says and does things in the theatre of the world,"[33] and "arises out of the historical performance of God and resources the ongoing performance of the church."[34] Rather than faith speaking understanding, which is the preferred description of Vanhoozer for the church's performance, Vander Lugt and Hart opt for "faith seeking performative understanding," which would seem a more accurate description given the breadth of meaning included in performance

---

27. Vanhoozer, *Faith Speaking Understanding*.
28. Vanhoozer, *Faith Speaking Understanding*, 22.
29. Vanhoozer, *Faith Speaking Understanding*, 22.
30. Vanhoozer, *Faith Speaking Understanding*, 22–23.
31. Vanhoozer, *Faith Speaking Understanding*, 23. For similar definitions, see Johnson and Savidge, *Performing the Sacred*, 12.
32. Vanhoozer, *Faith Speaking Understanding*, 28.
33. Vander Lugt and Hart, Introduction to *Theatrical Theology*, xiii.
34. Vander Lugt and Hart, Introduction to *Theatrical Theology*, xiv.

over merely speaking.³⁵ It is worth further noting that although Vander Lugt and Hart broadly agree with Vanhoozer's definition of drama as script that includes "plot, interaction of characters, conflict and resolution" there is a subtle difference in language use with the terms "theatre" and "theater."³⁶ For Vander Lugt and Hart the former of these describes the performance, hence "theatre" as performance, whereas the latter describes a place.³⁷ This author will follow Vander Lugt and Hart's more specific definitions as this project proceeds.

The dramatic model contrasts with a narrative approach in that narrative depicts action in the third person but is limited to description. Dramas can include this approach but, given the definition of theatre above, in essence, they center on dialogical action, moving beyond description and into performance where one person presents themselves to another in word and deed in space and time. "To conceive of the gospel as dramatic and theology as theatrical is to embrace a meaningful, imaginative vision for thinking about reality and about discipleship."³⁸ This call to participate in the action—to speak, communicate, make common one's understanding of one's faith commitment—means that, contra narrative theology, "disciples are not mere storytellers but *storydwellers*."³⁹ As Todd Johnson notes, faithful worshipers are to tell the story "by becoming the story."⁴⁰ In short, the dramatic model is apt for aiding in understanding what we are a part of and how we are to respond—perform—our parts.⁴¹ This theodramatic lens enables the parallel developments of more nuanced understandings of who God is and what God does, and what Scripture consists of and how we are to engage with it, to be pursued in greater detail. Prior to undertaking those dual developments, it is important to note a third point in the hermeneutical circle of first theology that has, thus far, only been hinted at.

Concurring with Vanhoozer, what was missing from his earlier work on first theology was the place of ecclesiology. Although the content of ecclesiology relevant to this work will be engaged with more fully

---

35. Vander Lugt and Hart, Introduction to *Theatrical Theology*, xiv.
36. Vander Lugt and Hart, Introduction to *Theatrical Theology*, xv.
37. Vander Lugt and Hart, Introduction to *Theatrical Theology*, xv.
38. Vanhoozer, *Faith Speaking Understanding*, 29.
39. Vanhoozer, *Faith Speaking Understanding*, 29.
40. Johnson, "Doing God's Story," 157.
41. For Vanhoozer's defense of the dramatic approach in response to various objections, see Vanhoozer, *Faith Speaking Understanding*, 239–52.

in chapters 4 and 7, it is important to mention its role in first theology. In a later collaboration with Daniel Treier, Vanhoozer notes of his original approach, "I now think that my first theology was too small, its 'domain of the Word' too limited."[42] Using the analogy of a boat kept from straying by being tied to an anchor (what they describe as "an anchored set"), Vanhoozer and Treier reframe first theology to include the church—signified by the boat—in contact with waves that represent the contemporary context and culture. The boat can move in response to the waves but is kept from straying too far by the rope of catholic tradition that keeps the boat attached to the anchor of the Trinitarian God revealed in Scripture and most clearly glimpsed in the life, death, resurrection, and ascension of the Son.[43] Although this, rightly, does not give the same level of authority to experience, tradition, or the church as that which is attributed to Scripture, there is recognition that the God revealed in Scripture is discerned and received as such by the church which is constituted, empowered, and guided by the Spirit.

Drawing on the work of liturgical scholar Lester Ruth, Todd Johnson notes how when exploring the question of "whose story is told?" in gathered worship, Ruth uses a spectrum of options between the "cosmic" and the "personal."[44] Engagement with the cosmic is characterized by locating one's performance within God's story in contrast to identifying the presence and work of God within an individual or community's personal story, often recounted through testimony. Although there is room for the whole spectrum in authentic Christian ecclesiology, Johnson draws similar conclusions to Vanhoozer, noting that "the cosmic story of God's redemption is primary and the subjective response is grounded in objective revelation."[45] Ecclesiology thus finds its way into first theology as the locus of the gospel's contemporary reception and embodiment. As the church receives the revelation of the primary performance of God in Scripture using a theodramatic model, we are able to say more about what Scripture is, who God is, and what it means to identify as the church and live wisely from within the drama.

In his exploration of wisdom and play focusing on worship and liturgy within a theodramatic approach, Jim Fodor draws from David Ford's work on Christian wisdom. Fodor states that "theatre and

---

42. Vanhoozer and Treier, *Theology*, 13.
43. Vanhoozer and Treier, *Theology*, 51–53.
44. Johnson, "Doing God's Story," 158.
45. Johnson, "Doing God's Story," 160.

theology are analogically related by virtue of play,"[46] where play can be "valued for its own sake," can determine its own meaning, and, where God's wisdom is involved in particular, be hope-filled and hope-inducing.[47] More will be said about the role of play as this work proceeds but, for now, it is helpful to offer further insight into the theodramatic nature of Vanhoozer's ecclesial analogy.

Where Vanhoozer wants to keep the boat anchored and restrained on the sometimes choppy waters of contemporary culture, Fodor wants to note the limited openness of the theodrama. The future is open to a degree because of the nature of play that God has created for creation to be involved in. Fodor uses Ford's dialectic between "wisdom of reserve" and "wisdom of ramification" to curtail this from drifting into seemingly out-of-control relativism, though, where the boat is cut loose from the anchor. Where a wisdom of ramification encourages an openness to improvise and explore how the script might be embodied in various contexts and cultures, moving with the undulating waves, a wisdom of reserve enables discernment of suitable and fitting performances and keeps the boat attached to the rope and anchor.[48] Such an approach continues to recognize the nuances of the particular scenes in which the church performs for their contribution to the shape of the ecclesial performance. The theodrama is thus perceived not as something external to be observed but something we are already participating in and to some degree shaping as we go. However, ecclesiology is also not treated as the norming norm with Scripture retaining that type of authority given whose story we find ourselves in and the tendency of the church toward sinful interpretations and performances in this act of the theodrama.[49] To continue on the hermeneutical circle in light of the present theodramatic model, we return to Scripture authored and discerned by the Spirit of God at work in the lives of individuals and communities.

46. Fodor, "Play," 126.
47. Fodor, "Play," 128.
48. Fodor, "Play," 147–48.
49. Trevor Hart offers a similar openness, noting that the "incomplete" nature of the meaning of Scripture requires readers and performers to bring it to completion. In this way, the text is not to be used as something to derive doctrines from by the church but is to be used to guide multiple, varied, and enfleshed performances that need not result in relativism. However, if doctrine is understood as guidance for performance, as Vanhoozer would suggest it should be, then not only has Hart thrown the metaphorical baby out with the bathwater, but he has also not made clear how, exactly, relativism is to be avoided. See Hart, "Beyond Theatre and Incarnation."

Vanhoozer had initially equated Scripture with the script of the theodrama in *The Drama of Doctrine*; however, on further reflection he notes the limitations of this as well as expands its definition: "Scripture remains the church's script, a divinely commissioned and authorized written witness to the ongoing drama of redemption, for which doctrine gives direction to disciples for understanding and participation."[50] However, it "is *not* a script in the sense of a detailed blueprint for action (or the future)."[51] In addition, though, it is also a transcript in that the authors, under the inspiration of the Holy Spirit, "have produced an authoritative record of God's work," as well as prescriptive, "authorizing spiritual medicine (e.g., the fear of the Lord; faith) that, if taken as directed, leads to beneficial and healthy results: wisdom, *salus* (welfare)."[52] Within the dramatic model, Vanhoozer also sees Scripture as stage lighting. Beginning with Gen 1:3 he states, "What illumines the stage is God's word, the word that spoke forth the created order in the beginning, the incarnate word whose activity eventually restores and perfects that original order, and the word written that attests to the Word through and for whom all things were made (Col. 1:16)."[53] Scripture as stage lighting is that which the Holy Spirit uses to light the path for disciples of Christ as it both points to Christ as the true light (John 1:1–9) who displays God who is light (1 John 1:5) while also enabling readers to see reality as it is (Ps 119). We can, therefore, within the dramatic model, view Scripture as script and prescriptive while also offering the transcript of God's interaction with creation that provides a light for the path of disciples.

When accepted as authoritative because of divine authorship, what Scripture reveals is a particular kind of God, who has authored the drama of salvation—hence theodrama—and who has therefore chosen to create and reveal Godself in particular ways in order to draw what God has created into eternal communion with Godself. Scripture becomes trustworthy in the sense of offering information and direction on how to participate well within the unfolding drama of God's relationship with creation because it bears witness to a God who claims to be faithful and the very definition of love, and then displays it in the life, death, resurrection, and ascension of the Son. In short, Scripture can be trusted in this sense because its divine author has proved trustworthy through

---

50. Vanhoozer, *Faith Speaking Understanding*, 24.
51. Vanhoozer, *Faith Speaking Understanding*, 24.
52. Vanhoozer, *Faith Speaking Understanding*, 24.
53. Vanhoozer, *Faith Speaking Understanding*, 63.

fulfilling promises within the economy of creation. Therefore "the ontology of Scripture is a function of what God has done and is doing with it, not of what its human users do with it."[54] What God has done and is doing with it is displaying the Trinity in the economy of creation as the one God of Father, Son, and Spirit who has "opened up, through Jesus' incarnation, cross and resurrection, a way to share in God's own perfect life."[55] The Trinity is, therefore, the gospel and is illuminated by the light of the world—Jesus Christ—who, enabled and empowered by the Spirit, displays the inner life of God in eternity in order to bring creation into union with himself, and, therefore, communion with God. This is why Scripture and God must be held together as first theology because the prior life and actions of this Trinitarian God, revealed most clearly in Christ, and as testified to in the Scriptures, should shape whatever else might be said and done in creation. A Christocentric entry into interpreting the theodrama is required because what is glimpsed in Christ in terms of human existence and the Trinitarian life is the clearest and fullest example provided for both who God is and what it means to live as a human made in the image of God within the theodrama. More will be said about this in chapters 3 and 6. Continuing to move around the hermeneutical circle of first theology, the very way that this God has chosen to commune with creation means that the Spirit-constituted church as the body of Christ must also be the place where the gospel is proclaimed and revealed, as the church, in a sense, is the goal of the gospel, seen only dimly in the present.

The drama, then, is one conceived and initiated by God into which we are cast as performers. It is in this sense that Vanhoozer, following Balthasar, can label it a *theo*drama in which "God and humanity are alternately actor and audience." He continues, "Better: life is divine-human interactive theatre, and theology involves both what God has said and done for the world and what we must say and do in grateful response."[56] Final eschatological communion will be communion between creation and creator as creation is drawn into the community of the triune fellowship of love, participating in the divine life and becoming whole yet without collapsing the creator/creature distinction. "The theodrama is essentially missional, the enactment of God's several overtures to the world; for God's communicative initiatives are first and foremost *missionary*

54. Vanhoozer and Treier, *Theology*, 74.
55. Vanhoozer and Treier, *Theology*, 68.
56. Vanhoozer, *Drama of Doctrine*, 37–38.

movements."⁵⁷ God goes out of Godself into creation to reveal Godself and draw creation into the divine life through the covenantal promise made good as a sign of God's faithfulness. God reveals Godself most fully in Christ and makes possible, in spite of the fall, the relationship humans in particular were intended for in terms of communion with God. It is the missions of the two hands of God that enable this: "The Father sends the Son in order to share his truth with others; the Father sends the Spirit in order to share the love he bears for the Son with others."⁵⁸ Using J. R. R. Tolkien's terminology, Vanhoozer defines this drama as "a *eucatastrophe*: a cataclysmic event with a beneficial effect."⁵⁹ Right reception of and response to God's love results in recognition that one's identity has been relocated "in Christ" as children of God (John 1:12–13). Vanhoozer settles on a five-act drama in which act 1 consists of Gen 1–11; act 2 is the rest of the Old Testament; act 3 focuses on the incarnation in the Gospels; act 4 is the era of the church from the sending of the Spirit until the eschaton; act 5 is the return of Jesus and consummation of creation at the eschaton.⁶⁰ Given this division of the action, it is in act 4 that we can locate the present scenes, and in which this work is set.

There is more that needs to be said about human identity and performance and the role of the church in enabling and supporting that within the theodramatic model. However, this must wait until later chapters. For now, it is enough to summarize that the method of first theology that involves the Spirited church engaging in the interpretation of Scripture to know God better and live wisely in the world is where this project begins. In response to the challenge of trauma in the world, this is where the church must turn in order to discern how to respond in a Christlike way that supports the drama's progression toward its rightful conclusion, while aiding those in its midst to find the healing that only God can provide. The model for approaching the subject in hand is a theodramatic

---

57. Vanhoozer, *Drama of Doctrine*, 68–69.

58. Vanhoozer, *Drama of Doctrine*, 70.

59. Vanhoozer, *Drama of Doctrine*, 38. In a similar way, Marilyn McCord Adams describes Christianity and the Gospel as "*tragi-comic*: grim realism that wins through to a happy ending" (Adams, "Eucharistic Drama," 217). However, this definition needs tempering with Ivan Khovacs's observation that Jesus does not straightforwardly fit the Aristotelian mold of a tragic hero (see Khovacs et al., "Intractable Sense," 50–53). Vanhoozer's choice of "eucatastrophe" is therefore more straightforward.

60. See Vanhoozer, *Drama of Doctrine*, 2–3; and Vanhoozer, *Faith Speaking Understanding*, 95–98, for a fuller exploration of options for dividing up the action.

one that understands creation as participating in the theodrama with communion with God its destiny.

Theodrama and Pentecostalism[61]

Picking up where I left off in *A Dramatic Pentecostal/Charismatic Anti-Theodicy*, this project continues my attempt to present an approach, this time to understanding and responding to trauma, that is compatible with and can be accommodated in Pentecostal theology and practice. Previously I have focused on developing an approach to lament that can find a home in Pentecostal theology and practice and, although this project has a broader ecclesial audience than Pentecostalism alone, the intent is that the approach to trauma developed here will also be able to be accommodated in Pentecostal theology and practice. Time and space do not allow a revised version of my engagement with Pentecostal hermeneutics from my earlier work. Instead, I wish to simply restate my point more extensively argued there that I believe the theodramatic model and method presented here continues to be conducive to a "Full Gospel" Pentecostal theology that affirms Jesus as Savior, Sanctifier, Baptizer in the Spirit, Healer, and Soon Coming King; anticipates and looks for the work of the Spirit in the present; holds a high view of Scripture; and recognizes that theology is something to be embodied with as much emphasis on orthopathos as on orthodoxy and orthopraxy.[62] As with my previous work, my key area of caution in presenting a theodramatic approach as conducive to Pentecostal theology and practice is what is meant when a high view of Scripture is proclaimed. Or more precisely, being clear on where authority lies.

As I have noted previously, it is commonplace in Pentecost hermeneutics to affirm a high view of Scripture yet give a significant amount of weight to the work of the Spirit. At face value, this seems unproblematic, but what it often equates to is giving the community an unhelpful amount of authority to discern a correct interpretation of the work of

---

61. I am here opting to define "Pentecostalism" using the fourfold grouping that Allan Anderson offers, building on the work of Walter J. Hollenweger. The four types of Pentecostalism presented by Anderson are "Classical Pentecostals," "Older Independent and Spirit Churches," "Older Church Charismatics," and "Neo-Pentecostal and Neo-Charismatic Churches." See Anderson, "Varieties, Taxonomies, and Definitions." Anderson suggests that what groups these together is a "family resemblance described in terms of an emphasis on the Spirit and spiritual gifts," 17.

62. Torr, *Dramatic*.

the Spirit and of Scripture. As noted above in the theodramatic approach proposed here, the community is the site of enactment of the gospel, but it is not the norming norm. Scripture is authoritative because of its divine author and the way the divine author has opted to use Scripture to reveal Godself as well as God's perspective of the theodrama and the role of human performers within that. This makes space for exploring what shape performance takes on different stages in creation. The work of the Spirit is then that of aiding interpretation and improvised Christ-like performance but always measured against the revelation of God in Christ displayed in Scripture.

One particularly important example to note where Pentecostal theology has engaged with the theodramatic model and method is in the work of Wolfgang Vondey. Vondey, in exploring the idea of "play" within Pentecostal theology and practice, highlights Vanhoozer's theodramatic approach as a possible friend to the Pentecostal approach he is developing.[63] However, having noted possible points of agreement, Vondey then dismisses Vanhoozer's approach as overly cognitive, desiring to make more space for the spontaneous work of the Spirit. Vondey explains, "For Pentecostals, theology is not 'Christo-dramatic fittingness,' as Vanhoozer puts it, but Spirit-energetic freedom."[64] In this view, "the Spirit is not the director of a scripted drama but the moral and eschatological imagination of the story itself and of its performance in the world."[65] For Vondey, Vanhoozer's approach is too tied to Scripture as the center of revelation to be performed in the world. Following Rickie Moore, Vondey instead suggests that "the person and community thus captured by God's pathos participate in the divine self-disclosure not by performing but by being themselves transformed into a voice that brings together the witness of Scripture and the Spirit of God."[66] As will become apparent in what follows, there is something to be said for Vondey's (and others') query about Vanhoozer's overly cognitive approach. However, Vondey's alternative seems to fall foul of the question of how the church is able to determine right performance or play within creation if Scripture is not

---

63. Vondey, *Beyond Pentecostalism*. We will return to consider the idea of "play" in later chapters in light of the importance Winnicott gives to it as a sign of healthy development. However, as will become apparent, although there is some overlap with what Vondey proposes and what will be developed as healthy play here, there are also important differences.

64. Vondey, *Beyond Pentecostalism*, 38.

65. Vondey, *Beyond Pentecostalism*, 39.

66. Vondey, *Beyond Pentecostalism*, 71–72.

retained as the authoritative benchmark, particularly the revelation of God in the incarnate Christ. As Vanhoozer has noted in response, the theodramatic view does not downplay the role of the Spirit either. Instead, it is the Spirit as "director," "enabler," "prompter," and "giver of life" that brings the church into being, dresses her, and unites her to Christ by working in the minds and hearts of disciples. It is this same Spirit that also inspired writers of Holy Scripture and illuminates it for current performers.[67] Vanhoozer may well be overly cognitive in his approach to formation and performance, but Vondey's approach seems to have far greater problems to face. That said, my proposal is still that following the theodramatic model through, including the corrections that will be made to Vanhoozer's overly cognitive approach in the following chapters, it is still a model and method conducive to Pentecostal theology.

Theodramatic Theology and Psychological Insights

A further methodological question remains though, before an outline of the rest of the project is provided. In what follows, given that trauma theory and Winnicott's work will be engaged with, how does this method and model accommodate a multidisciplinary approach, as it must? Joanna Collicutt, in exploring the use of psychology when studying the Bible, suggests that "the first step in evaluating the usefulness of psychology in approaching the Bible is to be clear *which* psychology we mean."[68] This is certainly a question that will require answering but, arguably, this is not the first step.[69] The first step, as noted above is to be clear on what one thinks the Bible is and therefore how it is to be engaged with. Regardless of which psychology one engages with, there is a significant difference between reading the Bible believing it to be the type of authoritative text proposed in this work, and reading it as a fascinating piece of literature on par with the works of Shakespeare, for example. So, to answer the question requires reminding ourselves that this project is rooted in Christian pastoral theology and is about how *Christian* communities care well for those who have suffered trauma, and the Bible and theology are approached in the way described above. With that in view, the interaction

---

67. Vanhoozer, *Faith Speaking Understanding*, 250–51.
68. Collicutt, "Bringing," 6.
69. For helpful introductions to psychology and biblical hermeneutics, see Rollins, *Soul and Psyche*; and Ellens, *Psychological Hermeneutics*.

between theology and psychology could be visualized as a conversation in which, as Watts describes, there is "co-ordination between two separate disciplines" that offer "complementary perspectives on reality."[70] However, the danger here is that in the "co-ordination," theology may become subservient to psychological agendas and perspectives when the perspectives fail to be "complementary." Collicutt brackets something similar to Watts's proposal under the broader heading of "Psychology and theology in creative dialogue." However, under the same heading, she also offers the alternative of "Using the insights of one to advance the agenda of the other."[71] This latter type, in conjunction with a further heading she proposes of "Psychology serving the church," is what is being attempted here. Theodramatic first theology provides the starting point for whatever may follow with a view to mining psychology for resources that advance the pastoral theological agenda. In a critical examination of psychological approaches to biblical criticism, Walter Brueggemann highlights the danger of what Collicutt refers to as "idealogical reductionism":[72]

> There is a danger, in the eclectic enterprise of psychological criticism, to impose a psychological theory on the text in a way that overrides the specificity of the text itself and that distorts the text in order to serve the theory that an interpreter may advocate.... Thus while theoretical reference points are important, in the end such criticism serves well only if it permits us to read and hear the text more discerningly.[73]

With Brueggemann's words of caution in mind, what follows is a multi-disciplinary approach that gives primacy to divinely authored Scripture as the norming norm for direction for faithful Christlike performances in the theodrama. Psychology—in this case, primarily Winnicott's theories—then takes what Vanhoozer would refer to as a "ministerial" rather than "magisterial" role as a tool used by theology and the Holy Spirit to aid in the task of directing such performances.

Although the focus will be on trauma-related psychology and the work of Winnicott, I also have sympathies with the school of thought known as "positive psychology." Within this developing school, flourishing

---

70. Watts, *Theology and Psychology*, 7–8.
71. Collicutt, *Psychology*, 45.
72. Collicutt, "Bringing," 20–22.
73. Brueggemann, "Psychological Criticism," 215–16.

is seen as the goal rather than the release from that which hinders.[74] The two, of course, go hand in hand but where the emphasis is placed in terms of the main goal can have a significant impact. The equivalent in theology is perhaps about whether salvation equates to creation flourishing as God intended or whether it equates to freedom from sin and its consequences. Of course, again, the two go hand in hand, but I will be suggesting that flourishing is the aim, and freedom from sin and its consequences is part of what enables that flourishing. To put it another way, we were created to flourish, which was then hampered by sin, rather than, we were created sinful with the aim of escaping and flourishing.[75]

I am not the first and neither will I be the last to bring into conversation theology and psychology in order to try to aid the church in being more fully and authentically the church. Examples abound in terms of drawing these two disciplines together. Neither am I the first to engage, theologically, with Donald Winnicott.[76] However, to the best of my knowledge, nobody thus far has explored how Winnicott's work around the maturational processes, the facilitating environment, and the development of the true self might be brought into conversation with theology with the aim of providing theodramatic guidance for Christlike pastoral care to those suffering from trauma.[77] In his fascinating exploration of connections between Winnicott's work and Christianity, Stephen Parker draws out the possible Wesleyan influences on Winnicott from Winnicott's childhood as well as discussing similarities and differences between Winnicott's theories and John Wesley's theology.[78] In a similar way, the present project aims to explore connections between Winnicott's work and biblical theology. However, where the present project differs is in the intent to use Winnicott's theories as an aid to illuminate aspects of

---

74. Seligman and Csikszentmihalyi, "Positive Psychology"; and Ambler et al., *Flourishing in Faith*.

75. As will become apparent, in the current project I am following a similar line of thought to that outlined by Matthew Anstey. See Anstey, "'And God Saw.'"

76. For example, see Parker, *Winnicott*; Hamman, "Restoration of Job"; Hopkins, "Jesus and Object-Use"; Middleton, *Abraham's Silence*, 235–36; Brueggemann, "Psychological Criticism"; Brueggemann, "Costly Loss of Lament," 102–4; Risser, *Creativity*.

77. Interestingly, James Samra in his study exploring Paul's understanding of maturity and maturation notes in the preface that he had used a psychological lens to explore the subject matter but then jettisoned that material. Given the language used it is possible that Winnicott may have been one of the sources engaged with. Although Samra provides an insightful contribution, it seems a shame that his work did not also include a psychological exploration of maturity and maturation. See Samra, *Being Conformed*, xi.

78. Parker, *Winnicott*.

the biblical texts to help the church find guidance there for better care of those who have experienced trauma.

Dustin Risser's work *Creativity, Theology and Posttraumatic Growth* is one of few examples where Winnicott's work is engaged with at length in conversation with contemporary trauma theory and Christian theology. Focusing on the area of Posttraumatic Growth (PTG) Risser states, "Throughout this work, I provide psychological and theological grounds for the application of creativity as an adjunctive and ongoing therapeutic support, which might mobilize the occurrence of PTG."[79]

In dialogue with Winnicott's work and contemporary research on PTG, while using Judith Herman's three-stage process of recovery as a framework, Risser explores the importance and usefulness of creativity and play while engaging the work of Moltmann and others to add a theological dimension to this exploration of creativity. The result of such dialogue is suggestions about how the church might be a place of safety that can facilitate creativity and PTG in particular ways. The present project is aiming at something similar yet starting from a theo-dramatic model and method in order to locate and respond to trauma from within that model, aided by Winnicott and others. In that sense, the current project is aiming at a more theologically rich and robust approach that offers further reflection on Christocentric anthropology and a eucharistic ecclesiology in the understanding of trauma, and how best to respond to its impact within the theodrama.

Tiffany Houck-Loomis also draws on Winnicott and others in her proposal and exploration of Job as a post-exilic counter-narrative to the pre- and exilic Deuteronomic covenant.[80] She explains, "My approach draws equally on the methods of historical-critical and ideological biblical criticism and from selected psychoanalytical theory about symbols in order to analyze how individuals and communities construct historical narratives as a way of processing life-shattering circumstances."[81] Houck-Loomis's work differs from the present in a number of ways, some of which will be discussed further below. Noteworthy at this point is that where the present work understands the Bible to be ultimately authored by God via human hands thus mediating insight into the nature of God and God's intent for and relationship with creation, Houck-Loomis's work seems to be founded on a different approach. Instead, she

---

79. Risser, *Creativity*.
80. Houck-Loomis, *History Through Trauma*.
81. Houck-Loomis, *History Through Trauma*, 1.

seems to believe that the Bible—or more precisely, the Old Testament, as there is no connection made to the New Testament or Christianity—is a human creation made sacred by how it is viewed and used by certain people. For her, a sacred text is "a text that withstands the test of time in its ability to enable individuals and communities to make individual and collective meaning."[82] This leads her to use Winnicott and others to aid in exploring why particular authors of parts of the Bible have created what they have in response to the trauma of exile. Rather than believing God to be the ground of being and creator of the universe, Houck-Loomis holds to a particular psychological theory of the self as a "universal and timeless reality of the psyche" and "an objective reality," which she claims prevents her from reading the biblical texts through her chosen lens anachronistically.[83] The present work holds a much higher view of the whole of Scripture—Old and New Testaments—and is more realistic about the subjective nature and limitations of any psychological theory of the self. In what follows, contra Houck-Loomis's approach, Winnicott's theories will provide a helpful analogical tool to aid in enriching a biblically rooted understanding of healthy human development and the environments and relationships that best facilitate that, particularly during post-traumatic remaking.

As will become apparent, there are a number of key points of contact between Winnicott's work and Vanhoozer's that have fueled my exploration of the conversation. What might prove puzzling to those familiar with Winnicott at this point, though, is why engagement with Winnicott was chosen around the subject of trauma when he wrote nothing specifically on trauma as understood in contemporary discourse. To give the game away regarding where this project will land, the answer is that arguably, when a reexamination of the *imago Dei* and ecclesiology is undertaken through a combination of a theodramatic lens and insights from Winnicott's theories, what will become apparent is that the church that takes such results seriously will naturally be more trauma-sensitive.[84] A temptation of approaching ecclesiology and theological anthropology

---

82. Houck-Loomis, *History Through Trauma*, 30.

83. Houck-Loomis, *History Through Trauma*, 16.

84. It is also noteworthy that leading trauma psychologist Bessel Van der Kolk makes positive reference to Winnicott's work regarding how to offer constructive care to children in particular. See van der Kolk, *Body*, 135–37. This highlights that Winnicott's pioneering work has stood the test of time for informing contemporary approaches to healing. Risser has made similar connections between Winnicott's work and contemporary trauma theory, which he then takes in a different direction. See Risser, *Creativity*, 23–27.

with the aim of helping the church be more trauma-sensitive is that the inclination may be to provide some sort of tool kit for when the worst happens—for which there is a place. However, I will try to show in what follows that if theological anthropology and ecclesiology are revisited through a theodramatic lens, using insights from Winnicott's theories, perspectives and practices will be naturally embedded within the church that will mean that trauma care will be something that the church is more naturally equipped to do as an extension of its daily life, rather than something it has to reach for and learn on the spot.[85]

Structure

As noted above, what follows is primarily the construction of a Christian theological foundation for informed pastoral care of those who have experienced trauma. With that in mind, although the chief aim is better-informed practice, the emphasis of the present work is more on the development of the theological foundations, which then lead to guidance for practice. To set the scene for the following chapters, chapter 2 will focus on defining trauma as used in secular models as well as mapping out how relevant phenomena have been approached from within Christian theological discourse. This will provide a good overview of the field to situate and differentiate the current approach. However, rather than jump straight to redefining trauma through the lens to be used in this work, the next steps are to explore what it might mean to be made in the image of God and how the church encourages and enables that to provide a backdrop for how trauma might be revisited through a Christocentric theodramatic lens.

Chapter 3 will focus specifically on theodramatic anthropology to define what it might mean to be made in the image of God and how that is fulfilled by Christ in order to locate our eschatological identity "in Christ." Further to this there will be an exploration of what it might mean to perform Christ. The reason for beginning here is that it seems wrong-headed to attempt to give guidance on good trauma care if we have no sense of what it might mean to talk of a healthy and whole

---

85. Arguably, one example where a bolt on toolkit type approach is employed is in Carla Grosch-Miller's *Trauma and Pastoral Care*. Although this is an excellent resource for church leaders, what I want to suggest in what follows is that trauma care can more naturally emerge from church practices if we begin by reassessing what it means to better support humans within the church in performing Christ in the world.

person. Without the revelation of the theodrama to ground this, clarity risks giving way to individual relativism that can offer little in way of direction for the church as the body of Christ to care for and guide each other toward wholeness.

Chapter 4 shifts the focus to the church as the community that can encourage and enable—or discourage and block(!)—human growth and development. This chapter centers on the identity of the church as the place where the gospel is enfleshed by recognizing the way in which the church is the theatre/theater of the gospel. At the heart of this is the Eucharist, which both provides identity and nourishes the church as it seeks to live out its life in a variety of contexts as the unified body of Christ. Relating this to the previous chapter and to the project as a whole, chapter 4 offers guidance as to how the church is to enable the flourishing of individuals in their development in Christ that in turn results in a more Christlike church. Chapters 3 and 4 together therefore provide clarity regarding the identity of individuals and the church in the theodrama as well as what healthy development looks like and how it might be achieved. These two chapters thus set the backdrop for how trauma may be interpreted and responded to from a theodramatic perspective.

However, what will be made apparent in both chapters is that engagement with Vanhoozer's theodramatic model offers much to work with but falls significantly short in key areas to do with how realistic development as individuals and the church, in Christ, might actually be achieved. To aid with this shortfall Winnicott's work is drawn into the conversation. Chapter 5 maps out key aspects of Winnicott's theories that will prove useful in the following chapters as a way of addressing the shortfalls in Vanhoozer's work.

Chapters 6 and 7 revisit theodramatic anthropology and ecclesiology respectively, newly equipped with Winnicott's theories established in chapter 5. Rather than offering an alternative to the theodramatic approach, this will provide rich and illuminating analogical insights that will correct and strengthen theodramatic anthropology and ecclesiology in key ways for the better enabling of human growth and development as *imago Dei* and the body of Christ. The result of chapters 6 and 7 is a refreshed understanding of what healthy development as a performer in the theodrama might look like and how the church best enables this.

Chapter 8 extends the conclusions of chapters 6 and 7 into the sphere of theodramatic trauma care as the project comes full circle, returning to the experience of trauma, to address the central question of the project.

With the rest of the project in view, the definition of trauma is reinterpreted through the Winnicottian-informed theodramatic lens developed in previous chapters before direction is given regarding how churches might better care for those who are traumatized in their midst. In doing so an answer is given regarding what Job's friends could have done.

This work is drawn to a close with a final conclusion in chapter 9. However, rather than offering a totalizing project that answers all questions—as if such a thing were even possible(!)—the conclusion bears witness to the journey thus far and invites ongoing dialogue with readers. The challenges of performing Christ on the local and global stage are constantly shifting and, therefore, so should theological work that is attempting to remain in step with the Spirit of God at work in church and world alike. The hope is that this contribution to the field might aid us to become more Christlike in ourselves and toward others, particularly those who have faced or are facing the suffering of trauma.

2

Trauma and Theology

Introduction

To LOCATE THE PRESENT work within the existing fields it is helpful to identify the shape and content of those fields. It will also be helpful to offer a working definition of trauma drawn from psychological, biological, and sociological perspectives as a window into how trauma is understood and responded to in those overlapping fields, not least because such fields have paved the way to describing and responding to such phenomena experienced by people. This chapter therefore begins by exploring what is being referred to by different disciplines when the term "trauma" is used. No one interprets and labels from a position of pure objectivity, meaning that each discipline and proponent is operating from somewhere, interpreting as they go. The point is not to engage in some lengthy discussion about hermeneutics but merely to highlight the fact that no one person or discipline has a monopoly on the definition of terms, and so the theodramatic perspective to be developed here has a place at the table.

There have been numerous engagements with trauma theory by Christian theologians in recent years, and so the second task of this chapter is to map that field of engagement specifically. As with any descriptive enterprise, groupings are always only provisional, heuristic tools used to help draw attention to what the user wants the reader to notice. That is no less the case here. The mapping work will group the various approaches in such a way as to try to display, as clearly as possible, points of significant similarity in focus, model, and method when grouping the various approaches. There is definite room for blurring of boundaries between groups, but the categorizing used should illuminate helpful similarities and differences with the chief aim of drawing attention to how the current project contributes to the field in a unique way. With a sense of direction in hand, we turn to explore definitions of trauma.

Defining Trauma

The term "trauma" finds its root in a Greek word meaning "wound." However, whereas our minds and bodies are often able to heal themselves when wounded, this is not the case with traumatic wounding. Hilary Ison states, "*Trauma* is defined as that which overwhelms our capacity to cope with our experience and breaks connections—to ourselves, to others, to resources, to our frames of reference."[1] Trauma is thus a disempowering experience of helplessness and loss of control in the face of potential annihilation where one's worldview and sense of meaning are fractured if not obliterated. Each individual and/or community has a pool of resources to draw from in their response to such experiences that will be unique to them, meaning each individual or community is therefore both vulnerable and resilient in different ways at different times. If the experience encountered requires a greater amount of, or different, resources to enable the sufferer to cope with the experience then typical responses that enable safety and protection become what Judith Herman describes as "overwhelmed and disorganized."[2] The lasting impact of this overwhelm affects both the physical and psychological human systems in a variety of ways and, as Bessel van der Kolk explains, "means continuing to organize your life as if the trauma were still going on—unchanged and immutable—as every new encounter or event is contaminated by the past."[3] It is this lasting impact that is designated as a type of Post-Traumatic Stress Disorder (PTSD). Rather than be categorized as a pathology, Peter Levine argues that PTSD is "the result of a natural process gone awry" given that humans, like other creatures, have the capacity, under certain circumstances to recover from potentially traumatizing experiences.[4] Although there is a uniqueness about how each individual

---

1. Ison, "Embodied," 47.
2. Herman, *Trauma and Recovery*, 50.
3. Van der Kolk, *Body*, 53.
4. Levine and Frederick, *Waking the Tiger*, 6.

experiences trauma, Herman highlights that there is usually a commonality about experiences that result in trauma where such experiences "generally involve threats to life or bodily integrity, or a close personal encounter with violence and death."[5] Herman further states, "The most powerful determinant of psychological harm is the character of the traumatic event itself" rather than the uniqueness of each personality.[6] What personality type does shape is the nature of the PTSD that is experienced as a result. The impact of the traumatic experience is thus shaped by our previous experience and resultant resources while also shaping our physiology and how we respond to new experiences.[7] But what is the impact of trauma on our minds, bodies, and relationships?

Given the focus of this work, it is not necessary to be too extensive in detail regarding the impact of trauma on mind and body but, for a church community to be better equipped to recognize, care for, and respond to those who are traumatized, having a basic understanding of impact is vital. Exploring this impact begins by outlining a simple model of the brain that focuses on three distinct yet interconnected sections. For this, we turn to Van der Kolk, as a leading expert in the field.

The first of these sections is the oldest part of the brain in terms of evolutionary development—sometimes called the reptilian brain—which has commonality with aspects of other ancient animal brains. This section develops first, pre-birth, and includes the brain stem and hypothalamus. Its main role is to keep balance (homeostasis) in the body by enabling the basic functions that keep humans alive—such as breathing, eating, sleeping, pain awareness, and the expulsion of anything the body finds toxic—to be carried out correctly.[8]

The second part is known as the limbic system or mammalian brain, "because all animals that live in groups and nurture their young possess one."[9] This part develops more fully after birth and is the key to emotional development in humans. It monitors whether something is a threat or to be welcomed and in so doing judges whether something is enjoyable or frightening. It is therefore a vital part of the brain for navigating interactions and determining what is essential for survival. As a part of

---

5. Herman, *Trauma and Recovery*, 49.
6. Herman, *Trauma and Recovery*, 82.
7. See Levine and Frederick, *Waking the Tiger*, 48–52, for Levine's discussion of factors that affect the impact of potentially traumatic experiences.
8. Van der Kolk, *Body*, 64–65.
9. Van der Kolk, *Body*, 56.

the brain that largely develops post-birth in the very early stages of a baby's life, the healthy development of this part, and therefore the person, is dependent on its environment and interactions. "Whatever happens to a baby contributes to the emotional and perceptual map of the world that its developing brain creates."[10] If a child is provided with a safe and loving environment in contrast to one that is experienced as unsafe and possibly threatening, the formation of the limbic system and the resultant emotions, sensations, and behaviors will be very different. "If you feel safe and loved, your brain becomes specialized in exploration, play, and cooperation; if you are frightened and unwanted, it specializes in managing feelings of fear and abandonment."[11] The neuroplasticity of the brain is such that if a particular circuit in the brain fires on a regular basis, the brain develops in a particular way and creates default responses. It is, for good and for bad, possible throughout life to rewire the brain depending on new positive or negative experiences that might be had.

When placed together, Van der Kolk refers to these two parts of the brain collectively as the "emotional brain."[12] They operate instinctively to keep humans safe and healthy and influence our decision-making and actions on a day-to-day basis in numerous ways that we are largely unaware of. The emotional brain is the part that kicks into fight-flight-freeze-flop-attach mode when a potential threat is perceived (see below).

The third part of the brain is much more complex than the emotional brain and is called the neocortex. Although there is a commonality with other mammals in this part of the brain, it is far more developed in humans and is much thicker. The neocortex processes the complex data taken in by our senses as well as engaging in abstract and creative thinking in the use of symbols and language in order to communicate with others in a reasoned and thought-through way. This is the rational planning and problem-solving part of the brain that also attunes humans to other humans and enables engagement in appropriate behavior.[13]

When the brain is functioning normally, all three parts work together to enable the human to live well in the world, including making sure potential danger is dealt with. When the possibility of danger becomes apparent, humans initially instinctively rely on their social and tribal

---

10. Van der Kolk, *Body*, 56.
11. Van der Kolk, *Body*, 56.
12. Van der Kolk, *Body*, 57.
13. Van der Kolk, *Body*, 66–67.

makeup and call out for help.[14] If the call is unmet or the threat to survival is immediate, this information is perceived via the senses and the limbic system processes the incoming information and in doing so sends it both to the amygdala in the reptilian brain as well as to the frontal cortex in the neocortex. Drawing on the nearby hippocampus that connects previous experiences to the current experience, the amygdala determines whether the current information suggests a threat to survival. If it does, it then sends a message to the hypothalamus and brain stem in order to activate the hormone system and autonomic nervous system (ANS)—specifically the branch known as the sympathetic nervous system (SNS)—which causes the body to respond in a suitable way. All this takes place quicker than the frontal cortex can respond to the information, meaning that the reptilian brain decides first what response is required and activates the body quicker than the brain can cognize what is happening. This results in the classic fight or flight response in which the brain prepares the body for one of these outcomes by releasing hormones that raise heart and breathing rates and blood pressure. Once the threat has passed, the brain activates the branch of the nervous system known as the parasympathetic nervous system (PNS) to slow down arousal and return the body to a normal state. If, however, the threat is inescapable, a further mechanism is activated whereby the result is a collapsed or frozen state.

Where a threat is wrongly perceived and the emotional response is not too strong, the frontal lobes in the neocortex will enable a slower more reasoned response that short-circuits the fight or flight instinct and the related stress. Achieving a healthy balance in terms of brain response enables prevention of under- or over-reaction to given situations.[15] However, whereas those who have experienced a correctly or incorrectly perceived threat to survival escape or live through it and then return, at some point after, to a normal state and can integrate their experience into their life, "traumatized people become stuck, stopped in their growth because they can't integrate new experiences into their lives."[16] This traumatized state is one in which the brain continues to prepare the body to respond to a threat that is no longer present, and the presence of this state manifests

---

14. Levine, *In an Unspoken Voice*, 98–99.

15. For a fuller explanation see Van der Kolk, *Body*, 86–101. Van der Kolk draws from polyvagal theory in the development of his own work, as does Peter Levine (see *In an Unspoken Voice*, 97–131). For various resources on polyvagal theory, see Polyvagal Institute, "Scientific Papers, Chapters."

16. Van der Kolk, *Body*, 53.

in the body in a variety of ways. As Levine notes, "Traumatic symptoms are not caused by the 'triggering' event itself. They stem from the frozen residue of energy that has not been resolved and discharged; this residue remains trapped in the nervous system where it can wreak havoc on our bodies and spirits."[17] People experiencing this traumatized state may try to avoid or protect against the experience or even try to create a false sense of control. But ultimately, if the trauma is not resolved, such attempts will be in vain. Given the avenues of fight, flight, freeze, or flop, inevitably the resultant traumatized state is either one of hyper-vigilance or one of hypo-vigilance or numbness. The challenge for those seeking to find a healthy path out of such a state is, first, becoming aware of it. As Van der Kolk explains, "The challenge is not so much learning to accept the terrible things that have happened but learning how to gain mastery over one's internal sensations and emotions. Sensing, naming, and identifying what is going on inside is the first step to recovery."[18]

It is helpful at this point to offer a little more detail in terms of the lived reality of traumatization in order to better equip the church to know how to spot signs and how to respond well. Van der Kolk states that "dissociation is the essence of trauma. The overwhelming experience is split off and fragmented, so that the emotions, sounds, images, thoughts, and physical sensations related to the trauma take on a life of their own. The sensory fragments of memory intrude into the present, where they are literally relived."[19] What adds further pain to this experience is that the triggers for reliving are varied and most likely the timing, content, and intensity of the experience are unpredictable. The first experience of trauma is relived and experienced in the body time and time again and, during these experiences, the brain prepares the body to respond as if the original event was reoccurring. One particular challenge for those who are traumatized is that the part of the brain that is able to distinguish between a previous experience and the present does not function as it should and so a finite event of the past continues to be confused with, and relived in, the present. A further issue is that the part of the brain that enables sensory data to be integrated in an ordered way into one's autobiographical narrative also shuts down during a traumatic experience, meaning that the event is not remembered as a coherent storied experience but, instead, "as isolated sensory imprints: images, sounds,

17. Levine and Frederick, *Waking the Tiger*, 19.
18. Van der Kolk, *Body*, 68.
19. Van der Kolk, *Body*, 66.

and physical sensations that are accompanied by intense emotions, usually terror and helplessness."[20] This means that there is an ongoing feeling of sensory overwhelm that is addressed by attempts at shutting down—either naturally or by the use of artificial aids such as drugs. In addition to the fight or flight response, some who experience trauma simply freeze or flop. The freezing or numbing response occurs when trauma cannot be escaped, and so the mind protects the individual by dissociating into an emotionally detached state that may feel like an out-of-body experience or dream-like state, affecting sensations and perceptions of time and reality. How this continues to manifest as dissociation in those who are traumatized is in what is termed "depersonalization." Here the brain decreases in activity, meaning that the person "cannot think, feel deeply, remember, or make sense out of what is going on."[21]

Judith Herman, also a leading expert in trauma theory and therapy, describes the symptoms of PTSD as "hyperarousal," "intrusion," and "constriction."[22] Hyperarousal is the ongoing "elevated baseline of arousal" that affects sleep patterns and health in a variety of negative ways where "traumatic events appear to recondition the human nervous system" which is now on constant alert ready for threats that have, in reality, passed.[23]

Intrusion is that which Herman uses to describe the way traumatic memory continues to impinge on the life of the survivor, disrupting relationships. Perception and time are affected by painful and fragmented traumatic memories that are "encoded in the form of vivid sensations and images" that continue to intrude on the survivor's life.[24]

Constriction is what Herman uses to describe choices that "narrow and deplete the quality of life and ultimately perpetuate the effects of the traumatic event."[25] Such choices are the result of a desire to avoid places, experiences or people that may trigger memories of the traumatic experience. Although constrictions in life choices continue to fuel avoidance of various triggers, they also prevent integration of the traumatic experience into the survivor's narrative, which therefore stalls the healing process.

20. Van der Kolk, *Body*, 70.
21. Van der Kolk, *Body*, 72.
22. Herman, *Trauma and Recovery*, 51. Levine proposes a similar list but with some variation in use of terms. See Levine and Frederick, *Waking the Tiger*, 132–43.
23. Herman, *Trauma and Recovery*, 53.
24. Herman, *Trauma and Recovery*, 55.
25. Herman, *Trauma and Recovery*, 69.

Herman refers to the "dialectic of trauma" as consisting of "intrusion and constriction" where the survivor is engaged in this dark tension of which neither offers a pathway to healing.[26]

To add more nuance to describing the much-varied impact of trauma, Herman goes beyond description of the impact of a single traumatic experience to suggest a spectrum that includes what has been termed "complex PTSD."[27] Herman states, "The responses to trauma are best understood as a spectrum of conditions rather than as a single disorder. They range from a brief stress reaction that gets better by itself and never qualifies for a diagnosis, to classic or simple post-traumatic stress disorder, to the complex syndrome of prolonged, repeated trauma."[28] This spectrum is able to encapsulate the core symptoms of the impact of trauma while including the important nuances within this core.

Herman further goes on to note that "recognition of the trauma is central to the recovery process."[29] In doing so she proposes a three-stage approach that seeks to respond to the disconnection and disempowerment of trauma by trying to aid the survivor to rebuild "trust, autonomy, initiative, competence, identity, and intimacy."[30] Preferring a modality shaped by psychoanalysis, Herman purposely warns against any approach that tries to cure found in the "medical model" and instead aims at the facilitation of empowerment with intervention being the exception rather than the rule. And as humans are deemed fundamentally relational, "recovery can take place only within the context of relationships; it cannot occur in isolation."[31] The three-stage process she proposes consists of "Safety," "Remembrance and Mourning," and "Reconnection" and, in various guises, has been successfully used by various practitioners.

The first of these stages, "Safety," is possibly the most important, without which further healing work cannot be successfully undertaken. As Levine notes, "To move through trauma we need quietness, safety, and protection."[32] Here the aim is to facilitate the survivor achieving the experience of a sense of safety in their own body to begin with and then work outward to experience safety in their environment and context and in

---

26. Herman, *Trauma and Recovery*, 69.
27. Herman, *Trauma and Recovery*, 174–78.
28. Herman, *Trauma and Recovery*, 174.
29. Herman, *Trauma and Recovery*, 186.
30. Herman, *Trauma and Recovery*, 191.
31. Herman, *Trauma and Recovery*, 191.
32. Levine and Frederick, *Waking the Tiger*, 35–36.

various relationships. "Because no one can establish a safe environment alone, the task of developing an adequate safety plan always includes a component of social support."[33] Again, although this requires specialist care, a suitable wider social network is required to enable healing and remaking, which may also mean letting go of people and/or situations that do not offer the necessary provision.

The second stage of "Remembrance and Mourning" involves a detailed retelling of the traumatic experience by the survivor. Of note here is that this retelling is likely fragmentary, due to the nature of traumatic memory detailed above, and that it will likely need to take place within a suitable group of fellow survivors, alongside one-to-one professional support.

> The survivor is called upon to articulate the values and beliefs that she once held and that the trauma destroyed. She stands mute before the emptiness of evil, feeling the insufficiency of any known system of explanation. Survivors of atrocity of every age and every culture come to a point in their testimony where all questions are reduced to one, spoken more in bewilderment than in outrage: Why? The answer is beyond human understanding.[34]

The remembering joins with and informs the mourning as old ways of being and perceiving are grieved as a way forward is sought that both integrates the traumatic experience into the survivor's life and narrative and begins to navigate a way of continuing relationships with those who continue to hold a worldview that the survivor is no longer able to subscribe to. This process involves both personal and internal work as well as outward testimony to the relevant group and professional who bear witness to the unique reality of each testimony, sharing the burden of the traumatic experience while standing in solidarity with the survivor.

It is important to note here that Herman's therapeutic modality may have the tendency to overlook what Van der Kolk refers to as "body experiences." Focusing on body experiences—what Levine refers to as the "felt sense"—could appear out of place in the remembrance and mourning phase of the process.[35] However, what has become apparent from trauma research is that although verbal expression has a vital part to play, there is

---

33. Herman, *Trauma and Recovery*, 231.
34. Herman, *Trauma and Recovery*, 258.
35. Levine and Frederick, *Waking the Tiger*.

often a need for those who have experienced trauma to become at home in the body again and feel real, either before, or alongside, verbal expression and processing.[36] This is so because "the act of telling the story doesn't necessarily alter the automatic physical and hormonal responses of bodies that remain hypervigilant, prepared to be assaulted or violated at any time."[37] And particularly so if Levine is correct in arguing that persisting post-traumatic symptoms are due to "incomplete *physiological* responses suspended in fear."[38] Trauma therefore often means that a story can be told in the past tense while the body continues to operate in a mode that acts as if the threat is current and active. It is also common, because of how the brain responds to trauma, for the person to not be able to retell the experience coherently yet, if ever. So, providing space and activities that aid in grounding the person, helping them to feel real, and able to manage the emotions that come with the traumatic experience are crucial. We will return to this in greater detail in chapter 8.

The final stage of "Reconnection" seeks to continue to push back against the disempowering and isolating effects of trauma by enabling the survivor to reengage with the world around them with a sense of hope and imagination despite what has been experienced. "The self-discipline learned in the early stages of recovery can now be joined to the survivor's capacities for imagination and play. This is a period of trial and error, of learning to tolerate mistakes and to savor unexpected success."[39] What is achieved is not a complete healing as remaking is an ongoing progress always susceptible to a degree of regression, dependent on new experiences and potential triggers. Instead, there is an integrated sense of self that now includes the traumatic experience in the current coherent remade worldview in which there is fresh hope and imagination about the content of the future.

This latter stage of reconnecting may still involve group work, but now the survivor is encouraged to engage in groups that do not contain people with a similar trauma history. "The survivor must be ready to relinquish the 'specialness' of her identity" and locate her experience within a broader perspective or differing perspectives without diminishing it.[40]

---

36. Van der Kolk, *Body*, 203–6.
37. Van der Kolk, *Body*, 21.
38. Levine and Frederick, *Waking the Tiger*, 34. Emphasis mine.
39. Herman, *Trauma and Recovery*, 296.
40. Herman, *Trauma and Recovery*, 344.

Herman sums up: "Trauma shames and isolates; the foundation of recovery is therefore in restored relational connections."[41]

Although much that Herman and others suggest for healthy post-traumatic remaking involves specialized group and one-to-one work, the nature of the explorations and questions suggests that a church that takes seriously supporting those in the remaking process will need to consider how not to hinder such explorations and instead explore how best to support such processes. As has already been noted above, supportive, safe communities are vital for both the prevention of the experience of trauma as well as aiding this remaking. What will be presented in the ensuing chapters of this work, culminating in the conclusion, is how the church and the underpinning Christian faith might particularly be able to aid with this remaking. We will return to Van der Kolk and Herman's work in chapter 8. Before moving to locate this project within the current field of theological work on trauma, though, it is important to highlight and recognize that traumatic experience, although often focused on that of individuals, has a far broader reach and way of being interpreted.

Beyond the Individual's Experience of Trauma

When I first began to write this section, the world was gripped by the COVID-19 pandemic, which individuals have responded to in different ways. I mention this because, although individuals have indeed been impacted by this global phenomenon, as briefly noted in the introduction, the impact is far greater than that, with wider society and culture shaping the interpretation and responses to trauma as well as being shaped by them. What Jennifer Baldwin highlights in a helpful way that is also present in a less defined way in Herman and Van der Kolk's work, and that needs to be borne in mind here, is that there are different types of traumas, that have very different effects. Separating types into "Primary," "Secondary," "Intergenerational," "Societal," and "Cultural" trauma, Baldwin draws attention to the complex nature of trauma as experienced by individuals who exist within wider families, societies, and cultures.[42] Altering Baldwin's categories slightly, it is helpful to briefly outline the far-reaching impact trauma can have.

---

41. Herman, *Trauma and Recovery*, 388.
42. Baldwin, *Trauma-Sensitive Theology*, 31–38.

As the name would suggest, primary trauma refers to first-hand effects of trauma-inducing events on individuals. Secondary trauma, according to Baldwin, refers to the experience of trauma due to something that happened to someone else close to the one experiencing trauma. She further suggests that secondary trauma can particularly occur among those in professions where individuals are regularly caring for others who have experienced suffering. In such settings, Baldwin states that secondary trauma can sometimes be referred to as compassion fatigue and may lead to burnout if unnoticed or left untreated. However, it is important to add some nuance here as Baldwin unhelpfully equates terms that others would want to separate and more tightly define.

Rather than simply using secondary trauma and compassion fatigue interchangeably, these two need to be distinguished from one another and sharpened in definition while adding the additional term "vicarious trauma." Vicarious trauma takes place in the therapeutic (or similar) relationship and occurs where the trauma of a client "disrupts" the therapist's "cognitive structures or schemas that anchor some of their basic beliefs about the world."[43] More specifically, this touches on "basic needs of safety, dependency, trust, power, esteem, and intimacy" to which they become vulnerable due to "empathic engagement."[44] When vicarious trauma occurs, the sufferer will display symptoms of trauma due to the cognitive impact. By subtle contrast, secondary trauma needs to be replaced with secondary traumatic stress as a more accurate term distinguished from vicarious trauma. Following the work of Charles Figley, Newell et al. note that "rather than focusing on the cognitive shifts in thinking that could potentially occur when treating trauma disorders, Figley's early conceptualization of secondary traumatic stress suggested that the clinician could actually mirror the symptoms of PTSD in the client to a lesser degree."[45] The outcome may look the same for the therapist, but the cause, and therefore the response required, may be subtly different when distinguishing between vicarious trauma and secondary traumatic stress. The first involves cognitive disruption, the second a mirroring that is not primarily to do with cognition.

Compassion fatigue is not to be equated to the first two terms discussed but, instead, might be better defined as a broader umbrella term that includes vicarious trauma and secondary traumatic stress but

---

43. Rasmussen, "Effects," 356.
44. Rasmussen, "Effects," 356.
45. Newell et al., "Clinical Responses," 309.

cannot be reduced to them. "Compassion fatigue is a more general, and perhaps more user-friendly term that describes the overall experience of emotional and psychological fatigue that mental health professionals experience due to the chronic use of empathy when treating individuals who are suffering in some way."[46] These differences are important to note in this work because the focus here is on trauma and post-traumatic remaking specifically. This means that because of the broad coverage of compassion fatigue as a term, it is vicarious trauma and secondary traumatic stress that is included in the focus of this work, rather than direct engagement with the wider field of discussion of compassion fatigue, although there will, of course, be overlap.

Intergenerational or multigenerational trauma refers to ways that the effects of traumatizing experiences on one or more members of a family can, particularly when left untreated, cause experiences and behaviors in following generations. This area of trauma studies potentially draws together the various strands of trauma definition referred to in this section in that cultural and societal trauma likely overlap with multigenerational trauma, as will be discussed below. Primary and secondary traumas are relevant here because primary trauma has been experienced at an individual or group level that, under the "multigenerational trauma" heading, is realized as a further primary trauma, vicarious trauma, or secondary traumatic stress in later generations. Some factors could likely contribute to this. A primary trauma may: lead to behavior toward later generations that results in further primary trauma (i.e., someone who has been abused becoming an abuser); result in behaviors and emotions that are then mirrored by later generations resulting in secondary traumatic stress; be recounted to later generations, resulting in vicarious trauma; lead to a combination of the previous three.[47] Behavioral studies as well as genetics, and particularly epigenetics, all contribute significantly to this discussion. The contribution of behavioral studies is hopefully obvious, but there is also research in epigenetics that suggests, although life events do not affect the structure of genes, they can affect the activity of genes and thus how they function, *and* that these patterns of genetic activity can be passed on to offspring.[48] The impact of trauma is, therefore, potentially far-reaching, and this becomes even more apparent as we turn our attention to societal and cultural trauma.

46. Newell et al., "Clinical Responses," 309.
47. Wiechelt et al., "Cultural," 175–77.
48. Van der Kolk, *Body*, 152.

Baldwin's use of societal and cultural trauma as separate experiences is misleading and ill-defined. Although not entirely clear, it would appear that Baldwin understands societal trauma to describe the experience of trauma by a particular society after the experience of a particular trauma-inducing event or experience such as the 9/11 attacks. Cultural trauma then seems to describe the way trauma continues to affect a particular culture if the wider society does not process it in a healthy way. What is telling here is that Baldwin does not define society or culture and how the two relate and draws from no academic research when proposing her categories. This begs the question of how the two categories can be separated out in such a clear way. Surely societal trauma is at the same time cultural trauma, as social groups are structured by, and find and make meaning via, their culture, so this would be the medium and location of trauma processing. What would it mean or look like to process trauma at a societal level but not at a cultural one? The answer is not clear, but Baldwin does point us toward something that is given greater clarity by other researchers—the presence of collective trauma as cultural trauma.

Arguably, "collective" and "cultural" are used synonymously, to describe the way a social group experiences and processes trauma. Linked to descriptions of the impact of trauma, above, members of a group experience a similar collective response that overwhelms resources and ruptures meaning and identity. "Members of the collective do not need to directly experience the event to feel the dramatic loss of identity and meaning that the trauma causes. Nor does the trauma have to be a sudden event; it can be a slow process that works its way into the psyche of the collective."[49] Drawing on the work of Kai Erikson and Jack Saul, Kate Wiebe has highlighted this "collective trauma" and explored how churches might understand and respond well to such a phenomenon.[50] However, it is worth noting that the process of healing is not a certainty as "when carrier groups lack the resources to disseminate trauma claims or social institutions constrain trauma claims, perpetrators of collective suffering can avoid assuming responsibility for the damage they have caused, and the healing components of the trauma process are stymied."[51] Linking back to intergenerational or multigenerational trauma, when this involves a collective that experiences trauma due to either a single event or wounding over a prolonged period, it may

49. Wiechelt et al., "Cultural," 174.
50. See Wiebe, "Collective Trauma."
51. Wiechelt et al., "Cultural," 174.

be defined as "historical trauma." The result of this if unresolved is a "historical-trauma response" that manifests in the same way, but on a multigenerational and collective scale, as that of primary trauma, and which then embeds in the culture of the collective.[52]

Bond and Craps highlight the preference for "cultural" over "collective" in the work of Jeffery Alexander and others when defining such traumas. The reasoning here is that "in order to be regarded as collective or national traumas, events have to be constructed as such in the public sphere."[53] This requires the shaping of the cultural narrative by a community or government leaders, media sources, and other cultural influences that are then bought into by individuals. This is not to suggest the trauma is not real and felt, but more to highlight the socially constructed nature of the identity and understanding of the nature of the trauma which then affects how it is used and responded to. Although this is to be distinguished from individual trauma and how it impacts the individuals, it does raise an important point about the possible need to overcome the victim-perpetrator binary when thinking about individual trauma. That is not to remove culpability from perpetrators nor blame victims and survivors in any way but more to draw out the relational nature of humanity and therefore the reality that trauma occurs within the wider social context.[54] Examples that draw this point out include the potentially traumatizing experience of working in a sweatshop that is caused not simply by an individual but by a larger system of which individuals are a part. A further example is the experience of so-called "moral injury." Grosch-Miller describes moral injury as "significant suffering that results from violations of a person's moral beliefs about themselves or the world, by what they did or didn't do, or by what they witnessed."[55] Although moral injury is rooted in shame or guilt and therefore distinguishable from PTSD, it is similar in symptomology, and moral injury often occurs in situations that are potentially traumatizing. Examples have largely been drawn from those in military service who may have experienced moral injury due to actions they have been ordered to undertake or refrain from, but moral injury can occur in many other settings.[56]

52. Wiechelt et al., "Cultural," 176–77.
53. Bond and Craps, *Trauma*, 101.
54. Bond and Craps, *Trauma*, 141–42.
55. Grosch-Miller, *Trauma and Pastoral Care*, 49.
56. Grosch-Miller, *Trauma and Pastoral Care*, 48–51.

In both cases, the categories of perpetrator and victim become blurred and potentially unhelpful as they no longer accurately represent the causes and experiences. Although the focus of what follows will be on creating church environments that facilitate remaking, it is important to have the complex nature of trauma definition and understanding as well as associated conditions in view to better approach developing suitable healing environments and practices.

Above we have been able to briefly draw to the surface the genetic, neurological, physiological, psychological, and social voices, all of which are important perspectives to bring to the table. This project will add a further theological voice as we proceed. To do that with greater clarity, it is important to locate it within the ever-widening and developing field of dialogues between trauma and theology, showing how this relates to and differs from other current work.

Contextualizing the Project

What follows is not meant to be an exhaustive literature review, but instead is intended as a heuristic tool that marks out the current field of work in order to locate the current project within it. As the current project is located specifically within Christian theology, highlighting of similar examples below is also limited to those who explicitly or implicitly would seem to locate themselves under that umbrella.

Pastoral Approaches

One approach taken by some scholars and practitioners is to focus primarily on the practical impact of trauma and what a good practical response might look like for individuals and communities. In this approach theology is a secondary exercise done in such a way as to fit in with what is presented as a clinical and universal understanding of trauma and best practice for care and post-traumatic remaking. This approach mines faith resources—the Bible, tradition, liturgy—for suitable resources that complement what is proposed as the correct way of seeing and responding to trauma. Practical theologian Carla Grosch-Miller is a good example of this type of approach. In *Trauma and Pastoral Care*, she provides clear and accessible resources that will serve leaders and congregations well in terms of understanding and responding to trauma, and so fulfills her aim "to equip and to encourage those who tend to the wounds to self, others and the communities that arise from traumatizing events."[57] Later in the book she engages with some biblical scholarship and Christian liturgy, as well as discussing the potential usefulness of worshiping communities for containing and directing vocalization and meaning-making. She also briefly highlights some endeavors in the area of theology and trauma. However, Christian theology does not, in any substantial way, appear to shape her understanding of what trauma is and what recovery, remaking, and resilience might mean. Instead, at the core is the belief that "as the survivor is the expert, the role of the accompanying pastoral carer is geared towards hearing them into speech as they find their way, respecting the survivor's autonomy and agency, and signposting resources."[58] There are fleeting mentions of the Bible and Christian theology and practice, and toward the very end of the book, there is a passing mention of the resurrection as a source of hope. But, given the way the text is focused on a supposed universal secularized interpretation of trauma and recovery, it would be easy enough to substitute other faiths in place of Christianity and mine their resources accordingly. Underpinning this approach appears to be something of an Enlightenment-shaped hermeneutic that presumes there is a shared universal understanding of the world, trauma, and remaking that we can all agree on, and that faith is a separate (and private?) realm of life from which the individual or community can draw when appropriate. The result is that no clear definition is given to what healthy remaking looks like—here we see glimpses of the post-modern turn to the subjective self—as it is for the individual or community to determine for themselves. I see the imperative to guard against destructive imposition from those seeking to care for and support those who are remaking and, as will become apparent, I agree with and support such protective measures. But, in what follows I will suggest that God alone is the expert in remaking and that when engaged with via a particular Christian lens and method more clarity can be provided about the nature of trauma and what healing looks like. From there, a clearer sense of the Christian community's understanding of, and response to, trauma can be offered.

A further example is that of Jennifer Baldwin in *Trauma-Sensitive Theology*. In the introduction she explains, "Trauma-Sensitive Theology is a venture into a re/formation of Christian theology and practice with

---

57. Grosch-Miller, *Trauma and Pastoral Care*, 3.
58. Grosch-Miller, *Trauma and Pastoral Care*, 159.

the intention of honoring the stories of faith that have nourished past generations while infusing those narratives with the wisdoms of contemporary knowledge in order to meet the variety of needs of persons and communities struggling under the burden of traumatic experience/s and response."[59] She further states that "trauma-sensitive theology is a theoretical lens, ethical commitment, and guide for praxis that extends in most areas of pastoral care, practical theology, pastoral counselling, liturgy, homiletics, and care for souls, minds and bodies."[60] Influenced by Paul Tillich, underpinning Baldwin's approach is, again, a method that prioritizes secular trauma theory and practice with a view to dialoguing the faith of an individual or community with such theory and practice to either make the theology conform or be reformed to fit. In a way that is more explicit than Grosch-Miller, Baldwin openly admits that her approach "can be incorporated in the pastoral theology and praxis across theological traditions, including and not limited to the Reformed, Lutheran, Evangelical, Augustine, Anglican, Free Church traditions, and across the World Religions."[61] Like Grosch-Miller, the first section of the book, on the subject of trauma, is accessible and insightful as a resource. However, given Baldwin's approach to theology, inevitably the theological work lacks substance, clarity, and rigor, and although references pointing to Christian theology are present—e.g., Christology, pneumatology, ecclesiology—they are barely recognizable as within the bounds of orthodox Christian theology, given how each area is forced into the service of what appears to be a predominantly pluralistic project.

Even more so than Grosch-Miller, although Baldwin's is aiming at a pastoral outworking of her project, the starting point is clearly not from within an orthodox Christian worldview and so the project unfolds accordingly. As already noted, the problem with such an approach is that although it guards against imposing a particular view and response on the survivor, it also lacks clarity, from an orthodox Christian worldview, on how trauma is to be defined and understood, what healing and remaking means and so how best to aid that. And, as with Grosch-Miller but to a different degree, there is the combination of a post-Enlightenment belief in universal access to some aspects of the world—trauma definitions and good care—while relegating faith commitment to another less important sphere of life. Similarly, this is then

---

59. Baldwin, *Trauma-Sensitive Theology*, 2.
60. Baldwin, *Trauma-Sensitive Theology*, 6.
61. Baldwin, *Trauma-Sensitive Theology*, 6.

mixed with a post-modern turn to the relative position of the individual or community when defining healing and remaking.

A very different approach included in this grouping is Deborah van Deusen Hunsinger's *Bearing the Unbearable*. In this work, Van Deusen Hunsinger examines "trauma from a number of interpretive frameworks that are then brought into dialogue with Christian theology," stating that "the overriding aim of the book is to illuminate the impact of trauma on people's lives and to present conceptual frameworks and practical strategies for healing, particularly in a North American context, from a center in the gospel."[62] The source of the healing work for Van Deusen Hunsinger is God in Christ by the Holy Spirit, meaning that although she engages with different disciplines, her approach to exploring and responding to trauma, in very practical ways, is to baptize various resources into the Christian faith using the insights gained by theorists and practitioners in service of the *missio Dei*.

Situating her work within the discipline of pastoral theology she understands such an approach as "first and foremost a theology of *God's care* for the world in Jesus Christ, in which we are invited to participate." She continues, "This means that all pastoral care depends on prayer, leads to worship, and trusts in the promises of God,"[63] since "Jesus Christ saves us from both the guilt and anguish of human sin, as well as the terror and trauma of suffering and death."[64]

Similar to Van Deusen Hunsinger and in contrast to Grosch-Miller and Baldwin, the approach of the current work begins by acknowledging and recognizing the belief that we all begin from a particular faith position and interpret our engagement with the world through the related worldview lens. To pretend otherwise, particularly when discussing trauma, is to make a serious error in how trauma is to be approached by a community that is seeking to follow and (within limits to be discussed) emulate Christ as Savior, Baptizer in the Spirit, Sanctifier, Healer, and Soon Coming King. Although different from Van Deusen Hunsinger in the use of a theodramatic approach and engaging with different dialogue partners, the location within pastoral theology and the overall aim of the present work is, broadly speaking, the same.

---

62. Van Deusen Hunsinger, *Bearing the Unbearable*, xii.
63. Van Deusen Hunsinger, *Bearing the Unbearable*, 2.
64. Van Deusen Hunsinger, *Bearing the Unbearable*, 15.

Constructive Theology

Baldwin's approach, in contrast to Grosch-Miller's, shifts the type of method used in trauma theology to what has been labeled as constructive theology. As will become clearer below, Baldwin bridges the two categories in what she produces and so could also fit into the "constructive theology" bracket—thus showing the demarcation of categories as a heuristic tool rather than truly representative of the reality of the field. However, although constructive theology is often driven by experience to reexamine doctrines to bring about change that enables healthier living, thus meaning that they are sensitive to and propelled by real-life situations, the emphasis is less on the practical application of the resultant changes in theology and more on the theological underpinnings of those changes. That is not to do a disservice to the vital work of constructive theologians but more to highlight the subtle distinction in focus between their body of work and those more classically bracketed as "pastoral." In a sense, both find a home under the broader umbrella of practical theology in terms of method, but with slightly different foci and aims.

This shift in focus is characterized by Karen O'Donnell and Katie Cross writing at the interface of feminist and trauma theology: "Feminist theologians and trauma theologians are both seeking to understand people's experiences and to reshape theologies in the light of that experience, so that they do justice to the real lives of real people."[65] Although there is acknowledgment of the variety of interpretations of trauma as well as approaches in theology to engaging with it, O'Donnell and Cross loosely group this work under the umbrellas of practical theology and constructive theology. Broadly speaking, they define practical theology as that which "seeks to engage critically with the dissonance between theology and lived reality."[66] Here they follow Richard Osmer's pattern of exploring what is occurring in a particular context before asking "why?" in order to move to suggest a way forward that is transformative. In an overlapping way, constructive theology is "understood as an approach to theology that recognizes the constructed nature of all theology and resists the 'systematization' of theology that seeks to create overarching narratives which ignore or exclude anything that does not 'fit.'"[67] This way of doing theology tends "to follow a process that begins with the recognition of

---

65. O'Donnell and Cross, Introduction to *Feminist Trauma Theologies*, xx.
66. O'Donnell and Cross, Introduction to *Feminist Trauma Theologies*, xxii.
67. O'Donnell and Cross, Introduction to *Feminist Trauma Theologies*, xxi.

the insufficiency of a doctrine or theology, proceeds through a 'thick' description of the reasons for the insufficiency, and results in the construction or reconceptualization of theology in the light of this."[68] A notable example is the work of Shelly Rambo.

In *Spirit and Trauma*, Rambo suggests that "trauma is what does not go away,"[69] and exists in life as something unintegrated, akin to an open wound. She characterizes the ongoing presence of trauma that lives in bodies, communities, memories, and attitudes as the ongoing existence of death in the midst of life. She notes that this "is not, however, a literal death but a way of describing a radical event or events that shatter all that one knows about the world and all the familiar ways of operating within it."[70] Beginning with the existential reality of trauma, Rambo seeks to explore what resources theology can offer to aid those who are traumatized to live with their experience, those who are supporting them to bear witness, and how both might find healing. She states, "I am seeking a picture of redemption that adequately accounts for traumatic suffering, that speaks to divine presence and power in light of what we know about trauma."[71]

Using methods from deconstruction and post-structuralism, Rambo seeks to guard against an overly triumphal linear move from death to resurrection that fails to account for and address the reality of trauma. Instead, she seeks to use trauma as a lens through which to explore the middle place of Holy Saturday where the Spirit might be understood to emerge from. What may be said about key aspects of theology must be reread through, and destabilized by, this lens as fresh definitions of redemption are sought that involve remaining in this in-between space and bearing witness to what remains there. Space does not allow for an extensive examination of this complex theological project. However, what is important to highlight with regard to the current project is the constructive method rather than the details of its use.

In a related way but more practical in focus than Rambo, Serene Jones purposely avoids a "systematic theology of trauma and grace" and instead seeks to represent the variety of nuanced ways that trauma impacts particular people's lives in particular contexts through a collection

---

68. O'Donnell and Cross, Introduction to *Feminist Trauma Theologies*, xxi.
69. Rambo, *Spirit and Trauma*, 2.
70. Rambo, *Spirit and Trauma*, 4.
71. Rambo, *Spirit and Trauma*, 6.

of related essays.[72] In doing so, she aims at exploring "how those various circumstances potentially challenge theological understandings of how grace is experienced, how Jesus' death is remembered, and how the ethical character of Christian practice is assessed."[73] In an essay exploring the allure of the cross, Jones helpfully notes that a totality of meaning of the cross is always out of reach. However, as she continues to take seriously the experience of those who have suffered trauma in the process of theological reflection and construction, she suggests, "the meaning that counts most on a day-to-day basis is the one nestled deep within the beholder's heart—and hearts are unwieldy and often unpredictable sites of meaning-making."[74] In a further essay on reproductive loss, Jones notes the importance of knowing one's audience and what they want to hear in the aftermath of trauma.[75] This is a point of possible contradiction in Jones's work and something we shall return to below. Is what people want to hear what they need to hear, and how does that affect theological reflection? Although not named explicitly, again there is the implicit belief, apparently present, that the survivor is the expert. However, the reason this may be a possible contradiction in Jones's work is because she also, in an earlier essay reflecting on the aftermath of 9/11, critiques the dominant themes in the storytelling provided by movies and TV programs from a Christian perspective. This suggests that from Jones's perspective, these industries might be giving people what they want, but from Jones's particular Christian perspective, it runs contrary at points to what she thinks is needed.[76]

In one essay, Jones suggests that where a systematic theologian may engage with trauma via the well-worn track of creation-sin-grace-eschatology, she instead opts for a story-telling approach.[77] Moving further in this direction, in the following essay, Jones draws on the work of Calvin to begin to offer a dramatic approach, something she continues to hint at in various places throughout the book.[78] As will become apparent in what follows, I am supportive of the dramatic approach and will push further in that direction in conversation with Kevin Vanhoozer's

---

72. Jones, *Trauma and Grace*, 22.
73. Jones, *Trauma and Grace*, xix.
74. Jones, *Trauma and Grace*, 73.
75. Jones, *Trauma and Grace*, see chapter 8.
76. Jones, *Trauma and Grace*, 23–42.
77. Jones, *Trauma and Grace*, 36–38.
78. Jones, *Trauma and Grace*, 43–67.

theodramatic model and method. However, in contrast to Jones, I do not necessarily see the need to separate doctrine from storytelling but think both can go hand in hand.

In *Unspeakable*, Sarah Travis follows in the footsteps of Baldwin, Rambo, and Jones in developing a "constructive theology for preaching."[79] Exploring what role preaching has to play for those who have experienced trauma, Travis poses and seeks to answer the question: "What is a credible expression of the gospel for those who have experienced an absence of grace, especially when the imagination may be incapacitated, and language loosed from its moorings?"[80] In doing so Travis is heavily influenced by Baldwin in Baldwin's development of a trauma-sensitive theology in which biblical references are largely absent. This combines with Rambo's unwillingness to move too quickly—if at all—to the resurrection, which then begs the question of where hope may be found, particularly in light of Paul's words toward the end of 1 Cor 15.

Travis suggests that in response to the oft-presented absoluteness and certainty of Christian truth, what is required is "a willingness to critique the theologies and central narratives of the faith in light of the human experience of traumatic wounding."[81] In doing so she proposes the preacher as one who bears witness,[82] and "as a midwife of the imagination."[83] She further proposes "trauma-informed scriptural hermeneutics" and the practice of "Bibliodrama."[84] This latter practice "is a form of role-playing or improvisation that invites people to interact with Bible stories for the purpose of education, community building, and therapy."[85]

The influence of Baldwin, Rambo, and Jones on Travis's work means that a similar result emerges that is overly dependent on the experience of the individual for the shaping of theology and practice and in which it is not clear what hope is offered to those living in the shadow of trauma. And although Travis begins to explore engagement with Scripture with a nod to a dramatic approach, this is largely underdeveloped. In contrast, although the approach to be developed below acknowledges the role of

79. Travis, *Unspeakable*, 9.
80. Travis, *Unspeakable*, 7.
81. Travis, *Unspeakable*, 54.
82. Travis, *Unspeakable*, 55–76.
83. Travis, *Unspeakable*, 79.
84. Travis, *Unspeakable*, 100.
85. Travis, *Unspeakable*, 104.

experience in the development of theology and the performing of the Christian faith, experience is not and cannot be the norming norm for the reasons presented above. But, in following Vanhoozer's theodramatic approach, the present work will push Travis's suggestion of the use of Bibliodrama further by suggesting the whole of life in relationship with God and God's creation is dramatic.

In *Broken Bodies*, Karen O'Donnell highlights three "ruptures" that she suggests characterize an experience of trauma—"bodily integrity," "time," and "cognition and language"—and then proposes that recovery involves stabilizing in these areas.[86] Although O'Donnell's project connects to her own experience of trauma and she names the church as "a traumatized body because it is constituted of traumatized bodies,"[87] she is clear that she is "not concerned with constructing a response to traumatic suffering."[88] Instead, she uses this lens of traumatic rupture as a way of breaking open previously held orthodox theological positions by locating the "Annunciation-Incarnation event" at "the core of Christian somatic memory" and then defining that as traumatic. This event is the point at which the perichoretic nature of the Trinity breaks into and connects with creation thus causing a traumatic rupture. This event, O'Donnell proposes, is then repeated in non-identical ways in various areas of church life, particularly the sacraments (by which she means the seven referred to by Roman Catholic and Orthodox Churches), in such a way that potentially ruptures the way these areas have been understood and embodied, suggesting they are sites of trauma and recovery. She states, "If sacraments are an exchange between humanity and divinity, then they are both the places where we lose ourselves and the places where we find ourselves—they are sites of both trauma and trauma recovery."[89]

O'Donnell tries to draw evidence from Scripture that Mary, in the Annunciation, experiences trauma. But this is largely unconvincing, as the text does not seem to offer the required level of detail, meaning O'Donnell is reaching for evidence to support her argument. Furthermore, her argument is not overly coherent and is difficult to follow, and seems to equate trauma with anything that creates any sort of rupture in the three areas noted above. This does create interesting openings for exploring understanding of bodily engagement with the sacraments

---

86. O'Donnell, *Broken Bodies*, 6–7.
87. O'Donnell, *Broken Bodies*, 201.
88. O'Donnell, *Broken Bodies*, 13.
89. O'Donnell, *Broken Bodies*, 185.

in the church but, at the same time, seems to water down what trauma is commonly understood to mean to healthcare professionals working with those who have experienced trauma. Bracketing sacraments as traumatic because "they rupture the ontological identity of the recipient," meaning "the recipient must reconstruct their identity in the aftermath of their sacramental experience," does not seem to find a natural home alongside trauma-inducing experiences such as abuse, loss of a loved one, or threat to life.[90]

In another essay O'Donnell draws out "four principles of constructive theology" that she observes as "at work in both feminist and trauma-informed approaches to theology."[91] These principles are: "a recognition of change or development taking place; a mandate to draw on resources both within and beyond the Christian tradition; an identification of a multitude of theolog*ies*; and finally the construction of a theology that is in continuity with the goods deeply embedded in the tradition of Christian faith."[92] Some of these principles and the general method of constructive theology resonate with the current project in certain ways. Experience is vital in the doing of theology, particularly when experience enables the prophetic exposure of the hijacking of orthodox theology for destructive ends. Where accepted orthodox theology has not helped those who have survived trauma to heal (and in some cases compounded their suffering), it has to be recognized that something needs to change. Constructive change can then be supported and aided by a variety of resources drawn from different disciplines and traditions. This can produce various theologies that are more appropriate to aiding those who have survived trauma. Where the current project differs from O'Donnell's characterization of constructive theology is with regard to her fourth point, which changes how the other points are understood.

I concur that theology needs to be constructed in continuity with "the goods" of the Christian faith, but O'Donnell fails to define what these "goods" are or what criteria we use to decide. The result is that experience is potentially given too much weight, meaning that, in theory, nothing that exists at the core of orthodox theology need remain if it contradicts the experience of an individual or community or the aims of a scholar's theological endeavors, and is considered to require revision or rejection. What I will be proposing below is that, although I am

90. O'Donnell, *Broken Bodies*, 174.
91. O'Donnell, "Voices," 5.
92. O'Donnell, "Voices," 5.

supportive of various ways of doing deconstruction and reconstruction as part of the theological enterprise that leads to good praxis and pathos, to speak of such a project as within the bounds of orthodox Christianity requires that some things are undeconstructable and not up for grabs and so form the core of "the goods" of the Christian faith to which O'Donnell refers. Here there is a danger that systematic and/or dogmatic theology is caricatured in opposition to constructive theology and then knocked down accordingly. O'Donnell states that "at the heart of constructive theology is a rejection of the idea that there can be a 'system' of theology that is complete, finished, and stands for all time."[93] It is true that many systematic and dogmatic approaches to theology could be accused of proposing such a system but to conclude that all do is reductionistic. Instead, it is possible to propose that a system of theology exists that is undeconstructable that we are never able to fully access due to the limited nature of human existence but can still glimpse while engaged in the reworking of our incomplete approximations—what some have labeled as "Critical Realism."[94] It is also possible to suggest that a system of theology that is undeconstructable exists that is revealed in non-contradictory ways to different degrees in different places and at different times. Such an approach upholds what might be considered a good of Christian faith found in systematic and dogmatic theology while drawing on the good work of constructive theology. This potentially avoids giving too much authority to experience while also avoiding operating out of a closed system of dogma. The theodramatic approach proposed in the previous chapter seeks to avoid the dual pitfalls of over-systematization and giving final authority to experience.[95]

---

93. O'Donnell, "Voices," 6.

94. For descriptions and examples of the use of Critical Realism, particularly in relation to reading the Bible, see Meyer, *Critical Realism*; Vanhoozer, *Meaning*, 320–23; Wright, *New Testament*, chapters 2 and 3.

95. In a similar way, Alex Wendel critiques Rambo and Jones for privileging subjective experience as that which shapes one's theology. Instead, Wendel proposes the "subjective revelation" of God, enabled by the Holy Spirit, as the starting point for offering a theologically informed understanding and response to trauma. However, given the sinful nature and limited perspective of humans, Wendel leaves unexplained the process required to discern truth from falsity when examining the supposed subjective revelation received by individuals and communities. Without an explanation of such a process, Wendel's theory is sound, but in practice, it is found wanting. Hopefully, what is proposed in the present work is a model and method that goes some way to avoiding this problem while recognizing that discerning genuine divine revelation is not straightforward and is an ongoing task. See Wendel, "Trauma-Informed Theology."

Before highlighting how the sub-discipline of biblical studies has engaged with trauma theory, it is important to note examples of constructive theology informed and shaped by trauma theory that are pastorally sensitive and more clearly fit within what might be termed orthodox Christian theology. It is this group that the theodramatic proposal explored in the remainder of the current work seeks to contribute to.

In *Dawn of Sunday*, Cockayne et al. aim to offer guidance to readers about how to make the church safer for survivors of trauma not simply in a passive way but also by actively seeking "to explore how the church can facilitate God's healing from the effects of horrors of this life."[96] By holding the tension between the reality of Holy Saturday and the hope of Easter Sunday they further state that "the metaphor of remaining in the dawn of Sunday means that we seek to understand the stakes of horrors and trauma in order to facilitate recovery in the church."[97] In doing so, Cockayne et al. base the hope and means of recovery firmly within the Trinitarian God of Father, Son, and Holy Spirit, and the church as the body of Christ—the place where this healing is facilitated and made manifest. In so doing they acknowledge the importance of empowering the survivor in their journey of healing and note that "while we seek to take seriously the reality of life's despair, we also seek to provide a Trinitarian, and ultimately ecclesiological, vision of recovery that is rooted in hope."[98] The focus on the Trinitarian God as the ultimate healer and the church as the location where the healing is facilitated is something the present work would concur with while also supporting the use of attachment theory as a way to explore both trauma and healing. Where the current project differs is in at least three ways. The first is a more detailed exploration of what healing of the individual means Christologically and eschatologically—what does it mean to experience healing as the image of God growing into Christlikeness? The second way is a particular focus on engaging with Winnicott's work as a window into what this growth might mean and how it might best be facilitated by the church. The third is the use of the theodramatic model as the controlling way of approaching the subject matter. More will be said about this in due course.

In *Trauma-Informed Evangelism*, Charles Kiser and Elaine A. Heath ask and seek to answer the question, "What does it look like to

---

96. Cockayne et al., *Dawn of Sunday*, 7. For Harrower's Trinitarian theology that underpins his approach in this work, see Harrower, *God of All Comfort*.

97. Cockayne et al., *Dawn of Sunday*, 7.

98. Cockayne et al., *Dawn of Sunday*, 8.

share the good news of Jesus, to make disciples of Jesus, among people who have been harmed in the name of Jesus?"[99] The focus of their work is, therefore, primarily about what shape evangelism could take in response to those who have been specifically traumatized by the church through some form of spiritual abuse. Heath in particular highlights what she believes to be a central task of the current and future church as "healing the wounds inflicted by Christendom."[100]

Beginning with Grounded Theory to explore key themes among interviewees, Kiser and Heath draw to the surface and define traumatic experiences of spiritual abuse wrought by the church on the lives of individuals under the guise of various forms of "supremacy."[101] With this in view, they then offer a Christocentric window into God's solidarity with and response to survivors of trauma by examining the death and resurrection of Jesus in conversation with theological voices "at the margins."[102] This provides the foundation on which to then suggest an approach to evangelism among survivors of trauma that contrasts with previous approaches.

The focus on developing a practical response to real-life situations of post-traumatic recovery built upon Christological engagement with trauma is not dissimilar to what will be proposed in this work and so is heartily supported here. However, the present work differs in a number of ways.

First the focus here is on a broader category of survivor than those who have been spiritually abused (although it would include such individuals). Secondly, the focus is less specifically on evangelism and more on how the church community supports and aids recovery more generally (although again, evangelism is included in this). Thirdly, the present work will more explicitly seek to define trauma from a Christocentric theodramatic perspective. Where trauma seems, in Kiser and Heath's work, to be a concept borrowed from non-theological sources that God engages with and heals, the present work seeks to offer a redefining of trauma from a distinctly Christian theodramatic perspective aided by other disciplines. The fourth and perhaps most important difference is the nature of the church community that Kiser and Heath propose.

---

99. Kiser and Heath, *Trauma-Informed Evangelism*, 3.

100. Kiser and Heath, *Trauma-Informed Evangelism*, 61. See Coolican, *Research Methods*, 280–81, for a helpful description of Grounded Theory.

101. Kiser and Heath, *Trauma-Informed Evangelism*, 49–59.

102. Kiser and Heath, *Trauma-Informed Evangelism*, 74.

They rightly critique various "supremacist" ideologies that have found their way into church theology and practice, often resulting in abuse, that requires calling out and rejecting. They also recognize the need for certain boundaries to be in place for a community to be safe and function in a healthy manner suggesting an approach of "Radical Inclusion."[103] What is not clear is what those boundaries are or how they would work in practice that does not fall foul of their critique of being potentially abusive. It is not clear, for example, where the line is between holding a legitimate, pastorally sensitive, orthodox, and biblically rooted practical position in which same-sex union is not recognized as "marriage" according to Christianity, and this being considered a supremacist approach that could be accused of abusing those who disagree with it. More generally, when does holding a particular theological view—as all do, even Kiser and Heath—become supremacist? The implicit contradiction in Kiser and Heath's work is that surely it is possible that they might leave themselves open to a similar critique in that they appear to be excluding anyone that does not agree with their particular ecclesiology of radical inclusion, which potentially could be received as harmful to individuals who do not agree with them. The mistake I want to suggest is being made here is that there can be a difference, not identified by Kiser and Heath, between holding a theological position and how that is worked out in practice. Holding a particular, recognized, orthodox position on a subject such as same-sex relationships does not mean that all those who hold such a position will outwork that in the same way. I would agree that some views have no place within orthodox Christianity (such as the superiority of one ethnicity over another), but there are others where the water is murkier and the challenge is less over the belief and more about how it is outworked in power dynamics. This returns me to the point regarding what boundaries are maintained, why, and how—all of which Kiser and Heath are sketchy on. The result is that such an approach seems to favor what suits a particular people group at a particular time and the resultant interpretation of Scripture to suit that group, which, at face value, is no better than any other context-driven interpretation and outworking in terms of method, supremacist or otherwise. Let me restate a crucial point here: I am not advocating for supremacist ideologies; quite the opposite! What I am again highlighting is that any approach that is primarily driven by the wants and needs of any particular people group

---

103. Kiser and Heath, *Trauma-Informed Evangelism*, 140–47.

at the cost of carefully discerned, and humbly and reflectively held, orthodoxy ultimately makes gods of humans, thus dethroning God in the process. The challenge for the present work is to propose an approach to being a trauma-sensitive church that humbly and carefully recognizes first and foremost the authority of God to define terms and what healing and wounding are, and then to pursue such healing with the help of God, all the time recognizing that "we see only a reflection, as in a mirror" (1 Cor 13:12). Hence the method and model utilized in what follows.

Biblical Studies

To locate the current project, a final theological sub-discipline that needs mentioning in the field of trauma and theology is that of biblical studies. In the opening essay in a collection of essays that emerged from an SBL conference focused specifically on trauma studies, Christopher Frechette and Elizabeth Boase explain how these recent studies are impacting biblical interpretation: "Trauma hermeneutics is used to interpret texts in their historical contexts and as a means of exploring the appropriation of texts, in contexts both past and present."[104] Although intertwined, the discipline of biblical studies has drawn on the insights of psychology, sociology, and literary and cultural studies to engage with biblical texts through the lens of trauma in both shorter papers focused on certain characters or books of the Bible and more lengthy discussions of the Bible's creation and composition.[105] Rather than producing a single method, this engagement has created a "heuristic framework" that, when applied to the interpretation of Scripture, "may offer new insights on questions in the area of systematic, moral, and pastoral theology, as well as inform pastoral praxis with those affected by trauma."[106] Megan Warner makes a similar point noting that a "reader-response" approach to hermeneutics has provided a particular "platform" for using a trauma lens but the same lens can also be employed when exploring the world behind and in the text.[107] Elsewhere she illustrates this latter point by exploring how the Bible is, largely, "written out of the experience of trauma."[108] David Gar-

---

104. Frechette and Boase, "Defining," 2.
105. Carr, *Holy Resilience*; Boase and Frechette, *Bible*; Garber, "Trauma Theory."
106. Frechette and Boase, "Defining," 13.
107. Warner, "Bible and Trauma."
108. Warner, "Trauma," 83.

ber Jr. also observes that "the use of trauma theory does not constitute a method of interpretation but a frame of reference that, when coupled with diverse forms of biblical criticism, can yield interesting results in the study of the biblical literature and the communities that produced it."[109] This has meant that engagement with trauma theory by biblical scholars is not limited to a particular genre as survivors of trauma use different genres to express and process their experience.

What this brief description of the landscape of biblical studies highlights is that there is no single method used by all when bringing a trauma lens to the Bible or bringing a biblical lens to a contemporary understanding of trauma. Instead, each approach is shaped by the beliefs each proponent holds regarding what they think the Bible is, who they think authored it, what hermeneutical method they use, and what they understand by the term "trauma."

One example, already noted above, is the work of Tiffany Houck-Loomis. As also noted, her approach does not see the Bible as holy or sacred in the way proposed here. This inevitably shapes her engagement with Scripture and the results of her engagement. She seems to suggest that Israel was not to blame for being exiled,[110] but created the "Deuteronomic Covenant," which then dominated Israel's national narrative, as a way of explaining Israel's exile by blaming them for breaking the covenant, and in so doing, failed to do justice to the traumatic experience of exile.[111] Job, in her view, is then created as a counter-narrative to interrogate and deconstruct this dominant narrative and propose an alternative that does not completely remove the covenant theology but is held in tension with it. To restate points already made, Houck-Loomis only concerns herself with the Hebrew Bible and seems to approach it as a human creation open to psychological interpretation. Further, Houck-Loomis rejects the approaches to trauma outlined so far in this work suggesting that too much emphasis is placed on communicating traumatic memories as part of the survivor's story. Instead, she prefers a psychoanalytical approach that considers the impact of trauma less directly.[112] However, first, Houck-Loomis never actually defines what she means by "trauma," which is problematic given the central place it takes in her work. Secondly, her dismissal seems

---

109. Garber, "Trauma Theory," 25.
110. Houck-Loomis, *History Through Trauma*, 165.
111. Houck-Loomis, *History Through Trauma*, 201.
112. Houck-Loomis, *History Through Trauma*, 81–82.

reductionistic given that not all approaches by those she seems to highlight have the goal she suggests.

In contrast, Megan Warner, having acknowledged the traumatic background to the creation of much of the biblical texts, reads them from within the Christian faith in such a way that her acknowledgment of the traumatic background and origins can act as a springboard to focus on a "pastoral and theological use of the Bible" to aid those who have been traumatized.[113] Warner therefore seems to hold a high view of Scripture—recognizing it as a key resource used by God to enable healthy living, in this case in response to trauma—and an understanding of trauma similar to that articulated in the present work. There is then the double use of contemporary trauma theory to aid understanding the background and content of the biblical texts so that those texts can then be used to care well for traumatized individuals and communities in contemporary contexts.

Although influenced by Houck-Loomis's proposal for how to read Job, Norman Habel is not dissimilar to the approach used by Warner.[114] Habel follows Houck-Loomis's view regarding when and why the book of Job was created but then uses some of the lenses of trauma theory noted in the present work to aid in interpreting the book. Rather than as a hermeneutical exercise, Habel seems more committed to reading Job with a view to shaping his and others' faith and actions in the aftermath of trauma than Houck-Loomis does. Again, we see how one's belief about what the text is and one's motive for reading it combined with what tools are used produces very different approaches.

A final example that also focuses on the book of Job is offered by Isabelle Hamley. Taking Job in its final form reading the poetry and prose together, Hamley uses a "narrative approach to the text."[115] Although using the term "trauma," Hamley resists reading a contemporary diagnosis onto the text but instead states that she "will seek to bring out the text's own language of mental distress in ways that suggest possible avenues of exploration for those seeking to understand how Scripture frames the experience of mental distress, and how Scripture itself provides resources to understand and respond to those who struggle."[116] In this example the tables are turned in that rather than reading current

---

113. Warner, "Trauma," 83.
114. Habel, *God Trauma*.
115. Hamley, "Patient Job."
116. Hamley, "Patient Job," 85.

definitions of trauma onto the text, Hamley does the reverse and uses the text as a divinely provided authoritative source for defining both mental health issues and healthy responses.

Although further examples could be cited to show different ways biblical scholars engage with trauma theory, hopefully, what is clear is that there is no single approach but instead each approach is largely determined by the particular beliefs and resulting method of each individual. The method and model employed by this author have been outlined above and although not from the same sub-discipline of theology as biblical studies, given the place Scripture holds in the method of doing theology employed here, the insights from biblical scholars on the subject of trauma and the various aspects of the Bible engaged with make an invaluable contribution to the theodramatic model being used. The intended aim of this project is guidance for good pastoral practice toward those impacted by trauma, all set on the stage of the unfolding theodrama. Therefore, it resonates with the approach of Hamley in that Scripture is the authoritative text that provides direction for contemporary living. However, whereas Hamley is reluctant to read contemporary paradigms back onto the text, the present work takes a similar line to Warner in using contemporary theories in a ministerial rather than magisterial way to draw out aspects of the biblical texts, otherwise overlooked, to enrich guidance for pastoral practice. Therefore, the use of relevant insights from biblical scholars in further elucidating Scripture and the direction God provides through it in the area of trauma will be of great worth as we proceed.

A Theodramatic Approach

Having briefly marked out contemporary contributions to the field, it is helpful to return to the method and model to be used in the rest of this work. We can recall that the central aim is to provide guidance for churches on how to care well for trauma survivors in their midst, addressing the question of what Job's friends could have done better. The model to be used will be a Christocentric theodramatic one that majors on the work of Kevin Vanhoozer. From within this model, it will be possible to construe the question of how churches care well for trauma survivors in a particular way. As noted above in the exploration of other approaches to trauma-informed theology, this approach provides a distinct and different way forward from what currently exists and so offers an alternative resource for those grappling with the questions related to this area of work. While aiming to be pastoral in focus—driven by the existential realities of "ordinary" life and offering guidance for good praxis and pathos—this approach will also retain key aspects of orthodoxy that are not considered to be up for grabs.[117] The theodramatic model and a particular Christological engagement with Scripture will be at the heart of this and shape how trauma is interpreted and understood in order to offer a distinctly Christian approach to pastoral care. Although experience—and particularly the experience of those affected by trauma—will be given significant consideration in the shaping of this project, what marks it out as distinct is that experience is not given the authority that it is in other approaches. Instead, divinely authored Scripture as the revelation of the drama in which we find ourselves and our identity will be given pride of place in terms of theological sources. This is so because it is the means through which God has revealed God's self, the plot of God's drama—the *theo*drama—what God is doing, and how we are called to respond to God's prior activity and invitation. Scott Harrower, with Rambo and Jones particularly in mind, offers a "horror reading" of Matthew's Gospel, which is his preferred term for what might otherwise be called a reader-response trauma hermeneutic. He does this to show what happens if a Gospel is read this way. His conclusion is that "this reading shows that offers made by trauma studies—the limited use of Scripture and the mirror reading—are not sufficient to redress the pervasiveness of horrors and their traumatic and overwhelming effects nor the skepticisms that arise. There are strong limitations to what trauma studies has to offer."[118] In fact, Harrower suggests that such readings potentially compound trauma and fuel paranoia. In contrast, in what follows definitions of what it means to be a healthy human being, how that is facilitated by other humans, what trauma means, and how the church might respond well to trauma will all be grounded in the revelation of Scripture while in conversation with other disciplines and

---

117. Acknowledgment needs to be made here to the work of Mark Cartledge and in particular to his categorizing of "ordinary," "official," and "academic" types of discourse in theology (Cartledge, *Testimony in the Spirit*, 18–20). Although these categories are not that explicit in the current project, it is the desire for the church to provide a theologically grounded and fitting practical response to the existential, "ordinary," experience of trauma that drives this project, meaning Cartledge's categories are present in the background.

118. Harrower, *God of All Comfort*, 116.

sources of theology. This will provide a Christocentric theodramatic approach to trauma and trauma response that can offer hope to those that most need it and direction to those trying to help.

Conclusion

In this chapter a brief overview of definitions of trauma has been provided followed by a more focused overview of Christian theological approaches to the subject and experience of trauma. What has been suggested in light of these various contributions is that although both secular and Christian engagements offer important and helpful insights, there is a gap in the field in terms of a more distinctly orthodox Christian approach both to defining trauma and offering guidance for good pastoral care. Following the more extensive discussion of method and model in the previous chapter, this chapter closed with a signpost toward the Christocentric theodramatic approach to trauma that is going to be developed in the rest of this work as a contribution toward filling that gap. Chapter 3 will begin constructing this approach by exploring what a Christocentric theodramatic anthropology might look like as the basis for how the traumatizing of humans might then be better defined and responded to.

3

A Christocentric Theodramatic Anthropology

Introduction

THE CENTRAL AIM OF this chapter is to tease out what a theological anthropology might look like through the lens of Kevin Vanhoozer's theodramatic model and method. As noted in chapter 1, the reason for beginning here is that to interpret and respond to trauma from within a theodramatic model, in a fitting way, we must first have a clear sense of what it means to speak of humans within the theodrama, and particularly humans as made in the image of God. We will then be able to proceed to explore the place of the church in aiding the flourishing of humans in the next chapter.

In what follows, this exploration of theological anthropology will begin by examining what might be meant by the *imago Dei* in relation to humans by looking at the original divine intent for the image bearers. Consideration will then be given to the effects of the fall on the image, the redeemed *telos* of the image bearer, and how that final state might be partially experienced in the present act of the drama. As the chapter draws to a close, we will be in a position to explore in the following chapter what the role of the church is with regard to enabling the flourishing of its members and, by extension, creation.

Performing the *Imago Dei*

Starting in the Garden

In an essay focusing on theological anthropology, Vanhoozer defines it as "the attempt to think through the meaning of the human story, as it unfolds from Genesis through the Gospels to the Apocalypse and as it is lived out before, with and by God."[1] Following Vanhoozer's model, the larger drama in which the human story is but a part is the theodrama of salvation—God's bringing into being, relationship with, and salvation of, the whole of creation. Whatever the details of the human performance are, it is to be lived out as a response to the prior activity of the transcendent creator God while also being lived out in the presence of the immanence of God, and most remarkably, is lived out to its fullest by God in the incarnation. As noted in chapter 1, the primary source of revelation in terms of the drama we find ourselves in, what parts we are cast in, and direction for fitting performance, as well as the authoritative window into the Trinitarian life of the divine author and actor and previous performances, is Scripture as script, transcript, and prescript.

So far, the term "performance" has been used in a more general way but it is important, as we proceed, to refine and highlight its definition: "The overriding imperative in performance is, as the etymology of the term itself indicates, 'to carry the *form* through (*per*).'"[2] To explore the performances of the *imago Dei* in the drama then is to explore what form is to be carried through in such performances.[3]

As Vanhoozer rightly observes, "Three indicative statements—all taken from Genesis, the book of 'beginnings'—form the leading themes in Christian reflection about human beings."[4] Received in faith, these texts act as the springboard into theological explorations of what it means to be human and perform *imago Dei*. In a way unique to humans, Gen 1:26 depicts God saying, "Let us make humans in our image, according to our likeness"

---

1. Vanhoozer, "Human Being," 159.
2. Vanhoozer, *Drama of Doctrine*, 253.
3. It is important to note here a key objection to the dramatic model raised by Michael Pakaluk. Pakaluk's objection is that dramas are representations of something else. So, how can this work if the theodrama is supposed to be real? Vanhoozer's response is that what is being worked out in the theodrama is that which is true in eternity (the economic is the immanent Trinity). What is being re-presented is the kingdom of God "on earth as it is in heaven" (Matt 6:10). See "Forming the Performer," 28–30, 43; *Faith Speaking Understanding*, 29–30.
4. Vanhoozer, "Human Being," 163.

which is closely followed in v. 27, by "So God created humans in his image, in the image of God he created them; male and female he created them." It is this latter verse that provides the first of our indicatives.[5]

The second indicative is found in Gen 2:7 where we read "then the Lord God formed man from the dust of the ground and breathed into his nostrils the breath of life, and the man became a living being." Further information is then provided in the third indicative in 2:18: "Then the Lord God said, 'It is not good that the man should be alone; I will make him a helper as his partner.'"

When these texts have been considered at various points in church history, the conclusions about the *imago Dei* have differed considerably. For example, some, following what Stanley Grenz refers to as the structural or substantial model, have understood "the *imago Dei* as consisting of certain attributes or capabilities lodged within the person."[6] More specifically emphasis was placed on the rational capacity or the will of the individual as that which is made in the image of God. Given that such views emerged in the patristic period there is evidence of the grappling with Greek philosophy in the development of such approaches. Aristotelian influences make reason that which separates humans from animals and Platonist influences privilege the soul or mind over the body. Although working out their approaches in very different ways, Irenaeus of Lyon and Augustine of Hippo are two particularly influential figures whose foundation for the doctrine of the *imago Dei* was a structural understanding.

As Cairns notes, "It is generally accepted that in the main Irenaeus based himself on a certain interpretation of Genesis 1.26, which says that God created man in his image, after his likeness."[7] Here, Irenaeus interpreted "image" to refer predominantly to reason and free will[8]— arguably more so free will[9]—but includes the body as well, given the image of God in the incarnate Christ that humans are growing toward.[10] Although something of the image remains in the post-fall human

---

5. Mark Harris offers a concise and fascinating summary of how v. 26 has been interpreted and the implications of it. See Harris, "Functional," 52–56.

6. Grenz, *Social God*, 142.

7. Cairns, *Image of God*, 80.

8. Irenaeus, *Against Heresies*, 4.4.3 (*ANF* 1:466).

9. Grenz, *Social God*, 145–46.

10. Irenaeus, *Against Heresies*, 5.6.1; 5.16.2 (*ANF* 1:531–32; 544).

condition, it has become corrupted.[11] The *likeness*, however, refers to that which was in embryonic form pre-fall and lost at the fall and consists of the presence of the Spirit of God in humans.[12] Irenaeus seems to have the eschaton in view when outlining a process of immaturity to maturity made possible by the work of the triune God whereby humans grow toward embodying the image *and* likeness of God.[13] Although Irenaeus included the body in his understanding of the image of God, this became less the case when "subsequent church fathers display a growing tendency to link the divine image with reason."[14]

Of note in this lineage is Augustine, who carries on Irenaeus's thinking regarding the difference between image and likeness that had continued to be dominant through the patristic period where likeness continued to be understood as an eschatological reality toward which humans were tending in relationship with God. However, unlike Irenaeus, Augustine's focus in exploring the nature of the image was entirely on the soul, with little interest in the flesh. More precisely, this image for Augustine was equated with rationality, free will, and love in that the ongoing development of Christlikeness involved growing in knowledge of God and in so doing discerning the eternal as reflected in the temporal, choosing to love that which is eternal.[15] Augustine developed his thinking most fully in *On the Holy Trinity* and understood this capacity to be that which remains in the post-fall soul even in a "defaced and tarnished" state.[16] Communion with God is thus possible only by the grace of God that reaches to the structural remnant to guide the corrupt image toward eschatological likeness.

Their influence continued through the work of such notable figures as Thomas Aquinas. Cairns notes of Aquinas that "what St Thomas did was largely to adopt what Augustine had taught, making it more explicit and modifying it to fit his own elaborate system."[17] For Aquinas, with God as the ground of being, all of creation, to some degree, is like God with those aspects of creation that have a greater capacity for reason and a higher

---

11. Irenaeus, *Against Heresies* 4.4.3 (*ANF* 1:466).
12. Irenaeus, *Against Heresies* 5.6.1 (*ANF* 1:531–32).
13. Irenaeus, *Against Heresies* 4.38 (*ANF* 1:521–22).
14. Grenz, *Social God*, 150.
15. Augustine, *On the Holy Trinity* 12.7.12; 14.17.23 (*NPNF* 1/3:159–60; 196).
16. Augustine, *On the Holy Trinity* 14.16.22 (*NPNF* 1/3:195–96).
17. Cairns, *Image of God*, 120.

intellect being made in the image of God.[18] Although under the clear influence of Aristotelian philosophy, Aquinas, similar to Augustine, understood intellect in the human image of God to be manifest in knowledge and love of God. Such intellect has a universal aspect in all humans but is sanctified and brought to completion only by the grace of God.[19] There is much complexity about Aquinas's position that need not concern us here.[20] The crucial point to note is that the image of God, as for Aquinas's predecessors, is located in the intellect, and this approach continues to have some level of influence on contemporary discussions.

However, such an approach is problematic in that it privileges one aspect of being human over others in a way that Scripture does not seem to support. Arguably, whatever we might be able to say of the image from Scripture, what we can say with a level of certainty is that to be human is to include, without exclusion or reduction, heart, soul, mind, and body (Deut 6:5; Matt 22:37; Mark 12:30; Luke 10:27). To privilege any aspect at the cost of another is to fragment or misrepresent humanity as made in the image of God.

A further problem with such a view is that if reason or intelligence is the measure of how much one images God, then a spectrum can be created that defines some as more human than others based on intelligence and mental capacity. This then creates the possibility of using this spectrum to marginalize and control others and possibly view those with a diminished level of mental health as less than fully human.[21]

A contrasting approach is the more recent "Relational" model, which privileges relationship over ontology regarding what constitutes the *imago Dei*. Without becoming too side-tracked, it is worth noting Elmer Chen's helpful observation that this category can be broken down further into two sub-categories: (i) the personal *imago Dei* and (ii) the Trinitarian Social *imago Dei*. Chen notes, "In the case of the former, the image is the *person* in community; in the latter, the image is the *community* of persons."[22] Emil Brunner stands as an example of the former with Karl Barth exemplifying the latter.

Brunner's work developed in conversation and disagreement with Barth, but the full details of that discourse need not concern us here.

---

18. Aquinas, *Summa Theologica* 1.93.2.
19. Aquinas, *Summa Theologica* 1.93.4.
20. Cairns, *Image of God*, 120–26.
21. Swinton, *From Bedlam to Shalom*, 24.
22. Chen, "Pentecostal," 102.

The central point to focus on is that for Brunner, humans are only fully so in community. Cairns describes Brunner's approach: "man cannot be man in isolation, he can only be human in community. And this human 'thou' is thus not something accidental to our humanity, but it is the very condition of our being man."[23] For Brunner, humans are begotten in the beginning by the divine Logos, and given life as a gift of love that flourishes through loving response, primarily to God who calls to them. As Brunner notes of human nature, it is "responsibility from love, in love, for love."[24] Even though sin prevents humans from knowing who to respond to and how, a remnant remains in each human in the form of moral responsibility that suggests an ongoing, yet shrouded relationship with Christ as the Word of God. Humans can only be reborn afresh by revelation of Jesus Christ through Spirit and Scripture, which shed fresh light on human origins and purpose and enable the loving response and formation of Christlikeness for which they were destined. This Christlike formation and loving response only occur in relationship with God and neighbor in such a way as to correspond to the incarnate Christ who loves both Father and fellow humans—"Man cannot be man 'by himself'; he can only be man in community. For love can only operate in community, and only in this operation of love is man human."[25] To image God in Christlikeness is, therefore, for Brunner, relational. When sin entered, humans retained what Brunner refers to as the "formal" image—"that which distinguishes man from all the rest of creation, whether he be a sinner or not."[26] However, sin eradicates completely the "material" image in that humans are neither aware of nor able to respond accordingly and fully to their calling as image bearers.[27] It is this aspect of the *imago Dei* that is restored through faith in Christ.

Barth, like Brunner, viewed anthropology through a Christological lens, arguing that the image can only be properly understood and developed through such a lens. Although initially in disagreement with Brunner, the later Barth also seems to suggest that something of the prefall image remained post-fall and prior to faith in Christ. For the current discussion, the key area where Barth differs from Brunner is regarding how the relationality of humans is the *imago Dei*. As noted above, for

23. Cairns, *Image of God*, 156.
24. Brunner, *Man in Revolt*, 99.
25. Brunner, *Man in Revolt*, 106.
26. Brunner and Barth, *Natural Theology*, 23.
27. Brunner and Barth, *Natural Theology*, 23–24.

Brunner individual humans image God in their relationships with others, but the image is still primarily in the individual in relationship. In contrast, Barth believed that corporate humanity is the image of God, basing this on a particular interpretation of the Genesis text in which Barth draws attention to the plural nature that humanity is imaging—man and woman made "in our image" (Gen 1:26) where, for Barth, "our" refers to the intra-Trinitarian relations.[28] The image of God is therefore found in the I-Thou relationship of man to woman and human to human, and in the ensuing confrontation of God in Christ toward humans. The former—a natural bond—is the image of the latter—a bond formed by grace—where the former is, to some degree, a universal visible to all and the latter only made visible by God in Christ.

Although there is merit in both approaches, the danger in emphasizing the relational or social aspect as the location of the *imago Dei* is the tendency to reduce persons to simply the sum of their relationships and to misinterpret key texts in Genesis. With Barth's approach particularly in view, although both Adam and Eve are mentioned in connection to God's image and likeness in Gen 1:26–27, in Gen 5:3 where Seth is described as the "image" and "likeness" of Adam, there is no female counterpart mentioned. Catherine McDowell notes that such a view "falls short in that it fails to ground its case *in the text* and within its biblical and ancient Near Eastern contexts. The result is that implications (i.e., an intimate relationship that humans enjoy with God but that animals do not) are mistaken for meaning."[29] Further, in the New Testament, Paul describes Jesus—an individual—as "the image of the invisible God" (Col 1:15), and although, as the body of Christ, the church may collectively be conceived of as an extension of that image, thus supporting a relational or social view, in Paul's writing, emphasis is arguably placed on right living by individuals as well as the collective church, as the image of God. In an extensive discussion of relevant New Testament texts, Craig Blomberg first concludes that "of all the options for understanding that image, this summary supports the moral or relational interpretation."[30] However, after further analysis, he

---

28. Barth, *Church Dogmatics* 3.1:191–98.

29. McDowell, "In the Image," 34. Middleton, *Liberating Image*, 23–24, makes a similar point noting the cultural influence on Barth's conclusions. It is also worth noting that Thomas Oord suggests that humans are not that different from other creatures in creation and thus seeks to downplay the distinctiveness of humans as the image of God alone. However, his interpretation of Scripture on which he bases this is unconvincing. See Oord, "Relational Love."

30. Blomberg et al., "'True Righteousness and Holiness,'" 77.

refines his conclusion to the moral interpretation alone.[31] This is not a new approach and is not without problems, which will be discussed further below but, returning to the argument for a relational/social position, it would seem that the biblical texts do not fully bear this out, and so it does not seem to get to the heart of the matter of what the image is that then enables and expects it to have particular types of relationships. Healthy relationships of various types, it will be argued here, are fundamental to being fully human, but humans cannot be reduced to being only the sum of their relationships as the image of God.

In addition to the indicatives noted above, Vanhoozer also highlights three ethical imperatives found in Scripture to aid in determining what it might mean to be made in God's image. The first of these is an emphasis on living a righteous and holy life by putting on Christ in order to become fully human (Eph 4:24).[32] Notably, both Luther and Calvin, in different but similar ways, point in this direction in their work.

Luther, in his *Lectures on Genesis*, does not dismiss or refute what we have called the structural model but neither does he follow wholly in this direction.[33] Instead, he proposes that the image "was something far more distinguished and excellent" further stating of the image "that Adam had it in his being and that he not only knew God and believed that He was good, but that he also lived in a life that was wholly godly, that is, he was without the fear of death or of any other danger, and was content with God's favor."[34] This righteous and holy life is now only accessible as a gift of grace from God made possible by Christ's death and resurrection. The formation of the restored image is brought about by Word and Spirit, begun in this life, and completed in eternity.[35]

Similarly, Calvin also draws out an ethical aspect of the image. In *Institutes of the Christian Religion*, Calvin, when discussing St. Paul's exploration of the restored image, states that "in the first place, he [Paul] mentions knowledge, and in the second, true righteousness and holiness. Hence we infer, that at the beginning the image of God was manifested by light of intellect, rectitude of heart, and the soundness of every part."[36] In a parallel fashion, in his commentary on Genesis,

---

31. Blomberg et al., "'True Righteousness and Holiness,'" 87.
32. Vanhoozer, "Human Being," 165–66.
33. Luther, *Lectures on Genesis*, 60–62.
34. Luther, *Lectures on Genesis*, 62–63.
35. Luther, *Lectures on Genesis*, 64–65.
36. Calvin, *Institutes* 1.15.4 (164).

Calvin states of the image in the pre-fall Adam, that he "was endued with a right judgment, had affections in harmony with reason, had all his senses sound and well-regulated, and truly excelled in everything good."[37] However, it is noteworthy in both cases that reason continues to have a significant place in Calvin's approach, which is not as prevalent in Luther's. Therefore, although Calvin's understanding of the image has a definite ethical imperative that was not as strong in previous approaches, the remnant of the structural approach is still apparent, particularly in Calvin's discussions about the soul.[38]

Although the unhelpful presence of the structural model lingers with all the problems noted above, and there is the beginning of a greater emphasis on a relationship with God as the way to inhabiting the *imago Dei*, it is the emphasis on righteous living as the mirror of God in the world, in Calvin's work in particular, that is of significance. Where problems occur, in addition to those that come with the structural model, are regarding the connection between the pre- and post-fall humans across the two testaments where neither Luther nor Calvin appear to make a satisfactory connection between the two.[39] A further point is that arguably the ethical imperatives describe what it means to live correctly as the *imago Dei* but still fall foul of McDowell's critique above as the results of living as the *imago Dei* are mistaken for descriptions of what the *imago Dei* is.

A further approach that builds on the indicatives noted above in the creation accounts is the functional model or what Vanhoozer refers to as the second imperative of "*the creation-cultural mandate*."[40] Recent proposals about the nature of the *imago Dei* have come from biblical scholars focusing specifically on the creation accounts. This involves using historical-critical methods to explore possible authorial intent informed by broader, relevant ancient Near Eastern sources. As Middleton notes, a conclusion Old Testament scholars reach is that "when the clues within the Genesis text are taken together with comparative studies of the ancient Near East, they lead to what we could call a functional—or even missional—interpretation of the image of God in Genesis 1:26–27 (in contradistinction to substantialistic or relational interpretations)."[41]

---

37. Calvin, *Genesis*, 1.1.26.
38. Calvin, *Institutes*, 1.15 (159–70).
39. See Cairns, *Image of God*, 127–51.
40. Vanhoozer, "Human Being," 166.
41. Middleton, *Liberating Image*, 27.

Drawing on the royal undertones detected in the relevant Old Testament texts (incl. Ps 8), alongside examples from ancient Near Eastern cultures where kings and sometimes priests were understood as the image of the particular god in question, a conclusion reached is that what it is to be created in the image of God in the Hebrew Bible concerns how humans are to represent God in the world. And further, how they are to function as they share the rule and care of creation with the creator.[42] What sets the biblical drama apart is that *all* of humanity bears this image, not just kings and/or priests. John Walton argues that Adam (and Eve) in Gen 2 are established as archetypal royal priests in the sacred space of the garden of Eden and that this therefore provides the shape of intent for all humans.[43] N. T. Wright describes this vocation as, "looking after God's world is the royal bit, summing up creation's praise is the priestly bit."[44] Mark Harris suggests, "Humans have been given the task of putting God's kingship over the living creatures of the earth into practice, and it is this function that constitutes 'the decisive thing' about the image."[45] Such a view would be suspicious of attempts by systematic theologians, in particular, to read into texts influences from their systems and cultures that potentially lead to a forced misreading of the text.

However, the labeling of this as "functional" highlights that the focus here is on what the image of God *does* rather than what the image of God *is*. McDowell attempts to circumnavigate this issue by drawing attention not just to humans as representatives of God in the temple of creation but also as God's child. Drawing on the Genesis texts she states, "Humanity is defined both as God's royal 'son' and as living 'statuettes' representing God and his rule in his macro-temple, the world."[46] However, she still points back to Levitical laws as Old Testament examples of how the image is to live in the world as a sign of God's rule and kingdom. So, McDowell is still unable to elucidate what the *imago Dei* is without slipping into a functional description. In his discussion and advocacy of the structural approach (or as he labels it, "STIG," short for the "structural theory of the image of God"),[47] Aku Visala notes that, in reality, there can be no appeal to a purely functional (or relational)

---

42. Middleton, *Liberating Image*, 27–29.
43. Walton, *Lost World*, 104–15.
44. Walton, *Lost World*, 175.
45. Harris, "Functional," 58.
46. McDowell, "In the Image," 42.
47. Visala, "Structural," 64.

approach that has no elements of the structural in it. This is so because to understand what function one is to carry out and then go on and do requires some sort of intellectual capacity, and the nature of the functions in question requires relationships of particular kinds for which humans were made.[48] He therefore also highlights that any single model is susceptible to the ethical critique of the structural model leveled above in that if relational capacity or functionality alone is the measure of the image of God in an individual then if one is lacking in that specific way one may be perceived as less the image of God than someone who does not lack in the same way. Middleton further notes when it comes to Old Testament scholars settling on the functional model, they "tend to be notorious in their hesitancy to make broad theological pronouncements based on their research, preferring instead to remain submerged in the textual and linguistic minutiae of their discipline."[49] In addition to the reasons stated previously, a further reason, therefore, for engagement with Vanhoozer's theodramatic approach is that it seems to attempt to hold the tension between biblical and systematic scholarship with an eye to practical living and does not seem to want to pigeonhole the *imago Dei* into one of the models thus far discussed.

The final ethical imperative noted by Vanhoozer concerns humans being in right relationship with the self, the other, creation, and most importantly, with God.[50] Humans are to live into their createdness and in so doing bring praise and glory to God. This sense of completeness is depicted in the resurrection—preceded and enabled by God—as a wedding feast (Rev 21) and Sabbath rest (Heb 4:9–10) and is something humans as made in God's image are to live toward as a teleological end. Of such an eschatological approach to the *imago Dei* Ted Peters comments, "The Easter Christ as the divine image is our prototype. We live now as the *imago Dei* insofar as we live in him, insofar as we participate in the reality of the eschatological resurrection into the new creation."[51] Again, this focus does not get to the heart of what the *imago Dei* is, instead drawing attention to what it does in order to embody and display the *imago Dei*. However, Peters's point about growing into Christlikeness as the fullness of the image of God moves us in a helpful direction, and we will pick up

---

48. Visala, "Structural," 67–68.
49. Middleton, *Liberating Image*, 30.
50. Vanhoozer, "Human Being," 166–67.
51. Peters, "*Imago Dei*," 95.

Vanhoozer's discussion of what being "in Christ" might mean for humans as the image of God, below.

If the *imago Dei* cannot be reduced to rational capacity, relationships, or ethical imperatives but has something to do with all of these as well as being the chosen creatures in creation to represent God as God's children in God's creation-temple, how might the subject of theological anthropology be revisited to integrate these? Here we turn to a theodramatic approach to the *imago Dei* to attempt to hold the indicatives and imperatives together.

A Theodramatic Anthropology as Vocation

Influenced by certain Trinitarian theological anthropologies, Vanhoozer uses the understanding of the Trinity as three persons-in-relationship comprising the one God as a foundation on which to build his theological anthropology. The model of God as "being-in-communion" provides Vanhoozer with a lens through which to understand humans as persons-in-relationship without reducing the human creature to either individuality or relationships alone. "The human creature is neither an autonomous individual nor an anonymous unit that has been assimilated into some collectivity, but rather a particular person who achieves a concrete identity in relation to others."[52] He further states, "The person is rather an irreducible ontological reality that cannot be defined in terms of something else."[53]

Building from this foundation Vanhoozer opts to further flesh out the shape of the image through speech agency in particular: "The model of the self as speech agent may prove to be particularly fruitful for theological anthropology in so far as it specifies the nature of personal relatedness (namely, being-in-communication) without collapsing the person into the process."[54] For Vanhoozer, to focus on speech, or communication more broadly, as a (the?) defining factor of being human is not to exchange one model for another but to offer something that is a non-reductive, integrative lens that provides insight into the broad individual yet relational nature of humans.[55] Rather than privileging mind

---

52. Vanhoozer, "Human Being," 174–75.
53. Vanhoozer, "Human Being," 175.
54. Vanhoozer, "Human Being," 175.
55. In *Faith Speaking Understanding* Vanhoozer states, "if action 'speaks' louder

or soul over body, or vice versa, Vanhoozer attempts to hold the two together in a holistic manner by labeling humans as "doing" rather than simply "thinking" beings. "To act means to take an initiative, to begin, to set something in motion. In thinking the mind alone is active; but doing engages both mind and body."[56] The actions of humans (which includes speech, and communication more generally) take place in a "web of relationships" that influence without exhaustively determining humans. This is, of course, a two-way street in that humans also, therefore, influence this web. This further highlights Vanhoozer's intent to define humans as beings-in-communicative-activity who are intended for, and shaped by, relationships but, as persons, cannot be reduced to those relationships. "Individuality refers not to some underlying substance so much as to one's particular and typical pattern of communicative relations."[57]

The focus on humans as beings-in-communicative-activity may be novel but is it theologically grounded? Vanhoozer here returns to his point about the beginning of theology by stating, "The communicative agency which defines our identities and bestows our role is God's self-communicative activity in creation, Christ and Pentecost."[58] Following Barth but baptizing Barth's approach into his own, Vanhoozer suggests, "God's being is a being-in-communicative-act."[59] The points being made here are twofold: First, God initiates all communicative acts by engaging with that which God has created—God and God's activity is prior to anything else. Secondly, something of what it is to be made in the image of God is, therefore, the ability to respond to God in a similar fashion to the way God communicates with humans: "Humans are communicative agents like God because God is the one who goes out of himself in communicative action (for example, the incarnate Word) for the sake of entering into a dialogical relation with another."[60] To communicate means to

---

than words, then faith speaking understanding involves both verbal and nonverbal modes of communication: words and deeds" (1).

56. Vanhoozer, "Human Being," 175.

57. Vanhoozer, "Human Being," 176.

58. Vanhoozer, "Human Being," 176. Janet Soskice has pursued a similar pathway, arguing that in Genesis God is portrayed as "a semiotic God whose very Word is the power to create." She further states, "The cosmic Christology of the New Testament holds Christ to be a living, visible and audible Word made flesh." The God she then finds in Paul "is one who summons, speaks and names." See Soskice, "Creative Address," 200.

59. Vanhoozer, "Human Being," 176.

60. Vanhoozer, "Human Being," 176–77.

make common and in this case, it is to make common for the sake of communion. Holding together the rational and relational aspects within the communicative paradigm, the human creature mirrors God in how it is made able to go out of itself to connect with others and, most importantly, with God. What is important to add here is that God is love (1 John 4:8) and as being-in-communicative act, it is love that God, therefore, communicates in going out of Godself to creation. This is done with the intent of drawing creation, and humans in particular, into this intra-Trinitarian fellowship of love.[61] What follows from this is that to mirror God is to mirror the love God displays in action: "We love because he first loved us" (1 John 4:19). Vanhoozer draws on the Latin root of "person"—*per-sonare*, "to sound through"—to illuminate his point regarding human vocation. The *imago Dei* can therefore be understood "as an *echo* of the divine being and of the trinitarian communicative relations."[62]

Rather than reject the attempts to define the *imago Dei* in the classical theological tradition, Vanhoozer navigates his own path by retrieving key aspects of the tradition while seeking to overcome perceived issues. Where the individual knower is shown to be fallacious due to the web of relations each human is formed by and exerts influence on, Vanhoozer draws from Jürgen Habermas to argue that being rational is still to be retained as a characteristic of the image but must be redefined as "a corporate communicative process" rather than something located entirely in the individual.[63] Reasoning is a communicative, community action that emerges from dialogue. Similarly, Vanhoozer addresses the importance of the whole person as image. Whereas, historically, a divide had emerged in discussions of morality, between outward behavior and dispositions of the heart, with various voices arguing for the determined actions of the human animal, Vanhoozer is keen to hold the two together to affirm the biblical image of humans created for a unified, psychosomatic, covenantal response to their creator. In this view, "'spirit' is not to be understood in terms of a Cartesian dualism between spiritual and spatial substances, but rather in terms of that which makes possible both consciousness and culture, namely, communicative agency. If the body is the *field* of communication, spirit is communication's guiding *force*."[64] The human being as the image of God is therefore an embodied rational

---

61. Vanhoozer, *Faith Speaking Understanding*, 67–68.
62. Vanhoozer, "Human Being," 177.
63. Vanhoozer, "Human Being," 178.
64. Vanhoozer, "Human Being," 179.

communicative image whose "personal identity is enacted as one puts the socially governed communication system into motion and initiates speech acts that interact with others."[65]

To draw together that which we have noted thus far, to be human in the image of God is to be created by God, to communicate with God and others in particular ways, within particular types of relationships, as enabled by God, for particular intended ends. "I" am created to relate to myself as "I" but only because I am created to respond to "you" as "you" and, most importantly, God as "you," and thus come to understand myself, God, and others as fully as possible within the theodrama, within the relations for which "I" am cast. Among these, covenantal response to the divine creator is the most important and the one from which all other responses are derived. This is not to privilege the individual over relations or vice versa but it is to recognize the human image of God as being-in-communicative-action. True identity, then, becomes about faithful covenantal performance rather than unchanging repetition—a point we shall expand on below. Although shaped by various factors and voices, not least the voice of God, the human creature is not simply determined beyond any sense of control or responsibility. Instead, there is communicative freedom to be exercised within the webs of communicative action as cooperation with the divine voice is enabled and embraced in order to grow into all that the human creature was made to be within the theodrama. And again, this cannot be an individual thing but something humans have the responsibility to aid one another in doing, for the good of all. "The church . . . exists as a gathered people by virtue of the divine call (*ekklesia* = 'called out of'). To be human is to participate in the covenant of divine discourse as a faithful hearer and speaker."[66] More will be said about the role of the church in the following chapter.

The initial state of the *imago Dei* in Vanhoozer's theodramatic anthropology can be summed up under the heading of "vocation." To be made in the image of God is to be called, or perhaps summoned, by the Trinitarian God who goes out of God's self to communicate God's self to us and draw us into covenantal relationship with God who is the ground and source of being. At core, the self is "known and called by God (Gal. 4:9; 1 Cor. 13:12)"[67] and "being in his image, can cry out, or talk back,

---

65. Vanhoozer, "Human Being," 180.
66. Vanhoozer, "Human Being," 183.
67. Vanhoozer, *Faith Speaking Understanding*, 116.

to God."[68] Such things as ethnicity, class, and gender are understood as significant yet secondary identifiers (1 Cor 12:13; Gal 3:28; Col 3:11).[69] Contrary to many contemporary voices, "our identity is not an arbitrary chosen role, but a matter of how we respond to our theological vocation to image God so as to glorify and enjoy him forever."[70] There are thus both indicative and imperative aspects to Vanhoozer's depiction of being human: "what we should do follows from the kind of creatures we are . . . . Being human means being summoned: to be male or female, to be free and responsible, to live well with others in justice and peace, to glorify God."[71] Vocation thus involves response as a grateful yet responsible creature tasked with witnessing to what God has done and is doing in the world while joining with God, by invitation, in undertaking and completing God's mission in the world—the *missio Dei*. And this mission aims at creation "becoming a 'communicant' in the life of God."[72] As partners with God in God's mission to creation, "human beings are God's physical representatives on earth: living icons, statues of flesh standing in for the king, emissaries able to engage in the varieties of communicative action that characterize interpersonal covenantal relations."[73] What one is, as the *imago Dei*, is thus intrinsically bound up in what one does.

The Defaced Image

However, in the third chapter of Genesis, the plot of the theodrama has a complication added to it by way of Adam and Eve performing in such a way that distorts and defaces the image. This occurs by allowing the speech of the serpent to have a level of authority it should not have had. The human performance does indeed develop in relationship with self, another human, creation, and God, but it does so in such a way as to distort those relationships and deface the image by becoming one who does not, primarily, give chief authority to the voice of God.

As with the discussion of the image more generally, the discussion of what remains and what is lost after the fall with regard to the

68. Vanhoozer, "Putting on Christ," 151.
69. Vanhoozer, *Faith Speaking Understanding*, 116–17.
70. Vanhoozer, *Faith Speaking Understanding*, 116.
71. Vanhoozer, "Human Being," 183.
72. Vanhoozer, *Drama of Doctrine*, 43.
73. Vanhoozer, *Faith Speaking Understanding*, 84.

image has provided various responses in church history. Of this issue Vanhoozer states, "Fallen human beings have the image of God formally (for example, the capacity to communicate with God and others) but not materially (for example, this capacity is not functioning correctly); there are patterns of distortion in our communication with God and others, and with ourselves."[74] Vanhoozer here follows a similar line to Brunner whereby sin impacts all humans, yet does not deface the image of God completely without remainder. This is further confirmed by Vanhoozer's summation that "communicative agency thus refers to something the human creature is and does. Communicative capacity corresponds to the 'formal' image which constitutes the human creature as human; communicative excellence—right relatedness with others and with God—corresponds to the 'material' image by which the creature is conformed to the image of Christ."[75] For Vanhoozer and for Brunner before him, something of the original image remains in the post-fall human creature. However, the human creature is now—as is played out in act 2 of the theodrama—unable to develop in the right direction in terms of the performance for which they were cast. The form being carried through is a distorted one, unable to create the plot resolution necessary to get it back on track. The required resolution must therefore come from the divine playwright, whose drama this is, and it comes in the form of God entering the stage as a human. The incarnate Son enters the stage in act 3 to display the kind of performance that truly images God while also making a way for the plot to be resolved and Israel, gentiles, and the whole of creation to be conformed to the performance for which they were intended. As Vanhoozer notes, "It is God's address to us in Jesus Christ that draws us forward eschatologically towards our destiny as human creatures."[76] Our focus in the following section is examining what it might mean to be eschatologically conformed to the image of Christ in the human performance of the *imago Dei* and how that might begin in the current act—act 4—of the theodrama of salvation.

---

74. Vanhoozer, "Human Being," 177.
75. Vanhoozer, "Human Being," 178.
76. Vanhoozer, "Human Being," 183.

Restoring the Image: Performing Christ

In the introduction to *The Drama of Doctrine* Vanhoozer states, "To be a Christian is to belong to Jesus' way, to be actively oriented and moving in the same direction as Jesus, toward the kingdom of God."[77] He further adds, "Following Jesus' way promotes human flourishing (*shalom*) and leads to the *summum bonum*: life, eternal and abundant."[78] Elsewhere, in a later text, Vanhoozer elaborates further on what following Jesus means: "(1) to understand the meaning of what Christ says in Scripture, (2) to respond to his instructions with obedience, and (3) to go after Christ or along 'the way' of Christ."[79] In the post-fall world, the crucial revelation of the theodrama is the incarnation in which something of the performance we are cast for is revealed as well as a unique divine performance that is the gateway for our eschatological performances. The dramatic self-communication of God which is both the source of creation and the ongoing engagement of God with creation is the ground for all other performances. This self-communication brings the drama into being and scripts the parts for which humans are cast. At the heart of the action is the covenantal relationship, and it is God who both initiates the covenantal relationship and sets the terms for fitting covenantal performance. The incarnation is then that performance that fittingly and completely fulfills the human covenantal responsive performance in a way that no human had been able to do before that point: "Jesus Christ is both God's fulfilled promise and humanity's right response."[80] To develop this further, "the content of *what is in Christ* is nothing less than true deity and true humanity. What we come to know when we see *what is in Christ* is the full measure of the love of God and the full stature of his human image. We come to learn about the reality of God's nature and human nature and about the reality of the relationship between the two."[81] In the post-Pentecost act of the drama, the church as the body of Christ is constituted and empowered by the Spirit of God to be "both audience and part of the action."[82] In this sense, Vanhoozer is drawing on the model of "participatory theatre" where the task of the individual as the image of God, and the

---

77. Vanhoozer, *Drama of Doctrine*, 14.
78. Vanhoozer, *Drama of Doctrine*, 15.
79. Vanhoozer, *Faith Speaking Understanding*, 1.
80. Vanhoozer, *Faith Speaking Understanding*, 85.
81. Vanhoozer, *Faith Speaking Understanding*, 90.
82. Vanhoozer, *Drama of Doctrine*, 79.

church as the company of actors, is to perform Christ—carry the form of Christ through—by improvising on the performance of Christ in the power of the Spirit. The so-called fourth wall of the theater is broken as the audience becomes performers. It is the incarnation that both provides the concrete example on which to improvise as well as enabling the drawing back together of the fragmented formal and material self. The relationship between Father and Son enabled by the Spirit is what the whole of creation and humans, in particular, were made for. "To participate in God is to align oneself with the pattern of communicative action that forms the heart of the theo-drama."[83] As Daniela Augustine notes, "The 'likeness of God' is not a distant mirroring of the divine image but the fullness of a communion and community with the creator through the incorporating and transfiguring work of the Holy Spirit."[84]

Before we go any further here, it is important for the sake of understanding Vanhoozer's theodramatic approach to performance in act 4, to give more detail regarding the terms used and his engagement with the pioneer of method acting, Constantin Stanislavski. We turn first to Vanhoozer's use of "the Method," which Stanislavski was famous for creating.[85]

Until Stanislavski, emphasis in acting had been placed on outward delivery only. The result was a rather exaggerated performance or mechanical acting. In contrast, Stanislavski wanted actors to aim for alignment between both the inner and the outer. It was not enough to simply offer an outward performance; the actor must become the part for which they are cast. As Vanhoozer notes, "The Method rejects over-acting, clichés, mannerisms, and all other such forms of *mechanical acting*. The great actor creates the inner experiences of his character, incarnates them, and communicates them to the audience."[86] A disconnect between inner and outer would embody something of hypocrisy in performance. Therefore, preparation for a true and full delivery must include, if not major on, inner preparation, which will require study, reflection, and imagination. Here Vanhoozer draws attention to Stanislavski's "magic 'if'": "Actors must strive to answer the question of what they would do *if* they were a certain character."[87] He continues, "Actors can avoid me-

---

83. Vanhoozer, *Drama of Doctrine*, 107–8.
84. Augustine, "Image, Spirit, and Theosis," 188.
85. Stanislavski, *Actor Prepares*.
86. Vanhoozer, *Drama of Doctrine*, 370.
87. Vanhoozer, *Drama of Doctrine*, 371.

chanical acting by asking, for example, 'What would I do *if* I were in Othello's position and *if* the circumstances that surround Othello were mine?' This 'if' transforms the character's aims into the actor's, as if by magic—hence Stanislavski's magic 'if.'"[88] Following this preparation through to its performance leads Vanhoozer to conclude, "We achieve truth on stage when we have faith in our parts, when we believe with sincerity in what we are doing, when we know who we are."[89] With a sense of "the Method" and the "magic 'if'" in play, it is important for understanding Vanhoozer's approach to the *imago Dei* to outline and clarify further terms he incorporates. We turn to a definition of fittingness.

Fittingness in performance needs to be understood within a drama that is occurring. In the case of the theodrama, "'fittingness' makes sense only on the assumption that there is a state of affairs—God's action in the world, the drama of redemption—against which one can measure the rightness or wrongness of a course of action."[90] With the drama playing out, "we are to fit into something that is already there: There is both a structured stage (creation) and determinate plot (the history of salvation)."[91] We can here build on a key point noted earlier: the whole drama—plot, scenery, and characters—is initiated by the Trinitarian divine playwright. Fittingness, for humans as the image of God, is therefore about responding to the divine covenantal call in the manner for which they were created, namely, to partner with God in enabling the plot to unfold in the intended direction by imaging Christ into the world. However, here we stumble on several other terms that Vanhoozer draws on to elucidate his approach.

To fit as best as one can in the salvific theodrama, one must be aware, as much as possible, of the "superobjective" of the drama in order to carry on the "through-line" of the plot in one's performance of *imago Dei*. In reference to the first of these terms Vanhoozer notes, "The ultimate point of a performance is to communicate what Stanislavski calls the play's main idea, or 'superobjective.'"[92] He continues, "*The ultimate goal of the actor, then, is not simply to play a role but to project the main idea of the play.*"[93] Applied to our current discussion, each performance

---

88. Vanhoozer, *Drama of Doctrine*, 371.
89. Vanhoozer, *Drama of Doctrine*, 371.
90. Vanhoozer, "Voice," 100.
91. Vanhoozer, "Voice," 100.
92. Vanhoozer, *Drama of Doctrine*, 372.
93. Vanhoozer, *Drama of Doctrine*, 372.

of *imago Dei* in seeking to perform Christ is therefore to offer a performance that embodies communion with God and the kingdom in which such a communion occurs. It is a responsive performance that reflects a particular type of relationship with God that is displayed within the world in how human beings relate to the world and cultivate the coming kingdom as the revelation of salvific covenantal communion between God and creation. The "through-line" of one's performance—actions, thoughts, emotions—should point toward this objective and so carry the drama forward.[94]

This is far more complex than it might appear though, as one cannot simply repeat the performance of Jesus in our own time and space, for at least two reasons. First, the discontinuity between Jesus' performance and ours due to Jesus being the incarnate Son of God and thus uncreated is, in certain important ways, unique. Created humanity is not able to redeem creation in the way God in Christ is. So, to attempt an identical repetition of the performance of Jesus is to misunderstand the gulf between fallen creation and the Trinitarian creator God. Secondly, in terms of what is plausible to repeat in seeking to imitate Christ in the way created humans are able and intended to, in order to be relevant and achieve their purpose, would need a kind of repetition that looks suitably different in different cultures and contexts. Vanhoozer defines culture as that which "refers to the beliefs, values, and practices that characterize human life together at a particular place and time."[95] He continues, "Culture sets the stage, arranges the scenery, and provides the props that supply the setting for theology's work."[96] Therefore, any attempt to perform Christ—carry the form of Christ through onto the created stage—must be culturally aware in order to do this in a fitting manner. For the actor seeking to perform Christ, answering the questions posed by the magic "if" will require awareness of the culture, context, Script, and previous performances in order to offer their own fitting performance. With this issue in mind, the questions that emerge are, how might a repetition of the performance of Christ be achieved, and what would such a repetition look like?

To answer this, we can turn to Vanhoozer's use of Paul Ricoeur's definition of two types of identity—*idem* and *ipse*. Drawn from Latin, these two definitions shed light on two different ways of understanding what might be meant by repeating the performance of Christ as *imago*

94. Vanhoozer, *Drama of Doctrine*, 371–72.
95. Vanhoozer, *Drama of Doctrine*, 129.
96. Vanhoozer, *Drama of Doctrine*, 129.

Dei in the current context. "*Idem*-identity," or what Vanhoozer relabels "hard-identity" refers to an exact repetition of that with which one is identifying. It "is the identity of sameness or permanence in time" that suggests no substantial change or difference.[97] Vanhoozer labels this "hard identity" because the term "'hard' connotes immutability and permanence."[98] For the reasons noted above, this is neither desirable nor possible in attempting to offer a culturally relevant, fitting, Christologically shaped performance of the *imago Dei*. However, there is a possibility for understanding and delivering such a performance by understanding identity in terms of *ipse*-identity.

Ipse-identity, or for Vanhoozer "soft" identity, refers to an identity that is unchanging in character and reliability. There is room for growth and change in terms of response and relevance to the shifting nature of culture and context, but there is something unchanging in terms of identity that is defined as character and constant reliability. "This kind of sameness partakes more of *narrative* than of numeric identity. For personal identity ('same self') allows for development, growth, perhaps even a certain degree of change in a way that *idem*, or 'hard' identity ('self-same'), does not."[99] When applied to the performance of the church or individual, this opens the door to the possibility of identifying with Christ, as enabled by the Holy Spirit, in order to carry on the through-line of the theodrama by performing *imago Dei* in the current culture and context, while avoiding static repetition and the pitfall of ignoring the creator/creature distinction. Such an approach is affirmed by Scripture in terms of being found in Christ and growing into Christlikeness as the redeemed *imago Dei* emerges and heads toward full eschatological redemption (Rom 6:10–11; 8:29; 13:14; 1 Cor 1:30–31; 2 Cor 1:21–22; 5:16–21; Gal 3:23–29; Eph 4:20–24; Phil 3:8–11; Col 3:9–11). What it might mean to be "in Christ" and how God enables and encourages the development of the *imago Dei* is discussed below. Before then, more needs to be said about how one is to perform Christ as the human image of God in the current act of the theodrama. For this, we turn to Vanhoozer's use of improvisation.

With Scripture as script and transcript, as well as being prescriptive, it offers insight into the *ipse*-identity of Christ that we are seeking to perform in a fitting way as the image of God. Improvisation helps enable

97. Vanhoozer, *Drama of Doctrine*, 127.
98. Vanhoozer, *Drama of Doctrine*, 127.
99. Vanhoozer, *Drama of Doctrine*, 127.

such performances by providing a way of performing that avoids static repetition yet encourages consistency. It does this by cutting a middle way between the dual dangers of ad-libbing and an inflexible preplanned response to the presenting situations. Ad-libbing, on the one hand, "is the theatrical equivalent of heresy, where one person stubbornly insists on going his own way instead of playing the game."[100] In many ways, this is largely what is played out as the sinful aspect of humans from the moment of the fall. Rather than being cast within an unfolding theodrama where the aim is to respond to the divine playwright/performer in such a way as to carry the drama forward, ad-libbing potentially takes the drama in directions the playwright neither intended nor wanted and thus potentially ruins the integrity and beauty of the plot. In a sense, ad-libbing ignores the bigger picture and the superobjective and answers magic "if" questions that are not helpful to ask. Such a performance ignores the performance of the other actors for the sake of the wants of the individual, and all at a cost to the plot, the individual, and the rest of the performers.

At the other extreme is a preplanned performance, by which is meant "the temptation to think out a course of action before saying or doing anything."[101] In some ways, this is similar to ad-libbing in that the focus is on the desire of individuals. However, whereas ad-libbing is about individuals' *response* to the action being determined by their own perspective and desires at the potential cost to the unfolding plot, preplanning attempts to take control of the drama and rewrite the action before it has happened, at a potential cost to the unfolding plot. Occurrences of this are legion in the Scriptures and beyond. Wherever the work of God in creation is overlooked or mislabeled due to it not fulfilling the expectations of those who have already decided what God should be doing, the error of preplanning is manifest.

Improvisation, in contrast to the opposing extremes, attempts to remain open to responding to the work of the playwright and other actors in the theodrama while also knowing what a fitting response might look like in given circumstances, as they arise. "The true improvisor is the one whose actions appear neither pre-scripted nor cleverly novel but fitting, even obvious. Christian theologians [and Christians more generally!] improvise whenever they act in ways that appear obvious *to one who fears God*, to one whose reflex (instinct) is the 'law' of the Spirit of

---

100. Vanhoozer, *Drama of Doctrine*, 338.
101. Vanhoozer, *Drama of Doctrine*, 337.

freedom."[102] Such a performance of improvisation requires knowing the plot, script, and performance history such that one is able to recognize the work of the Spirit prompting and directing in the past and present. With such knowledge and understanding at work, the actors are able to "accept" or "block" "offers" where "offers" are defined as "invitations to respond by extending the action and keeping the play going."[103] In so doing, they are able to carry on the through-line of the theodrama in a fitting way in the context in which their performance is taking place by either accepting, and thus continuing a particular constructive sub-plotline, or blocking a destructive sub-plotline. To recognize and incorporate the constructive offer into the larger plotline is to "overaccept," which is the aim of good improvisers.[104]

To be made in the image of God as performers in act 4 is to discern what a Christologically shaped, fitting, improvised, covenantal response to the communication of God in a given context is and perform accordingly, enabled by the Spirit and the guidance of Scripture. This requires a Spirited understanding of the theodrama and how one participates as well as the ongoing work of the Spirit to enable the development of a more Christlike nature in each performer, that is displayed in the performance given. As Vanhoozer states, "Christian identity is theodramatic: who we are is ultimately defined in terms of Jesus' person and work. As such, Christian identity is both gift and task."[105] To be in Christ is to find a new identity that is in fact our "truest identity."[106] To walk more deeply in this vocation is to actively participate in working with God and others to move the drama toward the superobjective of the banishment of evil from creation and the full communion of God and creation at the eschaton.

Thus far we can see from engaging with Vanhoozer what it might mean to say what the *imago Dei* was at creation, what the impact of the fall is, and how that might be overcome by the performance of Christ on the stage of the theodrama. Fulfillment of the image for created humans is experienced "in Christ" as Spirited Christlike performances are brought to bear by way of progressive sanctification of the image. However, there

---

102. Vanhoozer, *Drama of Doctrine*, 338.
103. Vanhoozer, *Drama of Doctrine*, 339.
104. Vanhoozer, *Drama of Doctrine*, 340.
105. Vanhoozer, *Drama of Doctrine*, 392.
106. Vanhoozer, *Drama of Doctrine*, 393. This will link to Winnicott's idea of the "True Self" developed further in later chapters.

are two further points to address before we can move on to looking at the church as image bearer and image enabler. The first is what it might mean to describe the image as "in Christ." The danger with this term is that, if misunderstood, it could be presumed to describe a collapsing of the creator/creature distinction, which is far from the intent of the term and something Vanhoozer is keen to defend against. The second point to consider here is how the divine playwright brings about the Christlike image in the human creature. This, of course, involves the work of the Spirit, but more can be said about how this is done and what the role of the creature and creator is in this process. We begin by defining "in Christ."

"In Christ"

Vanhoozer follows a line of thinking that is keen to retain the ontological distinction between creature and creator with the first being a contingent being and the second a necessary being, or rather, the source and ground of all being. He is therefore aiming to guard against any form of panentheism in the development of his position while maintaining that "communion is arguably the ultimate aim of all God's communicative action."[107] To do this Vanhoozer specifies two different types of participation: "a general cosmological participation in the Son through whom all things were made (Col. 1:16) and a more particular Christological abiding in the Son in whom there is reconciliation (2 Cor. 5:17)."[108] The journey for humans should be to grow from the general participation into the more specific as God becomes all in all. However, with the fall came a destructive rupture in the covenantal relationship that required the reconciling work of God in Christ. To become "participants of the divine nature" (2 Pet 1:4) within Vanhoozer's model means a "theodramatic participation" that involves responding in a fitting way to God's address by way of the Spirit.[109] Such a participation is defined as "fellowship, not fusion" where "communion with God consists in sharing the love the Father has for the Son in the Spirit" and this as a gift of grace.[110] In using the grammatical notion of the middle voice, where one is caught in the midst of doing and being done to, to parse "I participate,"

---

107. Vanhoozer, *Remythologizing Theology*, 280.
108. Vanhoozer, *Remythologizing Theology*, 281–82.
109. Vanhoozer, *Remythologizing Theology*, 282.
110. Vanhoozer, *Remythologizing Theology*, 282.

Vanhoozer suggests, "We participate in God as we actively image God—as we dramatize *theos*—yet it is ultimately the Spirit who recreates or 'makes common' the image of God in us by efficaciously ministering the word of God."[111] Participation, for humans, is thus caught up in the dramatic imaging of God in creation in the context and culture in which we find ourselves. To do this is to image Christ, made possible by the Spirit, so, participation results in performing the *imago Dei* while performing the *imago Dei* is active participation. However, there is still more to say here in terms of drilling down into what it might mean to say we are "in Christ" or have "union with Christ."

Drawing on St. Paul, Cyril of Alexandria, John Calvin, and John Owen, Vanhoozer proposes six theses that lay out his position.[112] The first suggests union as eschatological, that is, to participate in the history of Christ. Whereas to be on our own fallen path means to have our own storyline apart from Christ that results only in death, to be "in Christ" means to participate in the drama of Christ—in his death and resurrection (Rom 6:5) that leads to eternal life. By way of the Spirit, our old self dies, and Christ lives within us (Gal 2:20). We are a new creation (2 Cor 5:17) in anticipation of God's completion of the good work begun.

The second thesis suggests union is medial. This returns to our point above regarding the middle voice. To be unified with Christ is something we actively choose to participate in yet is also something enabled in initiation and process by the work of the Spirit. We are thus both object and subject simultaneously as the Spirit works within us to enable us to perform Christ.

The third thesis understands union as covenantal. Connected to the idea of union being about participation in Christ's history, this pushes that view further by highlighting that Christ fulfills the covenant with God for which humans were made and by his death and resurrection makes it possible for us to participate in that covenant in the way we were intended. It is therefore not enough to say union is about participating in Christ's history. That history needs to be qualified as the fulfillment of a particular covenant.

The fourth thesis is that union is dialogical. To be "in Christ" is to be drawn into the eternal Trinitarian conversation. Although Jesus is divine in a way we are not and never will be, we are invited and enabled to

---

111. Vanhoozer, *Remythologizing Theology*, 283.
112. Vanhoozer, *Remythologizing Theology*, 283–94.

converse with God by the Spirit because of Jesus' covenantal faithfulness for us. Rather than losing ourselves as the Spirit works to speak the Word in us in response to the Father, we instead find our true identity in this communion. "Union with Christ is not a fusion of horizons whereby one's individuality and name are absorbed into the Godhead but a dialogical union in which Christ's 'voice' dominates our thinking and feeling."[113]

The fifth thesis that makes up Vanhoozer's approach is that union is sapiential. He suggests, drawing from 1 Cor 2:13, 16 and Phil 2:1, 5, that the Spirit is the one who enables a wisdom beyond human wisdom by providing us with the mind of Christ. To participate as the *imago Dei* is thus to grow into the wisdom of Christ enabled by the Spirit.

The final thesis points toward the next chapter where we will discuss the role of the church in enabling participation in Christ and a true performance of the *imago Dei*. In this thesis, Vanhoozer suggests that union is ecclesial. This is so because to be "in Christ" is to be part of the body of Christ—the two are inseparable: "Union with Christ implies union with others."[114] To partake of the divine nature is to be incorporated which, by the very term, means to be found in the body of Christ, the church. In fact, returning to where we began with these six theses in terms of the eschatological aspect of union, Vanhoozer sums up this final thesis by stating, "The drama of redemption reaches a climax with the formation of a 'holy nation' or covenant people that participates in the theodramatic action precisely by proclaiming and practicing the light, life, and love of God (1 Pet. 2:9)."[115]

In drawing these theses together Vanhoozer states that participation is "a graciously enabled speaking engagement in what the Father is doing in Christ through the Spirit."[116] To participate in the theodrama in this way as the human *imago Dei* is to participate in the kingdom of God. To return to a core theme throughout this chapter, approaching an understanding of what it means to be made in the image of God begins with God and God's self-revelation in Scripture. What this reveals to us, according to Vanhoozer, is that fulfilment of the performative role is only achieved in cooperation with the Holy Spirit who enables us to be in union with Christ and so grow into the Christlikeness for which we were created, without collapsing the distinction between the creator and the creature. In uniting

---

113. Vanhoozer, *Remythologizing Theology*, 292.
114. Vanhoozer, *Remythologizing Theology*, 292.
115. Vanhoozer, *Remythologizing Theology*, 292–93.
116. Vanhoozer, *Remythologizing Theology*, 293.

with Christ in this way our history is redeemed and reformed as we are found afresh within the covenantal historical relationship between Father and Son and so are able to respond to the call of the Father by way of the Spirit that ministers the Word in and through us. It is only in this way that a fitting performance of *imago Dei* is both understood and achieved. It is for this role that we were created as asymmetric partners with the divine playwright who has authored a theodrama of communion. Nature and role are bound together as we seek to work with God to cultivate the kingdom of God on earth in our own performances, which will therefore include the banishment of evil as we look toward final consummation at the eschaton. This is the superobjective that guides our performances as we seek to carry on the through-line in our Spirit-enabled Christological performances on the context-specific stage of the theodrama. Before we conclude this chapter and look ahead, there is one final area of Vanhoozer's thought left to explore relating to the *imago Dei*. This is the mechanics of how the divine playwright works with the performers to move the theodrama toward the superobjective and bring to fulfillment the image of God in those who participate in Christ.

Dialogical Consummation and "Putting on Christ"

To address this issue, Vanhoozer draws on the thought of Mikhail Bakhtin and explores the divine-human relationship through the lens of the author-hero relationship found in Bakhtin's work. Reaffirming what we have already noted above, Vanhoozer states, "God is to our world, I submit, as an author is to the world of his or her text."[117] To qualify this further, however, he notes that God is authorial in the sense that God is transcendent, yet God is also immanent in terms of dialogue with humans and creation and governs and cares for the world by way of "triune providence." God is, therefore, "a *dialogical* author."[118] In terms of the *imago Dei* specifically, "God authors human creatures in his image to be willing covenantal agents."[119] God then initiates and binds Godself to a covenantal relationship with the human creatures in which they "exercise a secondary authorship, and hence genuine freedom."[120] With regard

---

117. Vanhoozer, *Remythologizing Theology*, 298.
118. Vanhoozer, *Remythologizing Theology*, 298–99.
119. Vanhoozer, *Remythologizing Theology*, 303.
120. Vanhoozer, *Remythologizing Theology*, 303.

to the Trinitarian aspect of the divine interaction, Vanhoozer states, "the Father takes the authorial initiative, the Son authorially executes and the Spirit authorially perfects each and every divine communicative act."[121] Again, with regard to the human image, what takes precedence is the divine Trinitarian relations which creation is being drawn into. To grow into the complete *imago Dei* is, therefore, to grow into Christ by way of the Spirit, made possible by the divine author's involvement on the created stage in interactions with creation.

We can affirm, therefore, that the image is to be conformed to the likeness of Christ by the Spirit and is a secondary author operating with a level of freedom. We can also affirm that the divine author is guiding via a particular type of interaction. Using Tolstoy as an example in literature and matching that with a dominant stream in classical theism, Vanhoozer is keen to avoid an approach whereby the author operates from the outside and determines the action of the drama, including the performance of the characters. This does not reflect what is revealed in Scripture in terms of divine-human interaction, and so Vanhoozer follows the example of Dostoevsky developed further by Bakhtin where the hero of the piece is allowed a voice and a say in the direction of the drama. If taken too far the risk is reducing God down to just another performer, but Vanhoozer argues it is possible to maintain author-hero dialogue in the shaping of the action without falling into this trap.

As already noted, to image God is to answer God's communicative actions in a particular way in order to be the secondary author or creator. The response offered is done with a degree of freedom and is something for which humans will be judged. God dialogues with Adam and Eve like no other creature such that "what makes men and women 'like God' has to do with their *being spoken to* and their capacity *to speak back*."[122] However, this is where drawing on Bakhtin helps avoid reductionistic pitfalls. Of humans as heroes, Bakhtin suggests, "A given human being is the condition of aesthetic vision; if he turns out to be a determinate object of that vision (and he always tends, and tends essentially, toward that), he constitutes the hero of a given work."[123] The author, although able to interact with the hero, does not fully determine the hero but instead interacts via dialogue. The author is able to see the biggest picture possible

---

121. Vanhoozer, *Remythologizing Theology*, 304.
122. Vanhoozer, *Remythologizing Theology*, 319.
123. Bakhtin, "Author and Hero," 230.

in terms of all that the hero and others have done, thought, etc., and so is able to judge fully how well the hero has responded to the author. Vanhoozer follows Bakhtin in this view of the author's "outsidedness" and suggests that this enables the author to be able to consider "*all* that a character is—his or her whole life."[124] For Vanhoozer, biblical heroes are those defined by their trust in, and obedience to, God and "'outsidedness' names the asymmetrical, nonreciprocal boundary that distinguishes author from hero and that is consequently an aspect of their relationship."[125] He further suggests "the author is outside the hero with respect to space, time, and the meaning of the whole."[126] The latter point is contentious, particularly with respect to time, in terms of genuine interaction with the hero. However, this need not concern us here as this issue, important though it is, does not significantly affect the key point of what it means to image God, and the author-hero relationship.[127] The key point is that the perspective of the author coupled with the capability and opportunity of the author in the author-hero relationship is such that the author is able to consummate the life of the hero by providing meaning that is otherwise out of reach for the hero. Theologically this offers an eschatological perspective in that the divine author is able to provide meaning by drawing the individual performance of the hero into the history of Christ and thus reinterpret the hero's performance.

This consummation takes place dialogically (through words) as the divine author interacts with the hero, groups, and nations to provide opportunities for fitting responses. "It is through the give and take of dialogue that a person—Bakhtin's 'voice-idea'—actualizes his or her potential, realizes his or her true self, and hence rings true or false."[128] This latter point will be particularly important further on in this work as we turn to think about how, engaging with Winnicott, the true self is aided to emerge within Christian communities, particularly in times of trauma. For now, however, it is enough to note that "our freedom is our answerability" and what we answer to is the call of the divine who

124. Vanhoozer, *Remythologizing Theology*, 324.
125. Vanhoozer, *Remythologizing Theology*, 325.
126. Vanhoozer, *Remythologizing Theology*, 325.

127. The problem here is that not only is it potentially unnecessary for God to be outside of time in order for the asymmetrical relationship and ontological difference to be maintained, it is also potentially problematic for the existence of a genuine relationship between creator and creature. For a helpful exploration of time with respect to God's relationship to creation, see Ganssle, *God and Time*.

128. Vanhoozer, *Remythologizing Theology*, 333.

consummates us in dialogue.[129] That said, there is a further problem to address: if post-fall humans are incapable of performing the part for which they were cast as *imago Dei* surely all that will be consummated is a fallen creature as, free though they are in one sense, they are also slaves to sin. Here Vanhoozer highlights again the work of the Son and Spirit in setting the hero free to be the true hero. "In the beginning, the Author created his heroes good, with an opportunity to become even better."[130] However, as we have already noted, the fall results in the defacing of the image as the humans, for whatever reason, offer a less-than-good response to the call of God. With this as the problem in the plotline of the drama, "the gospel *mythos* is the good news that the Author freely and lovingly consummates human heroes by entering into the story himself with both hands, Son and Spirit" where the human hero at the heart of the drama is the divine-human hero empowered by the Spirit.[131] To be set free to be the *imago Dei* is thus to be set free to find oneself in Christ, in the ways noted above. And here we reach the crux of how this actually occurs, how the image is to be restored to offer its most fitting performance. This is achieved by way of triune dialogical consummation where this "is a matter of God's acting not *on* persons but *within* and *through* them in such a way that precisely by so acting, God brings them to their senses and makes them into the creatures they were always meant to be."[132] So, dialogical consummation, in the aftermath of the life, death, resurrection, and ascension of Jesus and the sending of the Spirit at Pentecost, means that, when God chooses, God is able to enable a fitting Christlike response to God's own call in the life of the hero.

Although Vanhoozer emphasizes the work of God in the life of the hero as that which enables and initiates a fitting response and move toward Christlikeness, it would be a mistake to downplay the role of human activity in the process of putting on Christ. As we have already noted, Vanhoozer understands becoming Christlike as a gift given and a task to be completed. The gift aspect refers to being justified by faith whereas the task aspect refers to the process of sanctification whereby we grow into Christlikeness by cooperation with the Holy Spirit's

---

129. Vanhoozer, *Remythologizing Theology*, 335.
130. Vanhoozer, *Remythologizing Theology*, 342.
131. Vanhoozer, *Remythologizing Theology*, 356–57.
132. Vanhoozer, *Remythologizing Theology*, 370.

activity.¹³³ However, what does it actually mean to co-operate with the Holy Spirit and put on Christ?

In a paper exploring just this issue, Vanhoozer explains, "This process of maturation—the post-conversion process of becoming more like Christ, of 'growing up . . . into him' (Eph. 4:15)—is what I mean by *drama of discipleship*."¹³⁴ He continues this line of thought elsewhere suggesting, "The children of faith need the diet of doctrine, and considerable performance practice, if they are to develop into 'grown-up' disciples."¹³⁵ In this view, sin can be defined as not living as our true selves in Christ, with the mind of Christ and "to the extent that we fail to coincide with our true selves, then, all people Christians included, need therapy."¹³⁶ However, Vanhoozer has a broad view of therapy and understands both the Christian psychotherapeutic setting and a more traditional understanding of discipleship to fall within the definition of therapy. The reason for this is that both should be aiming to aid the disciple to have the mind of Christ in terms of how the self, world, and one's place within the drama are understood and related to. He even refers to the use of doctrine as psychodynamic therapy when making disciples as this "encourages disciples to internalize dispositions and habits of the heart that lead to a right participation in the theodrama."¹³⁷ In a paper presented to Christian psychologists and counselors Vanhoozer stated that he would "assume that Christian psychologists and theologians are engaged in a common enterprise, namely, interpreting God, world, and especially the self first and foremost by interpreting Scripture."¹³⁸ Within this assumption and his theodramatic model he brackets the counselor as an "acting coach" and understands their role as "training the client's mind, heart, imagination and will to think, desire, see, and act in ways that accord with the way things are as we know them to be through the biblical testimony to Jesus Christ, the one through whom all things were

---

133. Vanhoozer, *Faith Speaking Understanding*, 129–30.

134. Vanhoozer, "Putting on Christ," 148. There are echoes here of the work of James Samra in his exploration of Paul's understanding of maturity and maturation understood as a process where "the character of believers is aligned with or conformed to the character of Christ" through "post-conversion growth and development." See Samra, *Being Conformed*, 3.

135. Vanhoozer, *Faith Speaking Understanding*, 204.

136. Vanhoozer, "Putting on Christ," 149–50.

137. Vanhoozer, "Putting on Christ," 154n18. Vanhoozer credits Steve Porter for guiding him to this insight.

138. Vanhoozer, "Forming the Performer," 5.

made and in whom all things hold together (Col. 1:16–17)."[139] Although the Christian may already be in Christ in terms of justification, one's identity and worldview continue to be formed in terms of how one responds to God's continual work—leading back to the point above regarding dialogical consummation.[140] The question is, "Will we adopt ways of seeing, judging, and acting that form a pattern of right response to God's word and fitting participation in the drama of redemption?"[141] To adopt these ways—to have the mind of Christ—"is ultimately a matter of the Spirit illuminating renewed minds (Rom. 12:2) and cultivating patterns of embodied wisdom—lived knowledge—hence the drama (embodied action) of discipleship."[142] What is being proposed is a middle way between the extremes of a Pelagian-type approach that majors on the work of humans in putting on Christ, and an approach that believes that conformity to Christ is entirely the work of God with no human involvement. Instead, what Vanhoozer is suggesting is the belief that God has already achieved what we are called to embody and that the Holy Spirit, with the use of Scripture, is enabling an understanding and behavior that is closing the gap between heaven and earth, the now and the not yet, as we co-operate in this dialogical process. Such a process requires an "eschatologically charged imagination" as disciples live out more and more the reality for which they were created and are destined.[143] "The Holy Spirit creates a 'clean heart' and illumines our minds to understand the word of God, but it falls to the disciple to trust the word of Christ by stepping out and putting it into practice."[144] The Holy Spirit is the one who clothes the disciple of Christ with Christ by working from within and establishing union with Christ.

When faced with the question of whether presenting an exterior which is at odds with an interior in the process of sanctification amounts to the hypocrisy Vanhoozer is so keen to avoid, he takes his lead from C. S. Lewis. Lewis offers the idea of "good pretending" whereby one

---

139. Vanhoozer, "Forming the Performer," 10.

140. Vanhoozer labels this character development as "theodramatic self-understanding." *Faith Speaking Understanding*, 131.

141. Vanhoozer, "Putting on Christ," 154.

142. Vanhoozer, "Putting on Christ," 155.

143. Vanhoozer, "Putting on Christ," 163. In *Faith Speaking Understanding* Vanhoozer contrasts Heidegger's description of humans as being-toward-death with his own suggestion of being-toward-resurrection (62).

144. Vanhoozer, "Putting on Christ," 167.

behaves as if one has a particular quality and in so doing one moves along the journey to having it.[145] There are a number of behaviors, actions, and attitudes that the Scriptures direct us to put on but, as already noted above, to avoid the twin poles of Pelagianism and laziness is to recognize what is already true of one's identity in Christ as gift and begin to co-operate with the sanctifying work of the Spirit in becoming imitators of Christ, clothed with Christ's righteousness. With this approach presented, Vanhoozer states that "acting out what is in Christ has nothing to do with playacting or pretending. On the contrary, to act out our new identity in Christ—to put on Christ, the costume of Christ's righteousness—is gradually to realize, one day at a time, the truth of our 'eternal weight of glory.'"[146]

In short, Vanhoozer suggests that the use of doctrine in cooperation with Word and Spirit can enable the transformation of heart, mind, and imagination.[147] This is entwined with the transformation of actions and behaviors meaning that orthodoxy, orthopraxy, and orthopathos are bound up together in the process of transformation.[148] This use of doctrine could even be defined as "cognitive-affective-eschatological therapy."[149] In order to aid this transformation, in addition to counseling, Vanhoozer suggests cultivating the habits of reading Scripture, regular prayer, and engaging in regular corporate worship. We will explore the importance of the last of these in the following chapter, and hopefully the importance of reading Scripture is clear from the exploration thus far, but it is important to say more about prayer in the process of dialogical consummation.

Vanhoozer states, prayer is "that form of human communicative action that draws us into communion with the triune God and so helps us willingly to conform to the Father's purposes, will, and wisdom—in a word, to the image of his Son."[150] After the pattern of Jesus, seen par-

---

145. Vanhoozer, *Faith Speaking Understanding*, 120; Lewis, *Mere Christianity*, 155–56.

146. Vanhoozer, *Faith Speaking Understanding*, 129. Vanhoozer also draws on the work of N. T. Wright and Robert Roberts for support. See "Putting on Christ," 163–66.

147. Vanhoozer, "Putting on Christ," 167.

148. Interestingly, although Vanhoozer links orthodoxy and orthopraxy together, there is an absence of mention of orthopathos. However, given the holistic nature of the transformation toward Christlikeness that Vanhoozer describes, it would seem natural to use this term. See *Faith Speaking Understanding*, 119–20, 220–23.

149. Vanhoozer, "Putting on Christ," 168.

150. Vanhoozer, *Remythologizing Theology*, 378.

ticularly in the garden of Gethsemane, prayer is that mechanism through which the hero is dialogically determined—by God at work in the hero—to conform to a freeing obedient response to the divine author and is thus dialogically consummated: "*prayer is an asymmetrical dialogical interaction whereby God effects in us, through word and Spirit, a freedom of consent.*"[151] What Vanhoozer is ultimately proposing here is something of an "effectual call" whereby the hero is enabled to respond in a fitting way by God at work within them. Such heroes are brought to Christlike completion by being drawn into union with Christ by way of the Spirit in such a way that the call of God to a performance of this redeemed and restored image is irresistible. However, one wonders how this is any different from the determinism Vanhoozer was so keen to avoid. Perhaps one way around such a hurdle is to subscribe to some form of universalism. The alternatives appear to be either belief in a God who is not capable of dialogically determining everyone to perform fittingly or a God who chooses not to enable such performances in some. This has particular echoes of the same problem Augustine faced and similarly, at this stage, Vanhoozer has not managed to resolve it in an acceptable way. However, there are some helpful threads that can be pulled together as we draw this chapter to a conclusion and look ahead to addressing the role of the church in the flourishing of the *imago Dei*.

Theodramatic Anthropology and Post-Traumatic Remaking

Léon Turner has noted, in conversation with Vanhoozer's model, that there is a prevailing trend among psychologists to understand each self as actually a construction of various "subselves."[152] Within this view, adaptation to different situations is seen as a healthy aim but it brings into question how one might define the "true self" and if, indeed, such a thing even exists. However, Turner has also noted that some psychologists have attempted to address this one-and-the-many dilemma by way of a narrative

---

151. Vanhoozer, *Remythologizing Theology*, 382–83.

152. Turner, "Behind the Mask." In a prior, more extensive study of this topic, Turner refers to these as "sub-personalities" that are to be distinguished from "alternate personalities." The former can be held together in a healthy singular narrative diachronically—through time—while coexisting synchronically—at the same time. The latter, which may be pathological, instead provides individual, autonomous narratives, meaning there is no diachronic singularity. See Turner, *Plural Self*.

framework of the self in which the parts are integrated to make a meaningful, single, individual thus preventing "the pathological fragmentation of self into multiple and completely autonomous parts."[153] If Vanhoozer's dramatic model functions in this way, doctrine, Turner notes, could have "the capacity to provide the context within which the person as a whole is formed and acts" and thus aid those offering counseling in how they treat clients.[154] In response to this engagement, Vanhoozer is keen to note the biblically rooted evidence of how behaving differently in different situations is entirely compatible with retaining a single, identifiable self. He suggests it is the task of Christian psychology to aid in the unmasking of the true self that finds its identity "in Christ" as the truest, fullest response to the prior call of God to humans.[155]

However, helpful though it is to identify what is meant by the true self as the image of God, and the Christological shape that we are destined for, regarding the focus of this work, where Vanhoozer's approach begins to unravel somewhat is with the rather cognitive emphasis on how this unmasking and development of the true self is to take place. As we have seen regarding those who are traumatized, in the previous chapter, transformation and remaking will not simply happen by way of knowing the right information—identity, drama, etc. In response to Vanhoozer, Teresa Tisdale has made just this point, highlighting that "knowing" does not necessarily result in "freedom and abundant life."[156] Although the dramatic model helpfully seeks to unify the various aspects of being human that have historically been singled out as *the* aspect that images God, how Vanhoozer suggests one develops and unmasks the true self is not so encompassing. The emphasis on cooperating with the Holy Spirit by way of transformed understanding through doctrine leading to transformed behavior and affections—Vanhoozer's "cognitive-affective eschatological therapy"—seems far too narrow an approach. As Tisdale notes, "in my clinical experience a person's capacity to internalize the reality of who they are in Christ is *relationally mediated*, not mainly cognitively mediated."[157] She continues, "In fact, distress is often associated with knowing theological truth and yet being unable to experience the reality of it."[158] Instead,

153. Turner, "Behind the Mask," 39.
154. Turner, "Behind the Mask," 39.
155. Vanhoozer, "Continuing the Dialogue," 45–46.
156. Tisdale, "Formation," 32.
157. Tisdale, "Formation," 33.
158. Tisdale, "Formation," 33.

Tisdale suggests that "what is needed is sound doctrine that is embodied and dynamically expressed by a community of believers who love and care for others and who are the Spirit-empowered incarnational reality of God in our day."[159] Here there are echoes of Herman's first stage in the recovery from trauma of facilitating the feeling of safety both internally and externally for the trauma survivor.[160]

In response, Vanhoozer acknowledges the importance of relationship and the embodied nature of the people of God. However, he suggests that experience without doctrinal direction is blind and thinks "it highly significant that the apostle Paul associates transformation with the 'renewing of our minds' (Rom. 12:2) rather than the dynamics of relational mediation."[161] Again, a helpful point though this is, it seems clear both from the accounts of Jesus' engagement with people as well as direction given in Paul's letters that renewal of minds and imaginations is crucial, yet people are transformed by way of relationships where they feel safe and loved and transformed for relationships where they also feel safe and loved. To miss this point is to undermine the very nature of the *imago Dei* that Vanhoozer proposes.

In *Faith Speaking Understanding* Vanhoozer gives examples of how Christians faced with a variety of situations improvise due to knowing what a fitting improvised performance of Christ could look like in response to the situation at hand. One of the situations recounted is that of a church community's response to an air disaster. In his use of this as an example, Vanhoozer suggests that a doctrinally informed, fitting response in this context is less about explanations and more about equipping "disciples to become 'answerable' agents, persons who improvise Christlike, compassionate responses to all who cry out in the wilderness of pain, emotional trauma, and existential angst" acknowledging "that in certain situations lament may be the best response."[162] The irony of this example

---

159. Tisdale, "Formation," 33.

160. Herman, *Trauma and Recovery*. Lengthier engagement with Herman's stages will take place in chapter 8.

161. Vanhoozer, "Continuing the Dialogue," 44.

162. Vanhoozer, *Faith Speaking Understanding*, 197. In response to Vanhoozer's model, Chuck DeGroat critiques the overemphasis on the cognitive aspect of transformation and also suggests the biblical practice of lament as that which would seem to be highly valuable yet out of place in what Vanhoozer is suggesting (see DeGroat, "Parts We Play," 17–20). Here we see Vanhoozer acknowledge the place of lament, which fits with his understanding that crying out to God is part of our fitting response as the *imago Dei*. Yet, Vanhoozer always seems to return to transformation of minds by way

and others is that although cognitive-affective appropriation of doctrine did indeed seem to shape the performance of the church, as he points out, the fitting response to the needs of the traumatized is an embodied one not, primarily, a cognitive one. The odd thing about this example is that Vanhoozer seems to use it to support the high place he gives doctrine in transformation yet misses the equally important place of embodied mediation of the love, grace, and mercy of God that is equally significant in the transformation of those who are traumatized.

Conclusion

The main aim of this chapter was to bring into focus what a theological anthropology might look like through the lens of Kevin Vanhoozer's theodramatic model. With this has come an outline of where we find ourselves and what our role is within that drama. Given that God is the author and main performer in the drama, it is to be characterized as a theodrama and our role is one of asymmetric partnership with God in the mission of God to draw all creation into the relationship with God for which it was intended. To be made in the image of God within this model is to do with vocation—the ability to respond to the covenantal call of God as being-in-communication and in so doing communicate with God and creation to aid and participate in communion with the triune fellowship. To image God is to answer God's call and re-present God in creation as human beings who communicate God's light, love, and truth in order to draw creation into communion with God.

From the fall in Gen 3 onward, humans have been unable to live up to (into?) this role in the way the divine playwright intended, and so the author became an actor in the form of the incarnation to fulfill the vocation of humanity. The incarnation thus provides both the gateway and example for humans to image God, and it is this performance that humans are to improvise on together, with Scripture in hand, cooperating with the Spirit, growing in awareness of what the superobjective of the drama is and what it might mean to carry on the through-line in each scene.

What emerges from the exploration in this chapter, then, is that the model of the dramatic *imago Dei* gives helpful shape to what it might mean to image God as a human as well as direction toward how

of Spirit enabled appropriation of doctrinal direction for performance as the primary way of becoming our true Christlike selves. For a retrieval of lament that fits within the dramatic model, see Torr, *Dramatic*.

transformation into our Christlike true selves might take place. However, what is also apparent is that although Vanhoozer displays some awareness of what might be needed for the church to aid the emergence of the true self in those who are traumatized, he stops short of developing this in any detailed way. The present project will aim to address that shortfall in conversation with Donald Winnicott and others. Before we engage with Winnicott's work we turn to explore what it means to be the church through the dramatic lens.

4

A Theodramatic Ecclesiology

Introduction

HAVING PROVIDED A BRIEF overview of Vanhoozer's theodramatic model in chapter 1, in the previous chapter, we were able to use it as a lens through which to explore his development of a theodramatic understanding of humans as made in the image of God. Of particular note was the Christological shape that we are destined for as justified and located "in Christ." The current experience, in this act of the drama, is one of sanctification as what has already been achieved by God at Easter is brought to bear, as we cooperate with God, on our human form. However, there are at least two possible problems to be resolved as we continue to explore how this process can be aided in the present act of the drama. The first problem is how this might be achieved. As was noted in the conclusion to the previous chapter, Vanhoozer's somewhat reductionistic approach of relying on Scripture, doctrine, and Spirit alone does not appear to take into consideration the complexity of the fallen human condition, and particularly in this exploration, the specific complexity of those who are traumatized. However, there is scope for building on, expanding, and adjusting Vanhoozer's approach as we engage with the work of Donald Winnicott in the following chapters. Prior to that, though, we need to address the second possible problem. In focusing on the individual human as the image of God there is a danger of slipping into the error Vanhoozer has noted of alternative approaches whereby there is an overemphasis on the individual at the cost of the relational aspect of the *imago Dei*. To avoid this overemphasis, the aim of the present chapter is to explore the church—what it is and what it does—in the drama of salvation.

In carrying on the theme of the previous chapter, we will here explore the church by continuing to use Vanhoozer's theodramatic lens. This will involve, first, exploring what, or rather, who constitutes the church and what the role of the church is in the drama of salvation. We will then explore what the church does to fulfill this role inwardly, and outwardly toward the rest of creation. As with theological anthropology in the previous chapter, the subject of ecclesiology engaged with here is vast and diverse in terms of the various approaches to the subject. Therefore, to narrow the engagement, the focus here will solely be on the theodramatic ecclesiology developed in Vanhoozer's work. With a clearer picture of this in place at the close of the chapter, we will be in a better position to move forward in exploring what guidance can be offered to shape a more trauma-sensitive church. We begin by exploring who the church is and what the role of the church is in the drama of salvation.

The Theodramatic Church: Identity and Role

In continuing with the theodramatic model, Vanhoozer follows in the footsteps of Calvin, who viewed the world as the theater of God's glory.[1] As we noted in the previous chapter, "Theater is not a static thing but a happening, a happening that involves more than physical events. The medium of theater is not physical but personal: human action and interaction. Theater happens whenever one or more persons present themselves to others in space and time."[2] Therefore, theatre is to do with "*communicative action in word and deed*."[3] After the drama reaches its climax in act 3 with the events of Easter, followed by the ascension, the church comes into being at Pentecost, at the beginning of act 4—the act in which we still find ourselves.

In Jesus, God enters the stage in act 3 as a human and offers the perfect divine-human performance that carries on the through-line of the drama toward its superobjective of triune communion with the whole of creation. As the curtain lifts on act 4, the scene is set and the church is

---

1. Calvin, *Institutes* 1.14.20 (156).
2. Vanhoozer, *Faith Speaking Understanding*, 22–23.
3. Vanhoozer, *Faith Speaking Understanding*, 23. In n19 on the same page, Vanhoozer also acknowledges the place of silence and suffering within the drama.

cast in the role of the body of Christ—those who will continue to perform Christ, together, in order to continue the embodiment of the eschatological kingdom that Jesus displayed and initiated in word and deed.

In the previous chapter, we noted the intrinsic link between the role and identity of the *imago Dei*. In this chapter, we can note the same link regarding the church—what the church is constituted for (role) is bound up with who the church is (identity).[4] Also as with the *imago Dei*, it is important to highlight that the church only has an identity and a role because of the prior intent, work, and covenantal call of God: "The church is not a community of choice but has been brought into being by a divine initiative: an effectual call."[5] Vanhoozer further states, "The church is *constituted*—gathered and governed—by a divine covenantal initiative that is both the source of its identity and authoritative principle."[6] In exploring ecclesiology we return to the initiatory work of God as being-in-communicative-action as its foundation. Here we can remind ourselves that God created out of love with the promise of drawing creation into communion with the triune fellowship. The missions of Son and Spirit find definition from within this wider *missio Dei* and "what matters here is that the church continue the missions—the way, the truth, and the life—of Son and Spirit."[7] In doing so, "*the church is the company of the gospel, whose nature and task alike pertain to performing the word in the power of the Spirit*."[8] In a similar way, John Zizioulas notes that the church is "a way of being," and that in its communion it is both brought into relationship with God as Trinity as well as reflecting the nature of the Trinitarian communion in its own life.[9] This is so because "the being of God could be known only through personal relationships and personal love. Being means life and life means *communion*."[10] The church knows and reflects the prior and continual communion of God through the prior and ongoing presence of God in the church. "In a christological perspective alone we can speak of the Church as *in-stituted* (by Christ), but in a

---

4. In *Faith Speaking Understanding*, Vanhoozer is keen to highlight that the church is something done by a group of people who identify as the church and thus writes of "doing church."
5. Vanhoozer, *Drama of Doctrine*, 141.
6. Vanhoozer, *Drama of Doctrine*, 133.
7. Vanhoozer, *Drama of Doctrine*, 125.
8. Vanhoozer, *Drama of Doctrine*, 401.
9. Zizioulas, *Being as Communion*, 15.
10. Zizioulas, *Being as Communion*, 16.

pneumatological perspective we have to speak of it as *con-stituted* (by the Spirit)."[11] It is both the Son and the Spirit that bring the church into being and sustain her in her relationship with the Father and the world as she is drawn into the Trinitarian mission of drawing creation into communion with God. The Son calls the church into being, making communion with the Father possible by his death and resurrection, that the church may be transferred to the kingdom of God in Christ. But, as with the incarnate Christ, so with his body, it is the Holy Spirit that enables the church to perform in this role.

Following Vanhoozer, the identity and role of the church can be characterized as bound up in the threefold vocation of: (i) observing who God is and what God is doing, particularly in Christ; (ii) being conformed, together, to the pattern of Christ; and (iii) being distinct from, yet "observed by the world" with the aim of the world participating in what God is doing in Christ through the church.[12]

Audience

"The *mythos* of Jesus Christ—the drama of his birth, death, resurrection and ascension—is the divine communicative act of which the church is the effect and theology the response."[13] Or, put another way, "the church's task . . . is not to make something new but to describe and display newness that already obtains 'in Christ.'"[14] The church, as made in the image of Christ, is therefore, the "plot or pattern of his history."[15] However, in order to fully "describe and display" as "plot or pattern" the church must be an ongoing observer.

With Scripture in hand, one aspect of the role and identity of the church is as a spectator—the audience—to what God has done, is doing, and will do in the redeeming, and making whole, of creation. Although the church is the body of Christ, it is also not Christ and is therefore not able to make possible the reconciliation Christ achieves through his death and resurrection. For the church, full respondent participation in the theodrama requires awareness of the unique being-in-communicative

---

11. Zizioulas, *Being as Communion*, 140.
12. Vanhoozer, *Faith Speaking Understanding*, 139.
13. Vanhoozer, *Remythologizing Theology*, 357.
14. Vanhoozer, *Drama of Doctrine*, 200–201.
15. Vanhoozer, *Remythologizing Theology*, 293.

action of God within the theodrama. However, there is a danger here that a simple hypothetical linear approach may be proposed whereby first one observes, then one responds, of which there is some truth in this given the emphasis on the prior work of God. But, as Volf has noted, although belief may be logically prior to praxis as value-laden practices, this may not be the chronological process as practices, and performances may be engaged in prior to observations and interpretations enlightening such performances with fuller meaning.[16] Similarly, Bonhoeffer suggests an artificial separation between faith and obedience to highlight faith that justifies believers as logically prior to obedience. However, he then suggests that there is no such chronological distinction in reality between the two, arguing that "faith is only real when there is obedience, never without it, and faith only becomes faith in the act of obedience."[17] Obedience is thus "the consequence of faith" and "the presupposition of faith."[18] Both together are the correct response to the prior call of Jesus but the inseparable unity muddies the waters for those who gravitate toward a more linear model.[19]

In reality, then, the church is called to continually (re)turn to the drama of salvation as ongoing observers of what God has done, is doing, and will do, alongside developing its performance of Christ. This enables the church to remain vigilant to the threat of performance becoming detached from the dynamic ongoing direction and shaping of the Holy Spirit in conversation with Scripture, tradition, and experience on the one hand, and passive audience viewing on the wrong side of the fourth wall on the other. In this sense, the observing church is both prior to and working in conjunction with the performing church in an ongoing response to the prior and ongoing call of God in Christ.

---

16. Volf, "Theology," 255–62. In a similar way James K. A. Smith argues that worship precedes the formation, awareness, and articulation of worldviews and doctrine due to the kind of creatures we are and how we engage with creation. This means that we have a developing understanding of ourselves, creation, and God that cannot be fully articulated as knowledge. See Smith, *Desiring the Kingdom*.

17. Bonhoeffer, *Cost of Discipleship*, 21.

18. Bonhoeffer, *Cost of Discipleship*, 21.

19. Pete Ward also notes the blurring of distinct starting points in his exploration of practical theology. See Ward, *Introducing*, 3–5.

Participants

Rather than being reduced to simply audience, the church is also "*participatory* theater" cast as "both audience and part of the action"[20] within the wider theater of God's glory. Although the church cannot defeat sin and death and enable reconciliation, the church is the place where that defeat and reconciliation by God in Christ is embodied and displayed.

As with the individual image, the church takes Scripture in hand as that which transcribes previous performances, lights the stage for seeing it clearly, provides guidance for a fitting Christologically shaped, improvised performance, and gives the most complete overview of the theodrama into which we are to fit. It gathers as "the company of the gospel" and is "directed by 'just these texts' and their concomitant canonical practices."[21] As we saw in the previous chapter, the identity of redeemed humanity is found in Christ and the process of sanctification involves being clothed with this eschatological reality until God is all in all. In this sense, what was said of redeemed individuals in the previous chapter can be equally said of the church. The identity of the church as the body of Christ is found in Christ—"to 'walk in the truth' is ultimately to participate in the love of God by acting out our being-in-Christ."[22] In the same way that Scripture reveals the work of the Spirit in Christ as that which constitutes the Son and empowers him to obediently respond to the will of the Father, so it is with the church: "In the theo-drama, *the Spirit is the 'actor' whose body (the church) is to signify Christ*."[23] The church gains its identity from the calling into being by God to participate, with Son and Spirit in the *missio Dei*. "The church is the gathering of repentant sinners whom the Spirit constitutes as saints by uniting them to Jesus Christ."[24] The church is also then empowered by the same Spirit to implement the victorious and reconciling work of the Son at the cross in order to display and cultivate the emerging of the kingdom in the present scenes of the drama. The church is not just participatory theatre but more specifically "a theater of the gospel, or rather, a theater of triune operations."[25] The church gains its identity and role from being commissioned by God

---

20. Vanhoozer, *Drama of Doctrine*, 79.
21. Vanhoozer, *Drama of Doctrine*, 400.
22. Vanhoozer, *Faith Speaking Understanding*, 41.
23. Vanhoozer, *Drama of Doctrine*, 408.
24. Vanhoozer, *Faith Speaking Understanding*, 141.
25. Vanhoozer, *Faith Speaking Understanding*, 140.

to participate in the mission of God for the salvation of creation. With Vanhoozer we can state, "the church is the very form that the *missio Dei* currently takes. For the life of the church is to participate in and display that same love that the Father has for the Son, and that same obedience that the Son shows the Father."[26] But, with Vanhoozer we can go further and note that "the church is both a character in the drama of redemption and, in a real sense, the drama's goal."[27] This is so because the church, in a partial way in the current act, begins to display the communion with God and one another that the whole of creation was created for. The church is, therefore, "the embodiment of God's will-to-communion."[28]

Bearing Witness

Although the church is called to be audience and performer, participation in the theodrama as partners with God in the *missio Dei* means that the part the church is cast into is one that involves bearing witness to God's activity and the inbreaking of the kingdom to the rest of creation. One sense of being a witness is captured under the role of observer, where the church witnesses the being-in-action of God in the world. But to bear witness in the sense meant here involves communicating to those who have not yet traversed the fourth wall of God's love for creation, the inbreaking of the kingdom, and the invitation to come and participate. This bearing witness may be classed as "interactive theatre" where the fourth wall is demolished, and the audience is offered a part in the theodrama of salvation. The role of bearing witness therefore involves the church in offering a preview of the kingdom while also acting as a gateway to it for those who choose to join the interactive theatre of the church.

In summary, the church is called to be both audience and performer, witnessing and bearing witness to the ongoing loving activity of God in creation that constitutes the theodrama. As with the *imago Dei* in the previous chapter, the church, as the body of Christ, is to offer fitting improvised performances of Christ in the various scenes in which it participates, Scripture in hand, and building on the previous performances that have been handed on through history. In doing so, the church, constituted and empowered by the same Spirit that constituted

26. Vanhoozer, *Drama of Doctrine*, 72.
27. Vanhoozer, *Faith Speaking Understanding*, 150.
28. Vanhoozer, *Faith Speaking Understanding*, 151–52.

and empowered the incarnate Son, continues the missions of Son and Spirit which find definition and meaning within the broader *missio Dei* to creation. The church is thus the theatre of the gospel, where the good news is embodied while offering a partial glimpse into the superobjective of the drama—full Trinitarian communion with creation. However, although this provides us with a broad sense of the origin of the church and its *raison d'être*, more detail is required to explore what it means for the church to be the theatre of the gospel.

One way of digging deeper into Vanhoozer's ecclesiology is by exploring the eucharistic nature of the church as primary and how this informs its identity and role. To begin here is to return to Scripture as prescriptive, as well as the tradition of the church, and recognize that the community of followers is formed after the pattern of Christ's life, death, and resurrection. It is also to recognize that they find nourishment in corporate participation in the meal instituted by Jesus as the primary place in which the church meets with one another and God in acts of worship and fellowship. To say that the church finds its identity and role in Christ is to begin with the church as eucharistic in the shape it takes in bearing witness to and participating in God and the *missio Dei*. Drawing from the creedal categories of the church as one, holy, catholic, and apostolic, in what follows we will be able to briefly dialogue with Vanhoozer to further flesh out the identity and role of the eucharistic church. With that in place we will then be able to focus on what practices the church undertakes in rehearsing the kingdom, before finally exploring what practices it undertakes to bear witness to the world.

The Eucharistic Church

When the company "(*com* + *panis* = 'with bread')" gather to celebrate Holy Communion,[29] "the church represents the body of Christ, and Christ presents, makes present, his body."[30] Vanhoozer suggests that with Christ as both host and meal, "the Lord's Supper represents a condensed summary or summation of the climax of the drama of redemption—the creation of a new, unified body of Christ, the prime exhibit of God's kingdom on earth—and hence a summa of the gospel."[31] Within the words

---

29. Vanhoozer, *Drama of Doctrine*, 413.
30. Vanhoozer, *Faith Speaking Understanding*, 160.
31. Vanhoozer, *Faith Speaking Understanding*, 160.

and actions that constitute the celebration of Holy Communion—the performance of the church as it celebrates the inbreaking of the kingdom and the defeat of sin, evil, and death—we see echoes of act 2 in the theodrama as well as remembering act 3 and finding guidance for performance in act 4 with the anticipation of act 5. The echoes of act 2 are found in the links to the Passover and Exodus of the people of God from slavery in Egypt. There are also links to the sacrificial lamb used in Israel's worship, now replaced, once and for all, by Jesus as both priest and sacrifice. The meal is an obvious remembering of the last supper of act 3 as well as the death and resurrection of Jesus who, in this meal, invites and enables the church not just to come to the table, but also to participate in what he has achieved as they eat his body and drink his blood. This not only draws the church into holy union with Jesus but also into holy communion with one another—"Because there is one bread, we who are many are one body, for we all partake of the one bread" (1 Cor 10:17). As well as looking back to acts 2 and 3 to give shape and substance to the actions undertaken in this celebration, the Lord's Supper offers an eschatological window into the heavenly banquet of act 5. While physically enacting what is true of the church in holy communion with God and one another, the celebration of the Lord's Supper anticipates what will be when heaven and earth are entirely aligned. As Zizioulas observes, "The eucharist is the moment in the Church's life where the anticipation of the *eschata* takes place. The anamnesis of Christ is realized not as a mere re-enactment of a past event but as an *anamnesis of the future*, as an eschatological event."[32] This is a rehearsal where to rehearse "is a matter of doing something in the present that recalls something done in the past in preparation for something yet to be performed in the future."[33] The performance of Jesus in word and deed is the site of the inbreaking of the kingdom, and this is now extended into Christ's body, the church, as a sign and foretaste of its presence in the whole of the renewed creation.[34] However, as Marilyn McCord Adams has drawn attention to, in order for the Eucharist to be transformative and nourishing it also involves confrontation "with our own divided loyalties, with repressed memories, denied feelings, and hidden wounds."[35] When we refuse this engagement

32. Zizioulas, *Being as Communion*, 254.
33. Vanhoozer, *Faith Speaking Understanding*, 162.
34. For a similar exploration of the way the Eucharist draws together threads from the wider drama, see Adams, "Eucharistic Drama," 219–20.
35. Adams, "Eucharistic Drama," 216.

"liturgical neuroses" results where energy is redirected to obsession with the details of the performance or some destructive avenue.[36] As we will see, this makes creating a suitably safe and facilitating space all the more important. We will return to this point in later chapters. For now, to explore how the Eucharist shapes and informs the identity and role of the church in the theodrama we turn to the creedal categories of the church as one, holy, catholic, and apostolic.

One

We noted in the previous chapter what it means to be "in Christ" for the *imago Dei*. Here, we need to extend that definition with regard to the church to include being reconciled to one another as the body of Christ. The focus of the previous chapter was the individual *imago Dei*, but here we need to consider the collective identity of the church as the image of God displayed in the body of Christ. Where the emphasis in the previous chapter with regard to reconciliation, justification, and sanctification was on how that might be applied to the individual, here we need to recognize that an individual focus is a partial one because to identify as the justified image of God in the process of sanctification is to identify as part of the body of Christ and therefore not just reconciled with God but also reconciled with one another. For Vanhoozer, performers are called to "theodramatic participation (i.e., taking part in God's communicative action)" in which "the company of the saved (i.e., the church) is made up of communicants: those who commune with Christ as Reconciler, and therefore with one another."[37] Again we must remind ourselves that because God is love, love is the driving force behind the reconciliation achieved by God, which is being outworked in the church, and that this love is cross-shaped. In this sense, Vanhoozer defines the church as a group of amateurs—those that do what they do out of love: "As a company of amateurs, the church acts out of its love for God precisely by loving others who bear his image."[38] The church is called into being to "*display and exhibit the reconciliation already achieved through the death of Christ*," and it is therefore not possible to be the church as an individual because what it is to be the church is to be a group of individuals who collectively identify

---

36. Adams, "Eucharistic Drama," 216.
37. Vanhoozer, *Remythologizing Theology*, 282.
38. Vanhoozer, *Drama of Doctrine*, 442.

as the body of the Christ who has reconciled the world to God.[39] It is here that "God is visibly present primarily in those reconciliatory practices that take place *between* the members of this company."[40] As those who are "in Christ," the church is the place where that which is enacted has a Christological shape. In contrast to a utopian place the church is "to be a *eutopia*: a good place in which the good news of reconciliation in Christ is exhibited in bodily form."[41] For this to be the body of Christ means that there can be no division within the body, as this would not accurately display what it is to be found "in Christ" as Christ's body, yet, of course, there is division! However, in the same way that, in the previous chapter the gap was recognized between one's identity "in Christ" (justification) and being fully clothed in that in the present (sanctification), the same can be said of the church. Her identity is located "in Christ" as the body of Christ yet she is in the process of Spirit-aided embodiment of this prior to act 5 of the theodrama. Here we can remind ourselves of the point made in the introduction regarding method and ecclesiology whereby ecclesiology is not the norming norm in first theology but, instead, the locus of interpretation and enactment.

Following in the footsteps of St. Paul, in the church in Christ—the body of which he is the head—there is no slave or free, Jew or Greek (Gal 3:27–28) because reconciliation has taken place of which the church is the theatre. Jesus is our peace, breaking down divisions and ending hostility (Eph 2:14–16). The church's vocation of a "'ministry of reconciliation' (2 Cor. 5:18) is a mandate not to bring reconciliation about—only God can do that—but rather to bear witness to the reconciliation already won through the cross of Christ."[42] In contrast to other non-Christian communities, Vanhoozer writes of the church, "My working hypothesis is that Christian discipleship is distinct and unique because the practices of Jesus, and the politics of the kingdom of God, are distinct and unique by being hypermoral and eschatological rather than merely moral and ethical."[43] Vanhoozer's point here is that the church is not engaged in creating its own morality and achieving reconciliation in its own strength. Instead, the church is the Spirit-enabled and assisted community of those who are already reconciled and called into a drama not their own in order

39. Vanhoozer, *Drama of Doctrine*, 435.
40. Vanhoozer, *Faith Speaking Understanding*, 150.
41. Vanhoozer, *Faith Speaking Understanding*, 178.
42. Vanhoozer, *Faith Speaking Understanding*, 151.
43. Vanhoozer, *Faith Speaking Understanding*, 153.

to display a kingdom already in existence, which is breaking into the here and now specifically through this community. The church is, therefore, called to bear witness to and embody, as a eucharistic community, what God has achieved for creation. As an "image of the Kingdom," the eucharistic community should be a contrast to a society that is often fractured and fragmented to the point that "if the eucharistic gathering is not such an image, it is not the eucharist in a true sense."[44]

Holy (and Royal)

The church is also called to grow into the holiness that is already its identity. As Vanhoozer notes, "What God is ultimately authoring is a royal priesthood and holy nation (1 Pet. 2:9), a peaceable kingdom characterized by justice and righteousness where God's word rules in his people's hearts and minds just as it came to rule in King Hezekiah's."[45] The church is called to *be* holy—free from blemish and impurity—because as the body of Christ, its identity is already located in Christ and therefore one of holiness that is to be lived into. Vanhoozer suggests that "what makes the church 'holy' is not the ground on which it stands but rather what those who are gathered do there."[46] He further adds elsewhere that "the politics of God's rule are to be on conspicuous display in the church's common life."[47] In one sense this is true and will be further explored below when attention is turned to examining the inward and outward practices of the church. However, it is important to note that the external outworking of holiness is only possible because of the Holy Spirit at work within the church who is the same Spirit that constitutes the church as holy by locating it within a relationship to the head of the church—Jesus Christ. It is this relationship, primarily, that makes the church holy through no work on her part.

In thinking about holiness and sanctification—the Spirited process through which the eschatological holiness of the church is becoming a reality as the body is conformed to the sanctity of the head—we are again drawn back to the cross-shaped nature of the church. As Jesus took sin and death captive at the cross, destroying its power and defeating evil—that

---

44. Zizioulas, *Being as Communion*, 255.
45. Vanhoozer, *Remythologizing Theology*, 495.
46. Vanhoozer, *Faith Speaking Understanding*, 175.
47. Vanhoozer, *Pictures*, 42.

which opposes God in God's good creation—so too is the church called to take up its cross and follow Jesus. There is, most definitely, something important to say about the church taking up its cross that is to do with exposing and responding to structural evil in a Christlike fashion (see below). However, of particular importance here is that for the church to take up its cross is also to mean the putting to death of that which taints the holy theatre of the church. In this sense, the church is not just holy as the body of Christ, and thus called to put on holiness as part of its identity in Christ; it is also, therefore, to be a theatre of God's defeat of sin and death. The church "is God at work in his people, renewing and reconciling the world to himself. Such is the church's high and holy calling as a nation."[48] Rather than making a similar Pelagian slip that we noted Vanhoozer was wary of concerning the *imago Dei* in chapter 3, the church is not just called to live into its eschatological holiness. It is called to display this holiness, and the process of assuming it, to the world as a theatre that displays God's purifying work breaking into creation. We will return to the priestly nature of the church below. For now, though, it is important to reiterate that the church as those who re-present Christ, as the body of Christ, located in Christ are holy in their identity as the Spirit-constituted extension of Christ's holiness. And yet, they are growing into holiness as they cooperate with the Spirit's effecting work, prior to the eschaton.

Vanhoozer also describes the church as "royal theater": the place where heaven—the sphere of God's perfect rule—is intersecting with earth. Here, the church embodies and bears witness to the kingship of Jesus and therefore her own royal status as the body of Christ. To image God in creation has always had a royal category to it, as noted in chapter 3. However, with the defeat of evil at the cross and the ensuing inauguration of the kingdom of God brought to bear in the church, the church as royal theatre takes on a new dimension—or rather, begins to display a dimension for which it has always been destined. This is so because, with the "inaugurated eschatology" of the kingdom of God in the theatre of the church, the royal status of the church is not simply an eschatological title but emerges in the very structuring of what happens in the lives of disciples and the space in which church is done— "church" being both indicative and imperative.[49] In short, the church is

---

48. Vanhoozer, *Pictures*, 43.

49. I am here and throughout drawing on what N. T. Wright labels as an "Inaugurated Eschatology." By this, he means "beginning to live in the present by the rule of what will be the case in the ultimate future." Wright, *Evil*, 77. He further suggests that

royal theatre because the kingdom of God, as far as possible prior to act 5, is what is lived out by the church as the king's loyal subjects. As "that peculiar place where men and women freely and joyfully do the will of God on earth as it is in heaven" the church as royal theatre displays and cultivates something of the kingdom of God.[50] However, it would be a theatrical misunderstanding of the theodrama to confuse acts 4 and 5 by thinking that what the church displays in the present act is the entirety of the kingdom of God. Instead, although *"the kingdom of God, is what the church has to say and do that no other institution can say and do,"* Vanhoozer is keen to make the point that what is on display is not the kingdom fully present.[51] He states, "It would be presumptuous simply to identify the visible church with the kingdom of God. It is preferable to view the church as an enacted parable of the kingdom."[52] As a parable (or as he suggests elsewhere, "a moving picture"[53]) of the kingdom, therefore, "the church is a theater of the gospel in which disciples stage previews of the coming kingdom of God."[54] In a sense, the church is rehearsing the kingdom of God in its performances while offering a sign of the kingdom and anticipating its full arrival.

Given Vanhoozer's church tradition, he is keen to make the point that although the church is a kingdom of priests, it is "not literal priests," leaders are not special, and all have "access to God through Jesus Christ."[55] Of course, given one's tradition and theology, these points could be debated, and have been, extensively. However, such debates need not detain us here, as the more important point is that the holy, royal priesthood of the church is called to offer up bodily (Rom 12:1) and spiritual sacrifices (1 Pet 2:5) in worship and service of God in the world while also mediating the relationship between God and individuals, communities, and nations who, as yet, do not participate in the emergence of the kingdom of God on earth. All of this can be traced back to the vocation of Adam and Eve in Gen 2, as noted in the previous chapter. Andrew Malone in his clear and helpful study shows how Israel of the Old Testament is called

---

the church is therefore "to *implement* the achievement of Jesus and so to *anticipate* God's eventual world." Wright, *Evil*, 66.

50. Vanhoozer, *Faith Speaking Understanding*, 6.
51. Vanhoozer, *Drama of Doctrine*, 443.
52. Vanhoozer, *Faith Speaking Understanding*, 173.
53. Vanhoozer, *Pictures*, 29.
54. Vanhoozer, *Faith Speaking Understanding*, 59.
55. Vanhoozer, *Pictures*, 41.

to be a kingdom of priests (Exod 19:5–6), noting that "this title further clarifies their holy *status* as they celebrate their unparalleled proximity to Yahweh."[56] With this as their status and using a model of "graded holiness" that defines the variety of levels of holiness that are required at various proximities to God, Malone further notes that "all Israelites are to guard Yahweh's holiness and to advertise the privilege of being counted as his chosen attendants"[57] as well as having a "guarding function, keeping unready people from encroaching, to their detriment, on God's sacred space."[58] The role of priestly mediators before a God who desires communion with creation and particularly with his human creatures is therefore to make sure that humans are fit for such a relationship with such a holy God and to prepare them for such a relationship. Within the Old Testament context, the Aaronic priests, within the chosen people of God, mediate that relationship whereas the corporate priesthood of the nation of Israel acts as a mediator between God and the rest of creation. With the incarnation comes the fulfillment of the Aaronic priesthood in the life, death, and resurrection of Jesus as the ultimate priest that enables final and absolute communion between God and creation. With the new covenant in place, the Old Testament system becomes "cultically redundant" as Jesus' priestly ministry "renders all such earthly cultic ritual no longer necessary."[59] However, the church as collective corporate priest is the location where Christ's mediating work made possible by the Holy Spirit takes place as she is the place where conciliatory mediation occurs as well as taking on the role of "*communicative* mediator" regarding what is required of an audience that wishes to break the fourth wall to become a performer.[60] As we will see below when exploring the practices of the church, this involves displaying something of the kingdom and love of God to the world while praying for and inviting the audience to become participants and performers.

---

56. Malone, *God's Mediators*, 181.
57. Malone, *God's Mediators*, 181.
58. Malone, *God's Mediators*, 179.
59. Malone, *God's Mediators*, 186.
60. Malone, *God's Mediators*, 189.

Catholic

As we turn to the subject of catholicity, we are returning to issues of unity already addressed. However, the emphasis here is not simply on the need to be reconciled to one another as a sign of God's reconciling and unifying work with and within creation, but instead to recognize, encourage, and celebrate diversity within orthodox unity. To equate reconciled unity, as the one church, with uniformity as an absolute is to fail to recognize the contextually relevant calling of the church across time and space to display the diverse, yet orthodox, ways in which God is engaged with and the kingdom of God is made manifest in the church.

With Vanhoozer we recount the root of the word "catholic"—"from Gk. *kata* + *holos* = by the whole"—and in so doing recognize that the church as *koinonia* is not simply something that exists between those who gather physically at a particular time and place.[61] Instead, the church catholic is that which transcends both time and space incorporating those present on the world stage across the globe, and those who have performed Christ before us in the theodrama as the cloud of witnesses (Heb 12:1). As Zizioulas highlights, the church "is catholic first of all because she is the Body of Christ. Her catholicity depends not on herself but on Him. She is catholic because she is where Christ is."[62] The universal catholic church is given clarity about the theodrama and its identity within that through the creeds that developed from the early church councils and the localized confessions that followed. Although within the approach being proposed here Scripture is divinely authored guidance for fitting performance, as well as transcript, creeds are derived from Scripture, by the church, and passed on to provide clarity regarding what passes for right belief and fitting participation in the theodrama. The creeds provide clarity while also offering generous flexibility in terms of how such beliefs are lived out by the various companies of performers that constitute the church. In contrast, "the heretic chooses for oneself (Gk. *hairesis* = choice, that which is chosen) how to speak and act, even if it means speaking and acting contrary to the rest of the company of the baptized."[63] This is not to propose robotic mimesis—our previous discussions about the importance of correct improvisation should prevent us from venturing down such an avenue. The church is not a

---

61. Vanhoozer, *Faith Speaking Understanding*, 166.
62. Zizioulas, *Being as Communion*, 158.
63. Vanhoozer, *Faith Speaking Understanding*, 148.

museum! Instead, it is to recognize certain non-negotiable markers, that the church catholic has discerned and passed on, that give the theodrama in which we are called to perform, shape and content. "Creedal theology gives 'catholic' direction, general directions for the church at all times and places to follow; then confessions of post-Reformation Protestantism expressed the particular identity of companies of the baptized in specific geographical regions who faced particular theological problems."[64] In this sense, confessional theology is that undertaken by "churches that shared a particular history and geography, churches that became *regional theaters of the gospel.*"[65] This breadth of catholic performers called to transmit the one gospel in word and deed in their own particular scenes draws attention to the identity of the church as both catholic and evangelical. It is worth quoting Vanhoozer and Treier at length here:

> *Catholic* qualifies *evangelical*, for the gospel gathers the church, while *catholicity* designates the scope of the gospel's reception. To speak of *catholic* evangelical theology adds a crucial qualifier that *prohibits* any particular way of receiving the gospel from becoming too paramount while requiring all particular receptions of the gospel to be cognizant of what all other believers everywhere and at all times confess.[66]

The orthodox traditions of the church therefore act as the rope that links the anchor of Scripture and the boat of the contemporary church catholic in Vanhoozer and Treier's model noted in chapter 1. There is a recognition here that one expression of church can never speak the whole truth and that new situations and contexts combined with the illuminating work of the Holy Spirit may provide fresh insight into the Christian faith and how it is to be lived out by the contemporary performers. In this sense being catholic and evangelical, for Vanhoozer and Treier, involves a "'Pentecostal' plurality" of readings,[67] whereby "perspectives might be complementary rather than contradictory, with various lenses providing (epistemological) access to dimensions of the one (ontological) truth."[68] However, paradoxically, "although the catholicity of the Church is ultimately an eschatological reality, its nature is revealed and realistically

---

64. Vanhoozer, *Faith Speaking Understanding*, 148.
65. Vanhoozer, *Faith Speaking Understanding*, 149.
66. Vanhoozer and Treier, *Theology*, 114.
67. Vanhoozer and Treier, *Theology*, 121.
68. Vanhoozer and Treier, *Theology*, 167.

apprehended *here and now* in the eucharist."[69] When the Eucharist is celebrated and embodied, the variety of voices and cultures enabled and drawn together by the Holy Spirit live toward the full catholicity of their identity derived from the wholeness of Christ experienced in the bread and the wine. Each eucharistic local church is therefore both awaiting the full eschatological experience of its catholic identity while experiencing wholeness because it is eucharistic. And, returning to an earlier point, this dialectic tension of the historically situated and eschatological church is lived out as a eucharistic church that is instituted by Christ as its head, yet constituted across time and space by the Holy Spirit.

However, there is one more mark of the church to explore before we press on to examine in greater detail how disciples of Christ "do church" in concrete and specific ways that give content to the identity of the church and the role in which it is cast.

Apostolic

Apostolic is to be sent, but by whom, to whom, and for what purpose? Here we need to recall that the church finds its identity by being located "in Christ" and as such is called into being to continue the missions of Son and Spirit within the wider *missio Dei*. The Son and Spirit are sent into creation to salvage creation—make it whole—for fellowship with God. As the church finds its role within the missions of the Son and Spirit, we can say that the church is sent by God, constituted by, and in the power of, the Spirit to perform Christ for the world with the aim of participating in God's salvaging of the world as the place where the kingdom of God is glimpsed. Although, as noted above, the church is a glimpse of the end goal of union with one another and God, it is also the primary means God has chosen through which to proclaim the good news of what God has done and is doing, in word and deed, and thus is the gateway for non-Christians to the kingdom of God. The church is sent by God, to the world, to display the inauguration of God's victory over evil won at the cross and the emergence of the kingdom come, on earth as it is in heaven. By improvising on the performance of Jesus, the church is to prophetically expose the structural evil of opposing kingdoms and to invite the audience of the world to participate in this interactive, holy theatre of reconciliation that offers life-giving parables of the kingdom of God. In this sense, the

---

69. Zizioulas, *Being as Communion*, 144–45.

apostolic calling includes the calling to be prophetic, revealers of truth as well as priestly ministers to the world.

In exploring the relationship of church and world in the present act of the theodrama, Vanhoozer describes the church as "resident exiles." Similar to Israel, as the people of God in exile in foreign lands in the Old Testament, Vanhoozer draws on various New Testament texts to identify the church as in the world but not of the world.[70] The contrast that he then makes between Israel and the church is that Israel's exile was one of a foreign land as well as rule whereas for the church, land is of little concern. Here we encounter definitions of space and place. For Vanhoozer, drawing on the creation texts, space can be defined as an expanse that can be structured in a variety of ways. Place is defined not as a location within space as such but by how that particular part of space is structured and used. A place is a part of space that is loaded with meaning because of the shape of the action undertaken there. "What turns nondescript space into a particular place is what embodied persons experience or do there."[71] Linking this back to theatre, Vanhoozer states, "Space is thus the theater for social interaction; place is what those gathered make of it."[72] The church as resident exile is in a broad space where the place that is their own because of what happens there is surrounded by and often infringed upon by other kingdoms. The church is, therefore, "'in' the world in a spatial sense but not 'of' it in the sense that it is not under its sway; it is not 'in' the world in the sense of being under the sphere of its control. The term 'resident exile' captures the awkwardness, and the challenge, of this uneasy situation."[73] The church is thus apostolic, prophetic, and priestly because it is sent to those in foreign lands in order to bear witness to the inbreaking of the eschatological kingdom of God and call others to participate. As Vanhoozer notes, "The church worships (a kingdom of priests, offering up sacrifices

---

70. Vanhoozer, *Faith Speaking Understanding*, 179.

71. Vanhoozer, *Faith Speaking Understanding*, 174.

72. Vanhoozer, *Faith Speaking Understanding*, 174. Vanhoozer's definitions of space and place are not to be confused with those borrowed from Michel de Certeau by Peter Heltzel. Heltzel's uses of de Certeau's definitions put a more negative spin on "place" as that which is set and static in contrast to "space" which is "dynamic and open." Utilizing these definitions Heltzel proposes using liturgy in appropriate ways to change "places of despair" into what David Harvey refers to as "spaces of hope." This does not contradict Vanhoozer or the present project but simply uses language in a different way to propose a similar outcome to what will be presented here. See Heltzel, "Church," 252–54.

73. Vanhoozer, *Faith Speaking Understanding*, 179.

of praise and bodily life), proclaims truth (a chosen race of prophets, bearing witness to the word of God) and walks in the way of wisdom (a temple of kings who represent the holy nation)"[74] where "wisdom is the ability to see what is right and fitting in a particular situation given our understanding of the larger whole of which we are a part."[75]

So far, we have been able to map out, through a theodramatic lens, who the eucharistic church is and what role she is cast in. In the remainder of this chapter, we will turn our attention to key attitudes or dispositions and associated practices that the church engages in, in order to "do church," in the various scenes of the theodrama in which she finds herself. Our focus will first be on dispositions and practices the church is to foster as ways of initiating and forming the individuals that make up the church. As the eucharistic church, it is by returning to the celebration of Holy Communion that direction is found for forming and nourishing the church for service. Focus will then move to examining practices that flow out of the internal rehearsing as we explore how the church embodies Christ to and for the world. It is important to note here something of a thread that has run through the previous chapter and into the present one and underpins the celebration of Holy Communion. When humans come to participate in the theodrama generally and in Holy Communion as the body of Christ more specifically, it is only as a response to the prior work and invitation of God. To recognize this as we proceed to explore the attitudes and practices of fidelity, generosity, and hospitality highlighted by Vanhoozer is vital as these are not to be seen as human labels imposed on the being-in-action of God highlighted and celebrated in Holy Communion. Instead, they act as descriptors that draw our attention to what God communicates of God's self in the life, death, and resurrection of Jesus that we give thanks for in the celebrating of Holy Communion, but also seek to emulate toward one another and creation as we are nourished at, and sent from, the table to the world.[76]

---

74. Vanhoozer, *Pictures*, 44–45.

75. Vanhoozer, *Pictures*, 137.

76. Wolfgang Vondey, in a similar fashion within his development of a Pentecostal theology, uses the altar as the controlling metaphor to which Pentecostals come and go from out to the world. There is a similarity in movement here, but the narrative that shapes the Pentecostal identity and theology he is proposing has a different focus to that being proposed here where the Eucharist is that which shapes the identity and practices of the community. See Vondey, *Pentecostal Theology*, 5–10.

The Rehearsing Church

Vanhoozer suggests, "The company of faith is the place where the love of God and the truth of doctrine are demonstrated (i.e., acted out), both in the way believers interact with one another and with those outside the church."[77] In a sense, as well as offering a performance that, as the body of Christ, displays Christ to the world through a theatre of the gospel, the church in act 4 of the theodrama is also called to rehearse: "to retell and remember the main action of the play, to study their roles, to learn their lines until they know them by heart, to prepare for witness/performance in the world."[78] The church is, therefore, a school as well as a theatre.

The task of the rehearsing church is to form the performers as a holy nation and royal, prophetic priesthood—to aid in clothing the church, in co-operation with the Holy Spirit, with Christlikeness, as it is transformed by the renewing of minds (Rom 12:2). In this sense, the church is a holy temple, "a spiritual house where being 'spiritual' is a matter of having one's word and actions prompted by the Holy Spirit and conformed to the cruciform image of Christ."[79] We have already noted in the previous chapter, at an individual level, something of how this work is to be done. But, with ecclesiology in view here, we can extend what was noted in chapter 3 and focus on specific, practical ways in which the church contributes to the renewal of minds and hearts. In a general way, liturgy and acts of corporate worship are key to the discipleship of the church—"doxology precedes dogmatics."[80] This is so because it is through relationships with God, others, and the self, developed in worship, through word and action, enabling and honing participation in the drama of salvation, that disciples are formed into Christlikeness: "worship effects a catharsis that allows us to realize our true natures" as we are formed to be like Christ.[81] As was noted in the previous chapter, the same is true here in terms of the

---

77. Vanhoozer, *Faith Speaking Understanding*, 46.

78. Vanhoozer, *Faith Speaking Understanding*, 140.

79. Vanhoozer, *Drama of Doctrine*, 392.

80. Vanhoozer, *Pictures*, 118. Vanhoozer and Treier further make the point that, in addition to what was outlined in the introductory chapter of this work, "theologians easily forget that prayer is first theology." Vanhoozer and Treier, *Theology*, 149. James K. A. Smith equates liturgy to worship and makes a similar claim "that liturgies—whether 'sacred' or 'secular'—shape and constitute our identities by forming our most fundamental desires and our most basic attunement to the world. In short, liturgies make us certain kinds of people, and what defines us is what we *love*." Smith, *Desiring the Kingdom*, 25.

81. Vanhoozer, *Drama of Doctrine*, 410.

role of prayer in the formation of the church as the body of Christ. With Scripture as the guide for our words, "to pray the text is to acknowledge its author, to admit its claim, and to bring our desires into accord with those of God. Prayer is that canonical practice whereby we do not merely envision the theo-drama but *indwell* it and assume a speaking part."[82] To engage in not just prayer but the practices and liturgy of the church is to also recognize and acknowledge the work of the Spirit as the one conforming the church to Christ and thus, with Vanhoozer, recognize these as "*Spirited* practices."[83] *Lex orandi, lex credendi, lex vivendi* is shown to be true as Word and sacrament are engaged with as "holy props" being made efficacious by the Spirit and thus offering direction and sustenance for the performance.[84] As sacraments are engaged with, the past, present, and future of the theodrama are brought together for performers to discover their identity in, and be conformed to, Christ.[85] In this rehearsing, "the church is a celebratory theater that, through its liturgy and its life, inserts its members into the drama of redemption."[86] However, it is also important to acknowledge the connection between theology and worship whereby "*theology without worship is empty; worship without theology is blind.*"[87] Therefore worship and theological reflection must go hand in hand in the process of forming Christlike performers.

Before exploring how the eucharistic church fosters Christlike attitudes of fidelity, generosity, and hospitality, we turn first to briefly examine the initiatory sacrament of baptism as the gateway into the company of rehearsing performers.

Baptism

The sacrament central to admission into the church is that of baptism, and so it is where Vanhoozer begins in charting the rehearsal of the church.

---

82. Vanhoozer, *Drama of Doctrine*, 224.
83. Vanhoozer, *Drama of Doctrine*, 226.
84. Vanhoozer, *Drama of Doctrine*, 410.
85. Christopher Stephenson also proposes *lex orandi, lex credendi*, in an adapted way, as a window into Pentecostal theology. In his proposal, he is keen to highlight that one informs the other in a multi-directional way. Such an approach would be affirmed here with the caveat that Scripture, for the reasons suggested, continues to be the norming norm. Stephenson, *Types of Pentecostal Theology*, 112–19.
86. Vanhoozer, *Drama of Doctrine*, 410.
87. Vanhoozer, *Pictures*, 117.

In his own water baptism, Jesus identifies with God's people—Israel—and therefore the whole creation given Israel's mission to be a blessing to the world. John the Baptist famously queries Jesus' need for baptism, but the reason for Jesus' baptism is one of representation as well as a sign. In identifying with Israel and the world in baptism, the sinless Jesus assumes the role of representative of the sinful world that requires dying to sin and being reborn, to be led from slavery through the waters of baptism. Jesus' baptism as representative of the world is also a sign not just of his assumed role of representative but also of what, as representative, will be achieved by the Trinity in the death and resurrection of Jesus. As Jesus identifies with a sinful world in his baptism, so he will in his death and resurrection. With this crucial aspect of Jesus' ministry in view, we can return to the question of entry into the church and remind ourselves that to be a member of the church is to be found in Christ as part of the body of Christ and, therefore, in the kingdom of God. As Vanhoozer notes, "John's baptism sought to prepare disciples for the coming kingdom; Jesus' baptism effectively transfers them into that kingdom (cf. Col. 1:13)."[88] This is so because not only is our identity transferred to being in Christ in baptism, but, as John the Baptist highlighted to his hearers, Jesus baptizes with "'the Holy Spirit and fire'" (Luke 3:16). To be baptized with water in the name of the Father, the Son, and the Holy Spirit, as Jesus commands his disciples to do for others, is not simply to engage in a symbolic act, but "is a public declaration of an individual's initiation into the drama of redemption as an active participant, an outward expression of the inward grace of baptism by the Spirit, which effectively (albeit mystically) joins a person to Jesus' history."[89] To respond in faith to the prior work and call of God into union with him and fellow members of the body of Christ results in baptism as the rite that makes this union so.

In identifying with Jesus in baptism, members of the church are more specifically called to identify with Jesus in his death and resurrection as they turn away from the devil and all that seeks to draw the baptized away from Christ. To do this is to begin the journey of putting on the heavenly Christlikeness that is now one's identity as that which hinders this is put to death. However, following the account of Peter's preaching at Pentecost and the resultant repentance and baptism of many of his hearers, Vanhoozer draws our attention to what happened

---

88. Vanhoozer, *Faith Speaking Understanding*, 142.
89. Vanhoozer, *Faith Speaking Understanding*, 142.

next: "immediately after the three thousand were baptized, Luke tells us that those in the newly constituted Jerusalem church 'devoted themselves to the apostles' teaching [*didachē*] and fellowship [*koinonia*], to the breaking of bread and prayers' (Acts 2:42)."[90] He further notes that "in devoting themselves to teaching, the church is but responding to the second part of Jesus' Great Commission: 'teaching [*didaskō*] them to obey everything that I have commanded you' (Matt. 28:20)."[91] This highlights the fact that making disciples is less about the single moment of baptism and more about the process of how one is formed as a performer of Christ, post-baptism. This returns us to the church as a school where, having joined the company, the performers learn and rehearse the parts they have been cast in.

Whatever form teaching takes, it is indispensable to the life of the disciple. To return to Vander Lugt and Hart's definition, what is being enacted by the church is "faith seeking performative understanding."[92] To begin from a position of faith, as the starting point to journeying deeper into understanding the drama of which we are a part, to perform, in the most fitting way within the scenes in which we find ourselves, is what discipleship is about. As a living interpretation of Scripture, the church is not simply called to know information *about* the theodrama and the divine author but to learn how to be conformed to the pattern of Christ in relationship with God and other members of the body as it participates in a constructive way in the action. Space does not permit in-depth discussion of the complexities of biblical interpretation within the church here, but suffice it to say that engagement with Scripture in community with others and exploration and affirmation of creeds and confessions as part of one's identity as the one, catholic church in Christ is paramount to one's development as a disciple. The various concrete places and practices in which this takes place—preaching, teaching, small group discussion, recital of creeds, and confessions—are all of the utmost importance in the formation process and should not be used in a divisive or destructive way. And yet, a brief glance at either church history or the relationship between contemporary companies of performers yields ample evidence that unhelpful and destructive divisions do occur. However, as we return to the church as shaped and nourished by the celebration of the Eucharist, we can draw from key attitudes and dispositions

---

90. Vanhoozer, *Faith Speaking Understanding*, 143.
91. Vanhoozer, *Faith Speaking Understanding*, 143.
92. Vander Lugt and Hart, Introduction to *Theatrical Theology*, xiv.

that are rooted in the revelation of God in Christ as celebrated at Holy Communion. These attitudes offer not only important guidance for the rehearsing church as it seeks to perform Christ, but potentially offer an antidote to the divisions so prominent in church history.

Continuing in conversation with Vanhoozer, we can draw on his helpful highlighting of fidelity, generosity, and hospitality as the central attitudes derived from the revelation of God in Christ celebrated at Holy Communion as the framework to be used to explore what it means for the eucharistic church to rehearse. In Vanhoozer's discussion, he focuses on such practices as marriage and giving as ways in which some of these dispositions are displayed and honed. However, my suggestion here is that although these are activities that display central attitudes of the church, Vanhoozer starts in the wrong place. He moves through these attitudes and practices eventually getting to the Eucharist.[93] What I am suggesting is that, following baptism as initiation into the body of Christ, the next place to turn should be to the Eucharist as that which, when celebrated, most fully answers in word and action what it is we are being initiated into, why and how we are to be formed. Although Vanhoozer rightly notes that certain rites and practices in the church help members to grasp and participate more fully in the life of the church, the Eucharist as the meal instituted by Christ should be where we begin. It is only as we celebrate the Eucharist that the greatest light is shed on what fidelity, generosity, and hospitality look like when Christ-shaped.[94] As we venture to explore these dispositions, we therefore do so with the Eucharist at the heart of each one.

Fidelity

To focus on fidelity, Vanhoozer draws our attention specifically to the example of Christian marriage as a microcosm of covenantal relationship between God and humans. Again, we are drawn to the prior work of God with regard to understanding how the church is to respond to God and how marriage acts as an example of the fidelity the church is called to live out as a reflection of God's fidelity to creation. However, we need not

---

93. Although, to be fair to Vanhoozer, he does highlight the centrality of the Eucharist in other places in his work. See Vanhoozer, *Pictures*, 199, 248–49, 294–95.

94. Interestingly, Vondey highlights hospitality as a mark of the church but does not really anchor this in the hospitality displayed by God to creation as recognized and celebrated in the Eucharist. Vondey, *Pentecostal Theology*, 233–38.

wander into the contemporary quagmire of the underlying theological disagreements about the definition and outworking of marriage to draw out how fidelity is displayed by God in Christ and drawn attention to at the celebration of Holy Communion. Although I agree with Vanhoozer in his highlighting of marriage as a particular and concrete example of how the fidelity of God is to be reflected by the church in the world, as a time-limited type of relationship that will cease at the end of act 4 (Matt 22:30), I am more inclined to want to focus on how God's fidelity might be reflected in less specific types of relationship, particularly since not everyone is either called to or able to marry, Jesus being an important example. Interestingly, John Swinton, when suggesting church practices that might "absorb suffering" and aid the church to persevere in its worship and work, highlights friendship as part of the practice of hospitality.[95] He writes, "Friendship is a basic and vital human relationship that forms the social fabric of our lives. It is in and through friendship that we discover our identity, gain our sense of value and place in the world, and learn what it means to participate in community."[96] Although not mentioning the Eucharist specifically as that which in/forms our understanding and practice of friendship, Swinton does draw attention to the primacy of Jesus' example in how he treated others and ultimately his sacrifice for the whole of creation, that all may become friends with God. In contrast to cultures where friendship is often selected with those who are like us or for the sake of what can be gained from the particular friendship, Swinton highlights Jesus' "principle of grace" where friendship is not offered based on possible gain and is offered to all, recognizing a commonality that transcends usual categorization.[97] While recognizing the importance of good self-care for maintaining healthy friendships, Swinton helpfully summarizes, "Friendship embodies Christian community and the love and acceptance of Jesus and provides a safe space for growth and change. Friendship mediates love; perfect love drives out all evil."[98] It is this call to friendship and the fidelity on which it depends that provides the bedrock for the whole church in a way that marriage does not.

---

95. Swinton, *Raging with Compassion*, 4. Swinton here draws from Stanley Hauerwas regarding the establishment of communities that absorb evil and suffering. See Hauerwas, *Naming the Silences*.

96. Swinton, *Raging with Compassion*, 216.

97. Swinton, *Raging with Compassion*, 220–21.

98. Swinton, *Raging with Compassion*, 241.

Further nuance can be added to the nature of fidelity by following Sam Wells's distinction between "being with" and "working for."[99] For Wells, being with precedes working for and is the foundation on which working for is built. Wells suggests that being with finds its home in the Trinitarian relations and the nature of the relationship God intends to have with creation. Jesus—the one who saves—in his incarnation is to be called Emmanuel—God *with* us—but this does not replace doing for. Wells notes of Jesus, "He was for us when he healed and taught, he was for us when he died on the cross, he was for us when he rose from the grave and ascended to heaven . . . . But the power of these things God did for us lies in that they were based on his being with us."[100] Presence, connectivity, and relationships are what humans in the image of God were created for and what they desire and need. Fidelity after the pattern of God in Christ informs the nature of Christian relationships and should be based on a Christlike being with, that is the foundation of working for.

As can be noted at various points in Scripture, driven by love, the prior work of God seeks relationship with creation and particularly humans. In the Old Testament this is displayed first in God's relationship with Adam and Eve and then with Israel as God's representatives. In the New Testament, this is displayed in God's relationship with the church as the body of Christ. In the case of Israel and the church, marriage language is used to describe the covenantal relationship in which God shows fidelity to God's partner with the expectation of a mirrored response. The covenant is based, first and foremost, on the desire for a loving relationship—as Fretheim has noted, relationship "precedes the establishment of any covenant."[101] However, clarity is required regarding how this relationship is to work in practice—what attitudes and behaviors are un/acceptable. Such limits are marked out by what might be described as the contractual aspect of the covenant.[102] Although marriage—in the fidelity displayed by each partner to the other and, therefore, to God—is a sign and microcosm of the relationship the church is called to with God and one another, at a lesser level of intimacy, relationships characterized by sacrificial, loving desire to see the other flourish, yet with clear expectations in place, should exemplify all Christian relationships. What is remembered and

---

99. Wells, *Nazareth Manifesto*.
100. Wells, *Nazareth Manifesto*, 4.
101. Fretheim, *God and World*, 15.
102. For a more detailed discussion of the contractual and relational aspects of the covenant, see Torr, *Dramatic*, 143–45.

celebrated in Holy Communion is the ultimate example of fidelity in the sacrificial, loving yet boundaried relationship God makes possible with creation in Christ, by the Spirit. It is love-driven sacrifice for the flourishing of creation in that God gives of Godself in order to encounter death and overcome it for the salvation of creation. It is boundaried because a certain kind of response in word and deed is required to cooperate with the Spirit of God who aids us put on Christ. There are also expectations regarding what healthy behaviors and attitudes look like on both sides of the relationship. Vanhoozer suggests "Christian marriages participate in the drama of redemption when they model the covenant faithfulness that characterizes Christ's relationship to his bride, the church. Christian marriage is a microcosm of the communion of saints."[103] Drawing on this last statement, I want to highlight the point that, although Christian marriage may be a microcosm of the communion of saints, there is, therefore something of great importance to be noted about the cross-shaped friendships after the pattern of Christ, enabled by the Spirit that, in a less intimate way than Christian marriage, are the stuff of the communion of saints, that all are called to. Fidelity displayed by God to creation is something the whole church is called to, both to God and saint, in each relationship's own particular way. This becomes obvious when the new commandment central to Maundy Thursday is recalled together with the example of foot washing. In addition, it is noteworthy that Jesus states that his followers would be known by the love they display for one another which mirrors the love Jesus displays, not by the example of marriage specifically (John 13:1–17, 31–35). It is this sacrificial model of friendship that will live on into act 5 when marriage has ceased to function in the way it currently does.

Before moving on to explore generosity, it is important, under the heading of fidelity, to make mention of reconciliation as a crucial and cruciform feature of relationships modeled on Christlike fidelity. Again, Vanhoozer focuses on reconciliation that takes place between partners after a dispute, as one way in which the church enacts a theatre of reconciliation while practicing—in the dual sense of the word—fidelity that is demanded of those who are in Christ as a mirror of God's faithfulness to creation. This is, therefore, one way in which disciples are formed into the character of Christ. But again, it is important to highlight that although marriage may be one example of a relationship in which Christ-enabled and reflected reconciliation may be enacted, it is clearly not the only one

---

103. Vanhoozer, *Faith Speaking Understanding*, 155.

and arguably not the dominant example in the New Testament. Instead, it is reconciliation between fellow believers that dominates there and so must be given due attention in the contemporary body of Christ.

In terms of how the eucharistic company perform fidelity in specific acts of worship, attention here needs, perhaps, to be turned to ways in which what is believed is affirmed in word and deed. Each expression of church will vary regarding how it does this, but if fidelity to God and one another is to be encouraged then there are a number of practices that, likely, need to be considered. Space does not permit extensive examination here, but the first to be mentioned is the warning from the writer of Hebrews about not giving up meeting together (Heb 10:24–25). This must be combined with individual commitment to prayer and discipleship done in pursuit of cooperating with the Spirit clothing individuals with Christ. At the heart of both corporate and individual life as a performer of Christ must be a commitment to grow in Christlikeness as a response to God's love-driven fidelity and to therefore perform Christ by loving one's neighbor and fellow saint as oneself (Matt 22:34–40; Mark 12:28–34; Luke 10:25–28). Such an approach runs contrary to superficial consumerism that focuses only on what I want when I want it. As Peter Rollins would say, that way lies a "crack-house" church where I simply go to get my fix.[104] Instead, what the eucharistic company of actors perform as the body of Christ is commitment to God and one another that mirrors the loving commitment God displays to us in Christ as celebrated in Holy Communion.

In more detail, the discipline of confession done in a loving way that dispels shame and is, instead, aimed at reconciliation and mutual flourishing must be part of the community's life. As Bonhoeffer notes, "pious fellowship permits no one to be a sinner. So everybody must conceal his sin from himself and from the fellowship."[105] Such an approach is likely all too common and makes fellowship false and hypocritical. In living this way, sin isolates and takes hold, causing ever greater destruction and separating the individual from Christ—his cross and resurrection—and from fellow disciples. Instead, Bonhoeffer advocates for confession to a fellow Christian who also engages in confession. This confession of specific sins counteracts pride as the "root of all sin."[106] Bonhoeffer describes such acts of confession as "the profoundest kind of humiliation" as it

104. Work of the People, "Crack House."
105. Bonhoeffer, *Life Together*, 86.
106. Bonhoeffer, *Life Together*, 89.

draws into the light the darkness of sin and in so doing connects the one confessing to the cross of Christ where Jesus died in the place of all sinners and the power of sin was broken. In doing so the one confessing can "share in the resurrection of Christ and eternal life."[107] This experience of dying and living is a continuation of the sacrament of baptism in the life of the disciple and preparation for sharing in the Eucharist as one, holy body. Fidelity is not possible without the confession and absolution of that which seeks to divide and isolate. Bonhoeffer further suggests that confession needs to be made to another person who hears and absolves on behalf of Christ because confession to God in private will likely actually be self-confession and forgiveness. Although there is a place for this, he suggests that "self-forgiveness can never lead to a breach with sin" and that confession to a fellow disciple who also experiences the weight of sin and the release of forgiveness through their own confessions "breaks the circles of self-deception."[108] Rather than simply going through the motions, a community that encourages and facilitates this form of intentional confession is one that creates a safe space to break down barriers to the type of fidelity embodied by God in Christ and celebrated at the Eucharist and to which the community as the body of Christ is called to perform. "As the members of the congregation are united in body and blood at the table of the Lord so will they be together in eternity."[109]

Swinton selects forgiveness as another practice to resist evil in the church community—which sits alongside confession. However, rather than as an individual's momentary decision, Swinton presents the practice of forgiveness as a community practice that "is a way of life that produces a fresh understanding of the way that the world is and how we should respond as we experience it."[110] Again, although no mention of the Eucharist is made, Swinton focuses on the incarnation and particularly the Easter event as the example that should inform the need for and content of repentance as well as the possibility of forgiveness for all, regardless of the type of sin, given that the victory won at the cross is for everyone. In light of these beliefs, the community is called to repentance and forgiveness, embodying the forgiveness offered at the cross and embraced in the Eucharist. Repentance is the only avenue to the acceptance of forgiveness and the embodiment of reconciliation and so confession

107. Bonhoeffer, *Life Together*, 90.
108. Bonhoeffer, *Life Together*, 91.
109. Bonhoeffer, *Life Together*, 96.
110. Swinton, *Raging with Compassion*, 159.

within a community that continues to practice forgiveness is paramount to a church that seeks to embrace and reflect the fidelity of God. In the drive toward reconciliation and creating a community of forgiveness, Swinton is also realistic about the challenges of forgiveness and warns against making "*victims of grace*" by forcing people to forgive when they are not ready.[111] Instead, repentance, forgiveness, and reconciliation is likely a process that requires and feeds the fidelity of the community that is seeking to reflect the fidelity of God.

Regular affirmations of faith via declarations of what is collectively believed in the creeds, supported by acts of sung or said prayer and worship, can also display and foster fidelity regardless of worship *style*. However, when used as a hollow triumphalism that fails to acknowledge the spectrum of emotions that can be felt in a relationship with God and others, genuine, honest fidelity is exchanged for lip service that breeds false selves and relationships. More will be said about this in later chapters but, for now, it is enough to say that for fidelity to be nurtured, honesty must be encouraged and enabled without fear of rejection or condemnation.

Generosity

Vanhoozer notes St. Paul's often overlooked focus on giving within the early church communities.[112] In particular, with regard to our discussion of how the church rehearses the kingdom, generosity in giving is also a crucial way in which the actors participate in and bear witness to the theo-drama. This is so because in giving, the church acknowledges the prior generosity of God and responds, as the body of Christ, in a similar fashion with the resources available. Andrew Shepherd, drawing from Paul's letter to the Philippians, notes, "Having received the gift of Christ—a genuine gift, not earned, but offered freely—the ecclesia consists of a community whose self-earned *desires* have been put to death and in whom new desires and affections are emerging as a result of the work of the indwelling Spirit."[113] Shepherd here draws our attention not only to the prior work of God as the example and pattern for the church but also to the gift of God that the church receives for its existence, highlighting that "it is the reception of the free gift offered in Christ which provides the basis for our

---

111. Swinton, *Raging with Compassion*, 167.
112. Vanhoozer, *Faith Speaking Understanding*, 155–57.
113. Shepherd, *Gift*, 215.

ontological and therefore moral and ethical transformation."[114] Shepherd also warns against classifying who is deserving of giving to, as this goes against the generosity displayed by God in Christ for the whole world and likely blinds the giver to the eschatological potential contained within the recipient. Instead, the act of giving displays equality among the company of actors as the image of God, and a union between them as well as a union with God as the recognized source of what they have. "Generous giving is one way the church acts out not only the communion of saints but also the doctrine of providence. In giving to others, the church trusts God to provide for basic needs, as Israel trusted God to provide manna for their daily bread (see Exod. 16)."[115]

In a world where fear of scarcity, combined with a greed-ridden desire for more, results in inequality of resources at best and a violent defense, or claiming of resources at worst, trust in God for what is needed and equal sharing of resources to have everything in common (Acts 4:32) is crucial for rehearsing the kingdom and embodying "a new economy of mutuality."[116] Wells states, "*Generosity* is the virtue of abundance. Unlike charity, which assumes scarcity . . . generosity assumes abundance by investing in the still-not-fully disclosed gifts of the other."[117] However, generosity, as Vanhoozer notes, covers more than just money or resources. Generosity also includes forgiveness.[118] But "forgiveness presupposes sin. Sin is that inward curvature of one's existential spine that creates alienation between oneself and others. In sinning 'against' others, the sinner creates distance and division."[119] This, of course, runs contrary to what it means to be the body of Christ, and we here return to the practice of reconciliation. When sin has been committed in the church between one another, to harbor resentment without attempting to address the situation, forgive, and be reconciled, is to deny the gospel and disobey the head of the body. Again, God's prior act is one of forgiveness and reconciliation and the church is called to bear witness to and mirror what God has done. This is not to be mistaken for pretending that the sin committed did not hurt or was not wrong. Instead, it is to bring such acts

---

114. Shepherd, *Gift*, 223.

115. Vanhoozer, *Faith Speaking Understanding*, 156.

116. Shepherd, *Gift*, 222.

117. Wells, *Nazareth Manifesto*, 255.

118. Wells also highlights generosity as presence that aids the building of healthy relationships. See Wells, *Nazareth Manifesto*, 255–56.

119. Vanhoozer, *Faith Speaking Understanding*, 157.

into the light with a view to naming sin for what it is, so that repentance may take place, forgiveness be offered, and reconciliation be performed. "Disciples are never more authentic than when they ask for forgiveness and forgive others. Unlike the genuine communion of saints, the sanctimonious community conceals rather than confesses their sins to one another (Jas. 5:16)."[120] To forgive one another as the church is to take our place in the theodrama as the community that images God. "When saints forgive one another as they have been forgiven in Christ, they enter into the dramatic movement of God's own triune generosity."[121] In his groundbreaking work in The Truth and Reconciliation Commission of South Africa, Desmond Tutu anchored the process in a concept known "in the Nguni group of languages" as "*ubuntu*."[122] Complex and rich in meaning, when someone is said to have *ubuntu* it "means they are generous, hospitable, friendly, caring and compassionate. They share what they have. It also means my humanity is caught up, is inextricably bound up, in theirs. We belong in a bundle of life."[123] Applying this to all humanity, with a focus on "restorative justice" in the Truth and Reconciliation Commission, Tutu states, "the central concern is not retribution or punishment but, in the spirit of *ubuntu*, the healing of breaches, the redressing of imbalances, the restoration of broken relationships. This kind of justice seeks to rehabilitate both the victim and the perpetrator, who should be given the opportunity to be reintegrated into the community he or she has injured by his or her offence."[124] In a similar way, Volf argues for an embrace of the other in the aftermath of hurt caused "for only in mutual embrace within the embrace of the triune God can we find redemption and experience perfect justice."[125] Reconciliation of the whole of creation has been achieved at the cross (Col 1) and is to be lived into by creation with the church leading the way. However, Tutu and Volf are also keen to highlight, in their own ways, the challenge of this journey of forgiveness and reconciliation and the importance of naming and acknowledging the wrongs done and the hurt caused.[126]

120. Vanhoozer, *Faith Speaking Understanding*, 157.
121. Vanhoozer, *Faith Speaking Understanding*, 158.
122. Tutu, *No Future Without Forgiveness*, 34.
123. Tutu, *No Future Without Forgiveness*, 34–35.
124. Tutu, *No Future Without Forgiveness*, 51–52.
125. Volf, *Exclusion and Embrace*, 224–25.
126. Tutu, *No Future Without Forgiveness*, 216–20; Volf, *Exclusion and Embrace*, 224–25.

Here we see how generosity and fidelity overlap in the commitment to forgive and be reconciled. Faithfulness to God and fellow members of the body of Christ, after the pattern of God in Christ, should result in a sacrificial generosity that is willing to give, in whatever way is relevant and realistic, for the flourishing of the other and the body of Christ, trusting in the resources of God's loving provision.

There is also a generosity in orthodoxy, orthopraxy, and orthopathos that is required of those seeking to conform to Christ as one body. As Vanhoozer and Treier's "anchored set," discussed in chapter 1, illustrates, there may be limits to what classes as orthodoxy, but there is scope to have my limited and fallen perspective challenged and honed as, in an act of generosity, I give up absolute certainty for the sake of fresh, God-given, insight displayed in the lives of others. Such willingness may be glimpsed in how Scripture is engaged with, how the church engages in missional activities, how doctrines are defined and lived, and what shape and content corporate worship has. All such activities affirm what is orthodox while inviting the possibility of generosity within the one body of Christ and all are first and foremost centered on the example of God's generosity in Christ celebrated and participated in through the Eucharist, for it is in receiving that we are shaped to give accordingly.

Hospitality

"Hospitality is the fundamental gesture of God's grace, the opening up of God's 'household' (*oikos*), his own triune life, to 'strangers and aliens' (Eph. 2:19)."[127] We are here met again by Vanhoozer with the recurring theme that what is to be enacted by the company of the church is something that they also bear witness to as a prior movement of God in-communicative-action. God as love, with the intent and promise of triune fellowship with creation, becomes host to the guest of creation in God's interaction with creation. However, what follows is the intrusion of sin that Shepherd, following Zizioulas, understands "as a *perversion* of the personhood to which we are called" where "death is the ontological consequence of this failure of humanity to live as 'persons,' gift-bearers, offering our createdness back in praise and thanks to the Divine Gift-Giver."[128] In response to this situation, the divine host enters the stage of

---

127. Vanhoozer, *Faith Speaking Understanding*, 158.
128. Shepherd, *Gift*, 139.

creation as the rejected other. "As YHWH had journeyed nomadically with Israel in the harshness of the desert, so Jesus is born into the inhospitable and hostile realities of first-century Palestine, a world steeped in violence and political turmoil."[129] As the writer of Hebrews then makes clear, Jesus is tempted "as we are, yet without sin" (4:15) and as the perfect priest and sacrificial offering, offers himself as the perfect gift that breaks the transactional cycle of violence by continuing to open his arms of love to the world to the point of death. "Understood as a Trinitarian act and interpreting the terms 'substitution' and 'sacrifice' non-violently, Christ's death appears as the climactic expression of hospitality of the gift-giving God."[130] And this love-fueled hospitality is stronger than death and continues to beckon all to the resurrected life offered through the resurrected life of Christ. "The hospitable self is a catholic identity constituted by being *in* Christ and being incorporated with others into the life of communion within the *Ecclesia*."[131] A hospitable way of being is shaped by the experience and reception of hospitality from the divine host and, although Jesus is the center of the community, the Spirit continues to draw the community out to hospitality toward the Other. "It is such sojourning and careful attentiveness which provides the basis for the 'face to face' encounter and participation in table fellowship which follows."[132] What it is to rehearse scenes of the kingdom is, therefore, to perform Christ, as his body, in acts of hospitality toward one another and the world. Drawing on the example of Abraham, Shepherd highlights that "*responsibility for the Other stems from the prior reception of the gift of self-identity, the gift of being addressed, named and elected by the Divine Other.*"[133] The hospitality industry is big business in the contemporary world with hotels and hospitals deriving their names from the Latin for "host" or "guest"—*hospes*. However, "our particular concern is how disciples live out union with Christ by inviting others into their home and family and what makes Christian hospitality a characteristic scene of congregational life."[134] To address this point Vanhoozer draws us back to the source by highlighting a significant difference in the teaching and actions of Jesus. Whereas hospitality is usually offered at a price, the command and

129. Shepherd, *Gift*, 147.
130. Shepherd, *Gift*, 159.
131. Shepherd, *Gift*, 189.
132. Shepherd, *Gift*, 251–52.
133. Shepherd, *Gift*, 122.
134. Vanhoozer, *Faith Speaking Understanding*, 158.

example of Jesus is one in which those who are particularly invited are those who can offer nothing in return (Luke 14:13). "Offering hospitality to those who are unable to return the favor mirrors the unconditional hospitality of God."[135] The point here is motive—hospitality that comes with a price tag is driven by gain that favors and is focused on those who can afford it. Hospitality that seeks no gain from the guest is one that is driven by a love-fueled desire to see the other flourish, which mirrors the hospitality offered by God to creation. What further mirrors God's hospitality is when one considers the slippage in the root word for hospitality. John Caputo notes that hospitality "is made possible by sustaining an interior contradiction: welcoming the '*hostis*,' a stranger who may be a guest in need of a 'host' or who may be someone 'hostile' (same word!) who may do you harm."[136] He continues, "If you remove the risk, you remove the teeth of the hospitality."[137] Hospitality then is not only about concern for the other but is risky business!

There is a further point to be made here regarding hospitality that pushes it toward curiosity. A hospitality that welcomes with no expectation of return can be further developed if the host is also curious—curious about how the other sees and engages with God and the world with a view to both growing through interaction and dialogue. Hospitality finds meaning in mirroring the example of Jesus. Curiosity finds meaning in recognizing human fallenness and limits. To be curious in hospitality is to both recognize one's limited perspective and also to be open to and invite the possibility that the guest has something to teach about what it means to perform Christ in particular scenes. This crosses over with the approach to orthodoxy mentioned above in that space, time, and understanding are given generously in the belief that others may offer fresh insights into what shape orthodoxy, orthopraxy, and orthopathos might take in the scenes of the theodrama in which we find ourselves. Here, sacrificial fidelity, generosity, and hospitality that are rooted in cross-shaped love, intersect as the commitment to God and neighbor, in the conforming to Christlike performances, leads to the opening up of spaces in which others are welcomed and can be learned from in the embrace of mutual flourishing.

As will be discussed in later chapters of this work, hospitality that welcomes and makes honest relationships possible is hospitality that can

---

135. Vanhoozer, *Faith Speaking Understanding*, 158–59.
136. Caputo, *Hoping Against Hope*, 89.
137. Caputo, *Hoping Against Hope*, 89.

lead to transformation. This is what we find displayed in the life, death, and resurrection of Jesus remembered and engaged with at Holy Communion. It is this meeting of people where they are that enables the possibility of transformation mediated through relationships. A hospitality that expects too much of recipients upon entry is no hospitality at all and is either repulsive or, again, leads to the development of false selves and communities that mistake hospitality for controlling conformity that encourages the separation of one's outer world from their inner. More will be said about this as we proceed. For now, it is enough to highlight the theodramatic shape of the eucharistic company of performers that seek to embody and reflect love-driven divine modes of being defined as fidelity, generosity, and hospitality.

In this celebration where God is both host and meal, we are reminded of God's generosity and hospitality in Christ that is the very reason why we are able to be the body of Christ in this meal. God's fidelity to creation and the promise of redemption, salvation, and fellowship with the triune God is what has caused God to enable covenantal fidelity on both sides of the relationship in Jesus' death and resurrection. It is the combination of this fidelity, generosity, and hospitality that finds its culmination in the possibility of union with Christ as the church, the body of Christ through this sacramental meal. In the performance of the Lord's Supper, following Calvin, Vanhoozer proposes that the church finds union with Christ by the Spirit operating through not just the elements of bread and wine but through the broader words and actions that give the performance shape and meaning: "the elements really communicate (i.e., make common, make personally present) Christ and nourish the soul by virtue of the Spirit, who raises communicants up to fellowship with Christ in heaven. The Lord's Supper is thus a concentrated form of the ministry of Word and Spirit that enlivens and strengthens faith."[138] The singing of hymns enables celebration, rehearsal, and consolation in embodied, corporate ways that make space for "acknowledging both present pain and future hope."[139] In the public reading and reflecting on Scripture, "the stories, songs, promises, prophecies and teachings of Scripture soften hearts, orient desires, sharpen tastes, form beliefs, shape imaginations and prompt actions."[140] It is these rich and varied practices of the rehearsing church

---

138. Vanhoozer, *Faith Speaking Understanding*, 164.
139. Vanhoozer, *Pictures*, 142.
140. Vanhoozer, *Pictures*, 187.

that continue to form the company of performers into their Christlike identity of prophets, priests, and a royal and holy nation.

However, as Vanhoozer goes on to note, "The Lord's Supper is a theater of the gospel inasmuch as it communicates this twofold *communio*: union with Christ and communion with one another in Christ."[141] This latter point brings to the fore the church as the theatre of reconciliation and more broadly the place where Christ is presenced. The church does not just give thanks for what God has done but seeks to embody its identity on earth as it is in heaven as the people of God where the kingdom of God is breaking in and being rehearsed. We return here to the catholic nature of the church as the whole company across time and space who are united in this bread and wine.[142] The local performance is church but not the whole church and it is important to be mindful of this. The final mark of the church as apostolic is where we turn next as we look at the church *ad extra*, sent to the world as the body of Christ to continue the ministry of Christ enlivened and empowered by the Spirit of Christ.

The Performance

Vanhoozer states, "The church performs the drama of doctrine when it embodies and enacts the way of Jesus Christ in the various concrete situations that comprise the world."[143] As has already been noted, the challenge for the church is to continue to offer fitting improvised performances of Christ in the current scenes of the theodrama in order to maintain the through-line and aid in moving the action toward the superobjective of the consummation of creation and communion with the Holy Trinity. Whereas in the previous section, the focus was on the action of the church in itself, living into its identity, here the focus is on the church in its missional role for the world where "the mission of the local church is to constitute itself as a theater of the gospel, walking the way of Jesus Christ across the stage of the world."[144] Or as Heltzel puts it, "Churches today need to learn how to translate the liturgical performance of Sunday

---

141. Vanhoozer, *Faith Speaking Understanding*, 164–65.

142. Shepherd highlights the reading of Scripture, the Lord's Prayer, and the Eucharist as separate "Identity-Shaping Practices and Sacraments of the Ecclesia." However, although I would agree that they are all significant, arguably prayer and the reading of Scripture should be part of the celebration of the Eucharist. See Shepherd, *Gift*, 236–41.

143. Vanhoozer, *Faith Speaking Understanding*, 170.

144. Vanhoozer, *Faith Speaking Understanding*, 173.

worship into street theatre freely performed throughout the week."[145] Here we therefore follow Vanhoozer and focus on the church as "a theater of the gospel in a double sense: the space designed for the performance of plays (place), and the lived presentation of dramatic action (people)."[146] The questions to be answered are, where is the church to be found, and how does the church relate to the world?

To address the first, we return to Vanhoozer's definition of place. The local manifestation is a context-specific, culturally sensitive, and relevant manifestation of the church universal. As has already been noted, the traveling company of the performing church is not to be confused with the total manifestation of the kingdom of God but, instead, is a parable of the kingdom—a preview of or window into the kingdom and gateway to it. In Vanhoozer's paradigm, the local manifestation of the church is also not to be confused with the geographical coordinates of the building or location where the company of the church might gather. Instead, the emphasis is on what action is performed there, why it takes place, and who does what: "church exists in the 'space' between its members, in the space of meaningful interaction."[147] When Jesus states that where two or three are gathered in his name, so he is there also (Matt 18:20), the point appears to be that the church as the body of Christ is not simply about people gathering with a shared belief but also about what those people do together in the name of Christ. Vanhoozer suggests that the performance of the church is not about possessing a land or trying to make a society Christian; instead, it is about those who are baptized into the body of Christ, located in Christ, putting on Christ as they offer parables of the kingdom by performing Christ in the meaning-laden action they undertake together. "As a local theater of the gospel, the gathering of disciples is a historically extended, socially embodied dramatized argument about the good news of Jesus Christ."[148] Returning to Vanhoozer's definition of the church as a eutopia—a good place—he states, "it is the place where disciples gather as a domain of Christ: 'our citizenship is in heaven' (Phil. 3:20)."[149] Elsewhere he further describes the church as a "culturally specific Christotope: a spatiotemporal manifestation of the new order 'in Christ.'"[150] Location

145. Heltzel, "Church," 261.
146. Vanhoozer, *Faith Speaking Understanding*, 171.
147. Vanhoozer, *Faith Speaking Understanding*, 175.
148. Vanhoozer, *Faith Speaking Understanding*, 175.
149. Vanhoozer, *Faith Speaking Understanding*, 177.
150. Vanhoozer, *Drama of Doctrine*, 358.

for the church is thus about recognizing that, as it gathers in a particular location on earth to do church, it is, at the same time when being and doing church, the domain of heaven. This is so because if the church is the body of Christ and is located in Christ in the ways defined previously, and Christ is in heaven—defined as the domain of God's perfect rule—then to be and do church is to perform on earth as it is in heaven. It is to be located on earth and yet perform within the heavenly domain of the kingdom of God. Following Vanhoozer's train of thought: "the church's 'place' is the space between two ages, the old age and the age to come. And this leads to the church's mission: to serve as a living preview of a coming 'attraction,' the 'new heavens' and 'new earth' (2 Pet. 3:13; Rev. 21:1), where God will be 'all in all' (1 Cor. 15:28)."[151]

Shannon Craigo-Snell, borrowing from Peter Brooks's typology of theatre, in conversation with Karl Barth, argues for a combination of "Holy Church" and "Rough Church" that avoids "Deadly Church."[152] Deadly Church is that which is well crafted and ordered but ultimately predictable and boring, managing God out of any involvement. Holy Church, by contrast, is "a wildly unequal partnership" that recognizes God's initiation, involvement, and direction, where God is revealed and known. Rough Church describes the earthiness of creation where God incarnates Godself in order to be revealed in accessible ways. Where Deadly Church is built around human attempts to access the Holy, Holy and Rough Church combined recognize the limits and brokenness of humanity, and yet are expectant and prepared to meet with the self-revealing author of creation (and the drama!). For this to occur "Immediate Church" that is rehearsed yet humble and ready to improvise combines with "Empty Church" in which space is left open for the involvement, invitation, and leading of God. In this space, Craigo-Snell suggests, "Our performance is disciplined in order to help us become more sensitive to the working of the Spirit in a whole-personed way, to get in on the action and participate in what the Spirit is doing in the world."[153]

With Christ at work, by the Spirit, in the lives of disciples, individually and corporately, the church is called to turn each space in which it performs scenes from the kingdom into a eutopian place of heaven on earth. But, if this is how we locate the church in the world, in the

---

151. Vanhoozer, *Faith Speaking Understanding*, 178.
152. Craigo-Snell, "Empty Churches."
153. Craigo-Snell, "Empty Churches," 110.

multiple scenes of the theodrama played out across time and space, we need now turn our attention to details of how the church engages with the watching world.

As resident exiles, Vanhoozer argues that the church in its interaction with the world needs to avoid the dual pitfalls of becoming like the world and complete separation from the world. The challenge is to retain the identity of holy and set apart and yet continue to interact with the world in order to display the kingdom of God and invite the world to participate. Vanhoozer again draws us back to the prior work of God in exploring what such a middle way looks like for the church. "God has already acted, reconciled the world, and proved himself faithful. The church does not need to redeem society as much as indicate that redemption has already taken place. The company of the baptized is charged simply with living out this evangelical reality: what is in Christ."[154] Vanhoozer further states, "The church is called not to lord it over, escape from, or even transform culture (and especially not to be transformed by it!), but rather to *communicate* to it. Specifically, the church is to communicate Christ, and what is in Christ, in everything that it says and does."[155] To communicate what is in Christ is to communicate a different story in contrast to the variety of other ways that the world attempts to layer meaning onto experience. We again return to the church as a spectacle or theatre whereby the watching world is not simply to hear a story being told but is to be invited into a lived experience of a different drama that will transform their perception of reality. Crucial to the church engaging in the kind of theatre for which it was cast is the recognizing by all that all are cast to perform, not simply the clergy! This is what Vanhoozer refers to as the "*playerhood of all believers*" which "involves the privilege and responsibility of interpreting the Bible and of living out one's interpretations with others."[156] This constant call to lived interpretation also makes for a biblical church whereby "it seeks to embody the words in the power of the Spirit and so become a living commentary."[157] The church is to be the most important example of interactive theatre in which those not currently participating are not simply spectating but instead are invited to participate as the

---

154. Vanhoozer, *Faith Speaking Understanding*, 181.
155. Vanhoozer, *Faith Speaking Understanding*, 182.
156. Vanhoozer, *Faith Speaking Understanding*, 183.
157. Vanhoozer, *Faith Speaking Understanding*, 2.

organic nature of the body of Christ continues to grow and change in response to God's activity in the world.[158]

It is important here to note that in walking the middle way of engagement without conformity to the world, there will be overlap with other non-Christian communities, but there will also always be significant differences. "Although the church works for the common good and advocates for forms of life that are conducive to human flourishing, its vision as to what these consist in may vary greatly from the prevailing cultural paradigms. God's *shalom* is not quite Plato's *Republic* or liberal democracy."[159] This may mean that at times the church is perceived as odd or foolish, and yet, this is to be expected as the prophetic aspect of Christ's ministry and, therefore, the church's identity, is enacted and subverts culture by unveiling its flaws and displaying a different kingdom. In living as a theatre of "holy fools" the church not only enacts parables of the kingdom but performs "the apocalypse: the end of the (old) world."[160] The priesthood of the believing church is also on display here as one that continues to pray for the world while seeking to guide the current audience of the church's parables of the kingdom toward participation in that kingdom.

As the school of Christlike improvisers who are continually learning and participating in the theodrama, to be the church *ad extra* is to collectively improvise on the divine performance of Jesus in relevant ways in the scenes in which they find themselves. As I have noted previously, Scripture is the norming norm in terms of measuring the suitability and fittingness of performance and within that, in particular, is a Christological key against which all performances are measured as the ideal. And yet, the challenge for the church in its embodiment of Christ is how it does this in a relevant way in the ever-shifting scenes of contemporary culture. "It is a delightful paradox: the church discovers even more of the mind of Christ as it seeks to translate and embody the wisdom that it has into various forms of life and thought."[161] This also means that as well as learning from Scripture and tradition, there is always much to learn from other

---

158. As Richard Carter and Sam Wells note, "The goal is not for the Bible to become a means of liberation through study, conscientization, and renewed praxis; the goal is for the drama of the Bible itself to enact and create a new reality, that all might be drawn into its action and become participants in the world it creates and makes possible." Carter and Wells, "Holy Theatre," 227.

159. Vanhoozer, *Faith Speaking Understanding*, 185–86.

160. Vanhoozer, *Faith Speaking Understanding*, 187.

161. Vanhoozer, *Faith Speaking Understanding*, 203.

expressions of church in the continuing challenge and joy of translating the gospel in embodied ways onto the world stage.

Vanhoozer draws attention to two concrete examples of where this improvised embodiment has taken place in the contemporary world. One of these—the response to an air disaster—was mentioned in the previous chapter, with the second being how churches in Thailand responded to a natural flooding disaster in 2011. Vanhoozer uses both of these examples to demonstrate how well-formed churches improvise on the performance of Christ in fitting ways in contemporary scenes. He also highlights that "disciples will respond differently than other caregivers because the Spirit of Christ has formed them, not least by means of the big theodramatic picture."[162] There are numerous examples that could be brought to bear as displaying what is being discussed here, but these two examples will suffice to act as a springboard that takes us forward into the rest of this work. In reference to the response by a Church of England vicar and his church to the air disaster, Vanhoozer focuses on how good use of doctrine in the formation of the church community has formed "persons who improvise Christlike, compassionate responses to all who cry out in the wilderness of pain, emotional trauma, and existential angst."[163] Regarding the need to learn by doing, as previously noted he also suggests, "The children of faith need the diet of doctrine, and considerable performance practice, if they are to develop into 'grown-up' disciples."[164]

We have then a strong base regarding theodramatic ecclesiology on which to build. A clear sense of identity and vocation has been elucidated as well as what a rehearsing church should focus on and then perform in the world. However, as with anthropology in the previous chapter, there is scope for critique and development as we conclude this chapter and look toward developing further what rehearsing and performing might look like for a church equipped to aid performers in the process of post-traumatic remaking.

Theodramatic Ecclesiology and Post-Traumatic Remaking

Although I concur with Vanhoozer's suggestion of the need for good doctrine as guidance for fitting performance in a variety of new and

---

162. Vanhoozer, *Faith Speaking Understanding*, 197.
163. Vanhoozer, *Faith Speaking Understanding*, 197.
164. Vanhoozer, *Faith Speaking Understanding*, 204.

evolving contexts, as well as ongoing rehearsals and performance practice, there is a need to deepen and enrich his proposal if the church is to be more trauma-informed in its performance. To have the life, death, and resurrection of Jesus as the central performance that sustains all others in the Eucharist, and provides direction for improvisation, is vital. But if we take Vanhoozer's helpful use of Stanislavski's method seriously, as we should, the "magic if" must also include enquiry into the psychological as well as the ontological aspect of improvising on the performance of Jesus as the church. *If* we enact the fidelity, generosity, and hospitality of God, with the help of God, important questions we should ask are, "Why does it have the positive impact that it does and how can knowledge of that enrich the content and understanding of our rehearsals and performance?" For example, to understand the nature of the fidelity we are called to, it is helpful to ask what the motive and impact of performing Christlike fidelity is and why, thus enriching our understanding of why Christlike fidelity matters and how it displays the kingdom of God. Exploring these questions further informs our understanding of the performance we are called to, what an enactment of heaven on earth might look like, and how it might aid others in their performances. As we focus in on the relevance of the discussed dispositions, attitudes, and actions of the church's performance for offering fitting post-trauma care, it is important to explore specifically how and why they might aid in the process of post-traumatic remaking. Here we can again reach beyond the sources of Scripture and tradition to psychological resources, not as an alternative, nor as an equal to Scripture, but to aid in deepening our understanding of Scripture and the resultant performances and doctrines. Such an enriching of the use of sources and exploration of motives and reasons for faithful performances can also contribute to broadening the means of formation for performance used in the rehearsing church. To return to a point made in the previous chapter, to rely on cognitive learning as the single most important method of forming the performer is not only to misunderstand the formation process but also to misdirect the church in how it aids best in this process.[165]

As an example, Vanhoozer, in various places, describes the church as a theatre of the defeat of sin and death in that, as the victory of God breaks into the church, it is the place where God's victory and kingdom are displayed as well as the cruciform power that brought that victory

---

165. To be fair to Vanhoozer, he does offer examples of formation that occur through art, such as singing (for example, see *Pictures*, 123–45). However, arguably, cognitive learning still takes precedent in his work regarding the process of formation.

about. The church is thus the temple of God's victory, the place where heaven and earth intersect.[166] Disciples are called to bear witness and testify, in word and deed, as "an active participant" in the implementation of God's victory on earth.[167] This includes participation "in the power of Jesus' suffering love" and where suffering is encountered, endurance is the answer through which disciples and the church are conformed to the cruciform image of Christ. I have noted elsewhere both the details and shortcomings of Vanhoozer's reductionist approach to endurance and so will not rehearse that objection here.[168] However, what is important to note is the overly simplistic way Vanhoozer seems to understand the experience of suffering and how the disciple and the church are to respond. Endurance is right, in a sense—we are called to run the race (1 Cor 9:24; Phil 3:12–14; Heb 12:1–2). However, what does it mean, in concrete practices, for the church or individuals within the body of Christ, who have experienced trauma, to endure, to keep going, not just in principle but psychologically, and how does the church enable this to happen? Further, what might be made of the concept of the church as a theatre of healing, further exploring the practice of hospitality, particularly for those who are traumatized? To answer these and related questions requires a psychological and relevant enriching of not only the nature of healthy human development but also how and why the church is to perform in such a way that enables and supports the healing of trauma.

Conclusion

In this chapter, we have briefly traced Vanhoozer's dramatic ecclesiology continuing the theme of beginning with the prior work of God who calls the church into being as the body of Christ. The one, holy, catholic, and apostolic church finds its identity and vocation bound up together in participating in the missions of the Son and Spirit, which are part of the all-encompassing *missio Dei*. The church is fed and formed in the Eucharist where it deepens its understanding and improves its performances through rehearsing scenes of the kingdom of God together. These scenes embody fidelity, generosity, and hospitality and find their origin in God's communication-in-action, particularly in Christ. They thus bear witness

---

166. Vanhoozer, *Faith Speaking Understanding*, 214–16.
167. Vanhoozer, *Faith Speaking Understanding*, 217.
168. Torr, *Dramatic*, 52–56.

to God and God's kingdom as well as producing parables of that kingdom for a watching world who is called to participate in this interactive theatre. The church, in its interaction with the world, improvises on the performance of Christ as it is clothed and empowered by the Spirit to continue to embody Christ in the world in word and deed. These performances in the contemporary scenes of the world are places where the church is and, therefore, where Christ is present, and so offer what may to some seem like a theatre of fools. Yet this is the theatre of the gospel that challenges social norms and imagination and invites spectators to participate in this, the great theodrama of salvation for the world. The church as school forms actors to enable them to participate in fitting ways to carry on the through-line of the drama to its superobjective of complete communion between the triune fellowship and creation. But the question that is left, hinted at but as yet unanswered by Vanhoozer at least, is what does it mean for the church to improvise on the performance of Christ in response to those who are traumatized? What could Job's friends have done and what does it mean for the church to aid in the process of post-traumatic remaking?

Drawing on the theodramatic *imago Dei* and church discussed thus far, the rest of this work will be concerned with building on this platform to answer just these questions. The next building block to aid us in doing that is to be found in the work of noted twentieth-century pediatrician and psychoanalyst Donald Winnicott.

5

Donald Winnicott's Object Relations Theory

Introduction

HAVING EXPLORED VANHOOZER'S THEODRAMATIC anthropology and ecclesiology in the previous two chapters, it became apparent from both that although Vanhoozer offers a helpful model for understanding how they complement and inform one another, when it came to the question of growing in Christlikeness in a post-trauma state, Vanhoozer offers very little. However, although Vanhoozer does not propose guidance for such situations, that does not mean that there is no potential in his model. In fact, quite the contrary. But, before we can resume the conversation with Vanhoozer's model to further develop this line of thought, we first need to bring a relevant dialogue partner into the discussion to aid in the intended development. In this chapter, we turn our attention to the work of the twentieth-century British pediatrician and psychoanalyst Donald W. Winnicott.

Winnicott is best known as one of the early developers and proponents of the psychological school of thought referred to as Object Relations Theory. What will hopefully become apparent as this and the following chapters unfold is that Winnicott's particular approach to the healthy development of babies and children, as well as adults in therapy, offers us a tool to explore healthy human development as depicted in the Scriptures. In particular, what Winnicott's work potentially offers is a way of developing Vanhoozer's theodramatic model to provide biblically rooted, theologically articulate, practical guidance on how to care well for, and provide the best environment and support for the Christlike flourishing of, those who have experienced trauma. Before we can get to that stage, we must turn our attention to exploring Winnicott's work.

This chapter will first provide a brief context from which to understand Winnicott and his work before proceeding to explore key aspects of his work in greater detail. Due to space constraints and the need to keep the focus on addressing key issues, attention in the main body of this chapter will be on those aspects of Winnicott's work that are deemed relevant to the proposed development that will occur in the following chapters.[1] Having explored the relevant sections of Winnicott's work, the chapter will conclude by pointing ahead to where Winnicott's work can aid in addressing the question of how best to care for and support those who are traumatized within the church community.

Setting the Scene

Lavinia Gomez notes that "Object Relations was originally a British development of Freudian psychoanalytical theory."[2] Although Freud's earlier work understood the mind to be primarily physiological and thus measurable, his later work, instead, began to explore the mind as something subjective—a site for experiences to be had that combined the complexities of internal and external relationships. The impact of this relational, subjective turn in Freud's thinking can be seen in the development of theories such as the Oedipus Complex and the internalizing of the parent figure in the form of the superego. This added a fresh layer to Freud's instinct-driven view of early human development.[3]

Although emerging through the work of key figures such as Melanie Klein and Ronald Fairbairn, Object Relations Theory (ORT) is often associated with the life and work of Donald W. Winnicott. ORT is so called because, in the move away from the instinctual emphasis apparent in Freud's earlier work, the replacement primary driver thought to be present in humans is relationship.[4] "Rather than seeing the human being as

1. For a helpful overview of the development of Winnicott's theories, see Abram, "Evolution."
2. Gomez, *Introduction*, 1.
3. Gomez, *Introduction*, 2–3, 12–13.
4. For a more detailed exploration of how Winnicott's theories relate to and differ from Freud's, see Loparic, "From Freud to Winnicott."

a system of biological drives, Object Relations places relationship at the heart of what it is to be human."[5] The use of the word "object" does not refer to something inanimate but has Freudian roots as that at which one's instincts are aimed. More precisely, in ORT, "object" finds meaning in relationship to the "subject." Here the object is the person that the subject is relating to in some way. This can be as a "part-object" in the sense that the baby relates to the breast of the mother when seeking food, or in the sense that one might reduce a person down to being foolish or wise by focusing on one characteristic as the defining factor. Non-human objects can be referred to in this schema but usually as something that finds definition by connection to humans, such as home or culture.

As creatures whose desire and need for relationship is basic, "Object Relations theories rest on the belief that the human being is essentially social: our need for contact with others is primary, and cannot be explained in terms of other needs or reduced to something more basic."[6] It is important to note here that the subjective and objective develop in tandem and are influenced by one another. As will become apparent below, the healthy development of the internal world is shaped by engagement with the outside world, and reciprocally, how the individual interprets and engages with the outside world is influenced by the development of the internal world.

Although seeming to perceive her work as a continuation of Freudian development, Melanie Klein was not scientifically trained and dispensed with the emphasis on biological instincts prominent in Freud's earlier work. Instead, Klein focused on the pre-Oedipal subjective inner world and how this shaped perception and engagement with the outer world and, how that engagement impacted the development of the inner world. Contrary to Freud's scientific approach, Klein focused on the experience of her patients and argued that the id, ego, and superego were present to some degree in the pre-Oedipal child. Her approach, as an analyst, was to explore this developing inner world. However, Klein was less interested than her contemporary and daughter of Sigmund Freud, Anna Freud, in the impact of parents and the wider environment and context in which the child was developing. Klein and Anna Freud are mentioned here in brief because, although space and focus do not permit us to engage at greater depth with their respective approaches, the

---

5. Gomez, *Introduction*, 1.
6. Gomez, *Introduction*, 2.

development of Winnicott's theories occurs in conversation with both but mainly Klein's.[7] Adam Phillips suggests that "His [Winnicott's] work . . . cannot be understood without reference to Klein. It is a continuous, and sometimes inexplicit, commentary on and critique of her work."[8] Although Winnicott affirms Anna Freud's interest in the impact of the family and context when exploring healthy development, on the whole, he is more influenced by Klein's belief and interest in the pre-Oedipal inner world of the child. This period of the child's life is where Winnicott would suggest both healthy and pathological development has its roots. However, Klein was more confident than Winnicott in what she thought could be known about the inner world of the child at this stage, whereas Winnicott was more comfortable with the unknown and "did not feel that Klein understood the nature of the mother-infant relationship."[9] Also, where Klein focused on the drive and capacity for knowledge as a sign of health, Winnicott, in his later work, replaced this with the capacity for play as well as offering a different understanding to both Klein and Freud regarding what they had labeled the "death instinct."[10] These links with Klein's work mean that mentions will be made of her work as we proceed to explore Winnicott's but, as Phillips also notes of these links, Winnicott "would . . . take from Klein what he wanted without becoming either a devotee or a connoisseur of her theory."[11] Although Winnicott is not necessarily the most innovative and original of the ORT theorists, he was able to communicate his theories more clearly and to a wider audience than other theorists, making him more accessible, particularly to those who are engaging with ORT from within other disciplines. This will prove particularly useful as we proceed.

Born in 1896, Donald Woods Winnicott first trained as a medical doctor specializing in pediatrics before later training as a psychoanalyst. Given his combination of training and experience, it is no surprise that central to his work was an exploration of healthy human development,

7. For a more in-depth exploration of Klein's work and how it related to Anna Freud's, see Gomez, *Introduction*, 29–53.

8. Phillips, *Winnicott*, 9.

9. Ogden, "Mother," 47.

10. For a helpful exploration of Winnicott's interpretation of the death instinct, see Abram, Introduction to *Donald Winnicott Today*, 3; and Abram, "DWW's notes."

11. Phillips, *Winnicott*, 47. See Ogden, "Mother," for an interesting exploration of how Winnicott's theories relate to Klein's.

focusing on the impact the mother-child relationship during the early years of a child's life has on this. Phillips notes of Winnicott's work,

> In the master-plot of human development that he worked on for over forty years, Winnicott tried to explain how the individual grows, through dependence, towards a personal way of being, how he becomes at once ordinary and distinctive according to the sense he has of himself, and how the early environment makes this possible. Growth was this ongoing task of psychosomatic integration.[12]

What will become clearer as we progress to explore Winnicott's work in greater depth is that the paradigm of the "good enough mother" and her care of her child during the crucial early stages of childhood development would come to be the central lens through which Winnicott viewed and understood a whole array of relationships. Jan Abram notes, "A sense of self rooted in the newborn's primary relationship is at the heart of his theoretical matrix."[13] As well as being helpful to remember when we reengage with Vanhoozer's work in later chapters, it is also helpful to bear in mind now if the reader feels the emphasis of the role of the mother is dated or lopsided. Noteworthy here is the culture in which Winnicott is developing his theories as well as reminding ourselves that it is also a paradigm that more fluidly represents other relationships. Although Winnicott focuses on the mother-child relationship, the father does still get mentioned as does the wider family and other social groups in terms of involvement in the healthy development of the child.[14] However, the mother as the primary caregiver is the lens through which Winnicott gives us access to his developmental theories.

Dependence to In(ter)dependence

As already mentioned above, Winnicott suggested that growth, the maturing of an individual, is a process that begins with dependence on the mother and moves, ideally, toward independence. In *Babies and Their Mothers* Winnicott suggests, "It can be said that the story of the growing child is a story of absolute dependence moving steadily through lessening

---

12. Phillips, *Winnicott*, 2.
13. Abram, Introduction to *Donald Winnicott Today*, 1.
14. See Winnicott, *Home*.

degrees of dependence, and groping towards independence."[15] However, although this process of maturation and growth is a core theme in his work, it would be a mistake to oversimplify Winnicott's understanding by suggesting that independence is ever achievable or actually desired. He tempers the above suggestion by noting, "A mature child or adult has a kind of independence that is happily mixed in with all sorts of needs, and with love which becomes evident when loss brings about a state of grief."[16] Here we see hints of Winnicott stepping back from the idea of maturity being equated with full independence, but he elaborates on this more clearly elsewhere writing, "Individual maturity implies a movement towards independence, but there is no such thing as independence. It would be unhealthy for an individual to be so withdrawn as to feel independent and invulnerable."[17] However, if healthy growth involves moving away from complete dependence toward independence, but to be fully independent is neither achievable nor healthy, then the question remains as to what Winnicott thought healthy development is aiming at. Establishing this will provide the starting point that propels us into exploring how this aim is achieved, and what helps and hinders it.

Although independence remains on the table as a quasi-aim, in a paper presented in 1963, Winnicott goes further by stating, "Independence is never absolute. The healthy individual does not become isolated, but becomes related to the environment in such a way that the individual and the environment can be said to be interdependent."[18] Toward the end of the same paper he states, "In this way a true independence develops, with the child able to live a personal existence that is satisfactory while involved in society's affairs."[19] When referring to the development of the child through adolescence and into adulthood, Winnicott makes mention of the continuing support of parents and others as new experiences in society challenge levels of tolerance and understanding in the maturation process. In this sense, there is a continual paradoxical relationship in Winnicott's work between the suggested aim of independence and the recognition that interdependence is what is really desired and achievable. One of the areas that contrasted Winnicott's work with Klein's was the importance Winnicott placed on recognizing the impact of relationships

---

15. Winnicott, *Babies and Their Mothers*, 83.
16. Winnicott, *Babies and Their Mothers*, 83.
17. Winnicott, *Home*, 21.
18. Winnicott, "From Dependence Towards Independence," 84.
19. Winnicott, "From Dependence Towards Independence," 91.

and context on the development of the individual. In a paper given to the British Psycho-Analytical Society in 1952, Winnicott recounts his excited declaration to the Society at an earlier point that "*there is no such thing as a baby*," clarifying this by stating, "if you show me a baby you certainly show me also someone caring for the baby, or at least a pram with someone's eyes and ears glued to it. One sees a 'nursing couple.'"[20] For Winnicott, before the formation of the individual, there is simply the "environment-individual set-up" that, with good enough provision, will develop into the individual in relationship with the environment.[21] Paradoxes are commonplace in Winnicott's theories, and this is one such example. As we will come to see, a healthy self for Winnicott is one that is integrated and feels alive yet is always impossible to fully define. Phillips summarizes Winnicott on the self: "We will gather from the contexts in which he was used by this powerful word that he was asserting the presence of something essential about a person that was bound up with bodily aliveness, yet remained inarticulate and ultimately unknowable: perhaps like an embodied soul."[22] Although Winnicott's emphasis is on the healthy maturation of the individual self, the paradox is that the healthy soul is not alive in a vacuum but is embodied within the world and in relationship with the world, and that this is so in a way that means independence would not be healthy. What Winnicott here seems to be playing with in his paradoxical way is the tension of a self that cannot be reduced down to only relationships and thus lose the uniqueness of the self but can also not be healthy apart from certain crucial relationships. The move toward independence continues the assertion of agency in the self, yet the unobtainable nature of independence prevents the demise of individuals made for healthy relationships. It is the development from what Winnicott terms the experience of "absolute dependence" to the experience of "toward independence" via "relative dependence" that will form the framework for exploring Winnicott's approach to the un/healthy development of the mature self within ORT.[23] For the sake of clarity, it is these three experiences that will be used in what follows, to explore in more detail how the development of an individual occurs pre-birth and through childhood. However, it is important to note that Winnicott did not offer a one-directional approach to development.

20. Winnicott, "Anxiety Associated with Insecurity," 99.
21. Winnicott, "Anxiety Associated with Insecurity," 99.
22. Phillips, *Winnicott*, 3.
23. Winnicott, "From Dependence Towards Independence."

Instead, healthy development is characterized by a growing repertoire of various maturational developmental experiences. "Maturity is then the flexible toleration of, and potential access to, a full and ever-increasing repertoire throughout life."[24] What this means in practice is that "a relation with external reality is dependent upon a capacity to relinquish this relation in a return to states of primary unintegration in which one can be, for example, 'miles away,' or simply, preoccupied."[25] More will be said about this state of unintegration as we proceed. We begin with the stage of absolute dependence.

Absolute Dependence

The stage marked as "absolute dependence" in Winnicott's framework covers, roughly, the time in a baby's life spanning from pre-birth to up to four months old.[26] The name for this experience is seemingly self-explanatory in terms of the baby's absolute dependence on the mother for all that it needs to survive and develop in a healthy way. However, this is more complex than it first appears. To proceed, it is helpful to begin to introduce a number of Winnicott's key terms and offer some of his definitions of more established ones.

Winnicott believed that humans would naturally grow in a healthy manner, barring hereditary issues, if the environment was good enough. He stated, "It is the innate tendencies towards integration and growth that produce the health, not the environmental provision. Yet good-enough provision is necessary, absolutely at the beginning, and relatively at later stages, at the stage of the Oedipus complex, in the latency period, and also at adolescence."[27] Winnicott referred to this good enough environment as the "facilitating environment." In using this term, Winnicott was referring to the environment provided for the healthy maturation of the infant to take place. "The environment, when good enough, facilitates the maturational process. For this to happen the environmental provision in an extremely subtle manner adapts itself to the changing needs arising out of the fact of maturation."[28] The term "'maturational

---

24. Phillips, *Winnicott*, 82.
25. Phillips, *Winnicott*, 82.
26. Abram, *Language of Winnicott*, 133.
27. Winnicott, "Providing for the Child," 68.
28. Winnicott, "Mentally Ill," 223. Elsewhere Winnicott offers a definition of his use of the term "infant" as the phase "prior to word presentation and the use of word

process' refers to the evolution of the ego and of the self, and includes the whole story of the id, of instincts and their vicissitudes, and of defences in the ego relative to instinct."[29] It is the processes involved in the healthy maturation of the child as facilitated by a good enough environment. We here begin to encounter Winnicott's understanding of the id and the ego and how they relate to one another. In a lecture on the sense of guilt, given in 1956, Winnicott recounts Freud's understanding of the id and ego and how they relate, noting of Freud that in his work, the id "referred to the instinctual drives, and the ego . . . referred to that part of the whole self that is related to the environment. The ego modifies the environment in order to bring about id-satisfactions, and it curbs id-impulses in order that what the environment can offer can be used to best advantage, again for id-satisfaction."[30] However, although Winnicott seemed to hold to Freud's definition of the instinct-driven id, he offers a different approach to the ego and how the ego and id relate to one another that displays his relational-as-basic understanding of humans. In a paper on ego integration Winnicott answers the question of when the ego starts with the slightly cryptic, "The answer is that the start is when the ego starts."[31] In the same paper, he defines the term "ego" as that which "can be used to describe that part of the growing human personality that tends, under suitable conditions, to become integrated into a unit."[32] He further suggests that "in the very early stages of the development of a human child . . . ego-functioning needs to be taken as a concept that is inseparable from that of the existence of the infant as a person."[33] In contrast, what might be termed "the self" does not come into being for Winnicott until there is a perceived differentiation from the world. The id relates to the ego in that "id-functioning . . . is collected together in all its aspects and becomes ego-experience. There is thus no sense in making use of the word 'id' for phenomena that are not covered and catalogued and experienced and eventually interpreted by ego-functioning."[34] Winnicott

---

symbols" or "a phase in which the infant depends on maternal care that is based on maternal empathy rather than on understanding of what is or could be verbally expressed." See "Parent-Infant Relationship," 40–41.

29. Winnicott, "From Dependence Towards Independence," 85.
30. Winnicott, "Psycho-Analysis," 16.
31. Winnicott, "Ego Integration," 56.
32. Winnicott, "Ego Integration," 56.
33. Winnicott, "Ego Integration," 56.
34. Winnicott, "Ego Integration," 56.

is here suggesting that impulses prior to the existence of the ego are to be ignored and are not id impulses. The id can only be named as such when the ego has begun and, under healthy conditions, is managed by the ego. To help with this management Winnicott also suggests that the infant uses a "superego." Again, following Freud, Winnicott held to the idea that the superego is the name given to forces introjected by the ego to aid with the management of the id which also aids in the development of a healthy sense of guilt.[35] However, where Winnicott differed from Freud is in Winnicott's beliefs that the superego development in boys was different to girls and that the superego, although shaped by father-figures in the child's life, is "subhuman" and more "primitive" in origin than human father-figures.[36] Also in contrast to Freud, Winnicott seems to focus more on the development of the ego and its use of the id in the development of a self that relates well to the world rather than as something that manages the id impulses. More will be said about the development of the ego and its relationship to the self and the id as we proceed. For now, it is enough to have in play these basic definitions.

A key reason for studying this time of maturation within the infant's life is that Winnicott believed that "the completion of these processes forms the basis of mental health."[37] He further stated that "the mental health of the human being is laid down in infancy by the mother, who provides an environment in which complex but essential processes in the infant's self can become completed."[38] Before exploring what Winnicott had in mind regarding good enough environmental provision at this stage, it is helpful first to clarify what Winnicott thought the baby was experiencing and what these complex and essential processes involve.

At the start, Winnicott believed the baby to be in an unintegrated state, suggesting, "It is useful to think of the material out of which integration emerges in terms of motor and sensory elements, the stuff of primary narcissism."[39] Present here are not only Winnicott's thoughts about the initial status of the baby as unintegrated but also his belief that instinctual healthy development, enabled by a good enough environment, would lead to integration. The unintegration Winnicott refers to here is one in which the baby is in a state where there is no sense of

35. Winnicott, "Psycho-Analysis," 18–19.
36. Winnicott, "Psycho-Analysis," 19.
37. Winnicott, "Paediatrics and Psychiatry," 159.
38. Winnicott, "Paediatrics and Psychiatry," 160.
39. Winnicott, "Ego Integration," 60.

a unified, individual self, consisting of a psyche-soma, and there is no sense of differentiation between self and world—me/not-me—or inner and outer world. There is also, therefore, no sense of present or history as neither time nor space are able to be perceived yet. This unintegrated state involves an experience of what Winnicott refers to as primary narcissism where "it is only the observer who can distinguish between the individual and the environment . . . and it is therefore convenient here to speak of an environment-individual set-up, rather than of an individual."[40] At this point, "it is necessary not to think of the baby as a person who gets hungry, and whose instinctual drives may be met or frustrated, but to think of the baby as an immature being who is all the time *on the brink of unthinkable anxiety*."[41] What holds this anxiety at bay is the environmental provision that will be examined below. Although the ego is in existence, it is fragile and weak and will require suitable environmental provision to develop in a healthy manner in relation to the id and the outside world. If done in a constructive fashion, the id impulses will strengthen the ego rather than overwhelm it.[42] This draws us back to exploring in more detail what a good enough facilitating environment entails in this stage of absolute dependence, and what the maturational processes consist of in the healthy development of the person as an integrated individual with a sense of self.

Prior to birth the mother, hopefully, is providing a suitable facilitating environment for her unborn child to develop in. In the immediate weeks following birth, the primary caregiver—usually the mother—continues to shoulder the main responsibility of providing this environment.[43] Winnicott was keen to stress that usually, the mother is instinctually able to carry out this role without much guidance or direction from health care professionals to the point where "doctors and nurses can make it their first duty not to interfere," and instead should offer "support-without-interference" as interference can cause problems for the child and mother.[44] He even suggested that psychiatrists, in the treatment of some patients, could learn from mothers in terms of how

40. Winnicott, "Depressive Position," 266.
41. Winnicott, "Ego Integration," 57.
42. Winnicott, "Capacity to Be Alone," 33–34.
43. For an overview of the role of the father in terms of environmental provision within Winnicott's work, see Abram, *Language of Winnicott*; and Reeves, "On the Margins." See also Winnicott, *Home*.
44. Winnicott, "Paediatrics and Psychiatry," 161–62.

they are able to provide a suitable environment and adapt to changing needs and circumstances.[45] Continuity of care by the same person is of the utmost importance for the healthy development of the child, meaning that Winnicott was concerned that newborns be kept with their mother as far as possible. We here see undertones of the influence of Darwin's work on Winnicott with particular regard to the mother's ability and instinct to adapt to the baby's needs to enable survival.[46] Winnicott labeled the initial intense experience of focus and adaption in the mother, "primary maternal pre-occupation" suggesting that it begins to occur during pregnancy and lasts for a few weeks after the birth. The nature of this experience for the mother is such that "this organized state (that would be an illness were it not for the fact of the pregnancy) could be compared with a withdrawn state, or a dissociated state, or a fugue, or even with a disturbance at a deeper level such as a schizoid episode in which some aspect of the personality takes over temporarily."[47] The mother, in this state of being, is temporarily focused on her baby to such a degree that interest in other activities and people is excluded. The mother is instinctually able to feel what the baby feels and in so doing seeks to discern and meet the various body and ego needs of the baby, enabling healthy development in the baby. The importance of mothers being able to provide this kind of care and attention is high as "the mother who develops this state . . . provides a setting for the infant's constitution to begin to make itself evident, for the developmental tendencies to start to unfold, and for the infant to experience spontaneous movement and become the owner of sensations that are appropriate to this early phase of life."[48]

Although the initial primary maternal preoccupation passes, the general instinct for adaption to need does not. Winnicott labeled the vast majority of mothers who are able and willing to instinctually continue to adapt to their children the "good enough mother." By this label Winnicott means one who "meets the omnipotence of the infant and to some extent makes sense of it. She does this repeatedly."[49] Winnicott is here describing the care the mother provides in this early stage in which she is able to discern, instinctively, the needs of the baby and offer continual adaptation to these physical and emotional needs. Doing

---

45. Winnicott, "Paediatrics and Psychiatry," 171.
46. For further exploration of this influence, see Phillips, *Winnicott*, 1–6.
47. Winnicott, "Primary Maternal Preoccupation," 302.
48. Winnicott, "Primary Maternal Preoccupation," 303.
49. Winnicott, "Ego Distortion," 145.

this repeatedly at such a fragile stage provides an "auxiliary ego"[50] for the baby's weak ego that gathers the experiences of the baby together in such a way that some sense of coherence is offered as a foundation for the baby to begin to experience integration and "unit status" whereby "the infant becomes a person, an individual in his own right."[51] When the mother responds and adapts in this way, "[a] True Self begins to have life, through the strength given to the infant's weak ego by the mother's implementation of the infant's omnipotent expressions."[52] The reference to omnipotence by Winnicott highlights the experience the baby has of being inseparable from the world and getting everything that is needed on demand at this point. Healthy development will require the child to gradually be exposed to reality in due course but, for now, the maintenance of this illusion of omnipotence is vital for the baby's experience of continuity and the strengthening of the ego.

Good enough mothers provide a good enough environment for their infant, meaning that such "environment provision in the earliest phase enables the infant to begin to exist, to have experience, to build a personal ego, to ride instincts, and to meet with all the difficulties inherent in life."[53] In the course of this phase of the mother-child relationship, "there comes into existence an ego-relatedness between mother and baby, from which the mother recovers, and out of which the infant may eventually build the idea of a person in the mother."[54] If the provision by the mother is good enough, the ego-relatedness at this stage of the relationship is what enables the "going on being" of the baby that will lead to healthy integration.[55] This going on being refers to the continuity of relatively uninterrupted adaptive care of the child provided by the good enough mother that enables integration of psyche and soma in time and

50. Winnicott, "Capacity for Concern," 75.
51. Winnicott, "Parent-Infant Relationship," 44.
52. Winnicott, "Ego Distortion," 145.
53. Winnicott, "Primary Maternal Preoccupation," 304.
54. Winnicott, "Primary Maternal Preoccupation," 304. For further discussion of the role of ego-relatedness by Winnicott, see "Capacity to Be Alone," 30–35; and Abram, *Language of Winnicott*, 42–43.
55. Jan Abram defines "ego-relatedness" as "the time when mother and baby are merged." She continues, "During this time of merger, when the baby sees the mother, he sees himself, and when the mother sees her infant, she remembers (unconsciously) her own early days and weeks, and this enables her to identify with her infant's needs, so that it is as if she sees herself. This is the mother in a state of primary maternal preoccupation." *Language of Winnicott*, 42.

space such that the ego develops, as does a sense of self "with a past, present, and future."[56] At this fragile stage, the provision of the mother also involves protecting the infant from anything that may impinge and interrupt the continuity of the going on being. Such impingements would require a reaction from the baby which, if too frequent and overwhelming, would lead to unhealthy defenses developing (more will be said about this below). Without this provision and protection, integration into a unit status would be very difficult.

In his thinking, Winnicott did not elevate mothers to the unreachable heights of perfection but instead characterized them as good enough in their adaptation and care to provide a good enough facilitating environment for the healthy maturation of their child. Even from the beginning, Winnicott suggested that where the good enough environment fell short of perfection the infant was able to bridge the gap: "The mental activity of the infant turns a *good-enough* environment into a perfect environment, that is to say, turns relative failure of adaptation into adaptive success."[57] As will become apparent when the experience of relative dependence is discussed below, the relative failure in adaptation will increase over time, but initially, the environment almost entirely cares for the infant who has, as yet, not reached an experience of integration and so cannot offer much in the way of self-care.

In the mother's adaptation to need, there are obvious requirements such as feeding and changing; however, what Winnicott has in mind when mapping out the details of the facilitating environment involves more than these regular functions. We here come to the importance in Winnicott's work of healthy "holding" that enables integration; "handling" of an infant that enables "personalization" and the role of "object presenting" that enables "object-relating."[58] The importance of good mirroring will also be briefly discussed. We begin with holding and integration.

Holding and Integration

As with other terms used by Winnicott, there is something obvious and self-explanatory about the place holding takes in terms of healthy provision for the baby. A baby that is held correctly is one who experiences a

---

56. Winnicott, "From Dependence Towards Independence," 86.
57. Winnicott, "Mind and Its Relation," 245.
58. Winnicott, "Ego Integration," 60.

sense of safety and comfort as their physical and psychological needs—as yet indistinguishable from each other—are met by the good enough mother. However, when Winnicott refers to holding, he appears to have in mind more than simply the physical act of cradling a baby in one's arms. "The term 'holding' is used here to denote not only the actual physical holding of the infant, but also the total environmental provision prior to the concept of *living with*" where "'living with' implies object relationships and the emergence of the infant from the state of being merged with the mother, or his perception of objects as external to the self."[59] Winnicott is here highlighting the totality of holding in the state of absolute dependence prior to the experience by the infant of a unified self, distinct from the outside world. The role of holding on the part of the mother involves physiological protection and a sensitivity to "touch, temperature, auditory sensitivity, visual sensitivity, sensitivity to falling (action of gravity) and of the infant's lack of knowledge of the existence of anything other than the self."[60] The care involved in holding includes twenty-four-hour-a-day provision and awareness of and adaptation to every changing need. Love from mother to infant is conveyed in this way and the "inherited potential" present in the infant becomes a "continuity of being" or "going on being" in the good enough holding environment. This provision, through protection and adaptation to need, made possible by the mother's natural instincts and ability to empathize with her infant in this state of ego-relatedness, forms the basis for the integration of the infant into unit status with an individual sense of self. The support to the fragile ego of the infant by the ego strength of the mother combined with the protection from impingement of the good enough holding environment facilitates the ego development of the individual and enables them to develop an ego strength that can control id-impulses. As the ego strength develops, the infant experiences an increasing number of periods of integration that gradually last for longer. This paves the way for the development of an awareness of the distinction between self and the outside world and between one's inner and outer world, that occurs in personalization.

---

59. Winnicott, "Parent-Infant Relationship," 43–44.
60. Winnicott, "Parent-Infant Relationship," 49.

Handling and Personalization

Winnicott states, "Handling describes the environmental provision that corresponds loosely with the establishment of a psycho-somatic partnership. Without good-enough active and adaptive handling the task from within may well prove heavy, indeed it may actually prove impossible for this development of a psycho-somatic inter-relationship to become properly established."[61] Handling, then, in Winnicott's framework is a specific aspect of holding where holding includes the broader environmental provision. The provision of good enough handling is that which lays the foundations for the infant to integrate the psyche and soma into a unified subject with an inner life and distinguish this unified self from the outside world. Winnicott elaborates, "The ego is based on a body ego, but it is only when all goes well that the person of the baby starts to be linked with the body and the body-functions, with the skin as the limiting membrane. I have used the term *personalization* to describe this process."[62] Elsewhere he states, "It is instinctual experience and the repeated quiet experiences of body-care that gradually build up what may be called satisfactory personalization."[63] In contrast, he gives the example: "If you have got a child's body and head in your hands and do not think of that as a unity, and reach for a handkerchief or something, then the head has gone back and the child is in two pieces—head and body; the child screams and never forgets it . . . . Then the child goes around with an absence of confidence in things."[64] Good enough handling therefore enables and encourages development into the individual psycho-somatic self that feels real and connected.

Object Presenting and Object Relating

Linked with the provision of suitable holding and handling, the mother also engages in the task of "object presenting" as part of creating a good enough facilitating environment for the infant. This object presenting will provide the basis for healthy object relating in due course.

As previously noted, in the stage of absolute dependence the infant, in the ego-related state with the mother, is unable to perceive the outside

61. Winnicott, "Ego Integration," 62.
62. Winnicott, "Ego Integration," 59.
63. Winnicott, "Primitive Emotional Development," 151.
64. Winnicott, *Home*, 145–46.

world as separate and other. The infant therefore experiences the illusion of omnipotence in which what is desired appears at the right moment and is present for the right amount of time. A challenge to the infant's perception of omnipotence at this point within the development of the infant would result in detrimental long-term consequences. To prevent such an outcome and maintain the illusion, the good enough mother presents the required objects, such as the breast, to the infant at just the right moment. It is worth quoting Winnicott at length here:

> The pattern is thus: the baby develops a vague expectation that has origin in an unformulated need. The adaptive mother presents an object or a manipulation that meets the baby's needs, and so the baby begins to need just that which the mother presents. In this way the baby comes to feel confident in being able to create objects and to create the actual world. The mother gives the baby a brief period in which omnipotence is a matter of experience.[65]

By this experience of omnipotence Winnicott means "more than magical control." Instead, the term includes "the creative aspect of experience."[66] As these experiences repeat, "the infant experiencing omnipotence under the aegis of the facilitating environment *creates and re-creates the object*, and the process gradually becomes built in, and gathers a memory backing."[67] Elsewhere Winnicott observes, "For this illusion to be produced in the baby's mind a human being has to be taking the trouble all the time to bring the world to the baby in understandable form, and in a limited way, suitable to the baby's needs."[68] Noting the importance of continuity of the environmental provision—including the one who is caring for the baby—he states, "Only on a basis of monotony can a mother profitably add richness."[69] This relating to objects in a subjective way involves creating rather than finding and enables the complex move from experiencing objects as subjects to relating to objects as objects, objectively perceived. This move is labeled "adaption to the reality principle" by Winnicott and others and will be discussed below when we explore the developments in the stage of relative dependence.[70]

65. Winnicott, "Ego Integration," 62.
66. Winnicott, "Communicating and Not Communicating," 180.
67. Winnicott, "Communicating and Not Communicating," 180.
68. Winnicott, "Primitive Emotional Development," 154.
69. Winnicott, "Primitive Emotional Development," 153.
70. Winnicott, "Communicating and Not Communicating," 180.

Mirroring

For Winnicott, one of the roles of the mother in this early stage is that of mirroring. Jan Abram notes of Winnicott's understanding of this: "His main thesis is that in order to look creatively and see the world, the individual must first of all have internalized the experience of having been seen."[71] During this stage, when the baby looks at the mother's face Winnicott suggests that "what the baby sees is himself or herself."[72] He continues, "In other words the mother is looking at the baby and *what she looks like is related to what she sees there*."[73] What should be happening in healthy development is "apperception," "the term Winnicott gave to the infant's subjective experience of merger with mother."[74] This enables seeing oneself through the process of first experiencing being seen by the mother. Apperception prevents the need for the ego to develop too fast into the stage of perception where perception "refers to the ability to see whole objects, which is the ability to differentiate between Me and Not-me."[75] As will be noted in the section on pathology toward the end of this chapter, forcing the ego to develop too fast by not good enough mirroring leads to problems with the healthy development of the self. Winnicott described the process of growth and interaction with the outside world by way of good mirroring as follows:

> When I look I am seen, so I exist.
>
> I can now afford to look and see.
>
> I now look creatively and what I apperceive I also perceive.
>
> In fact I take care not to see what is not there to be seen (unless I am tired).[76]

Here we see the movement that good mirroring enables toward healthy engagement with the outside world. More will be said about the development of this engagement as we proceed.

Although the illusion of omnipotence in this stage of absolute dependence as enabled by the good enough mother is beneficial to the baby

---

71. Abram, *Language of Winnicott*, 239.
72. Winnicott, *Playing and Reality*, 112.
73. Winnicott, *Playing and Reality*, 112.
74. Abram, *Language of Winnicott*, 240.
75. Abram, *Language of Winnicott*, 240.
76. Winnicott, *Playing and Reality*, 114.

to begin with, in Winnicott's framework, healthy maturation requires the infant to experience disillusion resulting in relative dependence as the adaptation to need begins to fail in a healthy way. As the mother begins to establish a regained sense of independence a change starts to occur in how the mother adapts to the infant as the relationship shifts to the experience of relative dependence.

Relative Dependence

Regarding the change in stages Winnicott states, "Just as I call the first stage 'absolute dependence,' so I call the next stage 'relative dependence.' In this way one can distinguish between dependence that is quite beyond the infant's ken, and dependence that the infant can know about."[77] The initial extent of adaptation to need enables the baby to retain the illusion of omnipotence in order to not be overwhelmed at such a fragile point in the development of the ego. However, as the baby grows in ego strength and develops a unified psycho-somatic sense of self, healthy maturation requires the ability to distinguish one's inner and outer world, to distinguish me and not-me in terms of perception of objects in the outside world, and to be able to relate to and use objects in a suitable way. For this to occur, the mother begins to fail in adaptation to need—what Winnicott refers to as "graduated de-adaptation"—to enable this awareness to develop, meaning the infant encounters an experience of relative dependence with disillusionment as a temporary consequence.[78] Winnicott describes this stage as "a stage of adaptation with a gradual failing of adaptation" and it occurs from roughly six months old to two years old.[79] However, it is important to note that gradual failure, under healthy conditions, does not compromise the caring and necessary provision that the baby requires. "The infant can only find an unmuddled presentation of external reality by being cared for by a human being who is devoted to the infant and to the infant-care task."[80] But, we need to examine in greater detail what is occurring at this stage of development and why. To delve more deeply into this stage, we turn to explore various aspects of development in Winnicott's theories that

---

77. Winnicott, "From Dependence Towards Independence," 87.
78. Winnicott, "From Dependence Towards Independence," 87.
79. Winnicott, "From Dependence Towards Independence," 87.
80. Winnicott, "From Dependence Towards Independence," 88.

do not necessarily occur sequentially but overlap in the stage of relative dependence. We begin with one of Winnicott's most well-known areas of work, Transitional Objects and Object Usage.

Transitional Objects and Object Usage

In the previous stage of absolute dependence, object presenting was discussed as a way that the good enough mother continues to maintain the necessary illusion of omnipotence for the infant. Object relating at that stage involved, for the infant, experiencing the object as a subjective object, created by the infant and part of the infant. With continuing good enough provision leading to developing ego-strength and a unified sense of self, a transition begins in how objects are related to by the infant that moves the infant toward perceiving objects as objects, objectively (although Winnicott suggests this transition is never completed!). Winnicott notes this to be a shift from the pleasure principle to the reality principle as gratification in the meeting of needs gives way to the perception of reality that is not within the infant's complete control, thus bursting the omnipotence bubble. It is within this process of change in perception of, and relation to, reality that Winnicott developed his theory of the transitional object.

It is important to note at this point that although the "transitional *object*" is most famously associated with Winnicott, his thinking on the matter was actually broader than just objects and also included transitional phenomena, such as a song or rhyme. Of this area of his work Winnicott explains,

> I have introduced the terms "transitional object" and "transitional phenomena" for designation of the intermediate area of experience, between the thumb and the teddy bear, between the oral erotism and true object relationship, between primary creative activity and projection of what has already been introjected, between primary unawareness of indebtedness and the acknowledgement of indebtedness ("Say: ta!").[81]

In short, Winnicott is exploring the experience of the intermediate area between the subjective and objective perception of the outside world by the infant, and the objects and phenomena that are related to in that area to aid in navigating the transition. The phenomena and objects included

---

81. Winnicott, "Transitional Objects," 230.

here are "an infant's babbling or the way an older child goes over a repertoire of songs and tunes while preparing for sleep . . . along with the use made of objects that are not part of the infant's body yet are not fully recognized as belonging to external reality."[82] The focus here is not the first object an infant relates to but the first object that is possessed by the infant in the experience of the intermediate area.

The transitional objects and phenomena noted by Winnicott are drawn into the infant's patterns of behavior as "not-me" objects over the course of time. Although they symbolize the breast to some extent, the value lies as much in the actuality to the infant of it *not* being the breast. The journey is taking place away from pure subjectivity in perception to one of objective engagement with the world and the transitional phenomena provide a window into this journey. Transitional phenomena are perceived neither as internal objects completely within the control of the infant nor objects in the outside world beyond the control of the infant. Instead, they occupy the intermediate space and can be manipulated by the infant. However, their worth is only present while there is the good internal object, which is dependent, in turn, on the provision of the good external object—the breast, mother, and general good enough environment. As the mother gradually fails in adaptation—in a healthy way—thus disillusioning the infant, the transitional phenomena fill the intermediate area between that which is subjective and that which is objective, between the pleasure and reality principles, in an experience of reality-testing. In the absence of near-perfect adaptation in the stage of absolute dependence, the infant draws on transitional phenomena to fill the area of illusion that is being opened up by intended failure in adaptation. This means that transitional phenomena will already be present in the infant's patterns of behavior before reality testing occurs but take on this new role as adaptation starts to fail. The phenomena will be something that offers properties that seem "to show it has vitality or reality of its own."[83] It cannot be changed unless by the infant and must be able to survive the love and aggression which may be visited upon it. Although it is not perceived to be external to the infant, neither is it a hallucination from within. This paradox of the intermediate area that navigates the ground between subjectivity and objectivity is not to be questioned by others but simply is, in the process of reality testing for the

---

82. Winnicott, "Transitional Objects," 230.
83. Winnicott, "Transitional Objects," 233.

infant, and this is an ongoing experience into and through adulthood. For Winnicott, this process ties in with weaning, which must occur to enable the development of a healthy relationship with the outside world but must also, as a microcosm of the wider failure in adaptation, occur progressively over time. A benefit of the transitional object for the infant is in its ability to ward off the anxiety that the infant may experience in the process of disillusionment. At some point in the development of the child, transitional objects and phenomena will lose their meaning to the child as the realm of illusion that the transitional object or phenomena occupy is taken up by aspects of culture more broadly.

As the infant transitions away from the realm of primary narcissism and the pleasure principle, employing transitional objects to enable this, there is also the development of the capacity for object usage by the infant. This is crucial for healthy engagement with the outside world, but it must be noted that when Winnicott refers to using an object, he does not mean "exploitation."[84] Instead, what is intended by the word "use" is the ability to perceive the not-me world as such and to interact with it.

The development of the capacity to use an object followed by the ensuing usage is dependent on the prior stage of object-relating as well as the ongoing good enough facilitating environment. Winnicott notes, "When I speak of the use of an object . . . I take object-relating for granted, and add new features that involve the nature and the behaviour of the object. For instance, the object, if it is to be used, must necessarily be real in the sense of being part of shared reality, not a bundle of projections."[85] He further states that "to use an object the subject must have developed a *capacity* to use objects."[86] The development of this capacity as part of healthy maturation must not be presumed to naturally occur but instead is dependent on the good enough care of the facilitating environment and provides the possibility of object usage. "This thing that there is in between relating and use is the subject's placing of the object outside the area of the subject's omnipotent control; that is, the subject's perception of the object as an external phenomenon, not as a projective entity, in fact recognition of it as an entity in its own right."[87] This capacity to use an object develops through the infant's attempts to destroy something that they perceive as not-me. At this stage, the

---

84. Winnicott, *Playing and Reality*, 94.
85. Winnicott, *Playing and Reality*, 88.
86. Winnicott, *Playing and Reality*, 89.
87. Winnicott, *Playing and Reality*, 89.

infant relates to objects as that which are external to them yet created by them. At some point, the infant then attempts to exercise their perceived power to destroy such an object. This enables the development of the capacity to use objects because the object is not destroyed and instead survives the attempts at destruction. With this comes a new experience for the infant: "The subject says to the object: 'I destroyed you,' and the object is there to receive the communication. From now on the subject says: 'Hullo object!' 'I destroyed you.' 'I love you.' 'You have value for me because of your survival of my destruction of you.' 'While I am loving you I am all the time destroying you in (unconscious) *fantasy*' . . . . The subject can now *use* the object that has survived."[88] It is worth noting here that, in Winnicott's theory, the object must do more than survive— "It is important that 'survive,' in this context, means 'not retaliate.'"[89] The object can now be perceived as having a life of its own and, having survived and not retaliated, can contribute to the life of the subject in relevant ways. It is the survival and non-retaliatory response of the object here that is crucial for the development of the capacity to use objects and the resulting usage. This is particularly important when the object in question is a person—such as the mother or therapist—or part of a person—such as the mother's breast. The object can now be used due to the strengthening sense of "object-constancy" made possible by the reality of surviving, while in fantasy always being destroyed.[90]

Objects gain a fresh sense of value for the infant through this process, which must also include people. Although inanimate objects are often first recalled when exploring the subject of object usage, Winnicott includes people within this bracket, whether that is the mother or the therapist in later life. As a child, the infant may attempt to destroy what it initially perceives to be the self-created breast as object. The mother's ability to neither be destroyed nor retaliate enables healthy development because survival results in the infant developing the capacity to relate to objects and people in a new way and use them, and non-retaliation results in the infant being able to progress in the development of the True Self. More will be said below about Winnicott's theory of the True and False Self but suffice it to say here that when a child or client tests the safety and care of the holding environment, in order for healthy maturation to continue, that environment must not react in a

88. Winnicott, *Playing and Reality*, 90.
89. Winnicott, *Playing and Reality*, 91.
90. Winnicott, *Playing and Reality*, 93.

way that would be detrimental to that maturation. The analogy holds in the therapeutic environment where the client may test the safety and care of that environment. In this setting, the therapist must attempt to provide a continuity of safe care rather than retaliating in a way that might further fuel a False Self in the client.

Aggression, Erotism, and Fusion

When Winnicott speaks of erotic impulses and aggressive impulses in the stage prior to integration, there is a lack of clarity in his work regarding exactly what he means. In his earlier work what he appears to have in mind is the impulse for need fulfillment in the case of the erotic and the impulse of spontaneous motility and energy in the case of the aggressive. This latter becomes aggressive when spontaneous movement is met with resistance. In the good enough environment, the erotic impulse is met with adaptive provision that brings a sense of fulfillment. In the case of the aggressive impulse, there is a level of resistance provided that does not cross over into impingement in order for the infant to experience the outside world and a sense of being alive. When this good enough environment is provided, there is a natural fusion of aggressive and erotic impulses whereby "that which is fused with the erotic potential is satisfied in instinctual gratification" with the excess of the aggressive impulse directed toward "appropriate opposition."[91]

This fusion appears to take place prior to reaching what he terms the "Stage of Concern" (see below). In the "Pre-Concern" stage, "the child can be said to exist as a person and to have purpose, yet to be unconcerned as to results."[92] Winnicott saw no need to mention sadism, hate, or envy at this point, contra Klein, as the infant has no capacity to experience such emotions prior to the stage of concern. These feelings, along with anger and the desire to destroy, for Winnicott, develop later and are signs of emotional growth. Winnicott suggests, "Destruction only becomes an ego responsibility when there is ego integration and ego organization sufficient for the existence of anger, and therefore of fear of the talion."[93]

However, in a later paper on "The Capacity for Concern" Winnicott credits Freud with the origin of the theory of fusion in which "the

---

91. Winnicott, "Aggression," 212.
92. Winnicott, "Aggression," 206.
93. Winnicott, "Aggression," 210.

baby experiences erotic and aggressive drives towards the same object at the same time."[94] Here Winnicott suggests that "on the erotic side there is both satisfaction-seeking and object-seeking, and on the aggressive side, there is a complex of anger employing muscle erotism, and of hate, which involves the retention of a good object-imago for comparison."[95] What is noteworthy here is that Winnicott seems to uncritically take on Freud's belief in the presence of hate and anger, which, in Winnicott's schema, the infant does not yet experience. Winnicott also notes that "in the whole aggressive-destructive impulse is contained a primitive type of object relationship in which love involves destruction."[96] Although there appears to be a lack of clarity here, Winnicott seems able to name that and move on stating, "Some of this is necessarily obscure, and I do not need to know all about the origin of aggression in order to follow my argument, because I am taking it for granted that the baby has become able to combine erotic and aggressive experience, and in relation to one object. Ambivalence has been reached."[97]

This latter point seems to suggest that the later description of fusion based on Freud occurs in the process of gaining the capacity for concern—hence the note about the achievement of ambivalence. One way to resolve the apparent contradiction of when fusion takes place and what it involves is to draw on a point made by Winnicott about maturation processes more generally. He states, "Indeed most of the processes that start up in early infancy are never fully established, and continue to be strengthened by the growth that continues in later childhood, and indeed in adult life, even in old age."[98] It is therefore possible that the fusion Winnicott is describing continues to happen at different degrees approaching and beyond the stage of concern.

Confusion aside, what Winnicott seems to conclude is that unit status has been achieved, there is a growing sense of me/not-me and the existence of an inner and outside world, and the mother is perceived as a single whole object to relate to in an objective way. There is also the ability to experience fantasies of ambivalence as an elaboration of the body-function experience. There is a sense of a psychosomatic self that has gained in ego strength and relies less on the auxiliary ego of the mother. It

94. Winnicott, "Capacity for Concern," 74.
95. Winnicott, "Capacity for Concern," 74.
96. Winnicott, "Capacity for Concern," 74.
97. Winnicott, "Capacity for Concern," 74–75.
98. Winnicott, "Capacity for Concern," 73–74.

is the "enrichment and refinement" of the "achievement of ambivalence" which will bring about the stage of concern.[99]

Winnicott notes that in Klein's work, she entitled the stage of concern the "Depressive Stage."[100] For Winnicott this occurs typically between six to twelve months old and "to reach the depressive position a baby must have become established as a whole person, and to be related to whole persons as a whole person" (Winnicott here includes the breast or body of the mother as a whole person).[101] The situation Winnicott describes is of "a whole human baby, and the mother holding the situation, enabling the child to work through certain processes."[102] Winnicott was keen to change the name of this stage because he suggested that the term "depressive" could confuse what was occurring in this process with the experience of depression, which was not what the stage referred to. For Winnicott, "concern" more accurately describes what is developing. As the experience of ambivalence is encountered in which aggressive-destructive and erotic impulses are fused and directed at a single object—the mother—"Concern refers to the fact that the individual *cares*, or *minds*, and both feels and accepts responsibility."[103]

Exploration of this stage aimed to address the question of how a shift in the infant from an experience of "pre-ruth to ruth" occurs.[104] To do this Winnicott noted his belief that prior to this stage being reached the infant holds a perception of two mothers—"the mother of the quiet phases, and the mother used and even attacked at the instinctual climax."[105] In his later work, he refers to these as "the environment-mother" and the "object-mother" respectively.[106] According to Winnicott's theories what is happening to the infant as the stage of concern is encountered is recognition that these two mothers are in fact one and there "is the beginning of the recognition of the existence of ideas, fantasy, imaginative elaboration of function, the acceptance of ideas and of fantasy related to fact but not to be confused with fact."[107]

99. Winnicott, "Capacity for Concern," 75.
100. Winnicott, "Depressive Position."
101. Winnicott, "Depressive Position," 264.
102. Winnicott, "Depressive Position," 264.
103. Winnicott, "Capacity for Concern," 73.
104. Winnicott, "Depressive Position," 265.
105. Winnicott, "Depressive Position," 267.
106. Winnicott, "Capacity for Concern," 75.
107. Winnicott, "Depressive Position," 267.

The object-mother is on the receiving end of the post-fusion attacks driven by the id instinct while the infant attacks and destroys the mother in fantasy. "It is not only that the baby imagines that he eats the object, but also that the baby wants to take possession of the contents of the object."[108] The mother must survive this attack and not retaliate but instead remain constant in quiet times as the environment-mother. The mother's consistent holding as this cycle is repeated numerous times enables the infant to unite the two mothers into one and begin to distinguish fact from fantasy as inner reality is separated from outer reality.

Upon achieving this uniting of the two mothers there occurs anxiety at the prospect of losing the mother by consuming her. With the survival of the environment-mother, there comes the opportunity for reparation by the child, which the mother remains present to receive. This possibility enables the anxiety to be held at bay and transformed into a feeling of guilt. What Winnicott also suggests occurs is the realization that the survival of the mother to receive reparative contributions means, for the infant, that they can be freer with their instinctual life. The repetition of this cycle of attack and reparation, all the time held by the consistent care of the mother, results in the development of the capacity for concern. "The infant is now becoming able to be concerned, to take responsibility for his own instinctual impulses and the functions that belong to them."[109] At this point, the mother's keeping of time with her auxiliary ego starts to become redundant as time becomes part of the infant's integrated self.

Why Babies Cry

In *The Child, the Family, and the Outside World*, Winnicott dedicates a chapter to answering the question, "why do babies cry?"[110] It may seem out of place to discuss this topic here rather than in the pathology section below; however, such a thought betrays the approach that presumes crying is a sign of something being wrong. Of course, there is some truth in that but what I wish to highlight here is that, for Winnicott, there is something inherently healthy about a baby's ability to cry and them using that ability.

---

108. Winnicott, "Capacity for Concern," 76.
109. Winnicott, "Capacity for Concern," 77.
110. Winnicott, *Child*, 58–68.

In total, Winnicott lists five kinds of crying. The main focus of the chapter is on crying that is to do with "satisfaction," "pain," "rage," and "grief." Mention of the fifth kind of crying is made at the very end and is labeled as "the crying of hopelessness and despair." Winnicott further notes of this kind that it is "the crying that other kinds break down into if there is no hope left in the baby's mind."[111] This kind would rightly be better placed in the pathology section, but the remaining four display healthy development in the infant.

With the first Winnicott notes the satisfaction and excitement that comes from some crying. He suggests, "We have to recognize that pleasure enters into crying as it does into the exercise of any bodily function, so that a certain amount of crying can sometimes be said to be satisfactory for the infant, whereas less than that amount would not have been enough."[112] The second kind, in contrast, is quite different. "The cry of pain is not in itself pleasurable to the infant and no one would think it was, because it immediately awakes in the people around the urge to do something about it."[113] This may be due to pain being experienced at that moment—and Winnicott includes hunger in that—or it may be due to fear of anticipated pain from prior memory, such as when a nappy change is due that will involve being taken out of warm, comfortable clothes. Again, this kind of crying is a sign of health in the sense that the infant's warning system is working, and they are growing in memory and somatic awareness.

The third kind of crying is also a sign of health and will be particularly important as this project develops. In the event of inevitable frustration, the infant will cry due to anger or rage. For Winnicott, this is a sign of hope because this angry crying suggests that the infant still believes something can be done to alleviate the cause of anger. "A baby who has lost belief does not get angry, he just stops wanting, or else he cries in a miserable, disillusioned way, or else he starts banging with his head on the pillow, or on the wall or the floor, or else he exploits the various things he can do with his body."[114] For Winnicott, a baby who can experience the full range of his rage, including destructive tendencies, is a healthy one. The good response to this is to continue with calm care and survive without retaliation. As discussed above, such a setup in

---

111. Winnicott, *Child*, 67.
112. Winnicott, *Child*, 59.
113. Winnicott, *Child*, 60.
114. Winnicott, *Child*, 62.

terms of the infant and the environment enables healthy object relations and usage by way of the me/not-me differential, as well as enabling the development of the capacity for concern. With regard to the result of not offering this kind of provision in childhood, Winnicott suggests of adults, "Some people go about the world terrified of losing their tempers, afraid of what would have happened if they had experienced rage to the fullest extent when they were infants."[115] Although Winnicott does not address it here, one would also assume from other parts of his work that environmental failure here is a contributing factor to lack of fusion between aggressive and erotic roots.

The fourth kind of crying is to do with grief. Here Winnicott notes how well adults have mastered the art of containing the emotions experienced as babies. He states, "We grown-ups, although we value these intense feelings of our infancy, and like to re-capture them at chosen times, have learned long since how to defend ourselves from being at the mercy of almost unbearable feelings, such as we were liable to as babies."[116] This can result in fear of feelings that in turn leads to not being able to engage with emotional depth. Potentially, this curtails loving others to any great length and with any great richness. As with crying due to rage, crying due to sadness or grief is a sign of emotional development and health. However, sad crying differs in a number of ways. One of these ways is the sound, which Winnicott thinks "has a musical note in it."[117] He continues, "Some people think that sad crying is one of the main roots of the more valuable kind of music."[118] This crying will likely evolve into a kind of singing that aids in getting to sleep. The production of tears is also more associated with sad crying than with rage.

Sad crying initially involves the feeling of responsibility for everything that is happening to the infant. Over time, however, the infant will work out where responsibility for different aspects of the environmental provision lies. The ability of sad crying suggests a development beyond the cause of crying due to satisfaction, pain, or rage. The significant difference with sad crying is the developed ability to take responsibility, which suggests the stage of concern has been reached. Good care at this point involves continued love while the infant naturally recovers from the sadness that may also contain guilt. Winnicott reminds his readers,

115. Winnicott, *Child*, 62.
116. Winnicott, *Child*, 63.
117. Winnicott, *Child*, 64.
118. Winnicott, *Child*, 64.

"Remember that there is no better feeling in infancy or childhood than that which belongs to true spontaneous recovery from sadness and guilt feelings."[119]

The Capacity to Be Alone

Winnicott understood the capacity to be alone as a sign of maturity in emotional development. However, what he had in mind was not to do with being physically alone as such but rather the capacity to be alone as an individual with a personal life, yet related to the outside world. He notes, "A person may be in solitary confinement, and yet not be able to be alone."[120] For this capacity to develop in healthy maturation, the paradox of being alone in the presence of another must be experienced. In Winnicott's theory, this most likely occurs "*as an infant and small child, in the presence of mother.*"[121] This experience begins in the state of "ego-relatedness" in which, as previously noted, from the infant's perspective, the infant and mother are merged together. The provision of the good-enough environment including adaptation to need results in a building up of "belief in a benign environment" such that unit status is achieved, and good objects are internalized and "are available for projection at a suitable moment."[122] Of particular note for the ego strength of the infant is the introjection of the "ego-supportive mother" that enables the infant "to be alone without frequent reference to the mother or mother symbol."[123] Ogden here helpfully clarifies that what is internalized is "not the mother as object, but the mother as environment."[124] This capacity to be alone in the presence of another leads to being able to experience unintegration (infant) or relaxation (adult) where it is "possible to exist for a time without being either a reactor to an external impingement or an active person with direction of interest or movement."[125] In such a setting the infant is able to have id-impulse experiences that feel personal and real and can be received by the mother as object. "A large number of

---

119. Winnicott, *Child*, 67.
120. Winnicott, "Capacity to Be Alone," 30.
121. Winnicott, "Capacity to Be Alone," 30.
122. Winnicott, "Capacity to Be Alone," 32.
123. Winnicott, "Capacity to Be Alone," 32.
124. Ogden, "Mother," 55.
125. Winnicott, "Capacity to Be Alone," 34.

such experiences form the basis for a life that has reality in it instead of futility."[126] The introjection of the environment means that in the course of time, one is able to be alone in the way described without needing anyone present, yet continue to have real and personal experiences and feel there is always someone else there.

Playing

We here need to make mention of Winnicott's approach to play. The reason why discussion of play comes at this point is its link in Winnicott's work to object-relating, transitional phenomena, and the capacity to be alone. It is in the intermediate space that is neither inside, nor external, yet outside the infant, that play takes place, and play for Winnicott is fundamental to healthy existence in various realms of life. Covering this broad impact of the capacity to play, he states, "*It is play that is the universal*, and that belongs to health: playing facilitates growth and therefore health; playing leads into group relationships; playing can be a form of communication in psychotherapy; and, lastly, psychoanalysis has been developed as a highly specialized form of playing in the service of communication with oneself and others."[127]

Following the descriptions of the development of object-relating and the use of transitional phenomena above, including the intermediate space that opens up between the infant and the outside world, we can add the development of the ability to play to the descriptions of what is occurring in healthy development. Where the infant continues to experience omnipotence due to the mother's adaptation and provision, in his later work Winnicott labels this space "an intermediate playground," explaining that "I call this a playground because play starts here. The playground is a potential space between the mother and the baby or joining mother and baby."[128] This play is exciting for the infant because of the precarious nature of the interaction between the infant's inner world and the control exerted over objects. The ability to play develops because of the good enough mother's continuing, reliable provision.

The next stage in the development of play in the healthy infant's life relates to Winnicott's work on the capacity to be alone. In healthy

126. Winnicott, "Capacity to Be Alone," 34.
127. Winnicott, *Playing and Reality*, 41.
128. Winnicott, *Playing and Reality*, 47.

development of the capacity to be alone, Winnicott adds the ability to play alone, yet in the presence of someone else. With the continuing provision of the mother, this enables the introjection of the environment such that the infant progresses to being able to play in the presence of another even when it is the memory of the other, in their absence, that is relied on.

The final stage of playing involves the mother introducing her own play into the infant's. Here "she finds that babies vary according to their capacity to like or dislike the introduction of ideas that are not their own."[129] It is this process that enables infants to progress from "playing to shared playing, and from this to cultural experiences."[130]

The True Self

Although the development of the True Self is something Winnicott is well known for advocating in his work, he offers very little in way of detailed description regarding what this might look like in an individual. Instead, he seems to suggest that this is what will naturally develop in one who has experienced a healthy facilitating environment resulting in healthy maturational processes. Although he never explicitly makes the connection, Winnicott's notion of the True Self appears synonymous with descriptions of a healthy ego and finds greater definition in contrast to the more detailed descriptions of the False Self, discussed below. He states, "A True Self begins to have life, through the strength given to the infant's weak ego by the mother's implementation of the infant's omnipotent expressions."[131] We see here that Winnicott draws us back to the importance of the provision of the good enough mother in the development of the True Self. Offering some description of its activity, he notes the primary rather than reactive nature of the True Self whereby it "comes from the aliveness of the body tissues and the working of body-functions, including the heart's action and breathing."[132] The True Self is "the summation of sensori-motor aliveness" and is the source of spontaneity and creativity that can use symbols in the intermediate space and feel real.[133]

---

129. Winnicott, *Playing and Reality*, 48.
130. Winnicott, *Playing and Reality*, 51.
131. Winnicott, "Ego Distortion," 145.
132. Winnicott, "Ego Distortion," 148.
133. Winnicott, "Ego Distortion," 149.

The above sections offer overlapping windows into Winnicott's theories of the healthy unfolding of important processes in infants. As has also been noted above, the stage of relative dependence is not the final destination in Winnicott's thinking. This instead may be labeled as "toward independence."

Toward In(ter)dependence

As already noted in this chapter, Winnicott characteristically provides the paradox of suggesting that the movement of healthy development is toward independence while also suggesting that such a conclusion is actually unhealthy—preferring interdependence—and unobtainable. However, once development through the stages of absolute and relative dependence has occurred the direction of travel continues toward independence. Winnicott describes this stage in the following way: "The infant develops means for doing without actual care. This is accomplished through the accumulation of memories of care, the projection of personal needs and the introjection of care details, with the development of confidence in the environment. Here must be added the element of intellectual understanding with its tremendous implications."[134] Elsewhere he notes in more detail the overlap between the various stages as the move is made away from dependence toward independence.[135] What is particularly important to highlight is that if the environmental provision has been good enough in the stages of dependence, the child will be in a strong position to navigate environmental failures at a later point due to the good internalized environment that is carried forward. There is also the expectation that relationships and social groups will be engaged with in a healthy way "without too great a loss of personal impulse and originality, and without too much loss of the destructive and aggressive impulses that have, presumably, found satisfactory expression in displaced forms."[136] The child is able to move in the space of society because there is something familiar about it from the internal patterns that have been building up in the course of the previous stages. "In ever-widening circles of social life the child is identified with society, because local society is a sample of truly

---

134. Winnicott, "Parent-Infant Relationship," 46.
135. Winnicott, "Providing for the Child," 66–67.
136. Winnicott, "Providing for the Child," 66–67.

external phenomena."[137] Winnicott describes reaching adulthood as having typical experiences such as finding one's place in society, marriage, and "some pattern that is a compromise between copying the parents and defiantly establishing a personal identity."[138] However, even with healthy development, let alone where there have been failures in provision, there is a strong possibility that situations will be encountered that overwhelm the resources of the individual. We here return to the heart of this work in thinking through what Winnicott's work might contribute to healthy development of the True Christlike Self, what that might mean for remaking in the aftermath of traumatizing experiences, and what the role of the church is within that process. Bringing Vanhoozer's voice back into the conversation, it is this we begin to turn to in the next chapter. To better prepare us for that we must also explore what pathological development looks like in Winnicott's work.

Pathological Development

Thus far we have explored Winnicott's theories of healthy development in early childhood and the facilitating environment and provision that enables the various maturational processes to occur. However, it is important to turn our attention to a brief exploration of the consequences when there are failures in provision. Engagement with this in the following chapters will aid with informing what poor care from church communities might look like, and the consequences, with a view to improving practice.

What may be noted from the exploration thus far in this chapter is the utmost priority, in the healthy early development of a child, of the provision of a good enough environment, including the good enough mother. Unsurprisingly then, the root cause of most issues in healthy maturation, in Winnicott's theories, is due to some sort of failure in this provision.

As already noted, although good holding and handling are quite literal in the early stages, they retain importance throughout development but change in definition to include a more analogical sense. When there is not good enough holding and handling any number of problems can occur depending on when the failure takes place and for how long.

---

137. Winnicott, "From Dependence Towards Independence," 91.
138. Winnicott, "From Dependence Towards Independence," 92.

When the infant is in the stage of absolute dependence, the provision of the mother is what keeps impingements to the going on being of the infant at bay. "Maternal failures produce phases of reaction to impingement and these reactions interrupt the 'going on being' of the infant. An excess of this reacting produces not frustration but a *threat of annihilation*."[139] It is possible that in later stages of development where the threat of annihilation is encountered due to gradual healthy failure in adaptation, but there is repeated recovery, this can produce ego organization that is able to cope with frustration. However, "the mother's failure to adapt in the earliest phase does not produce anything but an annihilation of the infant's self."[140] In response to such a threat, the True Self employs defense mechanisms that manifest in the construction of a False Self, which will be discussed below.[141] One such mechanism is that of disintegration. Noted above in the exploration of healthy development was the place of unintegration (as the infant equivalent of adult relaxation) in the presence of the ego support of the mother. When unintegration is experienced in the absence of the mother's ego support the result is the defense mechanism of disintegration. Winnicott describes this as "a defence that is an active production of chaos in defence against unintegration in the absence of maternal ego-support, that is, against the unthinkable or archaic anxiety that results from failure of holding in the stage of absolute dependence."[142] Although disintegration may not sound like much of a defense, a significant factor in its use is that it is created by and within the control of the infant rather than being left to the mercy of the environment for provision.

Overlapping with Winnicott's description of disintegration as a defense is the mention of depersonalization and dissociation. In the case of the former, where good handling in infancy enables good psyche-soma integration in the form of personalization, failure in good "body-care" results in depersonalization.[143] For Winnicott, where de-

---

139. Winnicott, "Primary Maternal Preoccupation," 303.

140. Winnicott, "Primary Maternal Preoccupation," 304.

141. Winnicott also links early impingement to the development of particular mental health issues (see "Psychoses and Child Care" and "Ego Integration"). However, it is beyond the scope of this author's field of knowledge and beyond the scope of this project to discuss such suggestions with any rigor or depth.

142. Winnicott, "Ego Integration," 61.

143. Winnicott, "Primitive Emotional Development," 150–51.

personalization is a threat, a form of psycho-somatic illness may result as a defense against that threat.[144]

Dissociation is also a result of "integration being incomplete or partial."[145] This presents as a splitting off of sections of the individual that manifest as separate entities. One such example is seen when there is a failure in the fusion of aggressive and erotic impulses. Winnicott is realistic about the task of fusion noting that "even in health it is an uncompleted task, and that it is very common to find large quantities of unfused aggression complicating the psychopathology of an individual who is being analysed."[146] However, if the level of impingement is too great during the stage when fusion should be taking place leading to the capacity for concern, or the mother does not "survive" the attacks, then there is a failure in fusion. The result of this is that concern cannot be felt, and the individual develops a False Self in which there is the erotic part and the aggressive part, un-fused. The former part does not feel real because of the lack of an aggressive component and the latter part, although feeling real, is ruthless, having never reached the stage of concern. In addition, the experience of excessive impingement that has required a reaction by the infant producing the lack of fusion means that, for the aggressive component to feel real, it needs opposition and persecution and so looks for this. However, "this represents a false mode of development since the infant needs continued persecution."[147]

A further defense mechanism that may be activated against the anxieties that occur in emotional development is the "manic defence." Here Winnicott draws on Klein's work to detail a defense against acknowledging and facing painful inner realities by denial of those realities and turning to either alternative inner fantasies or external reality. As Winnicott explains, the characteristics of the manic defense "are omnipotent manipulation or control and contemptuous devaluation."[148] Although some sense of manic defense can be healthy, it is largely problematic.[149]

In contrast to the defense mechanisms that result from poor adaptation to need regarding lack of provision, there is also the possibility of unhealthy mechanisms forming to respond to a lack of suitable

---

144. Winnicott, "Ego Integration," 62.
145. Winnicott, "Primitive Emotional Development," 151.
146. Winnicott, "Aggression," 214.
147. Winnicott, "Aggression," 217.
148. Winnicott, "Manic Defence," 132.
149. Winnicott, "Manic Defence."

separation at the right time. If the mother adapts too well to the infant's needs, thus not offering the child the experience of manageable frustration to enable the me/not-me differential to be discovered, then two options are available: "either being in a permanent state of regression and of being merged with the mother, or else staging a total rejection of the mother, even the seemingly good mother."[150]

Before discussing the formulation of the False Self, it is important to briefly note issues relating to what Winnicott refers to as the "anti-social tendency." Although this subject relates to slightly older children than has been the focus in this chapter and the majority of Winnicott's work, the roots of anti-social behavior are traced back to some level of deprivation in infancy. Connecting with the work of John Bowlby, Winnicott suggests that where there is anti-social behavior present, this is actually a sign of hope. The reason for suggesting this is that Winnicott believed that such behavior was a sign of seeking after something healthy and necessary that was lost during infancy. In one particular paper, Winnicott focuses on acts of stealing and destructiveness specifically as two dominant trends in anti-social behavior. He suggests,

> By *one* trend the child looking for something, somewhere, and failing to find it seeks it elsewhere, when hopeful. By the *other* the child is seeking that amount of environmental stability which will stand the strain resulting from impulsive behaviour. This is a search for an environmental provision that has been lost, a human attitude, which, because it can be relied on, gives freedom to the individual to move and to act and to get excited.[151]

Inevitably, the behavior develops because of an unhealthy failure in environmental provision at a crucial point in the infant's development.

The False Self

Winnicott famously develops the notion of the False Self in his work, whose "defensive function is to hide and protect the True Self."[152] As a general principle, the False Self develops due to a not good enough environment. More specifically for Winnicott, the etiology of the False Self

---

150. Winnicott, "Parent-Infant Relationship," 51.
151. Winnicott, "Antisocial Tendency," 310.
152. Winnicott, "Ego Distortion," 142.

is found in exploring "the stage of first object-relationships."[153] Here the infant is on the verge of integration, personalization, and the differentiation of the outside world of not-me from the inner world of me. Fusion will occur here, in a good enough environment, as will the capacity for concern, to be alone, and to relate to and use objects. However, if the mother fails to provide a good enough environment, there may be initial acts of protest but these "disappear clinically, only to reappear in serious form at a later stage."[154] In place of the True Self and protestations, a False Self develops in compliance with the mother and environment, in order to protect the True Self. In the place of spontaneity—a sign of the True Self—compliance and imitation develop to protect against exploitation and annihilation. "Through this False Self, the infant builds up a fake set of relationships and by means of introjections even attains a show of being real, so that the child may grow to be just like mother, nurse, aunt, brother, or whoever at the time dominates the scene."[155] In contrast to the True Self, "the existence of a False Self results in a feeling unreal or a sense of futility."[156] It is often restless and, due to the development in reaction to impingements, will search for impingements to react to.

In his exploration of the False Self Winnicott highlights his belief that it will develop in degrees depending on the severity of the environmental failure.[157] At one end, in extreme circumstances, the False Self presents as the real person, completely hiding the True Self. Inevitably, in relationships where a whole person is expected the False Self fails. In "less extreme" circumstances, the True Self is "acknowledged as a potential" and "allowed a secret life" while being defended by the False Self. This preserves the individual in "abnormal environmental conditions." "More towards health," the False Self searches for the right conditions for the True Self to emerge. Where there is a failure to find such conditions, new defenses are organized to protect the True Self which, in the worst case, Winnicott suggests suicide could result as a way of controlled protection from annihilation from outside factors. "Still further towards health" a False Self develops that identifies with those who care for the individual. "In health," the False Self still operates but only so as to enable acceptance in, and conformity to, certain social settings. A significant difference regarding the role of the

---

153. Winnicott, "Ego Distortion," 145.
154. Winnicott, "Ego Distortion," 146.
155. Winnicott, "Ego Distortion," 146.
156. Winnicott, "Ego Distortion," 148.
157. Winnicott, "Ego Distortion," 142–43.

False Self in the case of good health is that "the compromise ceases to become allowable when the issues become crucial. When this happens the True Self is able to override the compliant self."[158]

Conclusion

In this chapter we have been able to take a brief tour of the key theories involved in Winnicott's work on un/healthy infant development. Winnicott is not without his critics, but the aim of the chapter was less about interrogating Winnicott's theories and more to do with elucidation to enable theological engagement with them in the coming chapters. This is possible because, although Winnicott's main focus was on infants and, primarily, their relationship to the environment and their mother, as noted, this acted as an analogy for other settings such as the client-analyst relationship. What that means for this particular project is that similar links can be made that bridge over into theological discourse and related practice as Winnicott's theories provide an analogy to be used there. Engagement with Winnicott will therefore enable us to ask afresh what the True Self is and how this develops from a Christian perspective. It will also, along similar lines to Winnicott's emphasis on the good enough environmental provision, enable us to explore afresh the human/Israel/church-divine relationship as well as the role of the church in the development of the True Self. In a more focused way this then enables us to reengage with trauma theory and ask the specific question of how the church can care well for those who have been traumatized in a way that enables and supports post-traumatic remaking. It is important to be clear here that I am *not* suggesting that Christian theology dismiss professional specialist psychological therapies with a view to arrogantly substituting them for a "spiritual" response. As John Swinton and others have noted, this is heavily reductionistic and deeply unhelpful to those in need and those trying to help.[159] Instead, what is intended is aid in forming the church's understanding and response to those who are traumatized in a way that works alongside other complementary disciplines and approaches. With that said, we turn to explore afresh the True Christlike Self and the Facilitating Church.

---

158. Winnicott, "Ego Distortion," 150.
159. Swinton, *Finding Jesus*, 11–37; Webb, *Toward*.

6

Developing a True Christlike Self

Introduction

SO FAR IN THIS work, the issue of trauma has been discussed with a view to exploring how best the church, unlike Job's friends, can offer constructive care. Continuing the conversation with Kevin Vanhoozer's theodramatic approach started in previous work, I have outlined what a theodramatic anthropology and ecclesiology might look like with the intent of constructing direction for a fitting performance of the church caring for those who are traumatized. What was noted in the exploration of Vanhoozer's theodramatic anthropology and ecclesiology was the potential for such direction and the current lack in his theatrical paradigm. With that in mind, the previous chapter laid the foundations for drawing the work of Donald Winnicott into the conversation in order to use Winnicott's work as a constructive corrective and addition to Vanhoozer's approach.

What was noted when discussing the experience of trauma and the possibility of post-traumatic remaking and growth was the importance of a community that can offer a safe space and bear witness to the pain of the one suffering as part of supporting the remaking process. It was also noted that such a community can also enable the building of resilience in the face of potentially traumatic experiences. This raised the question of what it might mean for the church to be that kind of community. Vanhoozer's model provides a theodramatic anthropology and ecclesiology that offers detail to what, from a Christian perspective, it means to be human and

DEVELOPING A TRUE CHRISTLIKE SELF 191

what we are growing toward as well as the role of the church in the *missio Dei*. However, what Vanhoozer does not offer is direction and a rationale for what Job's friends could have done better, or, therefore, what the church can and should do when those in its company experience trauma. In this chapter, the aim is to employ Winnicott's insights in the development of the theodramatic approach to anthropology explored in chapter 3. More specifically, the aim is to use Winnicott's work analogically to illuminate key aspects of healthy human maturation present in Scripture that have been overlooked. In the following chapter, the same approach will be taken to the theodramatic ecclesiology presented in chapter 4. Chapter 8 will then draw these two streams of development together and show how a church that takes such insights on board in its theology and practice will be better placed to support individuals in post-traumatic remaking. We begin by returning to theodramatic anthropology.

Returning to the Theodrama

A key point of overlap that acts as a helpful starting place for discussion is the recognition of the individual as a person-in-relationship. Recalling Vanhoozer's anthropology, he uses a particular model of the Trinity from which to illuminate his understanding of humans made in God's image. Drawing on the model of God as being-in-communicative action, Vanhoozer suggests that humans are vocational creatures created to answer back to God as they live into their role as co-missioned, asymmetrical partners with God in God's mission to creation of drawing creation into full relationship with God. In an analogous way to the persons that constitute the Trinity, humans are individuals that cannot be reduced down to relationships yet cannot—and are not intended to—live outside of relationship. And further, the matrix of relationships includes those with the creator and fellow creatures. Humans are to image God in the temple of creation in a priestly fashion that mediates God to the world and vice versa. Linked to this are the prophetic and royal tasks of speaking God's words of direction, affirmation, and rebuke and being the place of God's rule in their own thoughts and actions. The incarnate Christ offered the most perfect example of a human performance that integrates the roles of prophet and priest while displaying the kingdom of God. In addition, he offered the non-repeatable performance of sacrificial lamb and king in his death, resurrection, and ascension. To live into our role as the image of

God is to put on Christlikeness, aided by the Holy Spirit, while recognizing the crucial differences between Christ and created humans.

Arguably, the incarnation, death, resurrection, and ascension of the Son were required because sin had created an insurmountable block between being made good in the image of God and growing into perfect union with God. We noted in Vanhoozer's work that, similar to Brunner, he suggests that the fall results in the distortion of the material image of God, while the formal dimension of the image is retained. Humans are able to continue in dialogue with God but are unable to grow into their true selves without God's intervention in Christ. Following God's incarnate intervention, we noted that God sets free the human creatures to discover and perform their true selves—found in Christ. With Scripture in hand, improvisation is what is then required to continue the process of putting on Christ and performing as one's Christlike True Self, found in Christ. The obvious enrichment this adds to Winnicott's approach is that it provides a much-needed clear *telos* for the True Self as well as a wider dramatic setting for its understanding and development. Where Winnicott focused on the developmental processes, but with a lack of clarity regarding answers to key worldview questions, Vanhoozer offers the opposite. In Vanhoozer's work, there is clarity regarding who we are, where we are, what is wrong, what the solution is, and where the drama is heading.[1] The problem present throughout Vanhoozer's work is a lack of depth regarding how, in the details of daily life, we are to perform our true selves and break free of the various false performances so characteristic of the fallen existence in the theodrama. Vanhoozer offers us something in the sense of dialogical relations and the ongoing work of interpretation and improvisation as each individual, embedded within the community of the church, engages with Scripture, Spirit, and context in order to discern a fitting performance that opts for improvisation over ad-libbing and carries on the through-line toward the superobjective of the theodrama. As Turner noted, this provides a unified option for what is often experienced as a fragmented sense of self. Here the "magic if" has a sense of shape that we are to reach for as we seek to perform Christ on our various stages. However, although Vanhoozer highlights the renewal of the mind as the central focus of transformation, there seems to be a deficit concerning how such transformation is achieved, particularly when it comes to the

---

1. I am here drawing from questions that Brian Walsh and J. Richard Middleton identify the answers to as being the basis of our "faith commitments" on which our worldviews are constructed. See Walsh and Middleton, *Transforming Vision*, 35.

role of relationships, which, ironically, is key to his understanding of the Trinity and persons made in the image of God. Here we can switch over to explore what Winnicott offers regarding how, in greater detail and in a more realistic way, development and transformation might be achieved. I am, of course, not ignoring the work of God in this process as Winnicott seems to, but am, instead, attempting to draw out what might be of use from Winnicott's work in service of the development of the True Self, in cooperation with God, in the theodrama.

The Dependence of the Pre-Fall *Imago Dei*

Before rereading Gen 1–3 using Winnicottian tools, it is important to pause and briefly discuss the approach taken here to avoid the accusation of offering an interpretation the text does not support. As Peter Enns has helpfully highlighted, Genesis should not necessarily be read literally as a text that details the historical beginnings of creation and the human creatures within that as it is simply not that kind of text.[2] Instead, "Genesis is an ancient text designed to address ancient issues *within the scope of ancient ways of understanding origins.*"[3] John Walton similarly adds, "The Bible is not revealing science, and the biblical authors and audience would be neither aware of nor concerned with our scientific way of thinking."[4] Enns argues that Israel's authors and editors borrowed from similar stories found among ancient Near Eastern cultures in developing their own understanding of their origins and resultant identity—what Walton refers to as the "native cognitive environment."[5] The 'ādām of Gen 1 then represents the whole of humanity,[6] with Gen 2:4–24 offering a sequel in which a particular pair of humans are chosen by God for a particular role and task.[7] This role will involve working with God to bring order to a creation that is a mixture of "order" and what Walton refers to as "non-order."[8]

---

2. Although John Walton is an example of an Old Testament scholar who argues that Adam and Eve actually existed as specific people. See Walton, *Lost World*, 101–3.

3. Enns, *Evolution of Adam*, 36.

4. Walton, *Lost World*, 25.

5. Walton, *Lost World*, 25.

6. Walton offers a brief survey of the various uses of "adam" in Gen 1–5, noting that this would not have been the name of the first human but is a term used to convey information about these humans. See Walton, *Lost World*, 58–62.

7. Walton, *Lost World*, 63–69.

8. For Walton's categorization of "order," "non-order," and "disorder," see Walton,

Enns reads Gen 2:4-24 as a "proto-Israel" text where the humans in the garden are "a subset of the humanity" of Gen 1 parallel to the vocation of Israel.⁹ Following this line of thought he suggests, "The question is whether this Adam will be obedient to God and stay in Eden, or join the other *'adam* outside of the garden, in exile."¹⁰ A further complimentary proto-Israel way of reading the first chapters of Genesis that Enns suggests is from a Wisdom perspective with Proverbs in view. From this perspective, "the Adam story is about failing to follow the path of wisdom and reach maturity and not about a fall from perfection."¹¹ Using Walton's language, Adam and Eve failed to correctly partner with God to bring "order" where there was currently "non-order" and in doing so introduced "disorder"—the continuance of sin and death.¹² Added to this, the Old Testament does not seem to suggest that Adam is the root of all sin, nor that sin is hereditary given that Cain appears to have a choice about how he proceeds and Noah is described as "righteous" and "blameless" (Gen 4:7; 6:9). This is not to follow a Pelagian path either but more to push back against conclusions that the text does not support.

It is only when we get to Paul's letters in the New Testament that a more explicit argument for the fall of creation into sin and death as begun by Adam is made. Enns notes that "Paul's reading of Genesis is driven by factors external to Genesis."¹³ At the heart of Paul's theology and interpretation of Genesis is the life, death, and resurrection of the incarnate Christ for the whole of creation. If salvation is open to the whole cosmos via the mediating work of Christ, the disorder of sin and death are what the whole of creation is to be saved from and so, Paul concludes, sin and death have entered through Adam. The heart of the gospel Paul presents is true—all have sinned and are captive to sin and death because of the failure of Adam and Eve to successfully partner with God. But Christ has broken the chains of sin and death offering salvation for all, even if the Genesis text does not explicitly support Paul's interpretation. Paul's "Adam is . . . the product of a creative handling of the story. In that sense, Paul's handling of Adam is hermeneutically no different from what others were doing at the time: appropriating an ancient story to address

---

Lost World, 149–52.

9. Enns, *Evolution of Adam*, 61–76; Walton, *Lost World*, 177.
10. Enns, *Evolution of Adam*, 69.
11. Enns, *Evolution of Adam*, 142; Walton, *Lost World*, 144.
12. Walton, *Lost World*, 153–60.
13. Enns, *Evolution of Adam*, 87.

pressing concerns of the movement. That has no bearing on the truth of the gospel."[14] Although there is much more that could be said about the complexities of handling both the Genesis texts and Paul's letters, this will suffice to make the point that, although the scope of sin and death are universal in creation, as is the salvific work of Christ, caution must be taken when reading a fall paradigm back onto texts that do not necessarily support particular understandings of that paradigm. What we can take from this as we proceed is that a certain type of fall is recorded—one in which Adam and Eve of Gen 2 fall away from their vocation due to a desire to access wisdom that was not theirs to take—and that this results in a disorder that echoes through the whole cosmos. Although Genesis is also not a history or science book in the way we might understand such terms, it does still offer a window into the human vocation and condition, the intended process of maturation, and the kind of relationship with God and the rest of creation that would enable and be affected by those relationships. With that in view, what is offered below is arguably a plausible reading of those texts using contemporary psychological theory.

As noted in the previous chapter, central to Winnicott's work was the development of a True Self in contrast to a False Self. Whereas Vanhoozer offers us a Christological lens through which to view this idea of the True Self, Winnicott's work provides us with analogical material to aid in understanding how one grows toward this Christlike True Self. As also noted in the previous chapter, a core thread to Winnicott's work was his theory that the healthy development of the True Self involves progressing from absolute dependence toward independence, or rather interdependence. This provides us with a helpful window into the parts cast for humans as revealed in Scripture because, I will suggest, there is something of this revealed in the development of the *imago Dei*.

The *imago Dei* is, arguably, never destined for independence. Rather, quite the contrary in the sense that humans, like the rest of creation, are destined for union with God after the pattern of the Son as revealed in the incarnation.[15] However, we saw in the previous chapter

---

14. Enns, *Evolution of Adam*, 102.

15. Arguably, a central strand, if not *the* central strand, in the arc of the biblical narrative is the union of God and creation. This is initiated in the garden of Eden and even after the plot disruption of the disobedience of Adam and Eve, followed by the expulsion of the humans from the garden, which temporarily postpones the realization of this goal, God's love-driven faithfulness to creation results in God finding a way for that union to be realized by way of the death and resurrection of God incarnate. The Son who is eternally with the Father and participated in the genesis of creation (John

that although Winnicott initially proposes the idea of independence as the aim of healthy human development, he then tempers this by suggesting interdependence as a conclusion more in line with the relational core of humans. For the theodramatic perspective being proposed here, this destiny is still problematic when applied to the God-human relationship because interdependence suggests that both parties are, to some degree dependent on one another for a healthy pattern of life. This would seem true of human-human relationships but not God-human relationships as what is being proposed here assumes a perspective that categorizes God as necessary and the source of all being, and creation as contingent and created by God. In short, God does not need creation in any way for God to be fulfilled or complete as God is in no way dependent on creation. The superobjective of the theodrama is communion between God and creation for the sake of creation, not God.[16] Whatever we may say of the healthy development of the True Self must be qualified by Vanhoozer's point that humans gain their sense of purpose in discerning the voice of God and responding in a fitting way that carries on the through-line. Humans—and the whole of creation—are dependent on God for their existence and purpose and this is unchanging (Ps 104:29–30).[17] However, as well as it being an error to uncritically map Winnicott's aim of interdependence onto the *imago Dei* in the theodrama, it is also an error to suggest that humans simply remain in a state of absolute dependence. Instead, we require more nuance in engagement with Winnicott.

When rereading the God-human relationship revealed in Scripture with Winnicott's work in view, we are offered fresh insight into the desired process of maturation and the make-up of the facilitating environment. As already noted, the whole of creation is contingent and dependent for its existence on its creator—something, it would seem will always, to some degree, be true. The conclusion of the theodrama describes a creation where God is all in all as the waters cover the sea (Hab 2:13; 1 Cor 15:28). This would seem to suggest that a particular kind of

---

1:1–3) also enabled the reconciliation of creation (Col 1:15–20) to be realized at the eschaton (Rev 21:1–4).

16. It is noteworthy in Rev 21:1–4 that God comes to fully dwell with creation, yet it is God that removes from creation the effects of the fall. It is creation that requires healing by God; God does not require anything from creation to be whole.

17. In a similar way, Ann Ulanov in her engagement with Winnicott also highlights the importance of recognizing that healthy development for humans in their relationship with God involves dependence rather than independence or interdependence. See Ulanov, *Finding Space*, 120.

dependence on and relationship with God is required to be alive, free, and flourishing. Full communion and cooperation with God are not, however, about becoming a Christlike clone but are, instead—in agreement with Vanhoozer—about becoming truly who we were made to be. Dependence is, therefore, to some degree an important part of our developing True Self. However, what also seems plain to see from the outset of the theodrama is that this dependence does not equate to the initial stage of absolute dependence that Winnicott uses to categorize the stage prior to and immediately after birth. A glance at the creation accounts of Genesis may hint at a short-lived moment of a relationship that could be labeled absolute dependence in the sense of humans being created by God and placed in an environment also created by God in which humans are intended to flourish (Gen 1:26–30; 2:7–8). Further support could be added to this claim if particular evolutionary theories are engaged with that highlight possible ways that humans emerge and develop into the *imago Dei*.[18] Middleton draws attention to a possible developmental reading of the creation accounts making specific comparison between the first humans and children in the developmental process.[19] Such readings theoretically accommodate Winnicott's stage of absolute dependence. However, although humans are absolutely dependent on God for their existence, Winnicott's stage of absolute dependence, if it is there at all, rapidly transitions into something more akin to relative dependence in that humans are given a particular vocation that presumes a level of freedom and responsibility. In Gen 1:26–28, God creates humans as male and female and gives them their vocation of co-creator and ruler of creation. As God's representative, humans are to multiply and look after creation in the way God would.[20] We are reminded in Ps 24:1–2 that God is the creator of all, and the earth belongs to God. The human vocation is therefore one of tenant or steward for which they will be held accountable (Mark 12:1–12; Matt 21:33–46; Luke 20:9–19).

The sequel found in the second creation account adds further detail with a specific man being created and given life by the breath of God

---

18. See Visala, "Structural"; Van den Brink, "Questions"; Smith, "What Stands"; Middleton, "Reading Genesis 3."

19. Middleton, "Reading Genesis 3," 82. Irenaeus also made a similar comparison, although Middleton does not appear to reference that here. See Irenaeus, *Against Heresies* 4.38 (*ANF* 1:521–22). When using the term "first humans" and similar, I am referring to those traditionally named as "Adam and Eve."

20. Brueggemann, *Genesis*, 32–33; Wenham, *Genesis 1–15*, 33.

(Gen 2:7). He is placed in the garden of Eden to work it and protect it with strict instructions of what can be eaten and what cannot (Gen 2:15–17).[21] For now at least, the tree of the knowledge of good and evil is strictly off-limits and the transgressing of this rule is so serious that it carries a death sentence.[22] However, as Nicholas Ansell has argued, it is more than possible that the fruit of the tree of the knowledge of good and evil is only *temporarily* off limits until an appropriate time for humans to eat from it as part of the covenantal meal between God and humans, which follows a similar line of thinking to that of Enns and Walton regarding the acquiring of wisdom.[23] When understood in this way, transgression of the instruction not to eat of it does indeed lead to death, but a death that comes from being annexed from a close covenantal relationship with God in the garden where the tree of life can be accessed. "The disobedience and the deadly consequences come . . . in treating something that is only God's to give as a possession, as ours by right. Instead of being 'like' God by 'imaging' God, following the pattern of 1:26, Adam and Eve attempt to become like God by accessing the wisdom of God without respecting the covenantal nature of their existence."[24] The result is an end where they return to dust (Gen 3:19).[25] Given this reading of Gen 2 and 3, in light of Winnicott's work, humans at this stage of development could be characterized as not mature enough to cope with the responsibility that the knowledge gained from the forbidden tree would give them. Rather than that knowledge being entirely off limits, in the same way that a parent does not overburden a child with knowledge, information, and experiences they cannot yet bear, so too with God and the humans in the garden.

Placed in the garden of Eden, a companion in life and work is sought for the human from the other creatures. The process of discernment of a suitable partner is left to the human of whom no suitable partner is found among the other creatures. Instead, God divides the human to

---

21. Brueggemann characterizes the description of humans and their role in the garden as "vocation, permission, and prohibition." See Brueggemann, *Genesis*, 46.

22. Wenham, *Genesis 1–15*, 67–68.

23. Ansell, "Call of Wisdom," 40–41; Middleton, "Reading Genesis 3," 80–83.

24. Ansell, "Call of Wisdom," 41–42.

25. Walton notes that when humans are made from dust and return to dust, this is less about materiality and more about highlighting that humans were made mortal with immortality in reach while they remained in the garden of Eden with access to the tree of life. Once they were exiled from the garden, death is their eventual fate. See Walton, *Lost World*, 72–74.

create man and woman as equals and of the same kind of creature (Gen 2:18–22).[26] In this process, we again see that humans are dependent on God for their life and creation but are also given freedom within limits to make decisions for themselves as they interact with the world around them and grow in awareness, knowledge, and maturity while developing in their vocation. Within the limits and boundaries set for them by God, the fleeting initial moment of absolute dependence gives way to the ongoing stage of relative dependence in which healthy maturation can take place within the divinely provided facilitating environment. In the temple of creation, the humans are cast in the role of priests who mediate the presence of God to creation in their work and service and as royal images of the creator and ruler of creation in how they enable and maintain the ordering of Eden as the intersection of heaven and earth—God's sacred place of rule within creation.[27] It is worth noting here Winnicott's notion of mirroring, discussed in the previous chapter, whereby the baby begins to feel real by being seen by the mother. The internalization of this experience of "apperception" sets the foundation for perception of the self and the outside world. Arguably, what is occurring in the early stages of the creation of the human creatures is a sense of mirroring on the part of the divine parent. This means we can speak of these humans as made in the image and likeness of God because they see something of themselves when they are seen by God and when they look in the face of God. It is this initial ego support that also enables the human creature to then look at themselves and the world around in a creative and constructive way. This first seeing and mirroring by the divine parent enables healthy initial development of the first humans, which will come to be significant for how humans then see one another. This mirroring by God enables healthy development and formation of identity and a sense of being real which then continues beyond the initial act within the theodrama as the people of God are consistently called back to look on God in prayer as the source of their identity and vocation which, as Vanhoozer notes, are intrinsically linked.

However, where there is freedom to grow and develop there is the risk of destructive choices and a failure to live out the human vocation in a healthy manner. Whatever we make of the mysterious figure of the

---

26. Middleton, "Reading Genesis 3," 93; Wenham, *Genesis 1–15*, 68; Walton, *Lost World*, 77–81.

27. Middleton, *New Heaven*, 41–49; Malone, *God's Mediators*, 47–57; Middleton, *Liberating Image*, 77–90; Walton, *Lost World*, 104–15.

serpent in Gen 3, it offers a challenge to the path of healthy development for the humans as the serpent questions the maturational processes laid down by the creator.[28] To some degree, we depart from Winnicott here because the decision by the humans to listen to a voice other than God's presents as a drive toward independence that Winnicott may well have seen as positive, but in the theodrama is interpreted as quite the opposite.[29] In their response to the questions of the serpent, followed by the eating from the tree that was, at this point, forbidden, the humans seek to exchange their role as image bearers for that of God and in so doing strive for (unhealthy) independence. Where Winnicott suggests the idea of healthy maturation in the form of independence, with a more tempered development being interdependence, the very nature of the eternal ontological distinction between creator and creature means that such an achievement in the development of humans in the theodrama is not possible and attempts to achieve it are not beneficial. As noted above, it is distinctly possible that the fruit of the tree of the knowledge of good and evil may have been offered to the humans by God at some point further along in the maturing process, but it was always God's to give, not the humans' to take. In short, we here hit a limit to the parent-child or therapist-client analogy as a window into the divine-human relationship. However, to throw the baby out with the bathwater would be a mistake. Although following Winnicott all the way sets us in opposition to the theodrama, there are a number of insights gleaned from Winnicott's developmental theories that aid in illuminating the pre-fall state of humans in the garden and the relationships they are in.

As noted above, the state of the relationship with God, from a human perspective, is largely one of relative dependence, and, with Winnicott, we can emphasize that understanding what it means to be human

---

28. For an overview of different understandings of the serpent, see Ansell, "Call of Wisdom," 37–38; Middleton, "Reading Genesis 3," 84–86; Wenham, *Genesis 1–15*, 72–73; Bradnick, *Evil, Spirits, and Possession*; Walton and Walton, *Demons and Spirits*; Wright, *Satan*; Walton, *Lost World*, 128–39. Interestingly, Walton notes that the text does not say that the serpent was in the garden and so it is possible that Adam and Eve encountered what Walton categorizes as a chaos creature outside of the garden.

29. It is also worth noting that it would appear they did not listen properly in the first place. The woman—who was not created when God instructed the man about the prohibition (2:15–17, 21–22)—incorrectly recounts the instruction (3:3) adding the prohibition to touch the fruit, which was either miscommunicated to her by the man or misheard/misinterpreted by the woman. Middleton highlights further differences between the first instructions by God and the subsequent recounting by the woman, "Reading Genesis 3," 87–88.

in the image of God is not something undertaken in a vacuum. Where Winnicott makes the important point that there is no such thing as a baby, we can apply the same point to humans. This is not to reduce humans (or the baby for that matter) down to relationships alone but is, instead, about avoiding reduction in the other direction to humans being understood in isolation. Instead, the nature of humanity is only fully understood when considered in relation to God and the environment and as a single integrated unit that has relationships with God, creation, other humans, and the self. Although there is no sense in which God as spirit can physically hold and handle the newly formed humans, that is not to say that such environmental provision is not in place in other ways. The very act of creating order out of chaos including filling creation with life and vigor while enabling the ongoing production of life within creation (Gen 1:1–25) and then placing Adam (and Eve) in the sacred garden (Gen 2:15) with the tree of life suggests the provision of a particular kind of environment conducive to offering both security from overwhelming impingement as well as the opportunity for growth when the divine parent engages in planned failure in adaptation. This is something akin to Winnicott's description of holding.

Handling in the Winnicottian framework has to do with the care of the whole person in such a way that integration of psyche-soma is achieved, resulting in feeling real in one's body. Again, there is no actual physical handling as such by God, but there is the creation of humans as spirit enmeshed with a body (Gen 2:7). The point here is that there is, from the start, the creation of a human who is integrated and placed in a world where all parts of the integrated self are valued and provided for.

In terms of object presenting, it is interesting to note in the second creation account the sequence of creation; placing in the garden with a vocation; and provision of a suitable partner (Gen 2:5–9, 15, 18–24). The process of healthy maturation in Winnicott's theories involves the presenting of objects in such a way that progressively challenges the infant's false perception of omnipotence through gradual failure in adaptation as illusion changes to disillusion. Following the creation of a human in a world that provides for all initial needs, there comes the vocation of creation care which, although not to the same degree as is described in the post-fall state, offers some level of resistance that requires ingenuity on the part of the human (2:15). Object presenting turns to object relating and, finally, object usage, as the human potentially goes through the experience of encountering a world that does not simply produce what the human requires without any input on their part. This resistance without retaliation or destruction provides the experience of what Winnicott refers to as the intermediate space between pure objective reality and the world of illusions. That is not to say that what the human is experiencing is not real but instead to suggest that it is an interpretation of reality from a particular perspective enmeshed in the world, and it is a movement from an illusory world of the subject relating subjectively, to the subject relating to objects perceived with a level of objectivity.

This development continues with the introduction in the second creation account of the process of the creation of a suitable partner. Rather than simply creating a woman, God engages the human in the process giving them the opportunity to name the animals in the search for the right partner (2:18–21). Again, this would seem to fit the process already mentioned of object presenting leading to object relating and usage. Here we see God's awareness of the benefit of a partner for the human (18), but, rather than simply providing, God draws the human into the process by presenting all the current creatures for them to name (19). It is not too big of a leap to imagine that what might have been involved in this naming is, again, a resistance or failure on the part of the various creatures to fulfill the requirements of a suitable partner, yet continuing to exist (20), which in turn leads to them being found in the intermediate space by the human, as objective and thus nameable as "real." Relative dependence continues though as it is the consistent care of God who then does provide a suitable, equal partner of the same substance and value (2:21–24).

It is in the intermediate space that Winnicott suggests the infant learns to play while developing the capacity to be alone. Arguably, this is what is occurring in the creation accounts as creatures are brought before the human for naming and selection of a partner (2:19–20). As well as the experience of resistance, we see something similar to what Winnicott describes as the development of the capacity for play between parent and infant. The gradual failure in adaptation creates an intermediate space in which interpretation and interaction happen with some level of resistance to manipulation from reality now perceived with a level of objectivity. This, Winnicott notes, is exciting for the infant and, one can imagine, may have been exciting for the human in the garden. This giving of responsibility for naming and choosing, as well as the wider responsibilities of tending the garden, provides opportunity for the development of the capacity to be alone. As noted in the previous chapter, this is not simply about being on one's own but instead has more to do with being secure in oneself whether in the presence of another or not. This ability occurs because the infant is first able to play in the presence of the parent, introjecting that experience for future use. In the garden, something of this nature occurs when the human is in the presence of the divine parent while "playing" with the creatures. Once this capacity is established, another human is introduced with which to play, and the pair appear to be eventually left alone in the garden to continue in play. An imaginative suggestion here is that the capacity to be alone has been established in the first humans to the degree that they have introjected enough of the good environment and parent to respond in a suitable way to any possible impingements.

However, the theme of resistance resurfaces when the man and woman encounter the serpent in Gen 3. Having been given boundaries by God regarding what is currently permissible to eat in the garden and what is not, this is brought into question by the serpent, as are the consequences if this line is crossed (3:1–6). In a sense, the serpent offers further resistance because it challenges the makeup of the facilitating environment provided by God and so may be classified as an impingement. However, one would be justified in presuming that as the perfect creator and parent, God has enabled sufficient maturity to be reached by the humans for them to be able to cope with this resistance and impingement to their healthy development. In addition, but related, the narrative of Gen 3 also seems to imply a sense of distance between the humans and their divine creator-parent given the later point about them hiding as God returns to the garden in the evening (3:8). However, as is well known, this resistance and impingement are not met with a healthy response that keeps them within the realm of the facilitating environment but is allowed to destabilize the various human relationships as a consequence of "the Fall."[30] Arguably, what emerges in the place of a developing True Self as the image of God is a False Self. This False Self begins as soon as the humans opt to take a path directed by the words of the serpent toward unhealthy development.

Winnicott's understanding of the development of the False Self, generally speaking, is that it develops as a defense mechanism to protect the True Self from harm. The serpent is an impingement in that it interrupts and brings into question the maturational processes laid down by

---

30. Following James K. A. Smith, it is not necessary for the fall to be understood as a momentary event, but instead it could be understood as a process in which it would still retain its historical occurrence and impact. See Smith, "What Stands."

the divine parent. Given the flawless nature of the divine parent, it is safe to presume that the human children have developed to the point of having the ego strength to ward off the serpent's questions with suitable answers without the aid of the auxiliary ego of the divine parent.[31] Or else, they have the wherewithal to return to the safety of the divine parent (and the garden?) for further protection and guidance about how to respond to this unsettling impingement. However, for reasons that the text does not explain, what happens is compliance to the path laid out by the questions and suggestions of the serpent and by the peer pressure of one another. Arguably, something of the True Self drives this decision because, god-like (or more precisely, Christlike) status is what humans as presented in the theodrama are made for and so a desire to inhabit such a status is a desire of the True Self. However, the True Self presented by the theodrama is not to assume this status apart from within a perfect relationship with God. It might be suggested that this is more an act of defiance or rebellion to test the boundaries of God's love for God's children. However, the act of hiding when aware of the presence of God does not seem to support this. Instead, the actions of the two humans, fueled by the serpent's prompting, appear more like an attempt to protect their psychological core, the True Self, from the angst of never being fully realized by taking matters into their own hands.[32] This develops as a False Self because it sets a pattern of thought and behavior that will, throughout most of the theodrama, continue to draw each individual and community—including the church—away from the vocation of the True Self as developing into its fullness under the direction of, and in relationship with, the divine parent.

At this juncture, the conclusion that might be reached is that the continuing emergence of the True Self when faced with the serpent and the resulting peer pressure would have looked like a reiteration of the commands of God to the humans, by the humans, to the serpent much like the responses of Jesus to the satan in the wilderness (discussed below). However, it is perhaps important to stress the difference between the first Adam and the last in terms of ontological makeup and Trinitarian

---

31. The presumption about the nature of the divine parent drawn on here is not explicit in the text in question but is deemed an acceptable presumption given the general revelation of Scripture and orthodox Christian doctrine that has developed from that.

32. Interestingly, Brueggemann seems to reach a similar conclusion, noting that the scene "presents a prism through which the root cause of anxiety can be understood." See Brueggemann, *Genesis*, 53–54.

relationship. That said, even Jesus in his facing of the cross and resultant death engages in the practice of lament—something we shall return to below. The point here is that, rather than a simple reiteration that repeats the internalized world and relationships laid down thus far in the divine parent–human child relationship, what is perhaps a more realistic expectation is something akin to the cry of an infant when the parent has been gone too long and the ego strength given by the internalized parent has been worn down to the point of the infant experiencing the anxiety of impending disintegration and annihilation. Ideally, at this point, the parent returns to comfort the infant, or else defense mechanisms of the False Self are employed to defend the True Self. That said, if the fall account is read in the light of Winnicott's work, behavior that would be expected when the parent is absent for too long in the face of existential anxiety is a cry for help. What might also be expected is the use of some sort of transitional phenomena to aid in the warding off of anxiety at a crucial point of change. However, for reasons we cannot fathom from the revelation of the text, the humans neither cry out nor use transitional phenomena but, instead, employ a False Self defense mechanism in response to the angst accentuated by the questions of the serpent about their going on being and healthy development. It is this pattern of opting for entire self-reliance in a bid for knowledge, power, control, survival, and, ultimately, immortality that has been at the center of the development of the False Self throughout the history of fallen humanity. The result of this, as is made clear in the rest of Gen 3, is the corruption of the relationships that humans have with God, creation, each other, and the self.

A Joban Alternative

Although not a creation account, it is interesting to read the story of Job in parallel for a contrasting response, in ancient Jewish scriptures, to impingement when in relationship with God.[33] Before proceeding, however,

---

33. Gerald Janzen adds further weight to this comparison by drawing attention to the parent-child relationship as a metaphor for the divine-human relationship drawn from Mesopotamian religion and employed in Genesis (and other Old Testament texts) as well as in Job. Of the opening chapter of Job Janzen suggests, "In the questions which arise in 1:6–12, one senses the exploration of the possibility that the human as child, while continuing to be filially related to God, finally passes out of wardship and into shared responsibility for the 'inheritance' of the earth." Not only does this support the comparison with the Genesis account, but it also supports the use of insights from Winnicott's theories to explore the maturing from one stage of dependence to another.

it is important to note and acknowledge the challenges around classifying and interpreting the book of Job. Tiffany Houck-Loomis provides a helpful overview of the history of interpretation of the book of Job and in so doing draws attention to the lack of consensus about how it should be read, the dating, and genre.[34] This provides somewhat of a conundrum regarding how to engage with it. Given that my own specialty is not biblical studies as well as the space limitations and focus of the present work, I shall not attempt to wade into the quagmire that is discussions around the origins and message of the book.[35] However, given my own methodological leanings, I continue to read the book of Job in its final form and as part of the wider Christian biblical canon—as I have done elsewhere.[36] I therefore read it in light of the wider canon of Scripture and particularly in light of the revelation of God in Christ. Given God's affirmation of Job's speech at the end of the book, in contrast to God's anger at the responses of the friends, the focus here is specifically on exploring what it was that Job said and did that was "right," in comparison to the first humans depicted in Genesis, particularly as we use the tools of Winnicott to aid in that exploration. For the sake of the present discussion, the question of whether the story is literal is irrelevant given the focus. In the light of the wider canon, Job's response seems to be affirmed and so it is his response that will be concentrated on. However, it is necessary to set the scene for that response by noting the circumstances in which it occurs.

Similar to the first humans we are met with a voice of opposition and questioning, this time in the form of one of God's courtiers, aptly described as "the accuser."[37] This time, however, the questioning is directed at God about a human, who we are told is without sin (1:1). When the heavenly beings present themselves to God, the accuser is

---

See Janzen, *Job*, 39.

34. Houck-Loomis, *History Through Trauma*, 147–61.
35. For a helpful collection of essays, see Zuck, *Sitting with Job*.
36. Torr, *Dramatic*.
37. This character, drawing from the Hebrew for accuser or adversary, is commonly translated into English as "Satan." However, this is problematic given the definite article that always precedes it in the book of Job and the dating of the text. The definite article means it makes more sense to translate it as a description rather than a name, and the early dating of the text means that later development of the figure of Satan or the devil would likely not have been in view for the author. Therefore, to try to prevent unhelpful characterization from being read back onto this figure in the story of Job, the term "the accuser" will be used, following the NRSVUE translation. For a more in-depth discussion, see Clines, *Job 1–20*, 18–23; Middleton, *Abraham's Silence*, 69–71; Walton and Walton, *Demons and Spirits*, 215–17; Wright, *Satan*, 21–25.

with them, and God suggests that the accuser consider Job (1:8). Surely, the accuser questions, Job only fears God and turns from evil because God protects him and provides for him (1:9–11). The basic point seems to be that Job's relationship with God is nothing more than cupboard love. God, in response, gives the accuser permission to test that theory, seemingly sure that the accuser will be proved wrong (1:12; 2:4–6). And so, Job must endure several potentially traumatizing experiences in the seeming absence of God. Also of note is the possible blurring of what constitutes blessing and curse in the book given that the same Hebrew word is used for both. Does Job lead a blessed life in the fullest sense of the word given that he fears God but does not necessarily have a close relationship with God? Instead, possibly from a place of fear and anxiety, he makes sacrifices for his children, not explicitly desired by God, just in case they sin. This may suggest that Job believes in and fears an angry God who demands perfection from his creatures. Materially Job may be "blessed," but his perception of God seems off and this may impact his mental health and his related actions.[38] We can again refer back to Winnicott's paradigm to further illuminate what may be occurring and what can be learned from this.

In the face of experiences, possibly more terrifying than the encounter with the serpent for the first humans, Job's initial response, at first glance, offers an example of what the first humans perhaps should have done. In Job 1:21–22, we are told, "Then Job arose, tore his robe, shaved his head, and fell on the ground and worshiped. He said, 'Naked I came from my mother's womb, and naked shall I return there; the Lord gave, and the Lord has taken away; blessed be the name of the Lord.'" Even after the second attack on Job by the accuser Job continues in a similar way, in response to his wife (2:10). However, what rapidly becomes apparent is that such utterances appear more as robotic, pre-programmed repetition than the voice of the True Self. The defense mechanisms that have so far supposedly sustained the life and relationship he has known are further feeding the False Self. Or, as Hamley describes it, "The traditions of faith have become a substitute for truth-telling, and are unhelpfully reinforcing his distancing reaction."[39]

In the face of brutal impingement that again threatens existential disintegration and annihilation, and this in the seeming absence of God,

---

38. See Hamley, "Patient Job," 86–88.
39. Hamley, "Patient Job," 88.

Job first offered the defensive response of the False Self that seems to deny the reality of the pain and, emu-like, metaphorically buries his head in the sand. As noted above, such a response might be what we naively think the first humans should have offered, but what seems to be prized as healthy development as the story of Job unfolds is the honest articulation of pain, doubt, fear, anxiety, despair, and anger by Job. I say "prized" because, as noted above, as the story concludes we are told that from God's perspective, Job speaks rightly of God in contrast to Job's friends whom we will return to below in chapter 8 (42:7). In a similar way to the baby who cries for, and to, their parent in the face of what is felt as an overwhelming threat and anxiety, Job utters a similar cry, starting with lament into the ether (3:1–26) and moving to cries directed at God. As Middleton helpfully notes, "Job's honest voicing of his pain was appropriate, in contrast to that of the friends, who tried to defend God and explain Job's suffering."[40] He further highlights "that while the friends spoke *about* God, Job actually spoke *to* God. And that is what God wants, even if God has to correct the content of what Job says."[41] Contrary to many translations that render 42:6 as repenting *in* dust and ashes, thus seeming to support an interpretation that suggests Job's attitude and lament were something to repent of, I follow those who offer translations and interpretations that would more adequately account for and support Job's lament to God as being something God affirms and seems to encourage in the "Whirlwind Speeches."[42] This would seem to make more sense of the narrative of the book as well as the presence of two whirlwind speeches instead of one. In such a rendering Job would either seem to be repenting *of* dust and ashes and thus repenting of the passivity that the first whirlwind speech brings about, or Job is signaling that he is now aware that dust and ashes are called to honest conversation with God. Either way, honest speech before God is affirmed in contrast to the response of the friends.

Following the Winnicottian paradigm through, a further point to note is that in contrast to the development of the False Self in the response of the first humans to impingement, and the initial response of Job to impingement, the True Self can only develop in a healthy way in

---

40. Middleton, *Abraham's Silence*, 126.

41. Middleton, *Abraham's Silence*, 126.

42. See a more extensive exploration of my position in Torr, *Dramatic*, 164–68, and Middleton's most recent exploration of his conclusions from which I draw in Middleton, *Abraham's Silence*, 120–28.

the safe, holding, and facilitating environment provided by God in which cries of pain, need, and support can be articulated, heard, and responded to. The choosing to do otherwise and the setup of an environment that encourages and facilitates anything but this will ultimately run contrary to God's desire and provision for healthy maturation into our full vocation as children of God. This draws us into Winnicott's ideas of the transitional phenomena and the types of cries from babies.

As noted above, there is an absence of the use of transitional phenomena in response to the anxiety present in the fall accounts, as there is an absence of cries of any kind from the first humans. In contrast, what seems to be present in the story of Job is that initially, he uses the reiteration of God's sovereign control as a transitional phenomenon that fails to ward off anxiety and pain. At this point, the practice of lament is drawn on that appears to function both as a transitional phenomenon *and* as types of crying categorized by Winnicott, at the same time.

Walter Brueggemann, well known for his influential writing on the subject of lament, uses a transitional paradigm involving a move from "orientation" to "disorientation" in the relationship between God and Israel/individuals that eventually gives way to "re-orientation."[43] The "first move" from orientation to disorientation—much like Job's experience of loss and pain—is where lament breaks out as a vehicle to aid in maintaining an honest relationship with God amid suffering.[44] This is helpful to note because it appears to have parallels with Winnicott's move from illusion to disillusion in which transitional phenomena are employed to ward off anxiety, and cries of pain, anger, grief, despair, and hopelessness can be heard in the voice of the one lamenting. A further point of comparison is how memory is employed in the use of lament. Often the

---

43. Brueggemann discusses this paradigm in *Message of the Psalms*, 15–23, and "Psalms." Interestingly, in *Message of the Psalms* Brueggemann opts for "new orientation" as the final phase whereas in "Psalms" he opts for re-orientation. Both of these have merit in that there is something old and familiar and something new about this phase of the relationship between God and Israel. However, whereas I previously preferred "re-orientation" (Torr, *Dramatic*, 164–68), in more recent work I have switched to "renewed orientation" as, arguably, this more accurately reflects the tension of the new and the old that is present in this phase of the relationship. See Torr, "Winnicottian Approach," 53–54.

44. Brueggemann even draws attention to the parallels with Job by dividing Job up into three sections (Job 1–2; 3:1—42:6; 42:7–17) and suggesting, "This sequence nicely reflects the sequence of orientation/disorientation/new orientation that I have suggested for the Psalms some time ago" (*Theology*, 489). See also Torr, *Dramatic*, particularly chapters 5 and 6, for my more extended engagement with the form, content, and use of biblical lament.

central driving force behind the practice of lament is the individual or collective memory of previous experiences of a positive relationship with God in which God has been noticeably present and aided the sufferer or their ancestors in times of difficulty. Accounts of such periods are passed down through the generations and retained in the individual or collective memory—labeled by Brueggemann as the "core testimony." Lament—often involving a cross-examination of the core testimony with "countertestimony" from the current experience of suffering—is then driven by a belief that God is willing and able to affect change when new experiences of suffering occur based on the memories that have been passed down.[45] Similarly, according to Winnicott, infants at a certain stage of development can temporarily sustain themselves in the face of some impingements through the introjection of previous experiences of a good enough environment. When the impingent becomes too much, it is the hope of the return of the caregiver to resolve the situation that drives the crying. It is only Winnicott's fifth type of crying that suggests hope is lost. With this in view, we can reread the account of Job, in contrast to the fall narrative, as an example of what Winnicott describes as forms of crying one would expect to hear from a healthy child experiencing the anxiety of impingement yet with the hope of the parent's intervention. Combined with this is the use of this crying as a transitional phenomenon to be repeated as a source of comfort to ward off anxiety.[46] Here we are offered an alternative way of responding to anxiety and trauma compared with the fall account, illuminated by Winnicott's work, that, given God's response to Job in the conclusion of the story, appears to offer a healthier path for the True Self than we find in the fall account.[47]

A key plotline in the theodrama that is intrinsically linked to the superobjective of the communion of creation with the creator God is the expulsion of evil as a hindrance to the fulfillment of the superobjective. Although it is an interesting exercise to reread the creation and fall texts in light of Winnicott's work, it may appear that such a reading serves us no useful purpose post-fall. However, this is not true. Although post-fall,

---

45. For a more in-depth definition and discussion of Israel's core testimony and countertestimony, see Brueggemann, *Theology*, parts 1 and 2.

46. Ann Ulanov also suggests that contrary to Job's friends, Job destroys his image of God in his wrestling with God, enabling him to enter the frightening yet dynamic space where a fresh image can be born. See *Finding Space*, 114–16.

47. See also Torr, "Winnicottian Approach," for a further exploration of lament using insights from Winnicott's theories.

the plotline has the added complication of the expulsion of evil from within the human heart and mind, this is now simply included within the generally unchanged vocation of humans to partner with God in the flourishing of creation toward communion with the creator. With a generally unchanging vocation comes a generally unchanging process of maturation in so far as has been described. The added complication concerning humans is not that this process has changed as such, but rather that layers of defense mechanisms at individual and corporate levels have developed that produce varieties of False Selves that emerge to preserve the True Self in an often-hostile environment. Part of the challenge of plot resolution with regard to humans is the removal of False Selves in order to live out of one's True Self—"Wretched person that I am! Who will rescue me from this body of death?" (Rom 7:24). Here we dovetail with a number of points in Vanhoozer's work. In the aftermath of the fall, the theodrama repeatedly displays the inability of humans to fully recover their True Selves (although, as we will see, it does provide examples of what might aid that process). This recovery is enabled by the incarnation, death, resurrection, and ascension of the Son and the sending of the Spirit. As Vanhoozer highlights, to speak of the recovery of our True Selves, post-fall, is to speak of being in Christ in the ways discussed in chapter 3. However, to say that this recovery is simply enabled by the work of God does not go far enough. Even though it will find a particular form in each of our unique lives, to speak of the True Self is to speak of a True, Christ-shaped Self to which we are being conformed. As Vanhoozer also notes, the process of living into this state, completed at our resurrection, begins now and occurs in cooperation with the work of the Holy Spirit. What Vanhoozer helpfully clarifies in a way that is glaringly absent in Winnicott's work is that to rightly speak of a True Self, we must begin by looking at the pattern to which our True Selves find definition and are to be conformed, which is God in human form, Jesus Christ. Here we can turn to the incarnation with Winnicott's insights in view to give further clarity regarding what it might mean for us to grow into our True *Christlike* Selves.

Jesus Christ as the Archetypal True Self

As I have noted elsewhere, something Vanhoozer offers in terms of hermeneutics is a typological reading of the Scriptures whereby the

Old Testament sheds light on the identity and actions of Jesus, and the identity and actions of Jesus as the incarnate Son and Messiah offer fresh insight into Old Testament texts.[48] As Paul notes, where we have the account of the first Adam in Genesis, in Jesus we have the account of the last Adam (Rom 5:12–21; 1 Cor 15:20–22). This is one example of where the incarnation derives meaning from the Genesis accounts of the first humans while also offering a fresh window into what their healthy development should have looked like. A full comparison rests outside the bounds of this work, but some crucial points of connection will suffice to illuminate a Christological trajectory for the healthy maturation of humans, even in a fallen world.

Although we know little of Jesus' childhood and development in the biological sense of the terms, we are made aware that he grew in wisdom (Luke 2:40, 52) and had human parents who appear to have been attentive to the task at hand. Beyond the connections to human provision, we are also made aware that from an early age, Jesus had a particular type of relationship with his divine Father. In Luke's account, Jesus, at the age of twelve, having traveled with his parents to Jerusalem to celebrate the Passover festival decides to stay behind when his parents begin to travel home, without telling them (Luke 2:41–44). After three days of searching, we are told that Mary and Joseph find Jesus in the temple amazing the hearers with his understanding as he engages with the teachers (vv. 46–47). His response to their mixture of emotions appears to be one of surprise that they did not automatically know where he would be—in his Father's house (v. 49). He returns home with them, and we are told he is obedient to them (v. 51). There is little to go on in this brief account without entering into speculation, but what does seem apparent is that there are differences of views regarding what relationships Jesus has and how they enable his development and affirm his identity. We are told by the writer of Hebrews that Jesus was without sin (Heb 4:15) despite being tempted as we are, so it does not fit to say that Jesus did something wrong here. Instead, we seem to be steered toward the possibility that his human parents did not understand who he was and what healthy development meant for him in terms of his relationship with his divine Father. This does not, therefore, present as an act of rebellion or a testing of boundaries and loving provision by his earthly parents. Instead, it seems to suggest a difference in understanding between Jesus and his parents about his

---

48. Torr, *Dramatic*, 115–30. See Vanhoozer, *Mere Christian Hermeneutics*, for his most recent work on this.

identity, relationship to God the Father, and how that is developing and being outworked, all of which Mary seems to wisely ponder or treasure in her heart (Luke 2:51). What seems clear is that Jesus, at the age of twelve, recognizes the divine nature of his eternal parent and the importance of that relationship for his well-being and development.[49]

This reliance on his divine Father for identity and direction as well as sustenance for that to which his Father had called him becomes more prominent in Jesus' ministerial life in all four Gospels. It is the voice of the Father that the onlookers appear to be able to hear in the accounts of Jesus' baptism (Matt 3:17; Mark 1:11; Luke 3:22) where the Father affirms the Son's identity and the Father's pleasure at the Son's obedience. Jesus regularly retreats to pray (Matt 14:22–23; Mark 6:45–46; Luke 5:16; 6:12) and finds his identity and mission in the direction given to him by his divine Father, particularly apparent in the Gospel of John (4:32; 5:19–29; 6:57; 8:12–59; 10:17–18; 12:49–50; 13:3–4; 14:10, 24, 28–31; 15:15; 20:21), even to the point of that restricting both the length of time that mission takes on earth as well as the geographical location of it within the wider *missio Dei* (Matt 15:21–28; Mark 7:24–30). Jesus also highlights that only the Father seems to know the timescale of the eschaton (Matt 24:36; Mark 13:23), and as Jesus approaches his impending arrest and death he grapples with obedience to this vocation in prayer to his Father (Matt 26:36–46; Mark 14:32–42; Luke 22:39–46; John 12:27). Finally, in Luke's Gospel, we are told that it is into his Father's hands that Jesus finally commends his spirit (23:46).

Broadly, what seems evident from the Gospel accounts is that where the first humans were disobedient out of anxiety leading to the development of a False Self to protect the True Self, Jesus is obedient entrusting the shape and direction of his life to his divine Father. This is not a status of absolute dependence—a stage which if Jesus encountered, we are not party to knowing about—but rather more like relative dependence. Jesus does not operate on his own authority or with a sense of direction for life that is independent of that given by God the Father. The True Self Jesus portrays is not one that will eventually break free from his Father and go his own way and neither, we may therefore assume, is that what humans and creation more generally, are aiming at. Instead, what is presented is a picture of one who is encouraged and enabled to develop in a particular direction, able to make decisions and take responsibility for them yet in

---

49. For a fascinating exploration of this encounter, see McGrath, *Jesus and the Gospel Women*, 22–25.

such a way that never runs contrary to the intent of the divine Father.[50] It is worth noting a Christological affirmation of mirroring present in this relationship between divine Father and Son. As noted above, Jesus' identity, according to the Gospel accounts, derives from his divine Father. We can recall from Winnicott's work in the previous chapter, and applied in this chapter to the first humans, that the ability to perceive the self and the world in a healthy way has to first be facilitated by the experience of being seen by the good enough parent. Jesus would likely have received a version of that in his early years from his human parents but in the descriptions noted there is evidence of a particular type of mirroring in the divine relationship that is retained even into a stage more akin to relative dependence. There is a continuing reliance upon the divine parent for the clarity of identity of the Son as well as direction for fitting performance on the created stage. This ongoing experience of the Son being seen by the Father appears to be the significant fuel for the Son's ability to perceive and interact with the world in a fitting manner. This becomes particularly apparent when, in the garden of Gethsemane and at the cross, the Son's ability to discern and agree to the divine plan appears harder than it has been at any other point in his life just at the same point as the divine Father appears hidden to the Son. From this, we may conclude that divine mirroring is crucial for clarity of identity and activity in the world and that Jesus has been able to introject the security of the facilitating environment provided by his Father in such a way that he is able to fend off temptation of various types, particularly in the seeming absence of the Father. This therefore also points to Jesus having reached the developmental stage of being able to be alone (while reminding ourselves that Winnicott did not necessarily mean physically alone, which would compromise orthodox Trinitarian theology!).

Turning to particular instances that give greater insight into the differences in development between the first and last Adam, it is instructive to look at Jesus' temptation in the wilderness. In the various accounts of Jesus' forty days and nights in the wilderness that occur straight after his baptism (Matt 4:1–11; Mark 1:12–13; Luke 4:1–13) the parallels between the first humans in the garden and Jesus' experience are noteworthy. Although the parallel may primarily be intended to be that of ancient Israel

---

50. It may be possible to make the case that being "born again" or "born from above" (John 3:3) includes turning away from striving for independence and toward some form of dependence on God as a more fitting performance of the human role in the divine-human relationship.

in the wilderness for forty years after the exodus, with Jesus taking on the role of Israel to resolve the plot issue caused by Israel's sin,[51] the temptation by the satan/devil evokes the scene in Gen 3 of the first humans contending with the serpent.[52] Jesus is explicitly faced with a voice that challenges various aspects of his healthy development and relationship with his divine Father. As Joel Green notes of the Lukan account, the encounter "is concerned with finalizing the establishment of Jesus' performative competence prior to his actual assumption of public ministry in the service of God's salvific aim."[53] The challenges offer temptation to abuse position and power and test God's provision unnecessarily, all of which, much like the first humans, would draw Jesus away from who he is at his core and the relationship with his divine Father that enables that.[54] Ultimately, there is the temptation to perceive the True Self as needing protection from possible threats such as malnutrition (Matt 4:3; Luke 4:3), or requiring a particular type of rule and position to be considered of worth or successful (Matt 4:8–9; Luke 4:5–7). Both of these potentially encourage the development of a caretaker False Self that does not trust the provision of the parent or that has not introjected the loving environment the parent provides that should shape and inform a high sense of self-worth. There is also the temptation to unnecessarily test the provision of the parent, something that would also signify a questioning of trust and whether the child feels loved and secure in the relationship (Matt 4:5–6; Luke 4:9–11). However, as is well known, the difference between the first humans (and Israel for that matter) and Jesus is that temptation does not give way to pursuing a path in which a False Self develops. Instead, Jesus resists temptation, continuing to trust in the provision of his divine

---

51. Green, *Gospel of Luke*, 192–93; Hagner, *Matthew 1–13*, 61–62; Morris, *Matthew*, 70.

52. Although Hagner's main focus is on the parallel between Jesus and Israel, he does make brief mention of the fall scene in Gen 3. See *Matthew 1–13*, 63–69. Morris also makes a fleeting connection in his commentary on Matthew's account, but he suggests it is Luke's account that makes a more obvious connection. See Morris, *Matthew*, 74. Nolland, in his commentary on Luke's account, draws out connections with both Adam and Israel. See Nolland, *Luke 1–9:20*, 182.

53. Green, *Gospel of Luke*, 191.

54. It is worth noting here that "tempt" may also be rendered "test" and that the focus of the testing is not on Jesus' discerning that he is the Son of God—as this is something he already knows—but is instead on him discerning what it means to perform as the Son of God in his incarnate form in this act of the drama of salvation. See Green, *Gospel of Luke*, 191–92; Hagner, *Matthew 1–13*, 63–65; Morris, *Matthew*, 70–71; Nolland, *Luke 1–9:20*, 178–79.

parent and living according to the guidelines laid down by the parent. As noted above, Jesus appears to have introjected the provision of his Father in order to be able to fend off impingement. In the case of the temptation texts, this becomes apparent in Jesus' use of biblical texts to rebut the words of the satan/devil (Matt 4:4, 7, 10; Luke 4:4, 8, 12). Even in the seeming absence of the divine parent—similar to Gen 3—Jesus is secure in being alone yet in a particular type of relationship with his divine Father in which he trusts his Father to provide, when required, all that is needed for Jesus to be his True Self. There is even a sense here that as part of Jesus' human development, he experiences resistance that enables a particular perception of reality and interaction with it. Regardless, what we see displayed in Jesus' response is the continuance of his True Self in the face of temptation to develop a False Self.

To take the question of resistance further, as an important developmental aid within the facilitating environment, we can look at other episodes in Jesus' life. Jesus regularly experienced resistance to his teaching and action from a variety of sources, all of which contributed to his perception of and engagement with reality. For example, in Mark 6:1–6 where Jesus is rejected at Nazareth, we are told that aside from a few healings, "he could do no deed of power there" (v. 5) and that "he was amazed at their unbelief" (v. 6). A further example where Jesus seems to learn about his relationship with creation and what shape that takes as he lives into his True Self is in his encounter with the Syrophoenician woman in Mark 7:24–30 (a Canaanite woman in Matthew's account. See Matt 15:21–28). Here we are told that Jesus enters the region of Tyre (v. 24)—a gentile territory. While there he is met by the woman, a gentile, who begs him to cast a demon out of her daughter (vv. 25–26). Jesus' response seems to suggest that his understanding of his life and ministry was that although salvation would eventually come to the gentiles, that time was not yet, as his primary focus, as directed by his Father, was on the Jews (v. 27). However, his comment about feeding children and dogs is met with a sharp response that seems to cause Jesus to rethink the strictures of his life and ministry in light of the woman's faith, resulting in his healing of the woman's daughter (vv. 28–30). In crossing into geographical territory unusual for a Jew to enter, to get away for a while, Jesus engages with a non-Jewish woman who challenges how his identity is to be lived out in his actions. Arguably this resistance facilitates a maturing of Jesus' understanding of the shape of his True Self and resultant behavior.[55] Confirmation of this maturing and learning may appear in the very next encounter. Although Mark does not make it clear, it is possible that this encounter also involves gentiles requesting help (vv. 31–37).[56] However, unlike the previous encounter, Jesus does not hesitate in responding with an act of healing, now from within a reshaped understanding of who he is and how that presents in his interactions with others.

These brief examples seem to indicate that, in contrast to experiences of controlling the elements, exorcism of demons, and healing of illnesses, Jesus faces experiences of resistance that reshape his self-understanding and how he relates to and interacts with the world around him, all of which enable maturation of the True Self. We can here link in the possibility of Jesus learning to play. As noted above, we know little of Jesus' childhood, so it is not possible to comment on Jesus' development in play at that stage of his life. However, if we refer back to Winnicott's belief that play is a sign of health that takes place in the intermediate space that recognizes objects that resist yet are able to be manipulated to some degree, we see Jesus doing this with words, actions, and objects on numerous occasions. Returning to the temptation texts noted above, when Jesus responds to the satan/devil with biblical texts, his use of those texts suggests he is able take them and "play" with them in such a way that they are able to be reused in an appropriate way in a new context. In the Sermon on the Mount, when Jesus further reinterprets the law, on five occasions he begins, "You have heard that it was said . . ." closely followed by "But I say to you . . ." (Matt 5:21–48). Again, we read of Jesus taking something that offers a level of resistance—the law created by God that Jesus has come to fulfill rather than abolish (Matt 5:17–18)—and reinterpreting and reapplying it in this new context. His statements about the destruction of the temple and it being raised (John 2:19), his taking the Passover meal and transforming it into the Last Supper infused with fresh eucharistic shape and

---

55. Joanna Collicutt McGrath offers a more detailed reading of this encounter with a similar conclusion to that presented here. See McGrath, *Jesus and the Gospel Women*, 26–37. Both Robert Guelich and Donald Hagner seem to suggest that Jesus was initially genuinely dismissive of the woman because of her ethnicity. See Guelich, *Mark 1–8:26*, 385–89; Hagner, *Matthew 14–28*, 440–43. Leon Morris, however, in his commentary on Matthew's account tries to soften Jesus' response in v. 26 by speculating about Jesus' facial expressions and tone of voice. However, there is nothing in the text that explicitly supports Morris's interpretation. See Morris, *Matthew*, 404–5.

56. Guelich, *Mark 1–8:26*, 393–94.

content (Matt 26:17–29; Mark 14:12–25; Luke 22:7–23; John 13:1–30; 1 Cor 11:23–26), as well as numerous parables, display a developed ability to play in the intermediate space.[57] All such examples arguably suggest that Jesus Christologically qualifies the activity of play as an important sign of healthy development and maturation and therefore this is to be encouraged and celebrated. Interestingly, further resistance is met when others refuse to engage in a healthy and helpful way in the play that Jesus is involved in such as the confrontation with Pilate. However, even here, Jesus plays with the notion of king and kingdom (John 18:28–40), and his ability to play in such a way that brings transformation of symbols and situations reaches its climax at the cross and finally the tomb. Here the resistance of torture and death and the related objects are met with the eucatastrophic play of transforming them into a site of hope, freedom, and life eternal where resurrection is encountered at a tomb usually associated with death and loss. Jesus is able to "play" to the point of bringing redemption, reconciliation, and freedom from the most hopeless and devastating situations—what Vanhoozer would label as improvisation that carries on the through-line of the theodrama toward its superobjective. The question for the church, which we will explore in the following chapter, is how we are to learn to join in this transformative "playing" of God in the world as we learn to introject the love of God and improvise on the divine performance of Jesus.

In connection to Jesus' experience of resistance, there is also something significant to suggest about object usage. This may seem like a strange parallel to draw as part of what Winnicott has in mind when discussing object usage is that the infant is moving to the reality principle and thus discovering through planned failure and the resultant disillusionment that they are not omnipotent after all. At first glance, this might seem difficult to apply to Jesus as God in human form, particularly if a high Christology is retained. However, if we take seriously the kenosis involved in the incarnation (Phil 2:1–12) then it becomes possible to say that the pattern for human development laid down by the Son in his performance involves learning some of the limits of living in the world in human form, and what is possible in interaction with the world where, as noted above, the Son is only able to do what he is guided to do by the Father. In addition, the Son's existence and obedient activity is only possible because of the work of the Spirit,

---

57. In John 2:21–22, the writer helpfully tells future readers of the nature of Jesus' playing with the image of the temple.

which Luke in particular draws attention to.[58] Jesus' process of healthy maturation thus, arguably, involves discovering his incarnate limits and how to "use" objects, in the way Winnicott uses that term. This also involves the planned healthy "failure" of the parent/s which, although we have no clear evidence regarding Jesus' human parents, we do have some evidence regarding Jesus' divine Father. Returning to the various experiences of resistance, particularly the temptation texts noted above, it is possible to suggest that Jesus was gradually exposed to this world at the appropriate time by the planned "failure" of God the Father and the guidance of the Spirit. This then enables the development of both object relating and object usage in the way that healthy human development in relationship with God should. Here we return to how Jesus responds to seemingly overwhelming impingement.

Returning to the passion and the cross we find scenes in the theo-drama in which cries of lament, in certain circumstances, are given Christological affirmation as belonging to the True Self. If we were to take just Jesus' response to the temptations of the satan/devil as a test case we could refer back to Job's initial response to the various traumatizing experiences and suggest that, through a Christological view of the True Self, this is what the first humans, acting out of their True Selves, should have done. We could also suggest that the biblically rooted responses of Jesus, emerging from a specific way of perceiving and interacting with his Father, creation, and the self, act as transitional phenomena at a point where anxiety needs to be kept at bay in the face of overwhelming impingement to his going on being. However, although such responses do seem to act as transitional phenomena, to presume this is the only way to maintain the True Self in the face of all forms of impingement is to be overly reductionistic. Such a narrow view is brought into question as we take into consideration the accounts of Jesus' amazement and learning when he faces resistance. Those alone may not be enough to persuade the reader that Job's response is justified through a Christological lens, but they move us toward further experiences of Jesus that should do just that.

As I have explored at length elsewhere, what we see in the garden of Gethsemane and at the cross is Jesus improvising on (and therefore playing with) performances from the Old Testament as he uses lament as

---

58. Luke more than the other Gospel writers highlights the involvement of the Spirit in the incarnate life of Jesus, noting the Spirit's involvement in his conception (1:35), baptism (3:22), filling and leading into the wilderness (4:1), and empowerment on leaving the wilderness (4:14).

the vehicle to enable honest communication to continue with his Father during a period of extreme suffering (impingement).[59] If we continue to affirm that Jesus always acted out of his True Self—as we must—then the performance of lament must have a place within that. Jesus' performance in the garden of Gethsemane and at the cross, as he encounters impingements to his going on being that threaten annihilation, displays a performance of the archetypal True Self when faced with resistance that crosses the threshold into a threat to the life of the True Self. With this in view, not only does Job's response appear justified and clarified as a response of a True Self, but this also sheds further Christological light on what a performance of the True Self might have looked like for the first humans and what it, therefore, might look like for those of us in the current act of the theodrama. There is a level of overlap here with my previous work on the Christological qualification and clarification of the use of lament, but I want to go further and explore how and why it works.

As has already been noted about Job, the significance of lament is not just that it keeps the conversation with God honest during great pain and the seeming absence of God. What we can say as we combine the insights of Brueggemann and Winnicott is that in the first move from orientation to disorientation, as impingement takes hold creating anxiety about possible annihilation, the practice of lament acts as both transitional phenomena—something to cling to, to ward off the overwhelming emotions that come with this experience—while also providing a verbal avenue for expression of anger, pain, and grief—which Winnicott highlights as healthy forms of crying in a developing infant.[60] To push the point further we can consider the same phenomena from a pathological angle by, with Winnicott, exploring what happens when such cries are not allowed for.

In the case of cries due to pain or anger, an infant who does not cry when in pain or feeling angry has likely lost the belief that the parent can bring about relief from whatever is causing these emotions. One might say that hope in help from the parent has been lost and a False Self develops as caretaker and protector. Mapping this over to the practice of lament

---

59. Torr, *Dramatic*, 176–85.

60. It is important to note that there is a difference in causation between anxiety resulting from planned failure in adaptation and that brought about by overwhelming impingement that threatens annihilation. There is likely a difference in intensity as well. However, the same responses of crying and the use of transitional phenomena hold in both with the difference being that the latter may have pathological results.

displayed by Jesus at the cross and by Job and the psalmist suggests that this practice is indeed a healthy, hope-filled one that continues to expect and desire aid from, and communion with, the divine parent amid the most pain-filled circumstances. When discussing both crying as a result of anger and sadness or grief, Winnicott is keen to note that healthy development of emotions requires healthy expression. It is true that in contrast to babies, adults are expected to be able to control their emotions to some degree. However, when this kind of emotion is curtailed too much, the result is a curtailing of the ability to feel the full depth of such emotion and a fear of one's emotional response—all of which results in a False Self, a self that is emotionally stunted and, thus, unable to cope well with others' emotions. It is hard, if not impossible, to develop into one's True Christlike Self if one is unable to develop in an emotionally healthy way, or not allowed or enabled to by one's family, community, or church. In this instance, what is dialogically consummated is a False Self. However, further discussion about the facilitating and curtailing of lament by the church community will be discussed in the following chapter as will how cries of hopeless despair might be met.

Conclusion

As this chapter draws to a close, we are in a position to suggest that the biblical picture of the first humans, Job and, most importantly, Jesus, seem to correspond in significant ways with Winnicott's developmental theories and that these theories have offered helpful insights with which to explore healthy maturation in the biblical texts. In the same way that there appear to be times in Jesus' life for making a trust-driven stand from a secure position *and* an anxiety-driven cry of lament from a place of pain, we must be able to make the same affirmation about the lives of all humans who are seeking to live out their True Self—including the first humans called by God. The choices of these first humans—and every human since then, including the nation of Israel—set in motion the emergence of False Selves. However, although one response that would have prevented that would have been the secure, trust-filled affirmation of the way of the divine parent, an alternative and seemingly acceptable response displayed by Job and, most importantly by Jesus, is one of lament—a questioning cry of pain from a place of anxiety demanding the presence and affirmation of God, if not a divine resolution to the presenting problem.

In the same way that Jesus makes prayer—communication with his divine Father—central to living out of his True Self, so created humans are called to do the same thing, in whatever form honest prayer takes. This draws us back to a central point in Vanhoozer's definition of the *imago Dei*—one who answers back to God in a particular way and works on God's behalf, in relationship with God, to participate in moving the theodrama toward its eschatological superobjective of communion with the creator. To be found "in Christ" is to be drawn back toward a pattern of life involving a particular type of relationship with self, God, and creation that has been achieved by Jesus on our behalf and that reshapes our own interpretation of our own lives. What insights from Winnicott's theories have helped us to see is that healthy development is not as straightforward as Vanhoozer's approach of learning how to improvise, rehearsing one's part, and, aided by the Holy Spirit, performing it. Job is an anomaly in that he was able to perform as a True Self despite his community; however, this is likely not the norm! What is required to enable the healthy development of Christlike disciples is a good enough environment that facilitates such growth and change. But what does that look like? In the next chapter, we will use insights from Winnicott's theories to attempt to answer that question. We will then be in a position to return to where this project began—with the subject of trauma—and make suggestions for how the church might better facilitate post-traumatic remaking.

7

The Facilitating Eucharistic Church

Introduction

HAVING EXPLORED WHAT HEALTHY and unhealthy development of the *imago Dei* might look like in the previous chapter, we turn our attention in this chapter to the role of the church in the process of healthy maturation. In the previous chapter, we were able to reread key biblical texts and themes using insights from Winnicott's theories in order to explore the processes required to enable the healthy development of the *imago Dei* into the True Christlike Self. However, although we can affirm Winnicott's point about humans being born with a natural inclination toward healthy growth—albeit attributing that inclination to the divine creator—we also must affirm with Winnicott the importance of good enough environmental provision to enable such growth. Although rereading biblical accounts using Winnicott's work offers us fresh insight into the processes of healthy development for humans, which is given Christological clarity and affirmation, what was left unaddressed in that chapter was how those processes are outworked in the current act of the theodrama. To grow into being the image of God in its full sense is, as we have noted in conversation with Vanhoozer in previous chapters, to "put on Christ" and take one's place in the body of Christ, the church. The provision to do that, as we have glimpsed in reexamining the Genesis creation accounts, Job, and the incarnation, continues into the present act in terms of what healthy development involves and what kind of environment is required. We noted in the account of Job that although his actions give us insight into what a healthy response looks like in painful circumstances, his friends do not offer him much aid. In the following chapter, we will return to the question of Job's friends—those who are supporting others who are experiencing trauma. But, to complete the foundations for that, we need first to explore more generally how the church facilitates healthy development in its members.

A criticism that could be raised here is that I am emphasizing the needs of the individual over the community—something of a modern-day consumerist attitude—that almost seems to use the community of the church for the needs of the individual. Such a view potentially misses the significant point that if individuals flourish as the *imago Dei*, then so should the community, given the nature of what such flourishing means. Hopefully the win-win of mutual flourishing proposed in this approach will become apparent as we proceed.

The chapter will build by first rereading the church's life using Winnicott's theories as an analogical tool by focusing on various aspects of Winnicott's good enough provision for healthy maturation and showing how such provision might aid the maturation of the disciple toward their True Christlike Self. This will link up with what Vanhoozer has termed the *ad intra* aspect of the eucharistic church. Once completed it will be shown how this relates to what Vanhoozer referred to as the *ad extra* aspects of the church and how such practices in total enable a unified, holy, catholic, and apostolic Eucharist-centered church to flourish. This process, combined with the previous chapter, will complete the foundations required for exploring the issue of what Job's friends could have done better—the subject of the next chapter. We begin by turning to the facilitating church environment.

The Facilitating Church Environment

A danger noted in engaging with Vanhoozer's approach thus far is that it appears overly cerebral in its understanding of individual and corporate flourishing. What is apparent from Winnicott's work up to this point is that although there is no engagement with the Christian theodrama as a worldview, there is great emphasis on the right sort of good enough environmental provision for the healthy maturation of individuals. My suggestion here is that it is possible to map Winnicott's insights into environmental provision onto Vanhoozer's theodramatic worldview in such a way that Vanhoozer's overly cerebral approach can be counterbalanced. My starting point for this is to propose that although God does take on a parental role—as per the previous chapter—that role is shared with the people of God in certain ways. In a sense, this meshes with the notion of the *imago Dei* being that which mediates the presence of God to creation and vice versa. Although God is the first, divine, parent, there is a clear mandate throughout Scripture that part of the task of the *imago Dei* is to mediate God's parental provision to others in community relationships. To image God in creation is to display in word and deed how God would operate under the same circumstances and limitations.

As has already been noted, the superobjective of the theodrama is the union between God and creation in a way that does not swallow creation up but provides it with life to the full, for eternity. We have also noted that a significant problem with the plotline of the theodrama that requires resolution is the fall. However we might understand the details of that, what it conveys is that humans failed to perform the part for which they were cast in a fitting way—and continued to do so—thus requiring the divine playwright to enter the stage in human form to resolve the plot issue of the entrance of evil and resultant suffering. The act in which we find ourselves is one in which humans are called and enabled by the Spirit to "put on" the improvised image of God incarnate, as they grow into their True Christlike Selves, noting that sin encourages the growth and maintenance of the False Self. The questions to be addressed here are how does that growing into a True Christlike Self happen, and what role does the church community play in facilitating it?

The obvious place to start as we map Winnicott's insights is with the church as parent who is good enough to provide the right kind of environment for growth.[1] It is important to note here that I am not suggesting that the church replaces God as divine parent or that a relationship with God is not important for each individual. I am instead saying that it is both/and, and that God intends a combination of the two. I will also be suggesting that humans take their lead from God's example, particularly revealed in Christ, when discerning what good enough provision might look like. In that way, this is a continuation of the task of improvising

---

1. Calvin and others got here before me with the idea of mother church (for example, see Calvin, *Institutes* 4.1.4 [2279])! However, with Winnicott's help, I am aiming to develop this idea in new ways.

on the performance of Christ, but as the whole company of performers. With that said we can return to Winnicott's model.

As in the previous chapter, it is important to begin the mapping process by first noting the points of dis/agreement around the subject of dependence and independence. As also noted in the previous chapter, where paths diverge is with regard to the *telos* of development. However, the divergence in this chapter is not to the same degree, as we are dealing, primarily, with human-human relationships rather than God-human relationships. The difference is that where a level of dependence on God by humans is intended to always be present in the healthy development of parts in the theodrama, the maturing of individuals in the church suggests a more equal *telos* for individuals in community—something more akin to the interdependence Winnicott edges toward in parts of his work. Eschatologically, there is the possibility to suggest a completeness to the process of moving toward interdependence. Prior to the eschaton, in a way similar to Winnicott, the processes are not so linear in that at various points in time for various reasons, individuals may move between the role of child and parent in the church community. However, that does not alter the role of the church as parent to some of the people, some of the time and it is that dynamic that we are focusing on here. Within that dynamic, individuals will likely experience the stages of absolute dependence and relative dependence as they develop and encounter life in all its pain and beauty, and it is those stages that continue to provide a helpful structure for our mapping work.

Absolute Dependence

In terms of the stage of absolute dependence, we are in good company in that Paul and the writer of the letter to the Hebrews both use related language to describe im/maturity in the church. In 1 Cor 3:1–2, Paul describes the church in Corinth as infants not yet mature enough in certain aspects of their development to move from metaphorical milk to solid food. The writer of the letter to the Hebrews uses the same idea to make the same point (5:11–14) meaning we are here developing an analogy already in use in the church. We can recall from Winnicott's work that the stage of absolute dependence includes a period of primary maternal preoccupation and is characterized by the natural ability of the good enough mother to adapt to the changing needs of the baby. The baby is in a fragile, unintegrated state in which the sense of self is not yet formed, and the ego is not yet strong enough to manage the id impulses. The mother's provision of a healthy facilitating environment is what enables the baby to exist in such a state and begin to develop in a healthy way without significant impingement. We need to remind ourselves that Winnicott used the term good enough because he recognized that perfection was out of reach for humans and that healthy infants were able to bridge the gap in development left by the good enough provision.

To map this over to the context of the church is not to make a direct transfer but is instead to note significant points of connection while recognizing the limits of the analogy. As has already been highlighted in reference to the sections from 1 Corinthians and Hebrews, the early church seemed more than aware of the fact that development as a follower of Jesus had significant parallels with child development. Although not using Winnicott's language (for obvious reasons!), there is a reasonably clear sense present in the New Testament of the needs of those new to the faith that required significant adaptation to need by the leader or community. In the Gospel accounts, although no hard evidence seems to be present regarding a stage of absolute dependence in the life of followers of Jesus, there is a clear sense in which Jesus engages in a process of teaching and forming the disciples in which he gradually exposes them to particular knowledge and experience. Perhaps most important is Jesus' gradual exposure of the disciples to his impending death and resurrection, which was met with varying responses (Matt 16:21–23; 17:22–23; 20:17–19; Mark 8:31–33; 9:30–32; 10:32–34; Luke 9:21–22, 43–45; 18:31–34)![2] After his resurrection, Jesus then appears to various disciples on various occasions, in some cases re-narrating the drama of salvation in light of Easter (Luke 24:13–27, 36–49). John's Gospel also recounts Jesus' promise to send the Holy Spirit to remind them of his teaching (14:26). All of the above highlights the role of both Jesus and the Holy Spirit in the process of enabling maturation in disciples. To some degree, we face a blurring of lines here. Jesus as God incarnate offers a window into divine parenting in how he reveals God to creation while also offering the primary example of how to care for one another as the body of Christ, the church. Further, he offers a window into the True Self in relationship with the Father that humans

---

2. The Transfiguration would provide a further example of Jesus exposing his disciples to fresh insights about his identity, his performance, and the drama in which they were cast.

are growing toward. These link together because it is as we grow into our True Christlike Selves that we are more Christlike in our nurture of others in the church, while remembering that nurture of others also involves them developing as individuals, as well as the whole body of Christ, in their direct relationship with God as the divine parent. Given the fact that the church is the body of Christ consisting of the corporate *imago Dei* and individual *imago Dei*, there is therefore a sense in which the church is called to blur the lines as it mediates divine parenting while also continuing to allow for direct parenting by the divine parent toward individuals. The Spirit of God is the one who effects both of these paths of nurture—within the church, mediated by the church, and directed to individuals. That said, Jesus' gradual nurturing of the disciples offers us both further clarification of the Father's method of parenting—as the Son reveals the Father—while also providing the crucial example of how disciples are to nurture others—the foundation of this being loving service of one another (John 13:1–17, 34–35). And, although the evidence is not explicit, the evolving adaptation to need by Jesus that includes the process of revelation and exposure to resistance suggests that it would not be out of place to characterize an early phase of the disciples' life in relationship to Jesus as one of absolute dependence. This Christologically qualifies the point that church and individual may pass through a stage of a type of absolute dependence.

In addition, it is also fair to follow Winnicott in affirming that there is no child (disciple) without the mother (Jesus or the church) and the environment. This is not to collapse identities into one another but is more to make the point that each disciple exists in a particular context (environment) and in a particular relationship with God and the church (parents) and it is not possible to speak of their development into a True Christlike Self without reference to the context and relationships. Where a line perhaps needs to be drawn is concerning the idea of primary maternal preoccupation. This is so because it is not clear or necessary that God needs to pass through this phase as a parent or that the church offers such a response to those new to following Jesus. Having said that, some of the ways in which Paul speaks of his attitude toward various church communities and how he urges them to be toward one another do not rule this out (e.g., 1 Cor 4:14–16; Gal 4:12–20; 1 Thess 2:7–12). It is, however, a minor point in comparison to the broader points being made here, namely, that adaptation to need is vital for healthy development in the church community and that the identity and development of the disciple are highly dependent on key relationships and environments which must be good enough for disciples to develop. However, we are here met with the question of what good enough provision might look like. To explore this, we return to Winnicott's areas of holding, handling, object presenting, and mirroring as we explore how they relate to the provision of the Eucharist-shaped church.

Holding

We can recall from chapter 5 that the importance of holding lies in the safety, protection, and provision offered by the parent in their adaptive response to the infant that meets the various needs of the infant. At a point of great fragility in the life of the infant, provision that offers good enough holding meets their needs and keeps overwhelming impingement to their going on being at bay. While the ego is not strong enough to cope with the demands of the outside world, the mother provides auxiliary ego support that maintains the illusion of omnipotence and total subjectivity. Again, for obvious reasons, a direct mapping does not work. However, what can be mapped across is the general need of the church to offer adaptation to the needs of those in their care, making responses, like parenting, case-specific. Exploration of the subject of holding is fundamental because it gives vital definition to the kind of environment in which healthy development and transformation can take place. Winnicott notes that holding never stops, it just changes depending on the context and needs of the individual. Holding may not mean physical holding when it comes to the church (although it might), but there is a sense in which the church is called to continually affirm the love and care of God mediated through the body of Christ. Connecting to Vanhoozer's point in chapter 4, the church is called to a life of fidelity, generosity, and hospitality, all of which mediate and reflect the love of God in Christ celebrated in the Eucharist. To be held in community life is to know that others in that community, as an act of love, are faithful to God and therefore one another in their desire to see each other flourish as *imago Dei*. To hold one another in the church is not to offer false hope to all that everything will always be simple and straightforward as a follower of Jesus, but instead to embody a way of being toward one another that, as far as possible, guards against overwhelming each other with more than can safely be handled on the developmental journey while providing, as far as possible, all that is needed to enable one another to flourish. At root, this looks like fidelity to one another anchored in love and sensitivity to others' needs and the work of God in one another's lives. It is not just the case that fidelity is a good thing—which it is—but that fidelity is a good thing because it creates a particular type of environment in which growth can occur. Winnicott notes that the constant stability of provision from the same person helps with the development of the infant. The same thing can be said with regard to disciples in community. Continuity of "holding" provision in the form of the Christlike fidelity described by Vanhoozer will significantly improve the development of individuals in the following of Jesus.

Holding is also a way of illuminating the kind of generosity God in Christ has offered to creation and which the church, therefore, is to offer to others in her midst. When the mother holds the child in a good enough way, it involves giving of herself and her resources in order that the infant may feel safe and loved. Such holding likely requires sacrifice on the part of the parent as their time and energy is directed at the nurture of the infant. Returning to the eucharistic community, this type of embodiment is exemplified in Christ celebrated at the Eucharist and should be something the Spirit-empowered and -directed church mirrors as it gives thanks for God's provision. Although guarding one's own reserves for the sake of resilience and a sustainable pattern of life is paramount, the generosity of resources required by the mother to aid the healthy maturation of her baby finds common ground with that which is expected of the church toward one another to aid in the healthy maturation of disciples. As noted in chapter 4, generosity when mentioned in the context of the church, often conjures up the subject of financial giving—a valid issue for discussion. However, in the context of the current discussion, generosity has a broader understanding that concerns discerning and sacrificially adapting to the needs of others to maintain a consistent holding environment for others to grow within.

Overlapping with love-driven fidelity and generosity is the practice of hospitality that finds significant points of contact with holding. Commitment to the nurture of another is rooted in love-fueled fidelity and generosity, but hospitality is what describes the facilitating environment of attentive protection and provision in which the infant is hosted and cared for by the parent who keeps destructive impingements at bay. The one who prepares the table in the presence of enemies (Ps 23:5) that might impinge on healthy development is the Christ who welcomes us to come and be nourished by the Spirit that unites us with Christ. This is mirrored when the church draws others to come, be fed, and cared for as transformation, healing, and maturation are effected by the Spirit through the church.

Before moving to handling, a further point about types and content of holding needs to be mentioned here. Holding can take the form of physical holding which, under the right circumstances and in a suitable manner, can be what is needed. However, holding may also take a more general form of the space one creates for another to enter that requires thought regarding the structuring of that space and atmosphere. In a more formal setting, this can include laying out clear directions for the "script" of the gathering—what will happen, how, and why. It can also involve what liturgy is used that can both convey the loving intent of the community as well as help give voice to emotions, thoughts, or questions that those present may not necessarily know how to articulate. Marilyn McCord Adams has noted the similarities between the consistency in the structure of Greek tragedy highlighted by Aristotle and the consistency of the structure of liturgy within the church. Arguably, it is the familiar in both cases that provides the safety necessary for the participants to be challenged in suitable ways by the content. She suggests, "Implicitly, such literary, theatrical, and ritual conventions promise to contain the confusion, to house the chaos occasioned by any challenges the drama might present."[3] Liturgy and the wider familiar structure of a church gathering thus offer a way of holding participants in a way that makes space for transformation but within a safe and familiar environment.

However, for the holding environment to be good enough, it must be prepared to continue to offer Christlike loving fidelity, generosity, and hospitality without shaming, rejecting, or retaliating, even if boundaries are pushed and tested. Obviously, there are issues of safeguarding to be considered for all involved, but rejection, retaliation, and/or shaming does not reflect the Christ who died at the hands of those he came to save and continued to love beyond death, and therefore is not part of the holding to be offered by the church (Luke 23:34). This may seem obvious but can so often be lacking in churches when an expectation of conformity to certain patterns of behavior within a certain time-frame is expected. Here, we return to curiosity as a further discipline to be fostered by the church. If the transformative and developmental work of a follower of Christ is ultimately effected by the Spirit then the question each church

---

3. Adams, "Eucharistic Drama," 212.

needs to ask when attending to one another is, "how do we co-operate with the Spirit of God at work in this person's life?" When such a question is asked with genuine loving curiosity, there has to be a readiness to revisit, reshape, and even jettison one's time-frames and methods. This is what Christlike holding in the eucharistic community demands of those aiming to be the body of Christ to others.

A further point to be added here is about holding that is done from a distance. Holding of another can be done in heart and mind as the church family commits to praying for one another.[4] This sort of holding is important in the shaping of the discipline of holding in the one praying and in the care of the one being held, as an act of engaging in the work of God who is the only one able to do the deep work of healing and transformation.

The good enough holding environment of the church thus needs to be one of adaptive and yet continual safety and provision for those who are most fragile, and it is to be characterized by fidelity, generosity, and hospitality rooted in love if it is to support healthy maturation of the True Christlike Self. Holding illuminates and informs what is displayed by God in Christ as celebrated and mirrored by the eucharistic body of Christ. If we turn attention to Winnicott's emphasis on "handling" infants as a subset of holding, we are offered further insight into how churches are called to function as parables of the kingdom.

Handling

Much like the above point about "holding," in the majority of cases we are here using the term "handling" in an analogical way within the life of the church, although, also like holding, not always. Physical contact in the right way at the right time can be deeply comforting and affirming. However, as we recall Winnicott's link between handling and personalization we are reminded that what good enough handling achieves in Winnicott's framework is the affirming of the whole person as a single unit. Within the good enough holding environment of the church, it is important, therefore, to recognize the whole person as *imago Dei*. Historically and in contemporary settings there has been the danger of compartmentalizing aspects of a person as well as an overemphasis on such aspects as the mind or soul over and above the body in a way that

---

4. Ulanov, *Finding Space*, 47–48.

finds a more natural home in the work of Plato rather than the Bible. Whereas health in Winnicott's work and, arguably in the Scriptures, involves the move toward, if not completion of, integration of mind and body, there has been a danger in the church of privileging the rational aspect of humans. At the other end of the spectrum, there has also, at points, been the risk of privileging experience over reason. "Handling" mapped onto the context of the church involves recognizing each individual as a whole person made in the image of God rather than privileging aspects of that person over other aspects. In turn, as we shall see in the following chapter, this will call for responding to the whole of the traumatized individual when facilitating healing and growth.

The contrast that we have noted in Vanhoozer's work is that although his account of the *imago Dei* embraces a holistic view of humans that majors on the improvised performance of Christ in context, there is a tendency to slip toward an overly cerebral method of formation that does not seem to recognize that formation and transformation is mediated through embodied relationships within the church. The point here is that life as the *imago Dei* involves heart, mind, soul, and body, and the good enough facilitating church must be one that recognizes this and tends to its members accordingly. Creation, the incarnation, and the resurrection all point to a God who values every aspect of creation and desires that it be salvaged in total. God loves creation and, in Christ, has reconciled creation to himself (John 3:16; Col 1:20). Using insights from Winnicott's theories, we can see afresh the value to God of creation and persons in total and therefore, the importance of the eucharistic community valuing and seeking to facilitate the integration of the whole person. To privilege one part of an individual—or for that matter one part of the body of Christ—over another is to discourage integration and worse, encourage disintegration. Instead, the enabling of the whole person to flourish as their True Christlike Self in relationship with God, self, others, and creation must be at the core of the theatre of the gospel.

Object Presenting

We turn now to the subject of object presenting, which may not appear at first glance to naturally connect with the role of the church in relation to the development of the True Christlike Self of the individual. However, there appears to be a definite tendency for God in the Old Testament, echoed by Jesus in the Gospels and then the early church, to engage with the healthy development of individuals by beginning where they are in terms of knowledge and understanding of the world before introducing teaching, perspectives, and experiences that will challenge that. Although this is not the maintenance of the illusion of omnipotence and the adaptation to every id-driven need of the child offered by the mother in the stage of absolute dependence, what is a point of similarity is the importance of not overwhelming the individual in each case with more than they can cope with while trust is built between the individual and God and the church community. Again, this links to love-fueled fidelity, generosity, hospitality, and curiosity in that Christlike object presenting prioritizes the development of the other and commits to sacrificially discerning how best to contribute to that. Examples of this are present in the way Jesus uses language and images that are contextually meaningful to provide familiarity and relevance for his hearers. The same is true with Paul at the Areopagus as he converses with his hearers (Acts 17:16–34). In a far more striking sense, this is also true of the incarnation in that God comes to humans as a human (John 1:14), thus presenting Godself in a way that is tangible and accessible based on where humans are beginning from, before displaying in his life, death, resurrection, and ascension what humans were made for (Rom 8:29–30; 1 Cor 15; Col 1:18). Although this aspect of Winnicott's developmental theories does not map directly, there is a sense in which the point about development and maturation being possible only where overwhelm is guarded against does illuminate the work of a church. This is particularly so where a church is so driven by the goal of transformation—and its particular interpretation of that—that it fails to take into account the starting point of each individual or the rate and path of healthy development unique to each individual. To present Christ to another in a way that is irrelevant or worse, overwhelming, is to be complicit in forcing the True Christlike Self of the other into hiding with the False Self emerging as protector, or by excluding the other because they do not mature in a particular time or way. Although a program model approach can have benefits for some, what Winnicott's work illuminates in Scripture is the importance of relationships that are tailored to the needs of others as foundational for healthy transformation and development.

Mirroring

Discussed previously is Winnicott's concept of mirroring in which the infant first experiences being seen by the mother, known as apperception. This experience of being seen, having the self reflected back in the face of the mother, is what enables the ego to develop the strength to eventually perceive the self and the world around. We will come to see the importance of mirroring when working with those who are traumatized in the next chapter but, for now, it is important to mention the more general importance of this in church life.

The identity of the church, like the identity of humans more generally, finds its ultimate definition in its creator. Where humans are made in the image of God, the church is the body of Christ and is called and enabled by the Spirit to mirror Christ to the world in its performance. In the process of maturation into one's True Christlike Self one's perception of the self must change as the move to fully put on Christlikeness is made. However, to be able to see oneself in this way—perception—there must be the experience of being seen this way and seeing oneself in the other—apperception. In the garden of Eden, this occurs as a direct encounter between God and the first humans. In the current act of the drama this encounter with God is mediated to some degree by the church. Mother church is thus cast in this maternal role of seeing—bearing witness—to those in her midst who, in her responses and actions, are able to both experience the face of God as well as themselves as *imago Dei* reflected back. This provides the bedrock and ongoing support for the emergence and development of the True Christlike Self.

Such a calling to perform Christ for others requires the discipline, as Vanhoozer has noted, of learning our parts and maintaining our relationship with the one who first sees us and who we are to mirror. We again return to the Eucharist as the central place where we are reminded of who God is, and what human shape God's dwelling takes in Christ for the world as we enter into prayerful and liturgically shaped and guided communion with one another and God in Word and sacrament. In this gathering, creation—bread and wine in particular—Scripture, liturgy, and song are used by the Spirit to reveal the presence of God who sees us and loves us as we are with a desire to transform us. It is this apperception of God, effected by the Spirit, mediated through the eucharistic gathering that enables the church to see itself and creation more and more the way God intends. Apperception—"You are my Son, the Beloved; with you I am well pleased" (Mark 1:11; Luke 3:22)—in the act of mirroring leads to perception of myself, others, and creation through a theodramatic lens. This, in turn, shapes the body of Christ to perform Christ to others by seeing them, as the image of God, loved as they are, with a desire for the True Christlike Self to emerge more and more. The body of Christ is both the receiver of God's prior perception in the act of apperception and the one who mediates God's apperception to others in its Spirited perception of creation. The church, as with God and as the place where God is mediated, must also be present to bear witness to the perception of the other as it develops in order to validate it as real and seen. Again, we can return to our core markers of fidelity, generosity, hospitality, and curiosity that, after the pattern of Christ, guide and shape how the church attends to others in such a way that enables them to feel real in the theodrama before God and God's people and to learn to mirror performances of Christ that are taking place before them, in how they improvise their performances. Mirroring is not parrot-like repetition but learning to improvise in ways that are in synchronicity with the Spirit of God at work in the church as each member finds their place in the body of Christ. Transformation via mirroring and attunement goes beyond and deeper than focusing solely on the mind and may not even begin with the transformation of the mind. More will be said about this in the following chapter.

Relative Dependence

Although all of the above are important beyond Winnicott's stage of absolute dependence in the healthy maturation of individuals, the stage of relative dependence brings additional direction for the facilitating church. Of note here are the areas of object usage, play, and transitional phenomena.

Object Usage, Transitional Phenomena, and Play

As was discussed in chapter 5, object usage is intrinsically linked to Winnicott's theories about transitional phenomena and play. We can recall that planned failure in adaptation or exposure to non-overwhelming resistance or impingement enables the infant to separate the me from the not-me as disillusionment at the lack of omnipotence is experienced. The reality principle is then encountered with resultant anxiety due to the transition. During this process, transitional phenomena are selected and used by the infant in the intermediate space that has opened up, as a way of keeping the anxiety at bay during the transition. Object usage occurs, as does the ability to play, when objects survive the attempts of the infant to destroy them, as this leads to a fresh experience of the world as other, outside, and objective. The ability to play develops as the infant interacts with an objective world that resists yet can also be shaped and changed. The capacity to be alone also develops due to good enough provision up to this point and as a result of the development of a sense of a subjective self in the world. The combination of these developmental strands enables the ability to interact and play with others in the intermediate space. We now need to map this over to the facilitating church.

A good place to start with exploring how the areas of Winnicott's work relate to the church is with the experience of resistance due to healthy failure in adaptation. Over the course of time, Jesus exposed his disciples to the reality of his impending execution and resurrection as necessary parts of the theodrama that would enable it to reach its superobjective. The disciples—most notably Peter—do not respond well to this experience, which impinges on their expectations to the point of overwhelm. Various responses emerge such as distraction by discussing who is the greatest (Matt 20:20–28; Mark 10:35–45) and Peter's rebuke of Jesus (Matt 16:22–23; Mark 8:32–33).[5] The point is that these are among many examples in the Scriptures where the people of God experience resistance and impingement sometimes to the point of overwhelm. Some of these occurrences, such as the one mentioned above, can be easily categorized as planned failure in adaptation—a purposeful exposure to reality that offers short-term discomfort but long-term maturation. It is important to note that not every instance of resistance and impingement is necessarily a planned failure—as will become blatantly apparent in the next chapter. However, life experiences combined with the formation of individuals by the church will often—much like Paul and the writer of Hebrews highlight—offer the opportunity to taste solid food in contrast to the prior feeding on milk. These transitions can provide the opportunity for growth toward a

---

5. Morris suggests that in Matthew's account, Jesus' interaction with the disciples regarding who is greatest comes sometime later than Jesus' third foretelling of his death. However, this need not be the case, as both Hagner (Matthew's account) and Evans (Mark's account) suggest one follows immediately after the other. It is this latter interpretation that is presumed here. See Morris, *Matthew*, 508; Hagner, *Matthew 14–28*, 578; Evans, *Mark 8:27—16:20*, 115.

more mature engagement with the world, God, others, and the self and enable the individual to "play" in the intermediate space.

Play, in the context of a Christian theodramatic worldview lived out by individuals within the body of Christ, can be defined as the interaction with that which is other than the self in such a way that there is the ongoing negotiation of what is possible in the space where the self and the other object or person interact—the intermediate space. This can be physical interaction but can also be playing with ideas or the inner workings of how one relates to another person, situation, object, etc. To return to the example used above of Jesus' revealing to his disciples what was going to happen to him and why, we can see a number of transitions taking place that enable the possibility of maturation of the disciples.

The revelation of the upcoming events is a failure in adaptation because Jesus implicitly challenges the image of messiah that the disciples had inherited and bought into. Presuming the disciples have the developed capacity, individually and collectively, to cope with this impingement, the path is open for growth. This growth comes in the form of a new awareness about how God is working in the world that cannot be controlled in some omnipotent way (Peter's rebuke of Jesus) but is something that resists such an attempt at control (Jesus' response). The result is not that Peter now has to come to terms with a world in which he has no control but rather that there is a change in his understanding regarding who God is, how God works within the world, and how Peter can interact in the intermediate space. This then impacts Peter's thoughts and actions as Peter learns to "play" in this ever-developing intermediate space.[6]

This and similar experiences of resistance and impingement highlight both the need for the church to engage in planned failures in adaptation as an aid to the maturation of individuals as well as the importance of transitional phenomena when such impingements are experienced. Peter's experience displays an implicit grasping after transitional phenomena in the face of the transition that is happening. In his case, it is a reaching for a narrative or memory that is familiar and keeps anxiety at bay. However, as noted in the previous chapter, biblical lament can also act as a transitional phenomenon required when an individual or group makes the first move from a place of orientation

---

6. Arguably, Jesus outlines the future trajectory of Peter's maturation in their post-resurrection interaction, recounted in John's Gospel (21:15–18). First and 2 Peter then display Peter's maturity in comparison to his earlier interactions with Jesus recounted in the Gospels.

in their relationship with God to a place of disorientation, as a way of keeping the True Self in play rather than a False Self emerging. The False Self potentially emerges because there is concern that if the emotions being experienced during this phase of transition were vocalized there would be rejection by the community and/or the object of the lament—in the biblical case, this is usually God! However, if this is being used as a transitional phenomenon, to shut such expression down would be catastrophic for the maturation of the True Self. The point here is that a good enough facilitating church embodying the type of holding environment characterized above must be one that gradually fails in adaptation in relevant ways but must also be one that enables and supports the use of suitable transitional phenomena to aid individuals to mature as well as providing safe space for individuals to learn to "play."

This ties back into continuing to provide good enough analogical holding and handling for individuals. The eucharistic company of performers, who are seeking to offer Christlike improvised performances, must be open to the "play" of new improvised performances when the context offers fresh opportunities to explore new interpretations of performing Christ in fitting ways, guided by the Spirit, in conversation with tradition and Scripture. At the same time, the church must continue to create a suitably safe environment and offer fitting transitional props for the performers to find when there is either planned or unplanned failure in adaptation to need. Good enough ongoing holding and handling guards against forcing transition in ways and at a pace that causes unhealthy impingement which would result in the emergence of the protective and defensive False Self. When planned failure is introduced, such as in church teaching where ideas, perspectives, and performances are challenged, the facilitation of play involves not forcing a perspective or pattern of performance that the individual does not want to receive—even if orthodoxy, orthopraxis, and orthopathos deem it correct. Trust in the work of the Spirit to enable change in all parties and dialogically consummate the True Christlike Self, regardless of how long it takes, must be maintained for the church to be the church. Even if views or performances run contrary to the core confession of the church as agreed in a particular scene of the theodrama, within what is deemed safe for all concerned, Christ-shaped, Spirit-enabled fidelity, generosity, and hospitality must continue to be offered. Alongside curiosity, such loving provision can then facilitate transformation as the work of God is discerned in the person's life.

Unplanned failure in adaptation requires that the church have rehearsed ways of enabling the True Christlike Self to continue to be performed. To explore what these ways might look like we return to explore why, in Winnicott's theories, babies cry.

Crying

We can recall that, except for the fifth type—hopelessness—Winnicott attributes the remaining four types of crying—satisfaction/excitement, pain, anger/rage, sadness/grief—to the life of a healthy infant. The first of these may find a point of connection in the healthy church in that crying can occur in acts of worship as a positive emotion induced by an experience of encountering God. This is likely to be accepted and handled much more easily than expressions of the remaining four. Returning to the practice of lament, so prominent in the Old Testament and with a lasting presence in the New Testament, we find that expressions of pain, rage, anger, sadness, and grief are located within that language and appear as normal, healthy, and acceptable aspects of Israel's worship. I and others have also defended the presence of lament as a normal and healthy practice in the New Testament, exemplified by Jesus and mentioned in the early church.[7] As noted in the previous chapter, the content of biblical lament makes space for the various types of crying Winnicott lists and possibly even has space for the despair and hopelessness that is characterized by Winnicott's final type.

As noted above, suitable safe space and guidance for expressions of painful emotions must be something the good enough church can provide to facilitate dialogical consummation of the True Christlike Self, but in discussion with Winnicott's types of crying it is possible to remind ourselves why this provision is important and suggest how the church can provide it. The first type—excitement/satisfaction—has already been mentioned above and finds an easier-to-handle place in church life. Cries of pain, anger, rage, grief, and sadness are less easy to locate with space for hopeless despair likely nonexistent. Yet, the importance of safe space for such expression is highlighted by what happens if such space and expression are not allowed. As previously noted, Winnicott suggests that all of these types of crying, except for the fifth, are healthy expressions of certain experiences that if curtailed lead to

---

7. For example, see Torr, *Dramatic*; Eklund, *Jesus Wept*.

problems with handling one's feelings of pain or anger, and negatively affect one's emotional development and engagement with others. It has also been noted that where expression is curtailed, there is the likely danger of a False Self developing to protect the True Self from harm and the possibility of exclusion from the community. A less than good enough church community is thus one that does not encourage and enable healthy expressions of emotion toward God and others and instead encourages emotionally stunted and shallow compliance by a False Self that results in a church that exists in a perpetual state of denial. This may look like a happier, more straightforward community on the surface, but it is likely a superficial one made up of people whose relationship with self, others, and God is largely a false one. True healing, reconciliation, and praise can only be experienced if true pain, anger, rage, sadness, and grief are allowed healthy expression before God and others.

However, there is room to go further concerning the role of the facilitating church and healthy crying that addresses the issue of what to do with cries of hopelessness and despair. When infants cry from pain, the antidote is the relief from pain combined with suitable holding and handling by the good enough mother. When anger and rage are experienced, the infant requires environmental provision that allows for expression and survives without retaliation—what can again be bracketed as suitable holding. An additional point concerning anger is that space and avenues to express that to God can aid in what Winnicott refers to as the fusion of the erotic and aggressive strands of being human—that which until fused separates the parent into two individuals who are experienced and responded to differently. The safe experience of God as nurturing provider, mediated by the church, combined with a safe space to express aggression and anger toward God, aided by the provision of the church, might possibly enable a fusion of images of God and effect a richer relationship with the one God who loves us and is able to cope with our anger, rage, and aggression.[8] The lack of this provision may encourage a splitting in terms of how God is perceived and related to.

When sadness or grief is felt, again there is a need for suitable holding and handling that does not curtail emotional expression. In each of these cases, there is the need for continual, good enough environmental provision that survives without retaliation and is able to hold and handle the infant in a suitable way. The church community has a vital role

---

8. Ulanov, *Finding Space*, 52, 57–58.

to play here when this maps over to its members. As the body of Christ and a royal priesthood, the church is the human representative of the divine parent who is called to provide suitable parental care to all God's children on God's behalf, mediating the provision of God, enabled by the Spirit of God. The cry of hopelessness and despair is voiced because whereas the expectation of intervention and change is still present in the cries of pain, anger, and rage, such expectation is absent in the cry of hopelessness and despair. At this point, another facet of the church's role comes to the fore that draws on the vocation of the priesthood of the church. Hopelessness and despair occur when the hope of the return of the parent to address the problem is lost. In this space, the wider church community is called on, in its priestly role, to keep hope alive on behalf of the sufferer. By this, I am not meaning imposing on the sufferer false positive emotion. Instead, what I am envisaging is a church that keeps telling the core testimony of the people of God and using that as fuel for its lament in conversation with the situation of the one in despair. Here the community of the church continues to affirm key aspects of the theodrama juxtaposed with the countertestimony of the one in despair. The priestly role of the church comes to the fore as the church community represents God to the individual in how they provide suitable holding and handling while also representing the individual to God in Christ enabled by the Spirit as they offer hope-filled cries of lament to the one they still believe can provide a positive way forward.

Even in such devastating circumstances as when a whole church community finds itself in a place of despair and hopelessness, there is still language to be used, inspired by past acts from the theodrama, recorded in Scripture, that is able to give expression to such emotions. Honest and raw expressions are made among the prayers of all the saints across the globe, some of whom will be offering prayers of hope-filled lament on behalf of despairing brothers and sisters known and unknown.

Revisiting the Rehearsing Church

Having mapped Winnicott's work on the healthy development of the True Self onto the church community as a facilitating environment, I am returning to Vanhoozer's focus on the church *ad intra* as the church rehearsing the kingdom. In doing this, the aim is to enrich Vanhoozer's suggestions for practice as the church aims to aid one another in putting on Christ and thus developing their True Self.

Something that Winnicott may have been reaching for without success, which is potentially provided for by Vanhoozer, is a metanarrative, or in this case, a theodramatic plot, that offers the participating company an integrating core testimony. Although Winnicott discusses the importance of play as a sign of health, and mentions the idea of being fully alive, aside from the psycho-somatic integration that he believes should be aimed for there is no mention of any over-arching plot in creation that might provide a richer sense of integration of the self. As was noted above, Turner has highlighted that modern psychology largely acknowledges the fragmented nature of individuals. This would seem to run contrary to what Winnicott was striving for in his work. However, it was also noted that Turner sees Vanhoozer's theodramatic approach as potentially providing an integrating narrative that can combat such a problem. This becomes particularly important when we consider the issue of identity and a sense of meaning that is strived for in life. Where Winnicott highlights the importance of good enough handling as a vital way of facilitating psychosomatic integration, corporate and individual life are integrated in conversation with what Brueggemann termed the "core testimony" of the people of God. This core testimony is embedded within Scripture as transcript, guidance that lights the way, and in prescriptive form. However, as previously noted, what is also present in Brueggemann's formulation and use of core testimony is the place of "countertestimony" that cross-examines core testimony with experiences that do not fit with what has been handed on. This will be discussed further when we come to explore the role of play in the rehearsing church. For now, it is enough to note the importance of the role of core testimony—the story of God's faithfulness to his word (Ezek 36:36)—as the integrative center of a community that is affirmed through the reading of, and reflection on, Scripture and that enables a sense of integrated identity for individuals and the community as an expression of *imago Dei* and the body of Christ.

As Vanhoozer has quite rightly drawn our attention to, the core testimony provides identity and meaning—a plot with a superobjective that shapes our performances. What is required for the body to be formed by the head, which is Christ, are lives that image, as far as possible, the fidelity, generosity, and hospitality that God has revealed to creation, in Christ, all of which is rooted in the love displayed by the God who is love. The church as a eucharistic community has at its center the life, death, resurrection, and ascension of Christ as performed and given meaning within the theodrama. This performance of Christ gives the community its identity and shapes her life in the world. However, what Winnicott's work has revealed is that healthy maturation cannot depend solely on sound doctrine, good teaching, or repetitive practice. Neither, arguably, can it be simply the result of the work of the Holy Spirit. All of these are important and aid healthy maturation, but a good enough *environment* is also vital and something for the rehearsing church to reflect on. However, the reality is that there is no single starting point in the development of an environment that embodies Christlike fidelity, generosity, and hospitality but instead, various aspects of church life intertwine to make up the rehearsing, facilitating, eucharistic church. We begin with prayer and worship.

Prayer and Worship

Adhering to *lex orandi, lex credendi, lex vivendi* inevitably means that there is an inseparable link between beliefs, actions, and emotions and how they are in/formed by involvement in the rehearsing eucharistic church while contributing to the shaping of the church community.[9] The rehearsing church is a church at play in its prayer and worship. As has been noted throughout this work, the church is only ever a Spirit-enabled response to the prior activity and call of God. The eucharistic facilitating church finds its shape and vocation by first experiencing being seen and met by God's being-in-action that they are then called to bear witness to and, where possible, mirror. Prayer and worship facilitate being seen and the play involved in learning how to see and live toward God, self, and creation with a unified heart, mind, and strength. Liturgy, song, and prayer combined with the reading, rereading, and reinterpreting of Scripture aided by creeds and confessions of faith draw individual and community into the intermediate space of discerning how to live well in relationship with God, the church, and the world from which a sense of the kind of environment the church is called to provide can emerge.[10] Of

---

9. I am indebted here to Steven Land's work exploring Pentecostal spirituality on which others have since built. Importantly, Land highlighted the interplay of beliefs, actions, and emotions in the theological enterprise and in one's spirituality. See Land, *Pentecostal Spirituality*; Stephenson, *Types of Pentecostal Theology*.

10. See Smith, *Desiring the Kingdom*, particularly chapter 5, for a helpful exploration of how different aspects of a church gathering aid in formation.

particular note is the use of song, as highlighted in Winnicott's work on transitional phenomena where he draws attention to the selection and use by infants of certain songs to ward off anxiety as well as the song-like sound of some forms of crying.[11] Prayer and worship therefore are multi-functional in shaping the company of performers.

A Safe and Hospitable Space

From the creative to and fro of prayer and worship in the intermediate space emerges a sense of what kind of environment best facilitates the development and maturation of the True Christlike Self and therefore what type of environment best supports authentic and life-giving prayer and worship. This is so because it is only as one engages in prayer and worship, individually and collectively, that one becomes more aware of the identity and vocation of individuals and the church, and what type of environment best facilitates the healthy flourishing of Christ-shaped identities and vocations. In a complementary way, as such environments are created and developed, a richer engagement in prayer, worship, and the flourishing of individuals and communities can occur. A good enough facilitating eucharistic church community is called to practice creating hospitable environments that are consistently safe and welcoming to all as a mirror of the divine example celebrated in the Eucharist. Where necessary and safe to do so, they must also be able to withstand rebellion and aggression without retaliation, and respond with loving continuity of care. This kind of good enough environment is founded on a love-driven desire to see the whole person of the other flourish as *imago Dei* and thus enable the church to be more fully the body of Christ. The goal is being with God and one another in the communion facilitated by the Eucharist, that stretches out into eternity. This is displayed in fidelity expressed in the consistency of care that mirrors the care shown by God to creation. Such an environment encourages authenticity and builds trust, making space for honest confession with no fear of rejection or destructive repercussions. Here the eucharistic church mirrors the divine to each other as it generously creates hospitable space for all to enter and know that the community and therefore the environment is one of love and fidelity rather than superficiality that is inconsistent and likely to reject.

---

11. For Winnicott's connection between "sad crying" and songs, see Winnicott, *Child*, 64.

We have noted above how mirroring maps over to the church and so it is important to make the point that the good enough facilitating church needs to be one that is willing and able to bear witness to one another's lives—to see one another through the eyes of God's love—and so enable those who may have often felt unseen to experience being seen in a new and life-giving way. This is again about making space and offering an environment that faithfully and generously demonstrates a loving commitment to seeing the other as made in the image of God with a story that is being integrated by the work of the Holy Spirit into the theodrama. This being seen enables fresh confidence and perspective to see the world around through new eyes and links to the development of discipleship discussed below. We will come to see in the next chapter how vital the discipline of bearing witness and mirroring is for the healing of those who have been traumatized.

Confession, Forgiveness, and Reconciliation

The nature of the environment being created is one that encourages and enables confession with a view to reconciliation between God and one another. Again, it is the consistent holding and handling shaped by the presence, word, and love of God, and the theodramatic plot reflected by the community, that enables this deep work to take place. To create this community, individuals must be willing to be attentive to the needs of others and the work of the Spirit in the lives of others and adapt—or fail to adapt where appropriate—in fitting and facilitating ways. Such attentive adaptation must be one that trusts the Holy Spirit to work at the right pace for the individual and so not fall foul of forcing maturation. There is a messy tension that exists here in how the core testimony and orthodox understanding of the plotline are maintained while offering consistent care and generosity mingled with curiosity toward those who question, challenge, and even rebel against this. Messiness occurs because of the nature of play that is to be encouraged in the intermediate space of discerning what, of the core testimony, is to be retained and what requires changing in the face of cross-examination by countertestimony. In terms of confession, forgiveness, and reconciliation, the facilitating community is to offer consistent loving care, even if wrongs need to be named, and regardless of how long the process—likely not linear—of confession, forgiveness, and reconciliation takes.

Discipleship

Linked to the practice of confession, forgiveness, and reconciliation and set within the broader definitions of prayer and worship is the ongoing work of discipleship in the community. The forming of the individual and community in tandem, after the pattern of Christ (of which confession, forgiveness, and reconciliation are a part), is severely limited if it is presumed that a program-style approach is the only way. That is not to say that programs do not have a place in the life of the church but more to say that presuming all followers of Christ start from the same place, progress at the same rate and in the same linear fashion, and should all look the same at the end of the process is incredibly naïve and hugely destructive to the people in question who are then reduced to objects manufactured on a conveyor belt. It also wrongly presumes that formation only happens in one direction—from master to novice. Programs can be a helpful tool used by some people, some of the time, but the healthy facilitating church is based on relationships that, through communication and listening, in the broadest sense of the terms, enable all members to discern how best to support one another in their mutual maturation toward their True Christlike Self.

The facilitating eucharistic church is to hold fast to creeds handed down and, more importantly, to the reading, rereading, and reinterpreting of Scripture as it prayerfully seeks to be a living hermeneutic through teaching, preaching, and wrestling with what it means to offer fitting Christlike performances in each scene of the theodrama. However, again, this is a messy business that requires fidelity to God and one another, as well as a generosity and hospitality that continues to maintain the safe and welcoming environment, noted above, while engaging honestly and lovingly in conversation with one another in the creative play-filled space between core testimony and countertestimony.

Although there is a sense in which a healthy community needs a core testimony to provide identity and meaning and a center to its worshiping life, countertestimony, that gives voice to the experiences that do not fit with the core testimony by cross-examining and interrogating the core testimony, also has a vital part to play. As I have already noted, the shutting down of countertestimony results in false compliance for the sake of inclusion, or exclusion from the community—neither of which is a satisfying and healthy outcome for either the individual or the community. In the case of the individual, the result is either the development of a False Self to protect the True Self from further harm while remaining a part of the community, or the experience of being excluded from the community as the True Self is considered unacceptable. In the case of the community, those who remain are those that present a False Self in superficial, inauthentic acts of prayer and worship, meaning that the community collectively has a culture that promotes and feeds the development of False Selves over True.

In contrast to a community that simply maintains the core testimony without room for anything else, what I am proposing is a curious and playful church community. As noted above, rather than being a label for pleasurable past-time, in Winnicott's theories play is how he describes the healthy interaction that takes place in the intermediate space. A playful church community continues to maintain the core testimony of the Christian faith while encouraging curiosity about how such beliefs might be reinterpreted and lived out in fresh ways in conversation with real-life experiences. We have seen that Winnicott describes a process taking place in an infant in which they first learn to play alone—as they experience resistance from the outside world while exploring what they can change and control—followed by learning to play with others. Although not necessarily quite as linear as this, the facilitating church enables and encourages the art of play in one's relationship with God as well as one's relationship with others. Curiosity comes in here as the facilitating church encourages maturation by encouraging individuals and the community to enquire and explore in prayer, reflection, and conversation as part of its worshiping life.

This brings us back round to fidelity, generosity, and hospitality as playing together also involves all three. Although we journey together, no two journeys of faith are the same, and yet the facilitating church seeks to be faithful in support of one another's discovering of their True Self. Hospitality is required as a safe space continues to be opened up where others are invited to come and play without fear of rejection or exclusion. Generosity is required because playing with others will almost certainly mean a clash of understanding around ideas, perspectives, and behavior at some point which will need individuals, and the community more generally, to not react but to pause and consider things from the other's viewpoint while discerning how best to provide good enough support for them in their development.

Play here dovetails with Vanhoozer's work on improvisation in that the facilitating church must be one that not only knows how to improvise but one that encourages exploration of what fitting improvisation looks like in particular scenes without being unnecessarily restrictive on possibilities. I am not suggesting an "anything goes" type approach that privileges the experience of individuals or communities over the guidance of Scripture and the creeds. Instead, I am highlighting the need to hold in tension that which is considered "orthodox" with the voices of those who are playing in the intermediate space by trying to discern what Christologically incarnating such faith means in the realities of life for those who are seeking to put on Christ.

Having applied Winnicott's theories to the rehearsing church, what remains in this chapter is to turn our attention to how the church engages with the world.

Revisiting the Performing Church

We can here return to Vanhoozer's emphasis on the church as a spectacle of holy fools that is neither separate from nor identical to the world, a group of resident exiles whose performance is to be a theatre of the gospel for a world audience to not just observe but to participate in. In chapter 4 it was noted how Vanhoozer focuses on place as the way a group organizes a space in time including what activities it undertakes there. Whatever we might say about the details of what constitutes a place where Christians gather, what interaction with Winnicott highlights is the importance of the nature of the environment that is created. A distinct mark of the Christian community, if not *the* distinct mark, should be, according to Jesus, the love that is displayed toward one another, and the world, even a world that persecutes and ridicules. The linking of the royal and priestly nature of the church should result in a place where the rule of the king is glimpsed—which is a rule founded on sacrificial love—and the community mediates God to the world while offering up prayers for the world. Returning to Winnicott, the church is called to display a way of being toward one another that is founded on a love-driven desire to see the True Christlike Self of the other emerge as the False Self falls away. This way of being finds direction and identity in Jesus Christ understood and experienced within the theodrama and should manifest in the ways noted above. This in itself should act as a spectacle for the world to see that stands in contrast to how other human groupings perceive and behave toward one another. But we must go further.

Many of Winnicott's theories emerged while working with adult clients who entered therapy or analysis. In the process of analysis, the client would often regress to a point of wounding or failure in provision from their past that was then addressed within the newly formed and substitutionary therapeutic relationship. Although I am not proposing that the provision of the environment of the facilitating church replaces specialist care by a trained practitioner, there is an insightful parallel that it is possible to draw here that we will return to in the following chapter. What the church potentially(!) offers to the world, as it carries out its priestly vocation, is a suitable facilitating environment, on behalf of and in cooperation with God the divine parent, in which the False Self of sin, constructed at least in part due to the wounding that occurs from living in a fallen world, can be begin to be removed. The performing church must therefore be one that engages with the other as one made in the image of God yet not explicitly imposing that lens without the ascent of the other. It must be a church that seeks to maintain its identity through playful interaction with the core testimony while seeking to embody the love of God toward the other. This must be done in such a way that suitable adaptation to need can be discerned and a mirroring can take place that listens and bears witness to the story of the other while presenting, at a suitable time and in suitable ways, the theodrama, and ultimately, Jesus, for the world to "play" with and through whose eyes they may see afresh.

The account of Jesus and the rich young man/ruler (Mark 10:17–22; Matt 19:16–22; Luke 18:18–23) may, at first glance, seem an odd choice for illustration but, I suggest, is instructive here. In Mark's account, Jesus is, once again, on the way somewhere (v. 17)—something that perhaps characterizes the dynamism of God and the fact that entering into a relationship with God, and by extension, the church, involves engaging in a process. The rich young man comes to Jesus with a desire to enter into eternal life (v. 17), presumably having recognized both that this has not yet happened and that he does not know how to amend this. As the conversation unfolds it becomes apparent that the key problem is with the place the young man has given wealth in his life, in the place of a relationship with the God who can transform him and draw him into the kingdom of God (v. 21. See also Jesus' response in vv. 23–25). Saddened by Jesus' response, the young man walks away, at this point unwilling to cooperate with Jesus in his transformation. There are a number of points to draw out here to aid in thinking about the facilitating church *ad extra* as the body of Christ.

First, Jesus is present, moving through the region, not hidden away anywhere, and it is his presence and the environment that he creates—the way space is arranged where he is—that draws the young man to him as well as the young man's belief that Jesus has something that he is currently lacking. As a traveling company that is seeking to improvise on the performance of Jesus, this is what the church should be doing. If the place where it resides is Christlike, it will attract those who are in need. Secondly, Jesus points the man toward God alone, who is good, while also highlighting that obedience to God cannot be shared with the love of money and must include care for those in need. Jesus here highlights the block in the man's maturation—the choice of wealth over a relationship with God—and in so doing introduces some resistance to the man, yet does so while loving him and because he loves him (v. 21). In this exchange we see love as the bedrock of Jesus' response, making the environment a safe one of invitation to change. However, Jesus is also uncompromising on what is required for transformation to take place. There are things that are malleable in this intermediate space that the man is invited to play with—how he perceives wealth, God, and God's kingdom—yet these perceptions and their related actions in life require the man to conform to Jesus' approach to such areas. Jesus does not shame or exclude the man; he simply loves him and invites him into a different way of being in the world that involves cooperating with God in the intermediate area of play. In choosing not to cooperate, the man excludes himself (v. 22) with the door always remaining open for him to return to the loving arms of Jesus and his followers.

The church *ad extra* is called to imitate an approach that travels through the world displaying a Christlike loving environment where others are invited to come, play, be healed, and be transformed. It is to be an environment that holds on to the hope of the inbreaking kingdom, displaying that in its consistency of care, yet not downplaying or shutting down the questions, doubts, anxieties, or fears of others. Although all are invited to come and play, this should not result in a wishy-washy compromise that simply gives the enquirer what they want. Instead, there is a call to hold onto the core testimony while allowing it to be cross-examined in an environment with clear boundaries, a door that is always open, and a love that never gives up, shames, excludes, or ends. Healthy play is encouraged as trust in the work of the Holy Spirit to bring about conformity to Christlikeness at the right time is deepened and relied upon.

Conclusion

Hopefully, what has become apparent here is not that I am contradicting that which was highlighted in chapter 4 as Vanhoozer's ecclesiology, but more that I am seeking to enhance the possibility of realistically living out such a community life by offering direction as to how that might be achieved. As has been noted, where Vanhoozer's approach seems to be lacking is with regard to more extensive exploration regarding what kind of environment encourages and enables the church to be one, holy, catholic, and apostolic as it seeks to live out its royal-priestly calling of a theatre of reconciliation offering parables of the kingdom. The aim of the above was to further enhance Vanhoozer's call to rehearse the kingdom by giving further guidance, drawn from Winnicott's work, on how the community can better contribute to fulfilling such a vocation and in doing so helping individuals to live more fully as their True Christlike Selves.

Mapping Winnicott's work over onto Vanhoozer's ecclesiology has illuminated and enriched it with regard to how the church, generally speaking, can be a facilitating environment for transformation into Christlikeness. This meshes with the work of the previous chapter on what it means to grow into our True Christlike Self by offering insight into what sort of environmental provision might better enable that to happen, all the time relying on the work of the Holy Spirit to effect suitable change through (and sometimes in spite of!) that provision. These two chapters taken together act as interlinked building blocks for the following chapter in which what has been mapped out here will be applied more specifically to the question of how best to aid those who are traumatized to grow into their True Christlike Self.

8

What Job's Friends Could Have Done

Introduction

SO FAR IN THIS exploration, we have continued a conversation with Kevin Vanhoozer's work started in a previous encounter by exploring a theodramatic anthropology and ecclesiology. Rather than doing that for its own end, the aim was to aid in exploring what the vocation and *telos* of human creatures are according to the theodrama and what the role of the church is in supporting and enabling healthy development. To enrich and extend Vanhoozer's approach, Winnicott's theories of healthy development of the True Self were drawn into the conversation. This has enabled a rereading of the theodrama to build on Vanhoozer's insights and offer fresh direction to the traveling company of performers regarding how to better improvise on the performance of Jesus in the current act, and aid others to do the same. However, rather than achieving the goal of the present work, they are only building blocks for what we now return to in this chapter as the central aim—addressing the question of what Job's friends could have done in seeking to care well for him in his traumatizing experience. Put another way, the question to be addressed is, what does it mean for the church to care well for those who have had traumatic experiences?

The current chapter will address that question by first highlighting the central role Scripture plays for the church in providing shape and content to the theodrama in which we find ourselves. This will enable a fresh examination of the definition and impact of trauma through a theodramatic lens that will frame the response of the church suggested in the rest of the chapter. Using the insights from Winnicott regarding healthy development and good enough environmental provision, what was presented in chapters 6 and 7 as the healthy development of the True Christlike Self and the facilitating church will be extended to suggest how what was presented there might be utilized by the church to aid in caring well for those who have been traumatized. In short, if the church takes seriously the insights provided by dialoguing Winnicott's work with Vanhoozer's in exploring healthy human development within a theodramatic worldview, care and support of those who are traumatized will be a natural extension of that provision. It needs restating here that what is being proposed as a good enough performance by the church is not meant as a replacement for specialist care by trained professionals for those who have been traumatized. Instead, what is proposed here should be complementary church provision that sits alongside and works with that specialist care while recognizing the place of such care within how God is interacting with, and bringing wholeness to, creation.

Scripture and Trauma

It is important to begin this section by noting that what follows is not intended to be used in a way that imposes this reading on the sufferer. As the central question that is being addressed in this work makes clear, the emphasis is on correcting Job's *friends'* approach and thus, in the current act of the theodrama, providing the church with guidance as to how to care well for those who have experienced trauma. In a similar way to how theological reflection on the origins and reasons for the existence of evil in God's good world may help prepare those offering pastoral care to do that better yet will likely not be brought into the pastoral encounter, the same principle applies in this section.

The Role of Scripture

As was noted in chapter 2, much theological reflection on trauma can tend to fall into the trap of giving authority for interpreting Christian Scripture and tradition to the sufferer. I say this is a "trap" because, although there is a validity that absolutely must be granted to the sufferer in what they are experiencing and how they are interpreting that, within the wider conversation within the church present and past there is a danger that if orthodoxy, orthopraxy, and orthopathos are entirely determined by the experience and interpretation of the sufferer then the inevitable conclusion will be that the prefix of ortho becomes redundant. In its place, experience becomes the norming norm. The challenge, then, is to continue not just referring to Scripture but to recognize it as the norming norm that provides the authoritative anchor for identifying the revelation of God to creation. At the same time, this belief needs to be held in conversation with the experience of others as fresh perspectives on the voice of God in Scripture are perceived, and the Spirit provides ever clearer direction for how to see and perform more like Christ in the roles cast for us.

In reflecting on what it might mean to be a trauma-sensitive church, we return to Vanhoozer's observation that whatever we may say about the nature of individuals or the church as *imago Dei* and the body of Christ respectively, we must always begin with the prior work of God to which we are always responding. This means that the identity of individuals and the church, when set within the theodrama, is ultimately determined by God and is to be dialogically consummated in relationship with God and others. Central to the life of any church must therefore be Scripture as that which continues to provide guidance for identity and performance for humans as Christlike images and for the church as the body of Christ. That is not to say that interpretation of and interaction with Scripture is straightforward and easy (something I have discussed elsewhere and will touch on again in what follows), but simply to say that Scripture is the norming norm that reveals the theodrama of which we are a part and thus gives definition and direction. For the community, this is crucial because it provides a particular worldview or lens through which to see God, self, others, and the world around in order to engage in a more Christlike manner. This view of and use of Scripture for the shaping of individuals and the community in cooperation with the activity of the Spirit offers the framework for understanding and responding to trauma outlined further below. To be a community that begins here is to be a community that is not held hostage to the ebb and flow of experience as the norming norm but is primarily anchored in the core testimony of Scripture and particularly in the revelation of God in Christ. However, that is not to say that experience has no place or currency in community, as the attempt to improvise on the performance of Christ in our own contexts requires bringing that context and our experiences to the table as legitimate and real but not ultimately norming. In practice what this means is that Scripture is understood within the community as having a particular authority, because of who its ultimate author is, but is engaged in such a way that recognizes our fallen nature and therefore the impossibility of it being used in any totalizing way.[1] It is to be engaged with curiosity and humility in recognition of its authority as God's vehicle for self-revelation in tension with our partial, fallen, open-ended interpretations and given space for voices to challenge and question what the dominant interpretations are. This makes space for countertestimony, which will be explored below, and prevents the weaponization of Scripture against those who disagree and, in the case of those who are traumatized, are fragile and vulnerable. This transitions us from the "what" of Scripture in a trauma-sensitive church toward exploring the nature of trauma from a theodramatic perspective as we look to the script for guidance and clarity by beginning with a reminder of the nature and vocation of the human creature.

A Theodramatic Perspective on Trauma

As was discussed in chapter 3 in an exploration of the theodramatic *imago Dei*, the theodrama, and therefore the shape and content of the *imago Dei*, begins with God's actions of creating and calling, thus giving priority to the *imago Dei* as vocational—a response to the prior call of God. Set within the wider unfolding plot of the theodrama, this vocation involves living and working on behalf of, and in partnership with, God to bring about the union of God and creation in holy communion—the *telos* for which all creation was intended. Contained in the first humans described in Gen 1–2, and displayed fully in Jesus, are priestly, royal, and prophetic aspects. The *imago Dei* is to be the location of God's rule and sovereignty as the human creatures mediate the relationship between God and creation while acting as God's mouthpiece. For reasons not entirely clear, evil and the resultant experience of suffering impinge upon creation and so involvement for the human creatures in the *missio Dei* now includes the expulsion of evil from creation (and themselves!) as a subtask of cultivating the flourishing of creation as it moves toward union

---

1. This is another example of the approach known as "Critical Realism" mentioned in chapter 2.

with God. The life, death, and resurrection of Jesus are the climax of the covenantal relationship between God and humans as the point within the theodrama where God assumes humanity so that humanity and creation can be redeemed and salvaged from the mess created by sin and evil. In the current act of the theodrama, the church is tasked with living out an inaugurated eschatology. The through-line to be maintained in moving the theodrama toward the superobjective of communion between God and creation at the eschaton is one of cooperation with the Holy Spirit in living out the Christlike identity that, because of the incarnation, is already ours. And doing so, corporately, as the body of Christ. Whatever we may say of trauma, must be set within this theodramatic framework if we are to respond to it in a Christlike fashion. With an overview of the theodrama, and the role of humans as *imago Dei* within that, in place, we can revisit definitions and understandings of trauma.

We can recall that trauma is generally characterized as an experience whereby the resources of the individual or community are overwhelmed beyond their capacity to cope with the experience. As was discussed in chapter 2, there are then several neurological, psychological, and physiological consequences of this experience. It was also noted that although some experiences are likely to be traumatic, whoever it is that experiences them, trauma is less about the event and more about the person experiencing it in that two people could experience a similar event and yet only one of them would experience trauma.

Set within the framework of the theodrama, there are several points to note. First, trauma is characteristic of the harrowing reality of a fallen creation in that such experiences are the result of a world initially described as very good yet, post-fall, impacted and marred by evil. Whatever else we might say from here, I shall pin my colors of anti-theodicy to the mast and state that I do not believe that experiences of trauma, although sometimes redeemable, are justifiable or an intended part of God's good intent for humans and are not part of some secret divine plan yet for us to comprehend.[2] Instead, they are symptomatic of a world tainted by evil in need of redemption by its creator and any attempt to explain their usefulness from some grander perspective, such as a greater good argument for the existence of evil, only makes the problem worse for the sufferer and distracts the one offering care away from more useful and effective approaches to the person and situation.

---

2. For a brief exploration of anti-theodicies, see Torr, "Anti-Theodicies."

Secondly, and more specifically, because traumatizing experiences are those that overwhelm resources, they point to two significant realities about the post-fall world. The first is that traumatic experiences may be a sign that the impact of the fall on creation has resulted in the world around us presenting us with situations that we were not intended to have to cope with. Death is an interesting case in point here. It is debatable whether the death of humans was the initial intent of God or whether access to the tree of life was removed because of the fall. In her work on the problem of evil Marilyn McCord Adams classes death as a "horror" defeated by the resurrection.[3] In this case, although most people find ways of coping with the death of a loved one, or the prospect of their own death, it is noteworthy that such experiences are deeply jarring to humans and for many will leave significant and damaging lasting effects—hence the need for defeat in the resurrection. It is these lasting effects, characteristic of the experience of trauma, that suggest, within the framework of the theodrama presented here, that trauma highlights the reality of a post-fall world that pushes many if not most beyond what they were designed to cope with.

The second reality links to the first in that traumatizing experiences may also highlight the fact that our ability to cope with such experiences has been diminished by the effects of the fall. An example of this is how various activities or relationships are shown to increase resilience and yet trauma sometimes occurs because individuals or communities have not been able, or chosen not, to engage in those activities or relationships.[4] Although we can split the impact of the fall down into these two realities regarding why trauma occurs it is likely that, in most cases, trauma occurs because of a combination of the two.

Thirdly, because trauma has no intended place in the theodrama, the conclusion of the theodrama suggests that with the achievement of the superobjective comes the total eradication of all evil and suffering (Rev 21:1–4).[5] My reading of this leads me to conclude three important and intertwining points that, while not seeking to downplay the reality of lived trauma in this act of the drama, nor shut down the voices of

---

3. Adams, *Christ and Horrors*, 207.

4. For example, De Terte et al. explore various interlinking areas of life that contribute to the overall resilience of individuals and communities. See De Terte et al., "Integrated Model."

5. Adams also argues for the absence of horrors and their resultant impact in the new creation. See Adams, *Christ and Horrors*, 227.

those who live with such pain, do provide the possibility of hope for the sufferer. The first of these is the salvific antithesis to the problem noted above. Whereas trauma in this and previous post-fall acts of the theo-drama highlights the nature of creation as one that, in its fallen state, provides humans with experiences that are beyond their capacity to cope with, the redeemed creation in full communion with God glimpsed at in act 5 of the theodrama will present no such challenge. The second point provides a corresponding antithesis to the other point noted above about the current state of humans. Whereas humans currently have diminished capacities to cope with some presenting experiences that cause trauma, the new creation will contain humans who fully inhabit their Christlike vocation and identity as the image of God and, collectively, the body of Christ. The third point to be added here, implicit in the previous two, is that the new creation of the eschaton is not only one that promises a full and sinless existence in a world with no evil and suffering, but it must also include the redemption or eradication of memories of experiences that might continue to result in trauma.[6] Here, we peer into the mist in terms of the details of such a post-resurrection state with only the wounded yet resurrected Christ as a highly obscured window into that existence. How such a state will occur and whatever form it takes, the anticipation of it offers us hope because it is a state with a creation that cannot wound us and in which we do not carry the weight of previous wounds.

Fourthly, the mention of Jesus' post-resurrection wounds directs us toward a further significant point that enfleshes the hope of the eschaton. In the incarnation of act 3 of the theodrama we are offered various accounts of God assuming human form on the stage of creation to plumb the depths of evil in order to overcome it so that the promises of the new creation of act 5 are a possibility for the whole of creation. The details of how this is achieved need not concern us here, not least because we are not given access, in the biblical accounts, to much between the death and resurrection of Jesus.[7] There are those who have engaged in constructive speculation about what occurs in that scene in the theodrama and have then brought that into conversation with trauma theory.[8] I see little mileage in such endeavors as they are largely guesswork and thus offer no

---

6. For one defense of such an approach, see Volf, *End of Memory*, part 3.

7. Adams offers an interesting window into a possible Christology that would defeat what she terms "horrors." This could be used in a similar way to propose how trauma might be eradicated by God in Christ. See Adams, *Christ and Horrors*.

8. Rambo, *Spirit and Trauma*.

solid foundation on which to build. An avenue that some have pursued here is to suggest that Jesus experiences trauma in the incarnation so that he can stand in true solidarity with sufferers in the current act of the drama.[9] However, Karen Kilby's critique of what Kenneth Surin refers to as "practical theodicies" surfaces here.[10] The focus of such theodicies is the loving suffering of God, in solidarity with creation, as the means of redeeming creation.[11] Kilby likens such an approach to someone who treats themselves badly because they have treated their children badly. The proponent's argument here is that such a move enables the eradication of evil and suffering by giving it a place in the life of God who is then able to defeat it for creation. When illuminated in this way, an approach that requires that God experience trauma in order to redeem us seems unpalatable. There are further issues to this logic as well, such as, if redemption requires experience, then redemption from every experience of trauma would require Jesus to experience every unique occurrence of trauma, which, of course, he did not. However, returning to Vanhoozer here, redemption by God not only does not require Jesus to experience every kind of trauma, but it may also not require Jesus to experience any kind of trauma at all. We can recall that trauma is the result of an experience that overwhelms the resources required to cope with it, resulting in certain neurological, physiological, and psychological consequences. With that in view, arguably what makes Jesus' experience redemptive is that where all other humans are ultimately driven beyond their capacity to cope—even if that is only in the inability to turn away the inevitably of death—what makes Jesus unique is his ability to stare into the face of all that can consume and destroy humans and yet, unlike all other humans, *not* be overcome or overwhelmed. Jesus chooses to turn toward Jerusalem (Luke 9:51), knowing that he will also decide to lay down his life (John 10:18). He then appears to be in control of when he is to face his death (Luke 23:46; John 19:28–30). Of the passion David Bentley Hart suggests, "The cross is thus a triumph of divine *apatheia*, limitless and immutable love sweeping us up into itself, taking all suffering and death upon itself without being changed, modified, or defined by it,

---

9. Cockayne et al., *Dawn of Sunday*, 80–81; Jones, *Trauma and Grace*, xvi–xvii; Kiser and Heath, *Trauma-Informed Evangelism*, 73–84; Travis, *Unspeakable*, 33–35; Baldwin, *Trauma-Sensitive Theology*, 120–22; Harrower, *God of All Comfort*, 171–72.

10. Kilby, "Evil," 20–21; Surin, *Theology*, 112–41.

11. Two particularly influential examples of this approach are Moltmann, *Crucified God*; Soelle, *Suffering*.

and so destroying its power and making us, by participation in Christ, 'more than conquerors' (Rom 8:37)."[12] The parsing of the passion, for Vanhoozer, results in Jesus being described as encountering death—a choice that suggests control—as opposed to Jesus dying—which implies Jesus is at the mercy of and overcome by death. Using the grammatical principle of the "middle-voice," Vanhoozer describes Jesus' suffering in the passion as both active and passive—he is active in having something done to him.[13] Vanhoozer states, "The Son is neither merely active nor passive but medially involved—as Mediator—in a broader process (i.e., God's reconciling the world to himself) over which he is ultimately still Lord."[14] The difference is subtle yet crucial in that hope is generated not by an account of a god who comes and feels what we feel and is overcome as we are, yet somehow bounces back, but instead, by an account of the author of creation who encounters the destructive power of evil *yet is not overcome or overwhelmed by it* and therefore goes beyond what fallen humans entangled in a fallen world are able to do. What is required, and what I am suggesting is displayed to us, is not a traumatized God but one who is not overwhelmed by the effects of a fallen world. Hope is generated by the God who carves out a way through the waters for all those who would otherwise be overwhelmed and carried away.[15]

However, here we come to my fifth point, which concerns the role of the church in the theodrama. If the role of the church in act 4 of the theodrama is Spirited implementation of the victory of Christ as improvised performances of Christ in the various scenes of the act, displaying parables of the kingdom, then regarding those who are traumatized, what must be performed are ways of being the body of Christ that facilitate the move of the incarnation through death to life. There is a danger here that I could slip down an overly triumphant path found in some streams of Pentecostalism that proclaims total healing is available in the here and

---

12. Hart, *Doors*, 81. See also Hart, "No Shadow of Turning"; and Lister, *God Is Impassible*, for a more extensive discussion of divine impassibility.

13. Vanhoozer, *Remythologizing Theology*, 426–33.

14. Vanhoozer, *Remythologizing Theology*, 427.

15. Adams's approach to horrors is interesting here because what she attempts to do is to navigate a middle way where the incarnate Christ experiences the overwhelm of horrors in his human nature but not in his divine nature. This is an option worth exploring further, but most important for the current project is that she maintains that in order for God to defeat horrors in Christ, the divine nature of Jesus cannot be overwhelmed by horrors. See Adams, *Christ and Horrors*.

now and is simply in the atonement, there for the taking.[16] Such an approach, or similar, is overly triumphant, denies the reality of the present for those who have experienced trauma, and in doing so closes down spaces that should provide suitable care and support that facilitates healing and growth. The reality of this act of the theodrama is that although Easter and the ascension offer windows into what awaits creation, Jesus is the firstfruits (1 Cor 15:20–24) and creation will groan in anticipation of its redemption until the return of Jesus at the eschaton (Rom 8:23–24). For the church in this act, what is required is a culture that facilitates healing and growth for those who are traumatized, recognizing that this is not a quick, easy, linear process, and is ultimately the work of the Spirit that will find completion only in act 5.

Having laid out in this section how attending to the experience of trauma is to be done from within the theodramatic lens presented here, we return to Job and his friends as a case study of what not to do. The rest of the chapter will then focus on what it means for the church to offer the right kind of provision to aid in the care, support, and healing of those who have experienced trauma as it seeks to both rehearse and perform Christ.

Job and His Friends: A Case Study in What Not to Do!

Ideally, it could be argued, in what follows I would provide some case studies as examples of the kind of church environment I am proposing. However, I am wary of this. The reason for my hesitation is that no single case study or group of case studies would be able to be replicated for every (any?) other situation that a church may face. Contexts are unique as are the individuals that live in each. For example, what a safe, holding, and facilitating space looks like in one context to one individual or group may look very different in another. Although the directions proposed for a fitting performance are transcontextual, the Christlike form each takes will be unique to each context. So, I am not convinced that case studies in the present study are a good use of space (although I recognize their value more generally under other circumstances). My preference is for providing the stage directions and suggested props and lighting that have been proposed, leaving each expression of church to find its unique improvised performance. Having said that, returning to where this project

---

16. See Torr, *Dramatic*, chapter 3, for an exploration and critique of this view.

began and to its title, it is possible and valuable, I believe, to revisit Job and his friends as a case study of what *not* to do. J. Richard Middleton in his exploration of Job has proposed that seven options are offered in the book regarding how to respond to Job's situation.[17] Briefly exploring some of these potentially offers windows into contemporary church perspectives and performances that can help to highlight what poor performance in response to someone affected by trauma might look like and act as a springboard to offer direction for fitting performances.

After the horror of chapter 1 of the book of Job, the first option Middleton highlights is to bless God regardless—which is what Job initially does (Job 1:20–21).[18] As the story develops it becomes apparent that this is, at best, an immature faith unwilling to ask difficult questions and at worse, an act of denial that is driven by anxiety and fear in the face of a perceived angry God that demands perfection. In Winnicott's language, it is an example of a False Self protecting the True Self in the face of potential annihilation. In his recent commentary on Job in which he uses a "trauma hermeneutic," Norman Habel suggests that all Job's responses up to and including sitting in silence with his friends are "a form of pious denial" that may be "recognized as a psychological defense against trauma, a mechanism that disavows the harsh realities of the situation."[19] More specifically, Habel labels this initial response "a pious expression of worship."[20] Such an approach has found contemporary affirmation in the popular worship song "Blessed Be Your Name," which draws from Job's initial response.[21] Although the creation of this song may have been helpful for the composers, by becoming a mainstay of a particular style of worship it aids in affirming an unhelpful response in contemporary Christian culture. However, rather than the source, this worship song and similar are symptomatic of a broader church culture of "bless God regardless" which, in effect, creates distance in the relationship by not allowing honest conversation. In such settings, as with Job's response, there is likely no room for difficult questions to be explored, and no room to name and express the full range of emotions. Instead, it's a church of (largely fake)

---

17. Middleton, *Abraham's Silence*, 79–90.
18. Middleton, *Abraham's Silence*, 79–80.
19. Habel, *God Trauma*, 8. Where I disagree with Habel is in his inclusion of silence as denial. This may sometimes be the case but not necessarily, and in the case of Job it is not clear that silence is in fact denial.
20. Habel, *God Trauma*, 9.
21. Redman and Redman, "Blessed Be Your Name."

smiles and platitudes that only speak of the goodness of God, closing down questions or any other approach. Like a stick of rock, this culture will be threaded through the welcome, the worship, the prayers, and the sermon, creating an environment that promotes either a compliant False Self or the shaming and exclusion of the True Self seeking to process and heal from trauma. In the background may be a belief in an angry God who expects perfection, and so any hint of anything that might anger this God, leading to rejection and punishment, is either hidden or used to shame and control. Either way, this is a performance that fails to adapt to need in a suitable way and is to be avoided by a church that genuinely seeks to be trauma-sensitive and involved in God's healing work.

The second option Middleton highlights is to "curse God," suggested by Job's wife (2:9).[22] Obviously, one would not expect to find such an approach at the core of any Christian church as this seems to be a total rejection of God. However, Habel proposes that Job's wife making this suggestion draws attention to the failure of the "traditional teaching" that Job clings to and that she encourages him to reject.[23] In one sense this is no bad thing as it facilitates and encourages a cross-examination of the core testimony. But, it is unhelpful in that it does not facilitate the sufferer reaching their own conclusion but rather prescribes, at best, turning one's back on God, and at worse, suicide. For obvious reasons this is problematic, not to be advocated, and not likely to be found within any Christian church. Such interpretations of this exchange presume a clarity that Hamley questions, though. Instead, she notes the challenge of translating biblical Hebrew as it has no punctuation marks and the same word is used for blessing and curse.[24] She therefore concludes that Job's wife "could simply be stating her sadness before him, her fear that he is dying, her trust that he is facing death from a position of integrity. Or, she may be angry, feeling alienated and locked within her own grief, and seeing no future but death."[25] Job seems to understand her in a particular way (see below) but that does not necessarily mean he is correct. Although space does not permit further exploration here, the ambiguity named by Hamley does highlight the complicated way that different people who experience the same event may be affected by it and may relate to each other, meaning that any form of trauma and post-traumatic care must be able to recognize

---

22. Middleton, *Abraham's Silence*, 80.
23. Habel, *God Trauma*, 10.
24. Hamley, "Patient Job," 89.
25. Hamley, "Patient Job," 89.

the unique journey of each individual and be able to adapt accordingly. A church with an inflexible "one-size-fits-all approach" will not be a safe place for many undertaking post-traumatic remaking.

The third option, at face value, is not dissimilar to the first in that there is no questioning of the situation or one's worldview but this time, rather than actively blessing God in response, the option appears to be passive resignation.[26] Here Job briefly resigns himself to the ebb and flow of experience and opts to take it on the chin (2:10). As with option one, this does not promote questioning, resistance, or expression and so, for the same reasons, a church that embodies such an approach should be avoided. A unique point is the resignation, though, as this could suggest a disconnection with God—"What happens, happens, and there's nothing we can do, so we just need to get on with it." Given that the end goal of the Christian faith is a relationship with God and God's people, and healing only comes through a relationship with God and God's people, a church that does not encourage personal and corporate honest relationship with God, including expression of questions and the full spectrum of emotions within that relationship, should be avoided. This is likely a church that goes through the physical motions but is, in fact, what was referred to earlier as "Deadly Church" where upholding a certain way of doing things takes precedence over the facilitating of honest relationships with God and one another. Such an environment stifles play and therefore healthy development and healing as there is no space to explore, within the breadth of creedal Christianity, the variety of ways that God may desire to meet and heal people. Here, static repetition of the core testimony is the end rather than a means of facilitating a vibrant, healing, dynamic relationship with God. It may appear safe in that it is known and predictable, but the inflexibility makes it unsafe for anyone who does not go along with the rigid repetition as, again, there is no suitable adaptation to need. Fidelity is to certain propositions, not God, the source of being who calls us into

---

26. Middleton, *Abraham's Silence*, 80–81. See Hamley, "Patient Job," 89–90, for an exploration of an interesting alternative way of reading this verse in which Job's words could be translated as a statement rather than a question. Hamley also highlights that the narrator only notes that Job utters nothing sinful here rather than him not sinning at all. Hamley therefore opens the door to considering the possible inner turmoil that Job was experiencing at this point, in contrast to his speech, as he grapples with his faith and his recent experiences. This plays into the present discussion, as paying lip service to remain within a particular group and structure will be destructive in the long run if emotions that run contrary to such speech are not acknowledged and addressed in a suitable way.

dynamic relationships. Generosity is thin on the ground and hospitality is only extended to those who will follow this rigid path.

Options four, five, and seven cover "Nonverbal Mourning, Followed by Silence," "Protest/Complaint about Suffering," and "Direct Protest/Complaint to God" respectively.[27] These options are included, implicitly or explicitly, elsewhere in the present work in discussions of constructive and healthy responses to experiences such as Job's, and so are not discussed at length here.

Option six sees the friends in various and nuanced ways attempting to defend God and explain Job's suffering.[28] At a general level, the friends share a simplistic view of doctrine in which the sufferer is in the wrong and is therefore the cause of their suffering. As Hamley notes with an eye on contemporary application, "they represent the community of faith—those who gather and are supposed to hold the member in distress."[29] Given Habel's reading of Job, influenced by Tiffany Houck-Loomis's work, as a postexilic text that critiques the Mosaic covenantal theology of pre and exilic Israel, Job's friends, through this lens, represent different expressions of covenantal theology.[30] In each case, the solution is therefore to confess and repent in order to find healing and restoration. Inevitably, such a view shuts down the cries of the sufferer by attempting to argue them around to recognizing their part in their own downfall and the required solution. It displays an overconfidence in a doctrinal position that does not do justice to the complexity of creation and the wisdom of God. The self-assurance it displays makes no space for curiosity and shows fidelity primarily to each proponent's system, offering little in way of generosity or hospitality to the sufferer. However, there are subtle differences between the friends' approaches that can be teased out to give further nuance to types of contemporary church environments to be avoided.

Eliphaz the Temanite is the first to respond to Job and is characterized by Susanna Baldwin "as a 'legalist.'"[31] Having allegedly gained insight from divine revelation—what Habel refers to as "a weird 'charismatic' revelation about the nature of the human condition"—Eliphaz has then verified his approach through "personal experience and observation" and

---

27. Middleton, *Abraham's Silence*, 81–85, 88–90.
28. Middleton, *Abraham's Silence*, 85–88.
29. Hamley, "Patient Job," 90.
30. Habel, *God Trauma*; Houck-Loomis, *History Through Trauma*.
31. Baldwin, "Miserable but Not Monochrome," 360.

so Habel labels him as coming from the "prophetic tradition."[32] Eliphaz understands God to be "objective and impartial"[33] and upholds a covenantal approach in which "God blesses those who walk righteously, but brings cursing and destruction upon sinners (4:7–9)."[34] In Eliphaz's view, no created being is entirely innocent—meaning no one would be suitable to act as a mediator for Job, heavenly or otherwise. Humans are sinful and come from the earth, "itself the source of evil."[35] Therefore, even the righteous sin as well as being affected by the wicked. However, Eliphaz does not necessarily see Job as wicked, just not innocent. Clines suggests that Job's piety is the basis for Eliphaz's responses and that Eliphaz seeks to encourage hope and patience in Job, recognizing that he will not share the fate of the wicked.[36] As Eliphaz's argument progresses, he suggests Job is in denial about his state, or unwilling to admit his sin and repent and so seeks to show Job the error of his ways and lead him to a different way of seeing and living. Eliphaz's third speech is notably more aggressive and harsh. Clines suggests that although this could be due to his patience running out it may well be that, given the focus of the third speech, Eliphaz can find nothing that Job has done to be the cause of his suffering so turns his focus to social justice, resorting to blaming Job for "sins of omission."[37] Eliphaz uses this as one last attempt to bring Job to repentance. For Job, "this will mean internalising and keeping God's laws, purposely eschewing sin, and discarding his earthly securities in order that he might find true value in God (22:22–24)."[38] Different to the other two friends, Clines notes of Eliphaz that he "does not command, threaten, cajole or humiliate Job in any way, but enters into his situation with all the imagination and sympathy he can muster."[39] However, "the God of Eliphaz is the God of original sin, creating humans from the corrupt clay of Earth and destined to be sinners."[40] Habel even suggests that Eliphaz's response to Job is, ultimately, "abusive rather than therapeutic."[41]

32. Habel, *God Trauma*, 21.
33. Baldwin, "Miserable but Not Monochrome," 362.
34. Baldwin, "Miserable but Not Monochrome," 361.
35. Habel, *God Trauma*, 26.
36. Clines, "Job's Three Friends," 208, 211.
37. Clines, "Job's Three Friends," 214.
38. Baldwin, "Miserable but Not Monochrome," 366.
39. Clines, "Job's Three Friends," 201.
40. Habel, *God Trauma*, 26.
41. Habel, *God Trauma*, 24.

In subtle contrast, Baldwin characterizes Bildad "as a 'deist.'"[42] Similar to Eliphaz is the emphasis on God's justice, but Bildad is more "black and white" in approach, choosing not to work through the logic of his view with Job, as Eliphaz had done, but rather simply tell it as he sees it.[43] In a sense, he is also more humble than Eliphaz, claiming to draw solely from the wisdom of tradition rather than an alleged divine encounter. However, following Habel and Houck-Loomis, this tradition is still the tradition of covenant theology and so Bildad believes there are rules to the world God has set in motion—there is cause and effect. In this deistic and determinist view, the wicked are punished—like Job's children!—and Job needs to repent and display his righteousness if he wants his situation to change and not share the fate of his children. Given the laws of creation, this should result in God saving him. Habel notes, "*The inherited spiritual truths of most religious traditions may be appropriated, not only to sustain faith and inspire ritual, but also to provide a resource for pastoral care and trauma counselling . . . often with harmful outcomes.*"[44] Bildad's approach highlights this point.

Zophar, in Baldwin's categorization, is "a 'mystic,'" claiming access to knowledge that is largely beyond human understanding.[45] Habel suggests Zophar thinks he is "initiated into the esoteric mysteries of Wisdom that are normally beyond human reach."[46] However, Zophar fails to listen to Job properly and seems to misquote and misinterpret him, claiming that Job is hiding his sin.[47] "For Zophar, the heart of Job's problem is that he neither has access to nor understands the wisdom of God (11:4–12)."[48] Job is therefore not able to comprehend the extent of his sin and is hiding it, which has not escaped God's awareness. With his supposed mystical insight, Zophar seems to presume a superiority to Job in being able to diagnose both the problem and the solution. As with Eliphaz, Zophar dismisses the possibility of a heavenly mediator but does call on Job to repent and turn to God. Where Zophar differs from Eliphaz and Bildad is that his emphasis on the nature of Job's healing, if and when it comes, is less on the restoration of health, family, or possessions but more on

---

42. Baldwin, "Miserable but Not Monochrome," 360.
43. Baldwin, "Miserable but Not Monochrome," 367.
44. Habel, *God Trauma*, 40.
45. Baldwin, "Miserable but Not Monochrome," 360.
46. Habel, *God Trauma*, 55.
47. Baldwin, "Miserable but Not Monochrome," 370.
48. Baldwin, "Miserable but Not Monochrome," 372.

internal characteristics. However, for all his claims to mystical insights, Zophar's approach still rests on a covenant theology.

There are a number of points Baldwin draws out that Job's friends do seem to have correct. As highlighted by Eliphaz, "God loves righteousness and hates wickedness (38:12–15, 40:8–14)."[49] God also has complete knowledge of creation and created it with a sense of order, as per Bildad. Zophar is correct in highlighting that God is wise beyond human understanding. However, there is much that is incorrect and unhelpful. God's governance of creation is not as straightforward and transactional as that proposed by Eliphaz. Neither is God as standoffish as Bildad suggests but instead cares for his creatures, particularly humans. God is also neither abstract nor entirely out of reach, accessible only via "some sort of esoteric experience."[50] Baldwin sums up, "Eliphaz, Bildad, and Zophar spent this time presuming to speak authoritatively on God's behalf with apparently no desire to personally entreat him, and ultimately this renders even more considered aspects of their discourse morally irredeemable."[51] In addition, Clines notes that, unlike Job, the friends' respective perspectives never change or evolve.[52]

Churches with the hallmarks of Eliphaz and Bildad are ultimately overly simplistic and transactional, maintaining a view that believes the sufferer is the cause of their suffering and that they simply need to repent to amend the situation. Eliphaz's church is legalistic, subscribing to a strict adherence to a particular interpretation of the covenant, making no room for alternative interpretations, the complexity of God's dynamic creation, and the grace and mercy of God. Although there is a degree of patience that may give hope and comfort to the sufferer, this is likely short-lived and founded on the underlying belief that the sufferer must be at fault somewhere. The space is therefore inhospitable to the sufferer, there is limited generosity, and fidelity is to a particular understanding of right and wrong that likely benefits those in positions of power. This is further backed up by those in positions of power claiming divine revelation from encounters with God that affirm and are affirmed by the leader's experience. The encounter with Job shows how wrong this can be and the damage it can do. It does not create a safe environment that

---

49. Baldwin, "Miserable but Not Monochrome," 374.
50. Baldwin, "Miserable but Not Monochrome," 374.
51. Baldwin, "Miserable but Not Monochrome," 375.
52. Clines, "Job's Three Friends," 214.

facilitates healing and growth but rather compounds the confusion and pain of the sufferer while misrepresenting God.

The God portrayed and worshiped in Bildad's church is cold and distant and not interested or intimately involved in the life of the sufferer—again, a view that is damaging and to be avoided given how God is relational and heals *through* relationship *for* relationship. Bildad's church appears to worship a cause-and-effect system that God has instilled in creation and that God therefore abides by. This tradition has been handed on through the generations, is upheld by the leaders, and is expected to be abided by and not questioned. Such an approach will not do justice to the complexities of how trauma occurs and its effects, the result being that those who are in the process of post-traumatic remaking are likely to have further blame heaped upon them for their slow healing with a message—subtle or otherwise—of repent or face the consequences. Bildad's church does not see itself as facilitating a dynamic and healing relationship with a relational God and so is also not a safe or hospitable place for those involved in post-traumatic remaking.

Zophar's church will have similarities to Eliphaz's and Bildad's in that the sufferer is to blame for their suffering, and confession and repentance are required for healing to be found.[53] However, Zophar's church will proclaim healing via a mystical connection with God that promotes inner growth but pays little attention to external material remaking. Such a church potentially over-spiritualizes both the process and nature of healing. This may result in selling a *technique*, overlooking honest communication with God and a multidisciplinary approach to healing. There is also likely not enough emphasis put on the various external aspects of healing such as relationships with others, bodily health, a fulfilling vocation, and making sure life-affirming needs are met.

There are then, similarities and differences in the three friends' approaches, but none of them makes for a safe space for post-traumatic remaking. Beyond the differences between the three is perhaps the most important point that none of them show any sign of curiosity or a willingness to reflect on and cross-examine their own position in the light of fresh experience—in this case, the experience of the trauma of their friend. A church that is not willing to question God or their own beliefs in

---

53. There is, of course, a place for confession and repentance. However, when it is the only answer, the sufferer will be made to feel guilty about something they may not have caused and forced to engage in a practice that is not applicable and therefore not helpful and possibly even destructive.

the face of such experiences is not going to be a trauma-sensitive church and therefore not a place where those in the process of post-traumatic remaking will find their healing process facilitated.

The Facilitating Church, the Healing Church

Having situated trauma and its impact within the theodrama, and briefly explored the responses of Job's friends, we turn to explore in greater detail how the church might become more trauma-sensitive, offering practice guidance that is anchored in Scripture. To do this, we return to primary literature on trauma and post-traumatic remaking in order to dialogue with the work undertaken thus far in the present project and so demonstrate how the facilitating church presented in the last chapter is well placed to provide the necessary culture and environment for healing and growth to take place in the *imago Dei*. Proposed in what follows is that a church that aims to enable disciples to become their True Christlike Selves and offers good enough environmental provision to facilitate this is set up to provide constructive care for those who have experienced trauma.

In engaging with Vanhoozer, we have already seen how the Eucharist centers on the prior work of God in Christ to reconcile creation to Godself. We have also seen how the Eucharist is rooted in, and a reflection of, God's fidelity, generosity, and hospitality toward creation, which we are called to respond to and participate in. However, what needs to be explored here is what happens when we examine what this response and participation looks like in the light of trauma theory as an extension of our engagement with Winnicott.

Post-Traumatic Remaking

To be able to offer something substantial regarding the shape and content of Christian communities that can provide an environment that facilitates post-traumatic remaking, we revisit the impact of trauma on humans and what professionals specializing in post-traumatic care suggest is required of a suitable, remaking environment. To give structure to this section of the discussion we return specifically to the engagement with Van der Kolk and Herman begun in chapter 2.

We can recall that Herman has provided a now much tried and tested framework for the process of remaking that follows the three phases of "Safety," "Remembrance and Mourning," and "Reconnection."[54] It is also helpful to note Herman's point that "recovery can take place only within the context of relationships; it cannot occur in isolation."[55] Within suitable relationships, the aim is to try to rebuild "trust, autonomy, initiative, competence, identity, and intimacy" that assists and empowers the survivor.[56] Although these phases are primarily developed with professional trauma care practitioners in mind, they can help guide the practice of the facilitating, trauma-sensitive church in its role in the remaking process, and so, it is this process that will provide the outline for what follows.[57] In addition, Van der Kolk suggests there are three avenues for treatment of those who have been traumatized, and any combination of the three is usually explored depending on the needs of the individual. The three Van der Kolk mentions are: (i) Talking; (ii) Medicine and Technology; (iii) Body experiences.[58] For obvious reasons, exploration of the usefulness of the second of these lies beyond the scope of this work and the specialty of this author. However, it is worth noting that Van der Kolk is keen to show the unhelpful overreliance on medicine that, he argues, has not really aided much in addressing the issues of post-traumatic healing. In fact, what he suggests this overuse of drugs in response to a reductionist diagnosis of "brain disease" does is automatically rule out the exploration of communication, behavior modification, and environmental changes as possible methods for healing.[59] It also overlooks the possibility that humans might be able to aid in healing one another from within particular types of healthy relationships and communities. We will therefore draw on the avenues of talking and body experiences as we follow Herman's process within the environment of the church community. We begin by examining the nature and importance of safety.

---

54. It is important to note here that Herman recognizes and highlights the over simplified nature of this description of a process that is, in reality, far more messy and far less linear. See Herman, *Trauma and Recovery*, 223–25.

55. Herman, *Trauma and Recovery*, 191.

56. Herman, *Trauma and Recovery*, 191.

57. One example where a theologian has helpfully used Herman's stages is in Scott Harrower's work. See Harrower, *God of All Comfort*.

58. Van der Kolk, *Body*, 3. Van der Kolk then goes on to explore various specific methods for healing in greater detail in part 5.

59. Van der Kolk, *Body*, 36–38.

Safety

As has already been highlighted, healthy membership in a supporting community is shown to be vital for healing and developing resilience. Van der Kolk notes the similarity between children and adults, stating, "Frightened adults respond to the same comforts as terrified children: gentle holding and rocking and the assurance that somebody bigger and stronger is taking care of things, so you can safely go to sleep." He continues, "In order to recover, mind, body, and brain need to be convinced that it is safe to let go. That happens only when you feel safe at a visceral level and allow yourself to connect that sense of safety with memories of past helplessness."[60] He draws from studies conducted during the Second World War of children living in London who were moved to the countryside and relocated with other families for their own safety. Winnicott was involved in this study and the results were that those who remained with their families fared much better in terms of health than those who were relocated. The reason is that attachment to family and community offers the bedrock for resilience and recovery. "The role of these relationships is to provide physical and emotional safety, including safety from feeling shamed, admonished, or judged, and to bolster the courage to tolerate, face, and process the reality of what has happened."[61] "People who lack solid early attachment bonding to a primary caregiver, and therefore lack a foundation of safety, are much more vulnerable to being victimized and traumatized and are more likely to develop the entrenched symptoms of shame, dissociation and depression."[62] Remaking can be further complicated if the source of the trauma was a trusted person. However, the same principle still applies with regard to healthy relationships of safety and provision required for remaking, it is just that it will likely take longer and be more complicated to establish such relationships. Regardless, as Herman has highlighted, establishing safe places and relationships that enable and support the individual in feeling safe in their own body is essential for any positive progress to be made.[63]

Although these relationships are vital for healthy remaking, it is important to go further and explore why, beyond the obvious surface-level provision of safety, these relationships, where trust is (re)born, are

---

60. Van der Kolk, *Body*, 210. See also Levine, *In an Unspoken Voice*, 12–13.
61. Van der Kolk, *Body*, 210.
62. Levine, *In an Unspoken Voice*, 60.
63. Herman, *Trauma and Recovery*, 249.

so important. As has already been noted, trauma continues to be experienced when the body and brain continue to prepare for or respond to a threat that is no longer present. As has also been noted, humans are fundamentally social creatures. "For us as humans, it means that as long as the mind is defending itself against invisible assaults, our closest bonds are threatened, along with our ability to imagine, plan, play, learn, and pay attention to other people's needs."[64] Although the repair work will almost certainly involve specialist care, the community complements this by being a place of reciprocity rather than just a presence. For the person who has experienced trauma, reciprocity means to have the experience of "being truly heard and seen by the people around us, feeling that we are held in someone else's mind and heart."[65] For the community, this means meeting the individual on their terms, with a willingness and ability to lovingly withstand challenging behavior by the individual without shaming or excluding, while genuinely hearing and seeing the person. "The fundamental issue in resolving traumatic stress is to restore the proper balance between the rational and emotional brains, so that you can feel in charge of how you respond and how you conduct your life."[66] To aid in doing this the community can play a vital part in helping restore healthy self-regulation by first making sure it is a place of safety and calm.

Drawing on the work of Winnicott and others, Van der Kolk highlights the importance of healthy mirroring and attunement by the parent in early childhood.[67] Van der Kolk's research suggests that when the traumatized individual is unable to self-regulate, mirroring by, and attunement with, individuals or communities that provide a safe haven can begin to aid in enabling the ability to self-regulate.[68] The research from early childhood, as we have seen, shows that babies learn how to manage their emotions and self-regulate by way of good attachment, attunement, and mirroring from their primary caregiver. This being seen and the adaptive support of parental regulation at a point in a child's life when they are unable to self-regulate eventually instills in them the ability to do it themselves. It also creates an internal map of how to perceive and respond to the self and world, based on what was mirrored and the environmental provision. The same principle is true for those

---

64. Van der Kolk, *Body*, 76.
65. Van der Kolk, *Body*, 79.
66. Van der Kolk, *Body*, 205.
67. Van der Kolk, *Body*, 111–15.
68. Van der Kolk, *Body*, 330–46.

who are traumatized. What is required from individuals and communities is a safe space where attunement and mirroring by the individual and/or community offer the required support to the traumatized person that assists in their reactivation or learning of self-regulation. Although early maps wire the brain in particular ways, it is possible for this to be rewired based on further experience. Where the wiring that has happened is a result of trauma, thus creating a particular type of map, either through developmental trauma or a specific incident, it is possible to rewire the brain in a healthy way if there are individuals and communities that can aid in the mirroring and attunement that leads to healthy self-regulation and new internal maps.[69]

The underlying point here is that whatever other more specific provision might be offered, what is required from a community that is seeking to offer care and support is that it is a safe place that is attentive and adaptive to the needs of the one who is traumatized and is a place, therefore, where trust can be built without fear of rejection or exclusion. It needs to be a community that can mirror a healthy way of being, rooted in love, and is attuned to the needs of the other to aid with the (re)learning of self-regulation. In the previous chapter it was noted that a church community that creates a safe and hospitable space is essential for the healthy development of the individual as *imago Dei*. The loving fidelity, generosity, and hospitality of God celebrated at the Eucharist and mirrored by the Spirit-enabled facilitating church toward one another and the world is aiming to create an environment of consistent safety, calm, and welcome able to lovingly withstand the challenges that different people may bring without them fearing being shamed or rejected. In terms of being trauma-sensitive, for those who have been overwhelmed by traumatic experiences, consistency of provision of loving care with a desire to facilitate post-traumatic remaking is vital for that remaking to happen and resilience to be built. This extends the good enough provision of the facilitating church environment drawn upon in the previous chapter and shows its usefulness to those who have experienced trauma.

It may be argued that Job's friends were committed to him in their practice and that although unhelpful from our perspective, their words and actions came from a place of loving desire for him to admit fault in order to experience healing. Concerning post-traumatic remaking, we can circle back around to address the question of why Job's friends'

---

69. Van der Kolk, *Body*, 55–60.

fidelity was actually counterproductive. The hospitality of God recounted in the Eucharist is one that expresses fidelity to lovingly create space for transformation, healing, and healthy development to take place. Although Job's friends may have been faithful to him, rather than creating a safe space for him to experience healing from God, the space they created was a hostile and dangerous one in which Job not only had to cope with the trauma so far experienced but also had to cope with unfounded accusations from so-called friends. God alone knows absolutely what is required in the remaking process for an individual. The role of the church as it seeks to mirror the hospitality of God is to provide a safe and consistent space for the remaking to take place. To place an interpretation of the experience of suffering that they have not discovered for themselves onto an individual is to create a hostile environment that is potentially abusive and liable to make the situation worse. The orthodox faith of the church need not be compromised by the questions and situation of an individual. Instead, as will be discussed below, there should be, in a eucharistic trauma-sensitive community, the capacity to read the Scriptures, declare the basis of faith in creeds and confessions, *and* maintain a safe, hospitable environment in which traumatized individuals can feel safe, and able if/when ready to explore their pain and questions without fear of rejection, condemnation, or the expectation to tow a party line. Admittedly, this is not easy. However, that is not a good enough excuse not to aim for and work toward such provision.

In Winnicott's work, we have seen that environmental provision that does not hold and handle an infant well enough, does not protect from impingement, or does not suitably adapt, is one that does not enable healthy development and maturation. Considering the work on trauma that has been examined, it cannot be stated strongly enough how important the experience of safety is to the one who is in the process of remaking. They may not need to be physically held and handled but they need to feel safe and seen as a whole person. When prayer is undertaken in the community on behalf of another, this can be interpreted as a form of holding where someone is held in mind or heart as they are held in prayer. This form of holding displays fidelity in commitment to bring the person in question before God and ask for suitable provision and healing. As noted above, Van der Kolk suggests this form of holding—which I am here suggesting finds a place in the eucharistic community as an extension of Winnicott's work—is particularly beneficial to those who have experienced trauma while not in any way demanding anything from the survivor.

As was also noted above, the feeling of safety is significant for healing and the experience of being seen and listened to does positive work in the brain's function. After the initial period of possibly helpful silence, Job's friends not only fail to provide a safe environment, but they also fail to see and listen to Job effectively, thus compounding his suffering. In addition, having shown positive signs of good care in their silent dwelling with him, they then seem to run out of patience and exchange their silence for presumed knowledge about what the cause of the problems is and what remedy is required. This contrasts with Winnicott's work where the True Self emerges and develops when provided with a good enough non-conforming, suitably adaptive environment. The True Christlike Self, we have seen, emerges as the individual co-operates with the Holy Spirit in a safe environment that is provided by the body of Christ. By extension, post-traumatic remaking is enabled and supported by an environment that provides safety and consistent and suitable attentive holding and handling, while not forcing an interpretation or process for remaking onto the individual. It is only in a space deemed safe, and one in which the whole person is seen and thus held and handled, that the person is able to continue the remaking work of coming home to their body and engaging in top-down and bottom-up regulation (discussed below) in the face of previously overwhelming emotions.

In the previous chapter, we noted how Winnicott's developmental theories illuminate how generosity in the theodrama enables and encourages healthy maturation and flourishing. Where generosity in church settings often and notoriously focuses on financial giving, the focus there was more on the sacrificial provision of space, time, and resources in the form of patience and understanding. What is apparent from the trauma literature is that remaking takes as long as it takes. Levine observes, "Too much too soon, threatens to overwhelm the fragile ego structure and adaptive personality. This is why the rate at which people resolve trauma must be gradual and 'titrated.'"[70] This can be extremely challenging for churches that are program-driven and measure success by numerical growth in attendance or assent to doctrines. For a church to be trauma-sensitive, it must be willing to consistently prioritize creating space that is safe and not place time-bound pressure on

---

70. Levine, *In an Unspoken Voice*, 70.

individuals to reach some particular goal. Remaking within the theo-drama may be helped or hindered by the community but is ultimately the work of God. In the celebration of the Eucharist, the community is reminded of God's patience and generosity, which is to be mirrored, as well as the feast that only God can get us to.

When the patience of Job's friends runs out, the group takes turns to accuse Job. The need to continue to offer a safe space and loving presence that does not require conformity to some norm is too much for them to bear. Patience gives way to oppressive quick-fix methods that fail to attempt to discern where God might be in the midst of the situation, or even talk to God about the situation! The need to sort out the problem and move on takes control and the context rapidly changes for Job. How easy it can be for church communities to do the same thing when expectations regarding the healing process are not met, and the person becomes "a burden" and "a hindrance" to "progress." What might be a better model in thinking about the long road of supporting those in the process of post-traumatic remaking is what we find with the disciples' support of Thomas as he asks questions about the reality of the resurrection (John 20:24–29). There is no hint of impatience or exclusion by the ten who had already encountered the risen Jesus. Instead, there is, perhaps, a community that maintains a safe space for Thomas, in conversation and contact with Jesus, to draw his own conclusions as he attempts to put the post-resurrection pieces of his shattered life back together. Maybe here we see embodied Paul's call to walk "with all humility and gentleness, with patience, bearing with one another in love" (Eph 4:2) as the disciples try to "rejoice with those who rejoice; weep with those who weep" (Rom 12:15). There can be no fixed time frame for remaking—to reiterate, it takes as long as it takes—and so to impose one is to do unnecessary damage that either excludes the individual or forces a False Self to emerge to protect the True Self by conforming to the norms of the community.

The generosity that finds embodiment in the provision of safe space and time must also be one that focuses on being present and attentive, particularly when the instinct in the uncomfortable silences or the hearing of unsettling stories is to prioritize our need to be in control and fix the person. Although there is likely some good motive mixed in with this instinct, it will largely be driven by my needs rather than what is best for the one I am with.[71] Here, sacrificial generosity comes

---

71. In a similar fashion, Dick Blackwell highlights how, in the therapeutic setting, the instinct to "help" torture survivors is more to do with the therapist's needs than the client's. See Blackwell, "Holding."

into its own as we look to the example of the cross to offer guidance and inspiration for putting the needs of the other above my own as I operate out of a place of divinely enabled love.

It is this kind of love that we see offered by the good enough parent in Winnicott's work that then illuminates God's example to us that we should be seeking to emulate. When turned toward those in the process of post-traumatic remaking this kind of generosity is vital for the trauma-sensitive eucharistic company of performers to embody.

Remembrance and Mourning

Within Herman's model, much of the work of remembering and mourning is done within the therapeutic setting facilitated by a trained and experienced therapist. In such a setting the survivor will often retell the story of their experience of trauma while the therapist aids in reconstruction and interpretation. Herman notes that this has personal and social dimensions as the individual experience is integrated into a larger social narrative. The safe space created by the therapist enables the survivor to voice rage and anger while mourning the loss of long-held beliefs about how the world and faith were thought to operate. Different fantasies, such as revenge, can be explored in safety as, hopefully, a transition is made to a more settled and sustainable place marked by healthy self-love and a desire for justice. In all of this, there is no substitute for mourning.

Within this process, we can draw on Van der Kolk's descriptions of body experiences and talking as aids. In both cases, there are ways of physically and verbally engaging with the impact of trauma that ground the individual and aid them in the healing process.

Body Experiences

The two ways Van der Kolk notes for learning to manage and regulate emotions are via either the top-down approach or the bottom-up approach.[72] The top-down approach focuses on better monitoring of body sensations by the brain leading to a more regulated response. The practice of mindfulness is associated with this approach as it aims to notice the fluctuating emotions and related physical sensations with a level of compassion and curiosity that does not result in reacting prematurely to

72. Van der Kolk, *Body*, 62–64.

them.⁷³ This practice retrains the mind to observe rather than react in order to give the person a level of control over their response rather than them feeling at the mercy of their emotions. This, therefore, contributes to the aim of better self-regulation of emotions.⁷⁴

The bottom-up approach aims at recalibrating an autonomic nervous system that has been severely disrupted by a traumatic experience. To do this, body activities are engaged in that aid in recalibration. These include deep breathing exercises, movement, and where appropriate, touch. Where the sympathetic nervous system (SNS) is overactive, leading to hypervigilance, deep breathing aids recalibration by activating the parasympathetic nervous system (PNS) and so slowing the SNS and moving the person back toward a balanced state. However, particularly in cases where the person is experiencing hypo-vigilance, leaving them numb and shut down, bottom-up approaches can also include physical movement. The setting and type of movement can vary considerably. There is evidence to suggest that activities such as yoga, which combines breathing, movement, and meditation, can aid in experiencing and learning to manage emotions and physical sensations that may have been overwhelming or closed off.⁷⁵ Such activities may bridge the gap between top-down and bottom-up if they incorporate both the techniques of mindfulness as well as breathing and movement more associated with bottom-up approaches.

The importance of attunement and synchronicity returns to the fore when exploring body experiences as an avenue to healing. Where an individual has experienced trauma, being part of something bigger that involves attunement to, and synchronicity with, others and where embodiment of a role may be required, healing can be facilitated. Attunement and synchronicity tap into the natural community orientation of humans in such a way that recalibration can result from working with and being in sync with others. Embodiment of roles can also provide a way of processing traumatic experiences that can lead to healing.⁷⁶

Where appropriate, physical contact with another can be used as a way of reestablishing a healthy connection to one's body. Although specialist treatment is an important part of this provision, it is also something

---

73. For a helpful and accessible introduction to Mindfulness, see Williams and Penman, *Mindfulness*.

74. Van der Kolk, *Body*, 208–10; Boyd et al., "Mindfulness-Based Treatments."

75. Van der Kolk, *Body*, 263–76; Kamp et al., "Body."

76. Van der Kolk, *Body*, 330–46.

that, where permitted and done safely, can be an important aid in helping a person feel safe, accepted, grounded, and real.[77]

Moving forward in post-traumatic remaking involves being able to manage and master emotions that are either out of control or locked away. Body experiences provide ways of bringing emotions to the surface and under control in a way that encourages owning and befriending them rather than burying or feeling at the mercy of them. Connecting the mind, the brain, and the body as an integrated whole person is what is being aimed at.

By focusing on body experiences, we can dig deeper into the details of what a trauma-sensitive eucharistic community could provide in supporting healthy regulation while remembering that such provision is only ever support to the specialist work of trained trauma therapists. Drawing on Winnicott's theory of mirroring and the evidence of its usefulness in post-traumatic remaking, the calling of the body of Christ is not just to see the individual but, like the parent in Winnicott's theories, and God as parent to humans, to mirror a way of being in the world to those who have been traumatized that helps them to experience being seen as a whole person while building confidence to engage with themselves and the world around them. A mistake here would be to confuse mirroring with the prescriptive approach of Job's friends as they begin to speak. Instead, what is being proposed is that the community, in addition to creating a safe space, can present practices within that space for people to engage in as they feel able. As will hopefully become apparent, this is not to equate the church community with another secular group as what is of significant difference is not just that certain practices are engaged in but that they are done in the presence of God, toward God, with the aid of God and find particular meaning within the theodrama.[78]

An example of this is found in the facilitating of different expressions of prayer that do not require speech from the survivor. The practice of mindfulness as a way of learning to note emotional responses without being controlled or overwhelmed by them is well documented.[79] Guided prayer that incorporates this in such forms as Ignatian

77. Van der Kolk, *Body*, 215–17.

78. Although space limitations do not permit a full discussion, this could be a point of conflict for Christians wishing to engage in yoga, as some forms of yoga will operate from a worldview that stands in direction contradiction to an orthodox Christian worldview and so should be avoided.

79. For a helpful introduction to the compatibility of Christianity and mindfulness, see Stead, *Mindfulness and Christian Spirituality*.

spirituality does so in a way that facilitates the practice of bringing these emotions to God in order to engage with God regarding what to do with them. Of particular note is what is referred to as the "discernment of spirits." As David Lonsdale notes, the term "comes from the time when the variety and changes of often contrary feelings within the human person were attributed to the presence and action of 'good' spirits (the Spirit of God and the angels) and 'evil' spirits (Satan and his minions)."[80] Whether one strictly holds to such a view, the more important point is that the practice involves "a process of sifting our daily experience by noting and reflecting regularly on our affective responses to God and to life and its events."[81] In doing so the aim is to assess what direction these emotions are pointing in—whether they are pointing toward a path of flourishing in free and healthy response to God or toward a path away from God. In Ignatian spirituality emotions that point individuals toward God are said to offer "consolation" whereas those that point away from God offer "desolation."[82] Therefore, the discernment of spirits involves discerning paths that lead toward God.[83] Such discernment might occur in what Ignatian spirituality refers to as the "Examen." This form of contemplative prayer involves pausing to look back over a particular period (a day, week etc.), or an event, in the presence of God, in order to discern with God's help where feelings of consolation or desolation emerge. As noted above, this discernment can then lead to positive action in whatever form this may take.[84]

A church community that facilitates such practices as part of its provision mirrors and facilitates the hospitality of God whereby God meets individuals where they are to aid them in the process of salvation—being made whole. Again, this is not about being prescriptive about what the individual should think, feel, or do, and neither is it about trying to explain too much or cast blame. Referring back to the hospitality of God, revealed particularly in Jesus and continued in the church, this is about creating a safe space in which to begin to note and learn to integrate difficult emotions in the presence of God.

---

80. Lonsdale, *Eyes to See*, 96.

81. Lonsdale, *Eyes to See*, 95.

82. Lonsdale, *Eyes to See*, 97–98.

83. For a further exploration of discernment within Ignatian spirituality, see Thibodeaux, *God's Voice Within*.

84. Lonsdale, *Eyes to See*, 124; Thibodeaux, *Reimagining the Ignatian Examen*.

Similar aid is found when considering the bottom-up approach to regulation that focuses on managing and working with the body in relation to traumatic experiences. Again, we can draw on Winnicott's insights in the shaping of the eucharistic company of performers who take seriously what it is to be relational and embodied creatures. As recognition of, and care for, the body, as part of the whole unit, is crucial for psycho-soma integration in infants, so is the ability to connect with and recognize the storing of experiences in the body of those who have experienced trauma. As with the top-down approach above, where such an approach finds a home in the church community is unique in that it is set within the theodrama and therefore done in the presence of God with a particular view, held by the church, on the body and what it means to flourish as a person made in the image of God. As Winnicott noted, learning to regulate one's emotions, as an infant, is made possible by the ego support and mirroring of the good enough mother. The research on post-traumatic remaking takes this further by noting the power of attunement when an individual is placed within a group that is working together, such as a band, choir, group of dancers, or theatre company. Where the individual is out of touch with their body or has lost (or never had) the ability to regulate emotions, healthy attunement can be facilitated by being part of a group with which one has to synchronize. This synchronicity offers the same support as the good enough mother provides for the infant who is not yet integrated and able to regulate their emotions. The church community is ideally placed to provide unique and crucial support in several ways.

Music, singing, and dancing are no strangers to the theodrama finding a consistent home in how the people of God express themselves and connect with God. By setting the post-traumatic remaking within a theodramatic model, there is the opportunity to bring together healthy corporate mirroring and attunement that recognizes the whole person as made in the image of God, set within a particular story unfolding in the presence of God. Where music and singing are used as the medium for aiding remaking, it can be undertaken as an act of worship that turns individuals toward God and sets them within this particular story while at the same time aiding regulation and body awareness leading to integration. Setting these avenues within the theodrama means that the music and singing are done with particular intent and with particular content.[85]

---

85. Vanhoozer seems to suggest something similar, but the present work seeks to enrich his observations by using particular psychological theories. See *Pictures*, 124.

The concern here could be that dovetailing the embodied activities of music, singing, and dancing with the label "acts of worship" risks creating a clash between the pain caused by the trauma that is being experienced when engaging in these activities and the positive affirmations about God and creation that are often equated with acts of worship. However, this is to mistakenly presume that worship always involves communicating only overtly positive content toward the object of worship. As I have argued elsewhere, the practice of lament so prominent in the Old Testament as well as continuing to be present in the New Testament may be considered as an act of worship too.[86] Cries of pain and anguish, desires for revenge, and pleas for help mixed in with doubt and questions when aimed at the divine covenant partner revealed in Scripture, who it is believed, can be present and affect positive change, may be considered acts of worship. The reason is that the motive for aiming such articulations at God, at least in part, is likely due to the belief that God cares and can do something to change the current situation. That may not always be the sole motivation, but where such a motivation is present, worship is taking place. And, even if on an individual level that motivation is not present, in the corporate affirmation of the core testimony, the body of Christ is maintaining this motivation, even while such testimony is cross-examined. More will be said about the place of lament in the trauma-sensitive church below. For now, it is enough simply to note that music and singing in such a community provide the opportunity for mirroring and (re)attunement, while embedding the group of individuals within the theodrama and engaging them in a relationship with God in acts of worship.

In a sense, given the overarching model of the theodrama being employed here, all activity discussed thus far regarding the church in act 4 might be considered performative. In the various explorations of how the eucharistic company of performers improvises, individually and collectively, on the performance of Christ in seeking to create parables of the kingdom that are trauma-sensitive and facilitating of remaking, we have been discussing the dramatic enacted in a variety of scenes. However, there is something more focused that can be said when considering the role of theatre.

Although Winnicott mentions theatre, it is not a major development in his work. However, as has been mentioned, the place of play in the development of the True Self is. As has also been noted, in

---

86. Torr, *Dramatic*, 217.

conversation with these ideas, a church community that takes seriously the development of True Christlike individuals must also take seriously the encouragement of play. In extending this to post-traumatic remaking, playing with others within the theodramatic setting could be extremely productive. If the Ignatian practice of praying by imagining oneself into a biblical scene can be extended to an embodied format, there is the possibility of specifically dramatic groups within the eucharistic community acting out previous scenes from the theodrama as a way of practicing attunement while also providing avenues for learning bodily awareness and emotional regulation in the process of performing a particular part. This combines a contemplative approach to prayer in which one is invited to imagine oneself into biblical scenes while being attentive to the impact, with the examples offered by Van der Kolk of engaging in theatre as an approach to (re)developing communal attunement.[87] If used in this way, there is scope for healing and formation facilitated by the body of Christ and enabled by the Spirit. I have here highlighted the possibility of the formation of a specific group but, in a sense, any gathering of the eucharistic company of performers is to collectively engage in performative acts that are to enable and encourage communion with God and others around the bread and wine. In such gatherings the past is remembered, and the future anticipated in the nourishing of the community in the present. In such gatherings, where there is participatory music, singing, and actions, all have the potential to be safe spaces of mirroring and (re)attunement that facilitate whole-person involvement and the learning of emotional regulation. However, that presumes several things that need to be noted.

First, the question of play and conformity returns us to the importance of a safe environment. For gatherings to be trauma-sensitive, the hospitality provided must be genuine to the point of not forcing anyone to participate in a rigidly prescriptive way. The community has shape and identity in part due to actions it undertakes while at the same time recognizing that these actions flow out of the shape and identity. As was noted in the previous chapter, *lex orandi, lex credendi, lex vivendi* mean that prayer, beliefs, emotions, and actions are all connected to, and formed by, each other while recognizing Scripture as the norming norm. However, there is no space in the trauma-sensitive community for either forced participation or exclusion when the individual does not participate in the

---

87. Lonsdale, *Eyes to See*, 110–16; Van der Kolk, *Body*, 330–46.

desired way. That is not reflective of God's fidelity and hospitality, and for good reason. True Christlike Selves develop and heal in safe spaces where participation is invited and facilitated but is not enforced. Play comes in here because for the space to be deemed safe, it must also be one in which those present are invited and made welcome to play—which may include questioning and boundary testing—with no fear of retaliation or rejection. False Selves emerge and further damage is done when individuals are not allowed the space to play and be. Such spaces will not be experienced as safe and so will not be places that facilitate remaking.

Secondly, in connection to the previous point about play, not only must the trauma-sensitive company create a safe space for play, but they must also be able to facilitate verbal expressions that cover the whole range of emotions. Here we return to Van der Kolk's work on articulation and expression of the impact of trauma.

Articulating and Expressing

Van der Kolk notes, "We may think we can control our grief, our terror, or our shame by remaining silent, but naming offers the possibility of a different kind of control."[88] The naming Van der Kolk refers to here involves bringing to speech the emotions and experience connected to the traumatic event/s. While hiding emotions from surface expression may feel like control, the reality is that these emotions are not being processed and managed in a healthy way, meaning that a lot of energy is being expended keeping oneself at the mercy of these emotions, which are likely manifesting in the body in unhealthy and disruptive ways.

To be able to communicate what has been experienced, and the accompanying emotions, can break down the isolation that is so damaging in trauma, as well as enable the renewal of a sense of identity and purpose in life. However, there are several important things to note here. First is how that communication is received. "Feeling listened to and understood changes our physiology; being able to articulate a complex feeling, and having our feelings recognized, lights up our limbic brain and creates 'aha moments.' In contrast, being met by silence and incomprehension kills the spirit."[89] Being able to feel safe enough to articulate something of the trauma, and then to experience a sense of being heard and

---

88. Van der Kolk, *Body*, 232.
89. Van der Kolk, *Body*, 232.

understood, enables progress toward healing. This requires individuals and communities that can provide such an environment and response.

A second point here is how we engage with and articulate what has happened. Neuroscience research has discovered that humans appear to have two distinct ways of engaging in and articulating self-awareness and these two ways are located in different parts of the brain.[90] The first is narrative self-awareness in which an individual creates an autobiography using the information at hand and connecting it into a narrative that can be adjusted as it is retold, and fresh information is incorporated. This approach has a linear view of time making it able to construct the narrative coherently. The second type of self-awareness is felt in the body and shifts with each passing moment. Given enough time and a safe environment, this can be accessed and brought to language. It is this latter form of self-awareness that requires accessing and embracing to be reconciled with accompanying emotions and make progress in remaking. This is particularly the case since the first type of self-awareness is located in a part of the brain that is usually knocked offline in the experience of trauma—which is why the coherent retelling of what happened can prove hard to provide. Also, there is a danger that retelling can be used as a way of being accepted in a community that is unwilling or unable to cope with the challenges of making suitable space for individuals to access and articulate their emotional self-awareness. As Van der Kolk notes, "Nobody wants to remember trauma. In that regard society is no different from the victims themselves. We all want to live in a world that is safe, manageable, and predictable, and victims remind us that this is not always the case. In order to understand trauma, we have to overcome our natural reluctance to confront that reality and cultivate the courage to listen to the testimonies of survivors."[91] Where a community can do this and, where suitable, offer words that can aid the articulation of emotion, there is the possibility of bridging between emotions held in the body and the language used to break down isolation, and process what has been experienced. Returning to a previous point, one way of doing this is by singing. By engaging in group singing there is the possibility of bringing to voice emotions while being attuned to, and in sync with, others and connecting with one's body in the process.[92] All of these are

---

90. Van der Kolk, *Body*, 236; Farb et al., "Attending to the Present."
91. Van der Kolk, *Body*, 194–95.
92. MacIntosh et al., "'Trying to Sing'"; Wang et al., "Music Interventions."

highly important for the journey of remaking and overlap with the body experiences discussed above.

One of the key problems that makes church communities trauma *insensitive* is the inability to offer safe yet honest ways of individually and collectively articulating painful emotions. Peter Levine refers to "pendulation" where there is a movement that swings between experiencing safety and exploring the disturbing impact of the trauma before returning to safety again.[93] This returns us to the importance of being able to create spaces of safety and hospitality as well as providing avenues for venturing into more difficult territory as and when the time is right to do so. Such movement can be enabled to take place within a church community if there is a consistently safe environment, the facilitation of honest vocalization of pain, and (when suitable) confession followed by genuine absolution. Here we combine Winnicott's work on play with his exploration of why babies cry. Connecting those areas with talking and being heard—where others continue to provide a safe environment while bearing witness to what is being articulated—the importance of countertestimony by the people of God comes to the fore. If a key feature of the eucharistic community is that it is one that facilitates, celebrates, and embodies reconciliation, then it must also be one that practices honest lament and confession properly.

To prize reconciliation in this way is to commit oneself to the processes that bring such a result about. These processes are neither straightforward nor clean but instead require the articulation of the various felt emotions as well as retellings of the story. Winnicott's work on play highlights the importance of being able to question the core beliefs of a community—its core testimony. To play, in this situation, is to be able to explore and examine how the world has been experienced and interpreted without censorship. Paradoxically, the community in which such cross-examination is taking place is called to create a safe space where the core testimony can continue to be held in tension with the cross-examination that comes from the countertestimony of those impacted by trauma. The hospitality of God, mirrored in the body of Christ, is one that, if it is mirroring such hospitality accurately creates ways of holding these voices in tension and without exclusion or imposed conformity, bearing witness to—hearing and seeing—the articulated emotion of those in the process of post-traumatic remaking. In so doing, it

---

93. Levine, *In an Unspoken Voice*, 78–82.

is facilitating the dialogical consummation of the True Christlike Self that the Holy Spirit is effecting. Winnicott's work on crying has shown us that to curtail the various types of crying is to encourage a False Self to emerge, meaning the True Self remains at least partially hidden and unable to be reconciled to God, self, and others. However, the role of the community in terms of safe presence is also vital in the absence of a clear and felt presence of God to the sufferer.[94] Again, referring back to Winnicott, when the parent is away too long, the crying turns to one of hopelessness. The body of Christ is called to continue to be present and bear witness in the absence of desired experiences of God as, paradoxically, a sign and an embodiment of God's presence.

To be a trauma-sensitive church is to be located within the theo-drama where final reconciliation is the goal between God and creation and among creation. This is a significant aspect of the core testimony that gives the community shape. However, safe space for play and crying must be available for those in the process of post-traumatic remaking, or else what will be formed in the performers are False Selves that have learned to conform to survive. Such a result is neither reconciliatory nor salvific and results from an environment that does not mirror the hospitality of God. This is the sort of environment provided by Job's friends that antagonized Job rather than helped him. It is only the God who encouraged Job's honesty that could bring about his healing.

Although confession might not necessarily seem to fit here, it does relate to the goal of reconciliation and communion and finds a particular place in the trauma-sensitive church. Although the lament discussed above relates to situations where the traumatized person might be the innocent party, there are occasions where trauma is experienced because of things done by the individual where guilt is carried—sometimes known as "moral injury," as discussed in chapter 2 above. The story may be different, but the need to speak out what has been done and articulate the

---

94. Both Harrower and Wendel highlight the importance of a safe and secure attachment to God, with Harrower suggesting a secure attachment to Jesus is where recovery begins (see Harrower, *God of All Comfort*, 173–75; and Wendel, "Trauma-Informed Theology," 21–22). In principle, I agree, but in reality, it is not that straightforward. Often those who have experienced trauma will likely struggle with an experience of an absent God or, worse, a God who is perceived as an enemy—something articulated in both Job and the Psalms. In such cases, the community of the church, contra Job's friends, must continue to hold survivors, mediating the love and care of God, while the remaking work is done. A safe and secure relationship with God is the aim, but getting to that is messy and mediated, at least in part, by human relationships, meaning it is far from a linear process.

connected emotions and experiences can still be vital. However, what is as important is again the safe space created by those who offer Christlike generosity and hospitality to these expressions without condemnation or exclusion as the community holds and handles the person and bears witness to the confession. Although absolution appropriately offered does not necessarily remove the pain and memories, it can provide a helpful building block in the remaking toward wholeness and reconciliation. Too often confession is either downplayed as between the individual and God alone or is presented as unimportant. Worse still, it may be weaponized as a way of exposing, condemning, and shaming some by those in positions of power thereby exerting toxic power and control. As we have seen in previous chapters, none of these avenues has a home within the eucharistic company that is seeking to mirror the hospitality of God's love-driven example toward creation. This is so because neither of these approaches facilitates healing and reconciliation.

The theatre of reconciliation and healing offered by a eucharistic company of performers seeking to embody and facilitate True Christlike Selves is therefore one that must embody a certain type of fidelity and extend a certain kind of hospitality and generosity to be trauma-sensitive. Building on the provision of a safe environment, the embodiment of such Christlike fidelity, hospitality, and generosity facilitates and supports the messy and lengthy process of remembering and mourning that is central to post-traumatic remaking.

Reconnection

Of this stage, Herman writes, "The self-discipline learned in the early stages of recovery can now be joined to the survivor's capacities for imagination and play. This is a period of trial and error, of learning to tolerate mistakes and to savor unexpected success."[95] At this point, the survivor is reconnecting with the self and the broader world, while opening up the possibility of a positive future. A reconfigured worldview emerges with a fresh sense of meaning that can accommodate the reality of the trauma experienced. At this stage, it is important to mix more deeply in groups that do not share the same experience of trauma yet do not diminish the experience that has been had and the continuing impact that such an experience has on someone in the process of remaking.

---

95. Herman, *Trauma and Recovery*, 296.

Given the unique nature of each individual, the reconnection stage that Herman outlines will look different for everybody. However, if the eucharistic facilitating company of church performers seeks to enact the performance direction offered in this and the previous chapter, the church should be a safe place for each trauma survivor to continue to play in the intermediate space between their experience and the core testimony of the church. With their fellow performers, Script in hand and guided by the Spirit, they should be able to find ways to discern what it might mean for them to improvise on the performance of Christ in the scenes in which they find themselves as they develop toward the full embodiment of their True Christlike Self. Here there may well also be a shift from being primarily a welcomed guest to becoming the host to others as they live into the priestly mediatorial role of the church, while prophetically unveiling the kingly rule of God glimpsed in the traveling troupe of performers.[96] Reconnection then becomes about reconnecting to life in all its splendor as the eternal kingdom is experienced—if only partially—in the now as a window into what is yet to arrive fully in act 5 of the theodrama. There may likely be a sense in which one is haunted by the ghosts of trauma, even as a follower of Jesus in the current act, but a reconnection with the full theodrama offers the hope-filled reminder that this is not the end of the story.[97] The good news to be proclaimed and performed by the eucharistic, facilitating, trauma-sensitive church is that healing and wholeness can be experienced as a foretaste of the final act as the remaking and reconnection continue.

Conclusion

Having constructed the necessary building blocks in the previous chapter, it has been possible in the present one to return to the main question at the heart of this work and explore what Job's friends could have done. Setting trauma and post-traumatic remaking within the theodrama

---

96. It is important to note here that although I am suggesting that the community has been the host to the one in the process of post-traumatic remaking, in reality, the roles may not be that clear. The reason for this is that it could be argued that the one doing the remaking has also, in certain ways, played host to the community as the community has been invited into the life of the survivor. Therefore, there is slippage in terms of who is host and who is guest. However, hopefully the point I am making about the changing nature of the survivor's relationship to the community is still clear.

97. For an example of a theologian grappling with this experience, see Jones, *Trauma and Grace*, 151–65.

gave fresh insight into how it might be perceived and interpreted by the trauma-sensitive church as it attempts to live out its vocation as the eucharistic company of performers that is the body of Christ in the world. The conversation between Vanhoozer and Winnicott had aided in clarifying the shape of the True Christlike Self and the role of the church in supporting such a development in individuals. In this chapter, it was possible to extend that insight to provide stage direction for how the church can care well, improvising on the performance of Jesus, for those who are in the process of post-traumatic remaking. By exploring the eucharistic shape of fidelity, generosity, and hospitality in the context of post-traumatic remaking it was possible to provide some guidance for what Job's friends, and therefore what we, could do to better care for Job and others affected by trauma. As we move toward the conclusion of this work the question that remains is, where now?

9

Conclusion

IN A SENSE, DRAWING this project to a close is only really the beginning, or more accurately, a continuation, of an exploration. Driven by my experience, the aim has been to answer the question, "What could Job's friends have done?" as a way of helping myself, while hopefully aiding the church more broadly, to reflect on how to care well for those in the process of post-traumatic remaking. In doing so I have used a Christocentric theodramatic approach, largely drawing from the work of Kevin Vanhoozer, in conversation with the work of Donald Winnicott, to offer guidance and a rationale for what fitting performances in the current act of the theodrama might entail for a church that is seeking to be trauma-sensitive. The terrain covered has involved exploring what it might mean to perform as *imago Dei*, how the church best facilitates and enables that, and specifically what it means for the church to facilitate and enable that for those in the process of post-traumatic remaking. In so doing, I have hopefully offered a fresh voice that will provide further material to keep the conversation about how to best cooperate with God's healing work in the church moving in a positive, Spirited direction. From here, the invitation is to the reader/s to explore improvised performances under the direction offered in this work that might better provide fitting Christlike care for those who have experienced trauma. Inevitably this will highlight avenues overlooked or not explored here, as well as flaws or shortcomings in the theory and the proposed practice. However, in such cases, a further invitation to continue the conversation is implicit, as we strive to grow together in our love of God and one another.

As I pause to reflect on the preceding pages, I am aware that I could be accused of setting the bar too high, that what I have presented is an attempt at performance direction for the perfect church, and that if any church tried to measure itself against the material presented here, it would only ever be faced with its shortcomings. This is an important point to note but in a sense is an old problem in new clothing/language. The call to Christlikeness in the pages of Scripture is always one toward the perfection for which we, collectively and individually, were made and will experience at the eschaton—"Be perfect, therefore, as your heavenly Father is perfect," says Jesus in the Sermon on the Mount (Matt 5:48). Until Jesus returns, we are always moving toward perfection, growing into the holiness that is already ours "in Christ" while recognizing that the best we can offer can be good enough because of the death and resurrection of Jesus and the work of the Spirit to make up for the shortfalls in our actions and provision.

Reflecting on Job's prayers for his friends in the final chapter of the book of Job, Hamley notes, "For the community of faith to function properly, there needs to be an acknowledgement of failure, willingness for grace and openness to a new articulation of its journey with God. Job as a teaching book therefore takes seriously the fact that communities of faith will not respond well, and holds them responsible, but also prepares this same community to respond with grace to the failure of its members."[1] At the end of the book of Job, it would appear that the friends are repentant, Job is forgiving, and reconciliation may begin. All church communities will fail in their care of, and their learning from, those who have experienced trauma. However, as with Job's friends, a willingness to learn and grow means that failure is not the end of the road. What I am trying to encourage, then, is a church that strives for perfection while knowing that it is still loved and drawn forward by the God of love in spite of not always being good enough. To have nothing at which to aim results in striving for nothing and instead groping around in the dark, likely causing more harm than good. So, the material presented here is intended to challenge us as we seek to name and repent of our failures, yet inspire us to do better as we cooperate with the work of the Spirit to embody Christlike performances that offer safer, more love-filled environments for facilitating the process of post-traumatic remaking for the Jobs we are invited to sit with.

1. Hamley, "Patient Job," 94.

Bibliography

Abram, Jan. "DWW's Notes for the Vienna Congress 1971: A Consideration of Winnicott's Theory of Aggression and an Interpretation of the Clinical Implications." In *Donald Winnicott Today*, edited by Jan Abram, 302–30. Hove, East Sussex: Routledge, 2013.

———. "The Evolution of Winnicott's Theoretical Matrix: A Brief Outline." In *Donald Winnicott Today*, edited by Jan Abram, 73–112. Hove, East Sussex: Routledge, 2013.

———. Introduction to *Donald Winnicott Today*, edited by Jan Abram, 1–25. Hove, East Sussex: Routledge, 2013.

———. *The Language of Winnicott: A Dictionary of Winnicott's Use of Words*. 2nd ed. Abingdon, Oxon: Routledge, 2018.

Adams, Marilyn McCord. *Christ and Horrors: The Coherence of Christology*. Cambridge: Cambridge University Press, 2006.

———. "Eucharistic Drama." In *Theatrical Theology: Explorations in Performing the Faith*, edited by Wesley Vander Lugt and Trevor Hart, 203–23. Eugene, OR: Cascade, 2014.

Allen, Leslie C. *Psalms 101–150*. Word Biblical Commentary 21. Nashville: Thomas Nelson, 2002.

Ambler, Gillies, et al., eds. *Flourishing in Faith: Theology Encountering Positive Psychology*. Eugene, OR: Cascade, 2017.

Anderson, Allan. "Varieties, Taxonomies, and Definitions." *Studying Global Pentecostalism: Theories and Methods*, edited by Allan Anderson et al., 13–29. London: University of California Press, 2010.

Ansell, Nicholas John. "The Call of Wisdom/The Voice of the Serpent: A Canonical Approach to the Tree of Knowledge." *Christian Scholars Review* 31.1 (2001) 31–57.

Anstey, Matthew P. "'And God Saw It Was Good': The Creation of Wellbeing and the Wellbeing of Creation." In *Flourishing in Faith: Theology Encountering Positive Psychology*, edited by Gillies Ambler et al., 55–64. Eugene, OR: Cascade, 2017.

Aquinas, Thomas. *The Summa Theologica*. Translated by Fathers of the English Dominican Province. Benziger Bros. ed. Grand Rapids: Christian Classics Ethereal Library, 1947.

Augustine. *On the Holy Trinity*. Translated by Arthur West Haddan. Revised and annotated by W. G. T. Shedd. *NPNF* 1/3:1–228.

Augustine, Daniela C. "Image, Spirit and Theosis: Imaging God in an Image Distorting World." In *The Image of God in an Image Driven Age: Explorations in Theological Anthropology*, edited by Beth Felker Jones and Jeffrey W. Barbeau, 173–88. Downers Grove, IL: InterVarsity, 2016.

Austin, J. L. *How to Do Things with Words*. Oxford: Oxford University Press, 1962.

Bakhtin, M. M. "Author and Hero in Aesthetic Activity." In *Art and Answerability: Early Philosophical Essays by M. M. Bakhtin*, translated by Vadim Liapunov, edited by Michael Holquist and Vadim Liapunov, 4–256. Austin: University of Texas Press, 1990.

Baldwin, Jennifer. *Trauma-Sensitive Theology: Thinking Theologically in the Era of Trauma*. Eugene, OR: Cascade, 2018.

Baldwin, Susanna. "Miserable but Not Monochrome: The Distinctive Characteristics and Perspectives of Job's Three Comforters." *Themelios* 43.3 (2018) 359–75.

Barth, Karl. *Church Dogmatics*. Edited by G. W. Bromiley and T. F. Torrance. Translated by J. W. Edwards et al. Vol. 3, *The Doctrine of Creation Part 1*. Edinburgh: T & T Clark, 1958.

Blackwell, Dick. "Holding, Containing and Bearing Witness: The Problem of Helpfulness in Encounters with Torture Survivors." *Journal of Social Work Practice* 11.2 (1997) 81–89.

Blomberg, Craig L., et al. "'True Righteousness and Holiness': The Image of God in the New Testament." In *The Image of God in an Image Driven Age: Explorations in Theological Anthropology*, edited by Beth Felker Jones and Jeffrey W. Barbeau, 66–87. Downers Grove, IL: InterVarsity, 2016.

Boase, Elizabeth, and Christopher G. Frechette, eds. *Bible Through the Lens of Trauma*. Atlanta: SBL, 2016.

Bond, Lucy, and Stef Craps. *Trauma*. Abingdon, Oxon: Routledge, 2020.

Bonhoeffer, Dietrich. *The Cost of Discipleship*. Translated by R. H. Fuller and Irmgard Booth. London: SCM, 2015.

———. *Life Together*. Translated by John W. Doberstein. London: SCM, 2015.

Boyd, Jenna E., et al. "Mindfulness-Based Treatments for Posttraumatic Stress Disorder: A Review of the Treatment Literature and Neurobiological Evidence." *Journal of Psychiatry and Neuroscience* 43.1 (2018) 7–25. https://doi.org/10.1503/jpn.170021.

Bradnick, David. *Evil, Spirits, and Possession: An Emergentist Theology of the Demonic*. Leiden: Brill, 2017.

Brueggemann, Walter. "The Costly Loss of Lament." In *The Psalms and the Life of Faith*, edited by Patrick D. Miller, 98–111. Minneapolis: Augsburg Fortress, 1995.

———. *Genesis*. Interpretation. Louisville: John Knox, 1982.

———. *The Message of the Psalms*. Minneapolis: Augsburg, 1984.

———. "Psalms and the Life of Faith: A Suggested Typology of Function." In *The Psalms and the Life of Faith*, edited by Patrick D. Miller, 3–32. Minneapolis: Augsburg Fortress, 1995.

———. "Psychological Criticism: Exploring the Self in the Text." In *Method Matters: Essays on the Interpretation of the Hebrew Bible in Honor of David L. Petersen*, edited by Joel M. LeMon and Kent Harold Richards, 213–32. Atlanta: Society of Biblical Literature, 2009.

———. *Theology of the Old Testament: Testimony, Advocacy, Dispute*. Minneapolis: Augsburg Fortress, 1997.

Brunner, Emil. *Man in Revolt: A Christian Anthropology*. Translated by Olive Wyon. London: Lutterworth, 1939.

Brunner, Emil, and Karl Barth. *Natural Theology*. Translated by Peter Fraenkel. London: The Centenary, 1946.

Cairns, David. *The Image of God in Man*. London: Fontana Library of Theology and Philosophy, 1973.

Calvin, John. *Commentaries on the First Book of Moses Called Genesis*. Translated by John King. Vol. 1. Grand Rapids: Christian Classics Ethereal Library, 1847.

———. *Institutes of the Christian Religion*. Translated by Henry Beveridge. Grand Rapids: Christian Classics Ethereal Library, 1845.

Caputo, John D. *Hoping Against Hope: Confessions of a Postmodern Pilgrim*. Minneapolis: Fortress, 2015.

Carr, David M. *Holy Resilience: The Bible's Traumatic Origins*. New Haven, CT: Yale University Press, 2014.

Carter, Richard, and Samuel Wells. "Holy Theatre." In *Theatrical Theology: Explorations in Performing the Faith*, edited by Wesley Vander Lugt and Trevor Hart, 224–40. Eugene, OR: Cascade, 2014.

Cartledge, Mark J. *Testimony in the Spirit: Rescripting Ordinary Pentecostal Theology*. Farnham, UK: Ashgate, 2010.

Chandler, Diane J. Introduction to *The Holy Spirit and Christian Formation: Multidisciplinary Perspectives*, edited by Diane J. Chandler, 1–16. Cham: Palgrave Macmillan, 2016.

Chen, C. Elmer. "The Pentecostal Doctrine of Spirit Baptism: A Theodramatic Model, with Special Reference to the Imago Dei." PhD diss., University of Birmingham, UK, 2017.

Clines, David J. A. "The Arguments of Job's Three Friends." In *Art and Meaning: Rhetoric in Biblical Literature*, edited by David J. A. Clines et al., 199–214. Journal for the Study of the Old Testament Supplement Series 19. Sheffield: Journal for the Study of the Old Testament, 1982.

———. *Job 1–20*. Word Biblical Commentary 17. Dallas: Word, 1989.

Cockayne, Joshua, et al. *Dawn of Sunday: The Trinity and Trauma-Safe Churches*. New Studies in Theology and Trauma. Eugene, OR: Cascade, 2022.

Collicutt, Joanna. "Bringing the Academic Discipline of Psychology to Bear on the Study of the Bible." *The Journal of Theological Studies* 63.1 (2012) 1–48.

———. *The Psychology of Christian Character Formation*. London: SCM, 2015.

Coolican, Hugh. *Research Methods and Statistics in Psychology*. Abingdon, Oxon: Routledge, 2019.

Craigo-Snell, Shannon. "In Praise of Empty Churches." In *Theatrical Theology: Explorations in Performing the Faith*, edited by Wesley Vander Lugt and Trevor Hart, 88–112. Eugene, OR: Cascade, 2014.

DeGroat, Chuck. "The Parts We Play: Anthropology and Application to Expand Vanhoozer's Proposal." *Edification: The Transdisciplinary Journal of Christian Psychology* 4.1 (2010) 17–20.

De Terte, Ian, et al. "An Integrated Model for Understanding and Developing Resilience in the Face of Adverse Events." *Journal of Pacific Rim Psychology* 3.1 (2009) 20–26. https://doi.org/10.1375/prp.3.1.20.

Eklund, Rebekah. *Jesus Wept: The Significance of Jesus' Laments in the New Testament*. London: Bloomsbury T&T Clark, 2016.

Ellens, J. Harold, ed. *Psychological Hermeneutics for Biblical Themes and Texts: A Festschrift in Honor of Wayne G. Rollins*. London: Bloomsbury T&T Clark, 2013.

Enns, Peter. *The Evolution of Adam: What the Bible Does and Doesn't Say About Human Origins*. Grand Rapids: Brazos, 2012.

Evans, Craig A. *Mark 8:27—16:20*. Word Biblical Commentary 34B. Grand Rapids: Zondervan, 1988.

Farb, Norman A. S., et al. "Attending to the Present: Mindfulness Meditation Reveals Distinct Neural Modes of Self-Reference." *Social Cognitive and Affective Neuroscience* 2.4 (2007) 313–22. https://doi.org/10.1093/scan/nsm030.

Fodor, Jim. "The Play of Christian Life: When Wisdom Calls to Wisdom." In *Theatrical Theology: Explorations in Performing the Faith*, edited by Wesley Vander Lugt and Trevor Hart, 126–52. Eugene, OR: Cascade, 2014.

Ford, Carla, and Andrew Ford. "Gratitude: A Theological and Psychological Perspective." In *Flourishing in Faith: Theology Encountering Positive Psychology*, edited by Gillies Ambler et al., 111–25. Eugene, OR: Cascade, 2017.

Frechette, Christopher G., and Elizabeth Boase. "Defining 'Trauma' as a Useful Lens for Biblical Interpretation." In *Bible Through the Lens of Trauma*, edited by Elizabeth Boase and Christopher G. Frechette, 1–23. Atlanta: SBL, 2016.

Fretheim, Terence E. *God and World in the Old Testament: A Relational Theology of Creation*. Nashville: Abingdon, 2005.

Ganssle, Gregory E., ed. *God and Time: Four Views*. Downers Grove, IL: InterVarsity, 2001.

Garber, David G., Jr. "Trauma Theory and Biblical Studies." *Currents in Biblical Research* 14.1 (2015) 24–44.

Gomez, Lavinia. *An Introduction to Object Relations*. London: Free Association, 1997.

Green, Joel B. *The Gospel of Luke*. The New International Commentary on the New Testament. Grand Rapids: Eerdmans, 1997.

Grenz, Stanley J. *The Social God and the Relational Self: A Trinitarian Theology of the Imago Dei*. Louisville: Westminster John Knox, 2001.

Grosch-Miller, Carla A. *Trauma and Pastoral Care: A Ministry Handbook*. London: Canterbury, 2021.

Guelich, Robert A. *Mark 1–8:26*. Word Biblical Commentary 34A. Grand Rapids: Zondervan, 2015.

Habel, Norman C. *God Trauma and Wisdom Therapy: A Commentary on Job*. Minneapolis: Fortress, 2024.

Hagner, Donald A. *Matthew 1–13*. Word Biblical Commentary 33A. Nashville: Thomas Nelson, 2000.

———. *Matthew 14–28*. Word Biblical Commentary 33B. Dallas: Word, 1995.

Hamley, Isabelle. "Patient Job, Angry Job: Speaking Faith in the Midst of Trauma." In *The Bible and Mental Health: Towards a Biblical Theology of Mental Health*, edited by Christopher C. H. Cook and Isabelle Hamley, 85–95. London: SCM, 2020.

Hamman, Jaco J. "The Restoration of Job: A Study Based on D. W. Winnicott's Theory of Object Usage and Its Significance for Pastoral Theology." PhD diss., Princeton University, 2000.

Harris, Mark. "The Biblica Text and a Functional Account of the Imago Dei." In *Finding Ourselves After Darwin: Conversations on the Image of God, Original Sin, and the Problem of Evil*, edited by Stanley P. Rosenberg et al., 48–63. Grand Rapids: Baker, 2018.

Harris, Tim. "Shalom, Gospel and the Mission of God." In *Flourishing in Faith: Theology Encountering Positive Psychology*, edited by Gillies Ambler et al., 65–80. Eugene, OR: Cascade, 2017.

Harrower, Scott. *God of All Comfort: A Trinitarian Response to the Horrors of This World*. Bellingham, WA: Lexham, 2019.

Hart, David Bentley. *The Doors of the Sea: Where Was God in the Tsunami?* Grand Rapids: Eerdmans, 2005.

———. "No Shadow of Turning: Divine Impassibility." *Pro Ecclesia* 11.2 (2002) 184–206.

Hart, Trevor. "Beyond Theatre and Incarnation." In *Theatrical Theology: Explorations in Performing the Faith*, edited by Wesley Vander Lugt and Trevor Hart, 30–43. Eugene, OR: Cascade, 2014.

Hauerwas, Stanley. *Naming the Silences*. London: T&T Clark, 2004.

Heltzel, Peter Goodwin. "The Church as a Theatre of the Oppressed." In *Theatrical Theology: Explorations in Performing the Faith*, edited by Wesley Vander Lugt and Trevor Hart, 241–82. Eugene, OR: Cascade, 2014.

Herman, Judith L. *Trauma and Recovery: The Aftermath of Violence—From Domestic Abuse to Political Terror*. New York: Basic, 2022.

Hopkins, Brooke. "Jesus and Object-Use: A Winnicottian Account of the Resurrection Myth." In *Transitional Objects and Potential Spaces: Literary Uses of D. W. Winnicott*, edited by Peter L. Rudnytsky, 249–60. New York: Columbia University Press, 1993.

Houck-Loomis, Tiffany. *History Through Trauma: History and Counter-History in the Hebrew Bible*. Eugene, OR: Pickwick, 2018.

Irenaeus. *Against Heresies*. ANF 1:315–567.

Ison, Hilary. "Working with an Embodied and Systemic Approach to Trauma and Tragedy." In *Tragedies and Christian Congregations: The Practical Theology of Trauma*, edited by Megan Warner et al., 47–63. Abingdon, Oxon: Routledge, 2020.

Janzen, J. Gerald. *Job*. Interpretation. Louisville: John Knox, 1985.

Johnson, Todd E. "Doing God's Story: Theatre, Christian Initiation, and Being Human Together." In *Theatrical Theology: Explorations in Performing the Faith*, edited by Wesley Vander Lugt and Trevor Hart, 153–77. Eugene, OR: Cascade, 2014.

Johnson, Todd E., and Dale Savidge. *Performing the Sacred: Theology and Theatre in Dialogue*. Engaging Culture. Grand Rapids: Baker, 2009.

Jones, Serene. *Trauma and Grace*. 2nd ed. Louisville: Westminster John Knox, 2019.

Kamp, Minke M. van de, et al. "Body- and Movement-Oriented Interventions for Posttraumatic Stress Disorder: A Systematic Review and Meta-Analysis." *Journal of Traumatic Stress* 32.6 (2019) 967–76. https://doi.org/10.1002/jts.22465.

Khovacs, Ivan Patricio, et al. "The Intractable Sense of an Ending: Gethsemane's Prayer on the Tragic Stage." In *Theatrical Theology: Explorations in Performing the Faith*, edited by Wesley Vander Lugt and Trevor Hart, 44–72. Eugene, OR: Cascade, 2014.

Kilby, Karen. "Evil and the Limits of Theology." *New Blackfriars* 84.983 (2003) 13–29.

Kiser, Charles, and Elaine A. Heath. *Trauma-Informed Evangelism: Cultivating Communities of Wounded Healers*. Grand Rapids: Eerdmans, 2023.

Land, Steven Jack. *Pentecostal Spirituality: A Passion for the Kingdom*. Cleveland, TN: CPT, 2010.

Levine, Peter A. *In an Unspoken Voice: How the Body Releases Trauma and Restores Goodness*. Berkley, CA: North Atlantic, 2010.

Levine, Peter A., and Ann Frederick. *Waking the Tiger: Healing Trauma*. Berkley, CA: North Atlantic, 1997.

Lewis, C. S. *Mere Christianity*. London: Fount, 1997.

Lister, Rob. *God Is Impassible and Impassioned*. Reprint ed. Wheaton, IL: Crossway, 2013.

Lonsdale, David. *Eyes to See, Ears to Hear: An Introduction to Ignatian Spirituality*. London: Darton, Longman & Todd, 2000.

Loparic, Zeljko. "From Freud to Winnicott: Aspects of a Paradigm Change." In *Donald Winnicott Today*, edited by Jan Abram, 113–56. Hove, East Sussex: Routledge, 2013.

Luther, Martin. *Lectures on Genesis: Chapters 1–5*. Vol. 1 of *Luther's Works*. Translated by George V. Schick, edited by Jaroslav Pelikan. Saint Louis: Concordia, 1958.

MacIntosh, Heather B., et al. "'Trying to Sing Through the Tears.' Choral Music and Childhood Trauma: Results of a Pilot Study." *International Journal of Research in Choral Singing* 8 (2020) 22–50.

Malone, Andrew S. *God's Mediators: A Biblical Theology of Priesthood*. Downers Grove, IL: InterVarsity, 2017.

McDowell, Catherine. "'In the Image of God He Created Them': How Genesis 1:26–27 Defines the Divine-Human Relationship and Why It Matters." In *The Image of God in an Image Driven Age: Explorations in Theological Anthropology*, edited by Beth Felker Jones and Jeffrey W. Barbeau, 29–46. Downers Grove, IL: InterVarsity, 2016.

McGrath, Joanna Collicutt. *Jesus and the Gospel Women*. London: SPCK, 2009.

McLaren, Brian D. *The Last Word and the Word After That: A Tale of Faith, Doubt, and a New Kind of Christianity*. San Francisco: Jossey-Bass, 2005.

———. *A New Kind of Christian: A Tale of Two Friends on a Spiritual Journey*. San Francisco: Jossey-Bass, 2001.

———. *The Story We Find Ourselves In: Further Adventures of a New Kind of Christian*. San Francisco: Jossey-Bass, 2003.

Meyer, Ben F. *Critical Realism and the New Testament*. Allison Park, PA: Pickwick, 1989.

Middleton, J. Richard. *Abraham's Silence: The Binding of Isaac, the Suffering of Job, and How to Talk Back to God*. Grand Rapids: Baker, 2021.

———. *The Liberating Image: The Imago Dei in Genesis 1*. Grand Rapids: Brazos, 2005.

———. *A New Heaven and a New Earth: Reclaiming Biblical Eschatology*. Grand Rapids: Baker, 2014.

———. "Reading Genesis 3 Attentive to Human Evolution: Beyond Concordism and Non-Overlapping Magisteria." In *Evolution and the Fall*, edited by William T. Cavanaugh and James K. A. Smith, 67–97. Grand Rapids: Eerdmans, 2017.

Migliore, Daniel L. *Faith Seeking Understanding: An Introduction to Christian Theology*. 2nd ed. Grand Rapids: Eerdmans, 2004.

Miller-McLemore, Bonnie J. "Introduction: The Contributions of Practical Theology." In *The Wiley Blackwell Companion to Practical Theology*, edited by Bonnie J. Miller-McLemore, 1–20. Chichester, West Sussex: Wiley & Sons, 2014.

Moltmann, Jurgen. *The Crucified God: The Cross of Christ as the Foundation and Criticism of Christian Theology*. London: SCM, 2001.

Morris, Leon. *The Gospel According to Matthew*. The Pillar New Testament Commentary. Leicester: Apollos, 1992.

Newell, Jason M., et al. "Clinician Responses to Client Traumas." *Trauma, Violence and Abuse* 17.3 (2016) 306–13.

Nolland, John. *Luke 1–9:20*. Word Biblical Commentary 35A. Nashville: Thomas Nelson, 2000.

O'Donnell, Karen. *Broken Bodies: The Eucharist, Mary, and the Body in Trauma Theology*. London: SCM, 2019.

———. "Eucharist and Trauma: Healing in the B/body." In *Tragedies and Christian Congregations: The Practical Theology of Trauma*, edited by Megan Warner et al., 182–93. Abingdon, Oxon: Routledge, 2020.

———. "The Voices of the Marys: Towards a Method in Feminist Trauma Theologies." In *Feminist Trauma Theologies: Body, Scripture and Church in Critical Perspective*, edited by Karen O'Donnell and Katie Cross, 3–20. London: SCM, 2020.

O'Donnell, Karen, and Katie Cross. Introduction to *Feminist Trauma Theologies: Body, Scripture and Church in Critical Perspective*, edited by Karen O'Donnell and Katie Cross, xix–xxv. London: SCM, 2020.

Ogden, Thomas H. "The Mother, the Infant and the Matrix: Interpretations of Aspects of the Work of Donald Winnicott." In *Donald Winnicott Today*, edited by Jan Abram, 46–72. Hove, East Sussex: Routledge, 2013.

Oord, Thomas Jay. "The *Imago Dei* as Relational Love." In *Finding Ourselves After Darwin: Conversations on the Image of God, Original Sin, and the Problem of Evil*, edited by Stanley P. Rosenberg et al., 79–91. Grand Rapids: Baker Academic, 2018.

Parker, Stephen E. *Winnicott and Religion*. Lanham, MD: Jason Aronson, 2011.

Pattison, Stephen, and James Woodward. "An Introduction to Pastoral and Practical Theology." In *The Blackwell Reader in Pastoral and Practical Theology*, edited by James Woodward and Stephen Pattison, 1–19. Oxford: Blackwell, 2000.

Peters, Ted. "The *Imago Dei* as the End of Evolution." In *Finding Ourselves After Darwin: Conversations on the Image of God, Original Sin, and the Problem of Evil*, edited by Stanley P. Rosenberg et al., 92–106. Grand Rapids: Baker Academic, 2018.

Phillips, Adam. *Winnicott*. London: Penguin, 2007.

Polyvagal Institute. "Scientific Papers, Chapters, and Interviews of Interest." N.d. https://www.polyvagalinstitute.org/scientific-papers-books-etc.

Rambo, Shelly. *Spirit and Trauma: A Theology of Remaining*. Louisville: Westminster John Knox, 2010.

Rasmussen, Brian. "The Effects of Trauma Treatment on the Therapist." In *Trauma: Contemporary Directions in Trauma Theory, Research, and Practice*, edited by Shoshana Ringel and Jerrold R. Brandell, 354–83. 2nd ed. Chichester, West Sussex: Columbia University Press, 2020.

Redman, Matt, and Beth Redman. "Blessed Be Your Name." Track 2 on *Where Angels Fear to Tread*. Thankyou Music, 2002. Compact disc.

Reeves, Christopher. "On the Margins: The Role of the Father in Winnicott's Writing." In *Donald Winnicott Today*, edited by Jan Abram, 358–85. Hove, East Sussex: Routledge, 2013.

Risser, Dustin S. *Creativity, Theology, and Posttraumatic Growth: The Sacred Impulse of Play and Transformation out of Tragedy*. Eugene, OR: Pickwick, 2022.

Rollins, Wayne G. *Soul and Psyche: The Bible in Psychological Perspective*. Minneapolis: Augsburg Fortress, 1999.

Samra, James G. *Being Conformed to Christ in Community: A Study of Maturity, Maturation and the Local Church in the Undisputed Pauline Epistles*. London: T&T Clark, 2008.

Searle, John R. *Speech Acts: An Essay in the Philosophy of Language*. London: Cambridge University Press, 1969.

Seligman, Martin, and Mihaly Csikszentmihalyi. "Positive Psychology: An Introduction." *The American Psychologist* 55 (2000) 5–14. https://doi.org/10.1037/0003-066X.55.1.5.

Shepherd, Andrew. *The Gift of the Other: Levinas, Derrida, and a Theology of Hospitality*. Cambridge: James Clarke and Co., 2014.

Smith, James K. A. *Desiring the Kingdom: Worship, Worldview, and Cultural Formation*. Cultural Liturgies 1. Grand Rapids: Baker Academic, 2009.

———. "What Stands on the Fall? A Philosophical Exploration." In *Evolution and the Fall*, edited by William T. Cavanaugh and James K. A. Smith, 48–64. Grand Rapids: Eerdmans, 2017.

Soelle, Dorothee. *Suffering*. Translated by Everett R. Kalin. Philadelphia: Fortress, 1975.

Soskice, Janet. "The God of Creative Address: Creation, Christology and Ethics." In *The Image of God in an Image Driven Age: Explorations in Theological Anthropology*, edited by Beth Felker Jones and Jeffrey W. Barbeau, 189–201. Downers Grove, IL: InterVarsity, 2016.

Stanislavski, Constantin. *An Actor Prepares*. Translated by Elizabeth Reynolds Hapgood. London: Bloomsbury Academic, 2013.

Stead, Tim. *Mindfulness and Christian Spirituality: Making Space for God*. London: SPCK, 2016.

Stephenson, Christopher A. *Types of Pentecostal Theology: Method, System, Spirit*. Oxford: Oxford University Press, 2016.

Surin, Kenneth. *Theology and the Problem of Evil*. Eugene, OR: Wipf & Stock, 2004.

Swinton, John. *Finding Jesus in the Storm: The Spiritual Lives of Christians with Mental Health Challenges*. Grand Rapids: Eerdmans, 2020.

———. *From Bedlam to Shalom: Towards a Practical Theology of Human Nature, Interpersonal Relationships, and Mental Health Care*. New York: Peter Lang, 2000.

———. *Raging with Compassion: Pastoral Responses to the Problem of Evil*. Grand Rapids: Eerdmans, 2007.

Thibodeaux, Mark E. *God's Voice Within: The Ignatian Way to Discover God's Will*. Chicago: Loyola, 2010.

———. *Reimagining the Ignatian Examen: Fresh Ways to Pray from Your Day*. Chicago: Loyola, 2015.

Tisdale, Teresa Clement. "Formation Through Grace and Truth." *Edification: The Transdisciplinary Journal of Christian Psychology* 4.1 (2010) 30–34.

Torr, Stephen C. "Anti-Theodicies." In *T & T Clark Handbook of Suffering and the Problem of Evil*, edited by Matthias Grebe and Johannes Grössl, 419–27. London: Bloomsbury, 2023.

———. *A Dramatic Pentecostal/Charismatic Anti-Theodicy: Improvising on a Divine Performance of Lament*. Eugene, OR: Pickwick, 2013.

———. "A Winnicottian Approach to Biblical Lament: Developing a True Self in the Midst of Suffering." *Journal of Psychology and Theology* 47.1 (2019) 48–65. https://doi.org/10.1177/0091647118795184.

Travis, Sarah. *Unspeakable: Preaching and Trauma-Informed Theology.* Eugene, OR: Cascade, 2021.

Turner, Léon. "Behind the Mask." *Edification: The Transdisciplinary Journal of Christian Psychology* 4.1 (2010) 37–40.

———. *Theology, Psychology and the Plural Self.* Farnham, UK: Ashgate, 2008.

Tutu, Desmond. *No Future Without Forgiveness: A Personal Overview of South Africa's Truth and Reconciliation Commission.* New ed. London: Rider, 2000.

Ulanov, Ann Bedford. *Finding Space: Winnicott, God, and Psychic Reality.* Louisville: Westminster John Knox, 2005.

Van den Brink, Gijsbert. "Questions, Challenges, and Concerns for Original Sin." In *Finding Ourselves After Darwin: Conversations on the Image of God, Original Sin, and the Problem of Evil,* edited by Stanley P. Rosenberg et al., 117–29. Grand Rapids: Baker Academic, 2018.

Van der Kolk, Bessel. *The Body Keeps the Score: Mind, Brain and the Body in the Transformation of Trauma.* London: Penguin, 2015.

Van Deusen Hunsinger, Deborah. *Bearing the Unbearable: Trauma, Gospel, and Pastoral Care.* Grand Rapids: Eerdmans, 2015.

Vander Lugt, Wesley, and Trevor Hart. Introduction to *Theatrical Theology: Explorations in Performing the Faith,* edited by Wesley Vander Lugt and Trevor Hart, xiii–xix. Eugene, OR: Cascade, 2014.

Vanhoozer, Kevin J. "Continuing the Dialogue: A Theological Offering." *Edification: The Transdisciplinary Journal of Christian Psychology* 4.1 (2010) 41–46.

———. *The Drama of Doctrine: A Canonical-Linguistic Approach to Christian Theology.* Louisville: Westminster John Knox, 2005.

———. *Faith Speaking Understanding: Performing the Drama of Doctrine.* Louisville: Westminster John Knox, 2014.

———. *First Theology: God, Scripture and Hermeneutics.* Downers Grove, IL: InterVarsity, 2002.

———. "Forming the Performer: How Christians Can Use Canon Sense to Bring Us to Our (Theodramatic) Senses." *Edification: The Transdisciplinary Journal of Christian Psychology* 4.1 (2010) 5–16.

———. "Human Being, Individual and Social." In *The Cambridge Companion to Christian Doctrine,* edited by Colin Gunton, 158–88. Cambridge: Cambridge University Press, 1997.

———. *Is There a Meaning in This Text? The Bible, The Reader and the Morality of Literary Knowledge.* Leicester: Apollos, 1998.

———. *Mere Christian Hermeneutics: Transfiguring What It Means to Read the Bible Theologically.* Grand Rapids: Zondervan, 2024.

———. *Pictures at a Theological Exhibition: Scenes of the Church's Worship, Witness and Wisdom.* London: InterVarsity, 2016.

———. "Putting on Christ: Spiritual Formation and the Drama of Discipleship." *Journal of Spiritual Formation and Soul Care* 8.2 (2015) 147–71.

———. *Remythologizing Theology: Divine Action, Passion, and Authorship.* Cambridge: Cambridge University Press, 2010.

———. "The Voice and the Actor: A Dramatic Proposal About the Ministry and Minstrelsey of Theology." In *Evangelical Futures: A Conversation on Theological Method,* edited by John G. Stackhouse Jr., 61–106. Grand Rapids: Baker, 2000.

Vanhoozer, Kevin J., and Daniel J. Treier. *Theology and the Mirror of Scripture: A Mere Evangelical Account*. London: Apollos, 2016.

Visala, Aku. "Will the Structural Theory of the Image of God Survive Evolution?" In *Finding Ourselves After Darwin: Conversations on the Image of God, Original Sin, and the Problem of Evil*, edited by Stanley P. Rosenberg et al., 64–78. Grand Rapids: Baker Academic, 2018.

Volf, Miroslav. *The End of Memory: Remembering Rightly in a Violent World*. 2nd ed. Grand Rapids: Eerdmans, 2021.

———. *Exclusion and Embrace: Theological Exploration of Identity, Otherness and Reconciliation*. Nashville: Abingdon, 1994.

———. "Theology for a Way of Life." In *Practicing Theology: Beliefs and Practices in Christian Life*, edited by Miroslav Volf and Dorothy C. Bass, 245–63. Grand Rapids: Eerdmans, 2002.

Vondey, Wolfgang. *Beyond Pentecostalism: The Crisis of Global Christianity and the Renewal of the Theological Agenda*. Grand Rapids: Eerdmans, 2010.

———. *Pentecostal Theology: Living the Full Gospel*. London: Bloomsbury T&T Clark, 2017.

Walsh, Brian J., and J. Richard Middleton. *The Transforming Vision: Shaping a Christian World View*. Downers Grove, IL: InterVarsity, 1984.

Walton, John H. *The Lost World of Adam and Eve: Genesis 2–3 and the Human Origins Debate*. Downers Grove, IL: InterVarsity, 2015.

Walton, John H., and J. Harvey Walton. *Demons and Spirits in Biblical Theology: Reading the Biblical Text in Its Cultural and Literary Context*. Eugene, OR: Cascade, 2019.

Wang, Crystal C., et al. "Music Interventions for Posttraumatic Stress Disorder: A Systematic Review." *Journal of Mood and Anxiety Disorders* 6 (2024) 1–10. https://doi.org/10.1016/j.xjmad.2024.100053.

Ward, Pete. *Introducing Practical Theology: Mission, Ministry, and the Life of the Church*. Grand Rapids: Baker Academic, 2017.

Warner, Megan. "Bible and Trauma." In *The Bible and Mental Health: Towards a Biblical Theology of Mental Health*, edited by Christopher C. H. Cook and Isabelle Hamley, 192–205. London: SCM, 2020.

———. "Trauma Through the Lens of the Bible." In *Tragedies and Christian Congregations: The Practical Theology of Trauma*, edited by Megan Warner et al., 81–91. Abingdon, Oxon: Routledge, 2020.

Watts, Fraser. *Theology and Psychology*. Aldershot: Ashgate, 2002.

Webb, Marcia. *Toward a Theology of Psychological Disorder*. Eugene, OR: Cascade, 2017.

Wells, Samuel. *A Nazareth Manifesto: Being With God*. Chichester, West Sussex: Wiley & Sons, 2015.

Wendel, Alex R. "Trauma-Informed Theology or Theologically Informed Trauma? Traumatic Experiences and Theological Method." *Journal of Reformed Theology* 16 (2022) 3–26.

Wenham, Gordon J. *Genesis 1–15*. Word Biblical Commentary 1. Grand Rapids: Zondervan, 1987.

Wiebe, Kate. "Toward a Faith-Based Approach to Healing After Collective Trauma." In *Tragedies and Christian Congregations: The Practical Theology of Trauma*, edited by Megan Warner et al., 64–77. Abingdon, Oxon: Routledge, 2020.

Wiechelt, Shelley A., et al. "Cultural and Historical Trauma Among Native Americans." In *Trauma: Contemporary Directions in Trauma Theory, Research and Practice*, edited by Shoshana Ringel and Jerrold R. Brandell, 167–205. 2nd ed. Chichester, West Sussex: Columbia University Press, 2020.

Williams, Mark, and Danny Penman. *Mindfulness: A Practical Guide to Finding Peace in a Frantic World*. Reprint ed. London: Piatkus, 2014.

Winnicott, D. W. "Aggression in Relation to Emotional Development." In *Through Paediatrics to Psychoanalysis: Collected Papers*, 204–18. London: Karnac, 1987.

———. "The Antisocial Tendency." In *Through Paediatrics to Psychoanalysis: Collected Papers*, 306–15. London: Karnac, 1987.

———. "Anxiety Associated with Insecurity." In *Through Paediatrics to Psychoanalysis: Collected Papers*, 97–100. London: Karnac, 1987.

———. *Babies and Their Mothers*. London: Free Association, 1988.

———. "The Capacity to Be Alone." In *The Maturational Processes and the Facilitating Environment: Studies in the Theory of Emotional Development*, 29–36. London: Karnac, 2007.

———. *The Child, the Family, and the Outside World*. Harmondsworth, England: Penguin, 1975.

———. "Communicating and Not Communicating Leading to a Study of Certain Opposites." In *The Maturational Processes and the Facilitating Environment: Studies in the Theory of Emotional Development*, 179–92. London: Karnac, 2007.

———. "The Depressive Position in Normal Emotional Development." In *Through Paediatrics to Psychoanalysis: Collected Papers*, 262–77. London: Karnac, 1987.

———. "The Development of Capacity for Concern." In *The Maturational Processes and the Facilitating Environment: Studies in the Theory of Emotional Development*, 73–82. London: Karnac, 2007.

———. "Ego Distortion in Terms of True and False Self." In *The Maturational Processes and the Facilitating Environment: Studies in the Theory of Emotional Development*, 140–52. London: Karnac, 2007.

———. "Ego Integration in Child Development." In *The Maturational Processes and the Facilitating Environment: Studies in the Theory of Emotional Development*, 56–63. London: Karnac, 2007.

———. "From Dependence Towards Independence in the Development of the Individual." In *The Maturation Processes and the Facilitating Environment: Studies in the Theory of Emotional Development*, 83–92. London: Karnac, 2007.

———. *Home Is Where We Start From*. Harmondsworth, England: Penguin, 1986.

———. "The Manic Defence." In *Through Paediatrics to Psychoanalysis: Collected Papers*, 129–44. London: Karnac, 1987.

———. "The Mentally Ill in Your Caseload." In *The Maturational Processes and the Facilitating Environment: Studies in the Theory of Emotional Development*, 217–29. London: Karnac, 2007.

———. "Mind and Its Relation to the Psyche-Soma." In *Through Paediatrics to Psychoanalysis: Collected Papers*, 243–54. London: Karnac, 1987.

———. "Paediatrics and Psychiatry." In *Through Paediatrics to Psychoanalysis: Collected Papers*, 157–73. London: Karnac, 1987.

———. *Playing and Reality*. London: Routledge, 1993.

———. "Primary Maternal Preoccupation." In *Through Paediatrics to Psychoanalysis: Collected Papers*, 300–305. London: Karnac, 1987.

———. "Primitive Emotional Development." In *Through Paediatrics to Psychoanalysis: Collected Papers*, 145–56. London: Karnac, 1987.

———. "Providing for the Child in Health and in Crisis." In *The Maturational Processes and the Facilitating Environment: Studies in the Theory of Emotional Development*, 64–72. London: Karnac, 2007.

———. "Psycho-Analysis and the Sense of Guilt." In *The Maturational Processes and the Facilitating Environment: Studies in the Theory of Emotional Development*, 15–28. London: Karnac, 2007.

———. "Psychoses and Child Care." In *Through Paediatrics to Psychoanalysis: Collected Papers*, 219–28. London: Karnac, 1987.

———. "The Theory of the Parent-Infant Relationship." In *The Maturational Processes and the Facilitating Environment: Studies in the Theory of Emotional Development*, 37–55. London: Karnac, 2007.

———. "Transitional Objects and Transitional Phenomena." In *Through Paediatrics to Psychoanalysis: Collected Papers*, 229–42. London: Karnac, 1987.

The Work of the People. "Crack House Church." N.d. https://www.theworkofthepeople.com/crack-house-church.

Wright, Archie T. *Satan and the Problem of Evil: From the Bible to the Early Church Fathers*. Minneapolis: Fortress, 2022.

Wright, N. T. *Evil and the Justice of God*. London: SPCK, 2006.

———. *The New Testament and the People of God*. London: SPCK, 1992.

Zizioulas, John D. *Being as Communion*. London: Darton, Longman & Todd, 1985.

Zuck, Roy B., ed. *Sitting with Job: Selected Studies on the Book of Job*. Eugene, OR: Wipf & Stock, 2003.